U0117729

3D Programming for Windows®:

Three-Dimensional Graphics Programming for the Windows Presentation Foundation

Charles Petzold

图书在版编目(CIP)数据

Windows 3D 编程:英文/(美)佩特索德著. –上海:上海世界图书出版公司,2009.1

ISBN 978 – 7 – 5062 – 9170 – 5

Ⅰ.W⋯ Ⅱ.佩⋯ Ⅲ.三维 – 动画 – 图形软件,Windows3D – 教材 – 英文 Ⅳ.TP391.41

中国版本图书馆 CIP 数据核字(2008)第 180649 号

Windows 3D 编程

[美]查尔斯·佩特索德 著

上海世界图书出版公司出版发行

上海市尚文路 185 号 B 楼

邮政编码 200010

(公司电话:021 – 63783016 转发行部)

上海竞成印务有限公司印刷

如发现印装质量问题,请与印刷厂联系

(质检科电话:021 – 56422678)

各地新华书店经销

开本:787×960 1/16 印张:28 字数:900 000

2009 年 1 月第 1 版 2009 年 1 月第 1 次印刷

ISBN 978 – 7 – 5062 – 9170 – 5/T·185

图字:09 – 2008 – 627 号

定价:188.00 元

http://www.wpcsh.com.cn

http://www.mspress.com.cn

Contents at a Glance

Table of Contents

What do you think of this book? We want to hear from you!

Microsoft is interested in hearing your feedback so we can continually improve our books and learning resources for you. To participate in a brief online survey, please visit:

www.microsoft.com/learning/booksurvey/

What do you think of this book? We want to hear from you!

Microsoft is interested in hearing your feedback so we can continually improve our books and learning resources for you. To participate in a brief online survey, please visit:

www.microsoft.com/learning/booksurvey/

Introduction

Microsoft Windows Vista is the first version of Windows to have built-in support for three-dimensional graphics. This 3D graphics support is integrated with the Microsoft Windows Presentation Foundation (WPF), the client application programming interface (API) that was introduced in 2006 as part of the Microsoft .NET Framework 3.0. Although .NET 3.0 is automatically included in Windows Vista, you can also install it under Microsoft Windows XP with Service Pack 2 or Windows Server 2003 with Service Pack 1.

This book shows you how to write programs targeting the 3D graphics API of the Windows Presentation Foundation—or "WPF 3D," as it is known to its friends. This book is essentially a comprehensive examination of virtually all the classes and structures in the .NET namespace *System.Windows.Media.Media3D*, with plenty of code and markup examples.

The Role of WPF 3D

WPF 3D is *not* intended for graphics-intensive point-of-view games; nor is it suitable for producing the next big-screen epic featuring three-dimensional rodents or ogres. Programmers who want to pursue those types of applications might be happier looking at Microsoft DirectX rather than WPF 3D.

WPF 3D is instead intended to give programmers the ability to integrate 3D into their client Windows applications. This use of enhanced graphics might be as subtle as fashioning a control that has a 3D appearance, or using 3D to display complex information, or mimicking real-world objects (such as books). The last chapter of this book has some examples of WPF applications incorporating 3D that I hope will inspire you.

Although WPF 3D is not intended for complex games or movies, it is definitely built for animation. WPF includes an extensive animation API and you can use that API with your 3D graphics. In this book I begin demonstrating animation in Chapter 2, "Transforms and Animation," and I never let up. Somewhat related to animation is data binding. You can move or transform 3D figures by binding them to controls such as scrollbars—another of my favorite activities in this book.

Although WPF 3D runs on both Windows Vista and Windows XP with .NET 3.0 installed, you don't get exactly the same features. Even on Windows Vista, the quality of 3D graphics is dependent on the video board you have installed in the computer. A video board with a better on-board graphics processing unit (GPU) can accomplish some feats that are too slow to be done entirely in software. WPF graphics capabilities are categorized by "tiers" that are described on this Web page:

http://msdn2.microsoft.com/en-us/library/ms742196.aspx

In particular, only with a Tier 2 video board installed under Windows Vista do you get anti-aliasing in 3D. (Anti-aliasing is the use of shades of color to minimize the stark "staircase" effect caused by using discrete pixels to represent continuous lines or surfaces.) In the grand scheme of things, anti-aliasing might not sound like an important feature, but it makes a *big* difference when 3D graphics are animated.

You might want to get a new video board for your forays into 3D graphics, but if you're writing applications for other users, you might also want to be aware of the limitations that some of your users may experience when they run your programs.

Your Background

In writing this book, I have assumed that you already have experience programming for the Windows Presentation Foundation using the C# programming language and the Extensible Application Markup Language (XAML) that was introduced as part of .NET 3.0.

If you're a beginning programmer, I recommend that you learn C# first by writing console programs, which are character-mode programs that run in the Command Prompt window. My book *Programming in the Key of C#: A Primer for Aspiring Programmers* (Microsoft Press, 2003) takes this approach.

If you're a programmer who has a previous background in C or C++ but has not yet learned about programming for the .NET Framework with C#, you might want to begin with my short book *.NET Book Zero: What the C or C++ Programmer Needs to Know About C# and the .NET Framework*. The book is free and is available for reading or downloading from the following page of my Web site:

http://www.charlespetzold.com/dotnet

If you're familiar with earlier manifestations of .NET but haven't yet tackled .NET 3.0, WPF, and XAML, my book *Applications = Code + Markup: A Guide to the Microsoft Windows Presentation Foundation* (Microsoft Press, 2006) is a comprehensive tutorial. Several aspects of WPF programming are more crucial for 3D than others. These are:

- XAML syntax, including data binding and resources.
- Dependency properties.
- Animation and storyboards.
- Two-dimensional brushes.

If you are an experienced WPF programmer but you prefer to code in Microsoft Visual Basic .NET or another .NET-compliant language, I can only tell you that many of the programming examples in this book are in XAML rather than C#. Learning at least to read C# code and mentally translate it into your preferred language has become a vital skill in .NET programming.

Three-dimensional graphics programming necessarily involves mathematics, but I've tried to presume a minimum of background knowledge. For example, I've provided refreshers on vectors, matrix algebra, and imaginary numbers, but I've assumed that you have no previous knowledge of quaternions.

However, I do want you to come to this book with a basic facility with trigonometry. I don't need you to reel off lists of common trigonometric identities, but you should have a good working knowledge of angles, radians, sines, cosines, and tangents. If you know without thinking too hard that there are π radians in 180 degrees, that the sine of 90 degrees equals 1, that the cosine of zero degrees also equals 1, and that the tangent of 45 degrees equals 1 as well, you should be in good shape.

Some of the WPF 3D classes are specifically intended to insulate you from heavier mathematics going on under the covers. Consequently, I cover those classes early in the book. Not until relatively late in the book do I get into the more mathematics-laden topics of matrix transforms and quaternions. Depending on your ambitions and aspirations regarding 3D graphics programming, you might find these chapters challenging or altogether too scary. Books are great for conflicts like that because:

■ You can skip something if you don't want to bother with it just now.

■ You can come back and read something later—perhaps more than once.

My objective is to help you, not torture you.

System Requirements

To compile and run the programs described in this book, you'll need:

■ Windows Vista, Windows XP with Service Pack 2, or Windows Server 2003 with Service Pack 1.

■ The .NET Framework 3.0. This is included as part of Windows Vista; for Windows XP or Windows Server 2003 you can download it here:

http://www.microsoft.com/downloads/details.aspx?familyid=10CC340B-F857-4A14-83F5-25634C3BF043

■ The .NET Framework 3.0 Software Development Kit (SDK), available as a DVD image here:

http://www.microsoft.com/downloads/details.aspx?familyid=7614FE22-8A64-4DFB-AA0C-DB53035F40A0

or as a Web install here:

http://www.microsoft.com/downloads/details.aspx?familyid=C2B1E300-F358-4523-B479-F53D234CDCCF

- Microsoft Visual Studio 2005 Standard Edition or Professional Edition.

- Visual Studio Extensions for .NET 3.0, available here:

  http://www.microsoft.com/downloads/details.aspx?familyid=F54F5537-CC86-4BF5-AE44-F5A1E805680D

In theory, you don't need Visual Studio to compile and run WPF applications. The .NET Framework 3.0 SDK includes a command-line program named MSBuild that builds WPF applications from C# project (.csproj) files. However, Visual Studio certainly makes WPF development easier.

The various links I've listed for downloading the .NET Framework, the SDK, and the Visual Studio extensions are all directly accessible from the 3D page of my Web site:

http://www.charlespetzold.com/3D

Go to the heading "Using the Book." Under that heading you'll also find a link to an Empty Project file for use with Visual Studio 2005, which is an approach to WPF programming that I prefer. (In fact, writing your own code rather than letting Visual Studio generate code for you is sometimes known as "Petzold style.")

At the time of this writing, the next version of Visual Studio (currently code-named Orcas) is available in a beta version. Orcas incorporates the .NET Framework 3.5 and the .NET Framework 3.5 SDK, and does not require any "extensions." As Orcas becomes more widely available, I'll have information about using it on the 3D page of my Web site.

For writing and experimenting with standalone XAML files, you can use XAMLPad, which is included with the SDK, or my own XamlCruncher, which you can install from the WPF page of my Web site:

http://www.charlespetzold.com/wpf

In particular, XamlCruncher 2.0 lets you load DLL files into the application domain. These files are then accessible to the XAML file you're developing.

Code Samples

All the code samples shown in this book (and some that are mentioned but not shown in these pages) can be downloaded from the book's companion content page maintained by Microsoft Press at the following Web site:

http://www.microsoft.com/mspress/companion/9780735623941

Purchase of this book gives you a royalty-free license to use any code samples (or modified code samples) you might find useful in your own programs, including commercial software.

(That's one of the purposes of this book.) However, you cannot republish the code samples. (That's why they're copyrighted.) Obviously I can't guarantee that the source code is applicable for specific purposes or even that it works right. (That's why it's free.)

If you page through this book, you'll notice that it has a number of pictures. Some of these are "screen shots" taken of the sample code running under Windows Vista. But others are diagrams and figures that help explain the concepts I'm discussing. All these other diagrams and figures were created with XAML files. The name of the particular XAML file is indicated in italics under each of these figures. You can find these XAML files in the Figures directory of the downloadable code. Running some of these XAML files requires loading the Petzold.Media3D library (which I'll describe shortly) into XamlCruncher 2.0.

Petzold.Media3D and Other Tools

The downloadable code for this book also includes source code for a dynamic-link library named Petzold.Media3D.dll that contains some classes that might be helpful in your 3D programming. If you're running XamlCruncher 2.0, you can load this DLL into the program's application domain and access it from XAML files that you create.

More recent versions of the Petzold.Media3D library are available for downloading from the 3D page of my Web site:

http://www.charlespetzold.com/3D

Purchase of this book gives you a royalty-free license to include this DLL with your own programs, including commercial software. You can also use any of the source code (including modified versions of the source code) in compilations of your own programs. However, I request that you do not distribute modified versions of the library itself. If you'd like to enhance the library in some way, do so by deriving from the classes in the library. I also ask that you do not distribute any of the source code that contributes to this library, either in a modified or unmodified state.

The Petzold.Media3D library is only one of several WPF 3D libraries available to the programmer. In particular, the WPF 3D team at Microsoft has put together a 3DTools library available here:

http://www.codeplex.com/3DTools

The WPF 3D team maintains a blog that often contains essential information here:

http://blogs.msdn.com/wpf3d

Support for This Book

Every effort has been made to ensure the accuracy of this book and the companion content. As corrections or changes are collected, they will be added to a Microsoft Knowledge Base article.

Microsoft Press provides support for books and companion content at the following Web site:

http://www.microsoft.com/learning/support/books

Questions and Comments

If you have comments, questions, or ideas regarding this book or the companion content, or if you have questions that are not answered by visiting the sites previously mentioned, please send them to Microsoft Press via e-mail at:

mspinput@microsoft.com

or via postal mail at:

Microsoft Press
Attn: 3D Programming for Windows *Editor*
One Microsoft Way
Redmond, WA 98052-6399

Please note that Microsoft software product support is not offered through these addresses.

Author's Web Site

Information specific to this book can be found on this page of my Web site:

http://www.charlespetzold.com/3D

Information about my other books, as well as a blog and miscellaneous articles, can be accessed from the home page of my Web site.

Special Thanks

Graphics programming in Windows has always especially appealed to me. In years gone by, I began writing books about Windows graphics programming—and even one about graphics programming for the OS/2 Presentation Manager—but something else always came up and these books were never completed. (Two covers of these abandoned books can be seen at the bottom of the Books page of my Web site.)

The prospect of writing a book about 3D graphics programming for Windows was very exciting. After I begged to write this book, my agent Claudette Moore and Microsoft Press Acquisitions Editor Ben Ryan helped make it reality. Thank you very much!

Apparently Project Editor Valerie Woolley and Technical Editor Kenn Scribner were sufficiently recovered from the experience of working with me on *Applications = Code + Markup* that we were able to reunite the "team" for this book. I am very thankful for their tireless work to help make this a book we can hold up with pride.

Positioned at the vanguard in the constant battle to prevent civilization from degenerating into chaos and brutality are copy editors. They help keep the English language clean from the evils of split infinitives, dangling participles, mismatched tenses, and the passive voice. I am forever grateful to the diligence of my copy editor Becka McKay in fixing my prose and helping me write with as much clarity as possible.

Eric Sink and Larry Smith graciously volunteered to read raw drafts of this book, and I am fortunate they did not also ask me to pay for the psychiatric counseling undoubtedly vital to their recovery from the experience. Their feedback and typo-detection skills were invaluable.

My friends at Microsoft continue to be generous with their knowledge and wisdom. From the 3D team I thank Daniel Lehenbauer, Jordan Parker, Adam Smith, Greg Schechter, and Peter Antal. I have also benefited greatly from the encouragement of Stephen Toub, Pablo Fernicola, Tim Sneath, and Paul Scholz.

In e-mails and blog entries, Larry O'Brien, Rob Hill, and Nathan Dunlap have given me advice and lessons. The inspiration for the StatePopulationAnimator program came from a discussion with Neil Devadasan.

And, of course, very much love and thanks go to Deirdre, who has helped make the past decade the very best years of my life.

Charles Petzold
New York City and Roscoe, New York
December 2006–June 2007

Chapter 1
Lights! Camera! Mesh Geometries!

Ever since artists of the Upper Paleolithic era began adorning cave walls with images of hunters and their prey, people have strived to depict three-dimensional, real-world objects on two-dimensional surfaces. Our newspapers, magazines, books, museums, scratchpads, photo albums, movie theatres, video libraries, and computers are filled with the results.

Human perception is so attuned to the three dimensions of the real world that we are easily persuaded to accept even simple drawings as representing actual objects. This, for example, is obviously just a geometric circle:

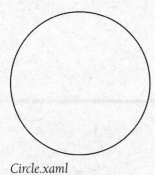

Circle.xaml

But add a little shading, and it becomes a ball:

Ball.xaml

You don't need any 3D programming to display such a ball: The interior of a circle is simply colored with a *RadialGradientBrush*. The color varies from red on the edges (rendered as gray on the page) to white at the point specified by the *GradientOrigin* property. Set the *Gradient-Origin* off-center to suggest a light source from the upper left, which has become a convention in on-screen computer graphics.

The following object is depicted solely by its edges, and yet it is easily recognizable:

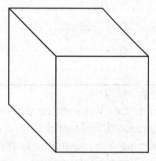

SolidCube.xaml

Although we can't see the entire object, only extreme skeptics would suggest that the back part of the object is much different from the front. An alternative version of the classic cube shows all the edges:

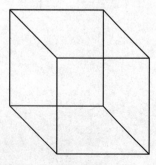

HollowCube.xaml

Our eyes and brain still want to see this as a cube, but they can't decide with any assurance which side is in the foreground and which is in the background. Rationally we can acknowledge that the figure is merely two squares with their corners connected, but this information barely affects what we clearly perceive.

We so much want to see three-dimensional objects in simple drawings that even something as impossible as this object seems oddly real:

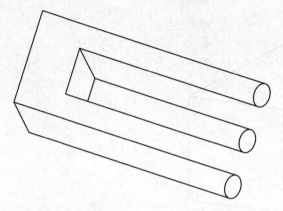

DevilsPitchfork.xaml

That monstrosity is sometimes known as the Devil's Pitchfork, and for good reason. I've often been tempted to try to build such an object, and there's always part of my non-rational brain that insists it can be done.

A sculpture in East Perth, Australia, has managed to mimic the famous triangle named after mathematician Roger Penrose but devised earlier by Swedish artist Oscar Reutersvärd:

PenroseTriangle.xaml

That Australian sculpture only seems to achieve this impossible design when viewed from two specific locations. Other impossible structures can be found in the works of Dutch graphic artist M. C. Escher, whose toyings with the conventions of two-dimensional representations of three-dimensional figures have delighted programmers and other techies for many decades.

What is this figure?

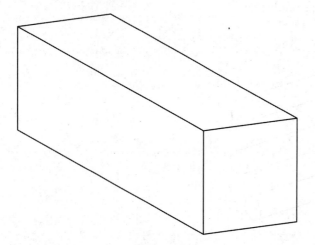

OrthographicSquareCuboidOutline.xaml

Mathematicians would recognize it as a square cuboid. A cuboid is a solid with six rectangular faces that join at right angles, where opposite sides are equal in dimension. If two of these opposite sides are square, the figure is a square cuboid. If all six sides are square, the figure is simply a cube.

Now, what is this figure?

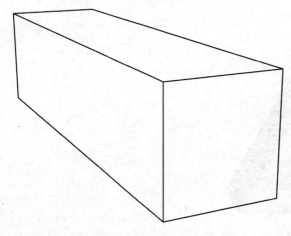

PerspectiveSquareCuboidOutline.xaml

The temptation is to say that this is also a square cuboid, because that is probably the simplest explanation. In fact, this is actually a more realistic view of a square cuboid than the first rendition. As everyone knows, objects farther from the eye look smaller, a phenomenon known as *foreshortening* or *perspective*. In real life, the square at the far end of the object would appear smaller than the square in the foreground.

The classification of the second long object as a square cuboid certainly doesn't negate the earlier verdict on the first object. It's just two different ways of representing three-dimensional figures on flat surfaces. In mathematics textbooks or engineering drawings, the version without perspective would surely be considered preferable. (Of course, you have to maintain a certain amount of trust that you aren't being deliberately deceived: the first of the two figures might have a larger back end reduced in size by a perspective rendition, while the second object could really have a smaller back end.)

Any method to render a three-dimensional figure—be it real, imaginary, or hypothetical—on a two-dimensional surface is known as a *projection*. The first square cuboid was rendered with a type of projection known as *orthographic* projection, from the Greek word *orthos* for straight. (Hence, *orthogonal* means perpendicular, *orthodontics* means straight teeth, *orthopedics* means straight legs, and *orthodoxy* means "straight beliefs.") The figure is projected onto a viewing plane by imaginary lines that are right angles to the plane:

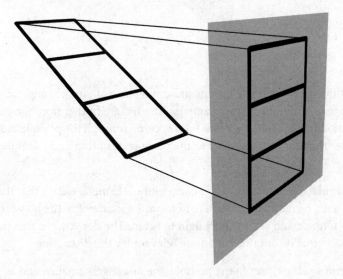

OrthographicProjection.xaml

Some distortion might be present—in this case the total height of the figure is not represented by the projection—but the most important characteristic of the orthographic projection is the preservation of parallel lines. Lines that are parallel in real life are parallel on the projection. Of course, the view of the three-dimensional object is different depending on the location of the projection plane. Technical drawings generally use several orthographic projections to show views of an object from several sides. Orthographic projections on parallel planes are identical.

In contrast to orthographic projection is *perspective projection*, which is based on the workings of the human eye. The eye is a complicated mechanism, of course, but for our purposes might be approximated by a pinhole camera. In a pinhole camera, all the light from a figure comes through a tiny hole and strikes a plane surface, onto which the figure is projected upside down.

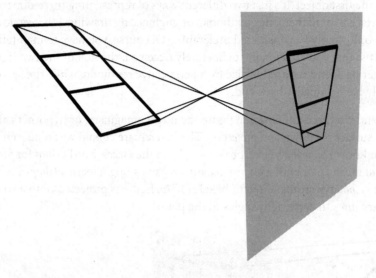

VisualProjection.xaml

The light rays passing through the pinhole do not strike the plane at uniform angles as they do in the orthographic perspective. Light rays from objects that are farther from the pinhole (such as the two projection lines at the top of this figure) come through the pinhole at a more acute angle to each other than for objects closer to the pinhole, resulting in the familiar fore-shortening effect.

The human eye and a regular camera work much like a pinhole camera, except that the pinhole is replaced with a lens. By refracting rays of light toward a focal point, the lens provides a larger aperture than a pinhole and allows more light to get in. The downside is that the lens cannot focus all distances equally. But this isn't quite relevant for the discussion.

As you move the projection plane closer to the pinhole, the image gets smaller, and as you move it farther away, the image gets larger. But the proportions among parts of the image remain the same. However, if you move the pinhole closer to the object, the projected front of the object gets larger in relation to the back, and perspective is exaggerated. If you pull the pinhole farther back, the difference in size between the foreground and background decreases.

In the human eye and the camera, the image on the plane is upside down. Partially to avoid upside-down images in diagrams such as these, the perspective projection is usually drawn like this:

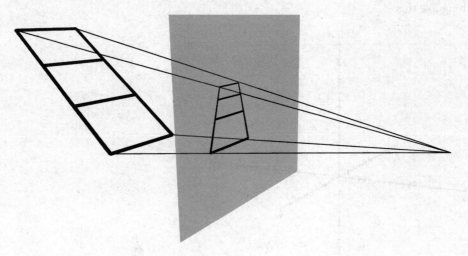

PerspectiveProjection.xaml

The pinhole has been replaced with a focal point, and the projection plane is now between the focal point and the object. But it's really the same geometry. As you move the projection plane between the focal point and the object, the projected image gets larger or smaller, but the proportions remain the same. Move the focal point closer to the object, and the perspective is exaggerated. Move the focal point farther back, and the perspective is decreased. If you move the focal point to infinity, the perspective projection becomes the orthographic projection.

The Microsoft Windows Presentation Foundation (WPF) three-dimensional graphics class library (which I'll often abbreviate as WPF 3D) performs all the mathematics necessary to project a three-dimensional figure onto a two-dimensional surface such as a computer screen or a printer page. You, the programmer, can select the type of projection you want by choosing one of the classes that derive from the abstract *Camera* class. The *Camera* class and its derivatives, like almost all WPF 3D classes, are defined in the .NET namespace *System.Windows.Media.Media3D*. The two classes named *OrthographicCamera* and *Perspective-Camera* perform the necessary transformations for the orthographic and perspective projection. WPF 3D also includes a *MatrixCamera* class for advanced purposes that can perform arbitrary types of projections of three-dimensional objects onto two-dimensional surfaces, but I won't be discussing that option until Chapter 7, "Matrix Transforms."

Of course, a camera is useless without something to point it at, so usually the first step in creating a three-dimensional scene in WPF 3D is to describe a figure in three-dimensional space.

Three-Dimensional Coordinates

WPF 3D uses a traditional three-dimensional coordinate system, generally pictured something like this:

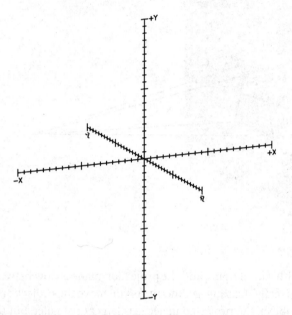

Axes.xaml

The three axes meet at an origin. Increasing values of X are to the right; increasing values of Y are upward; increasing values of Z come out of the computer screen and toward the viewer. This is known as a right-hand coordinate system: If you point the forefinger of your right hand in the direction of increasing X values and the middle finger points to increasing Y values, your thumb points to increasing Z values.

I said that the diagram shows how the coordinate system is "generally pictured" because it really depends on how you view it. You could view it from all different directions. Indeed, if I oriented the diagram so that the Z axis pointed *exactly* toward the viewer, the axis would be visible only as a point. The importance of the right-hand rule is this: Based on the direction of any two axes, you can always tell how the third is oriented by applying the rule.

Just as the two axes of the traditional two-dimensional Cartesian coordinate system divide the plane into four quadrants, three planes in the three-dimensional coordinate system divide space into eight octants. The eight octants don't have standard names, but the three planes are known as the YZ plane, the XZ plane, and the XY plane:

- The YZ plane consists of all points where X equals 0.
- The XZ plane consists of all points where Y equals 0.
- The XY plane consists of all points where Z equals 0.

You can visualize each of these three planes as dividing space in half, and it's convenient to use common words that correspond to the standard orientation of the axes I've shown in the previous graphic:

- The YZ plane divides space into *right* (positive X) and *left* (negative X).
- The XZ plane divides space into *top*, or *upper* (positive Y), and *bottom*, or *lower* (negative Y).
- The XY plane divides space into *front* (positive Z) and *back*, or *rear* (negative Z).

Each of the eight octants can then be described with a phrase such as "left bottom front." That particular phrase refers to all points where X is negative, Y is negative, and Z is positive.

Points in Space

A precise location in three-dimensional space is represented by a coordinate point traditionally notated as (X, Y, Z). WPF 3D defines a structure named *Point3D* that stores one of these coordinate points. The structure has three read/write properties named *X*, *Y*, and *Z* of type *double*, and a constructor that creates a *Point3D* object from its X, Y, and Z components.

Here's some C# code to create and initialize a *Point3D* object:

```
Point3D point = new Point3D(2.33, 1.5, -2);
```

In XAML, you represent a *Point3D* objects as a text string with spaces and/or single commas separating the numbers:

```
"2.33, 1.5, -2"
```

I tend to write my *Point3D* objects with spaces because it looks less cluttered to me:

```
"2.33 1.5 -2"
```

Very often, a WPF 3D application must specify an ordered collection of *Point3D* objects, and for that job you use the *Point3DCollection* class. This class has a method named *Add* that accepts an object of type *Point3D*. Here's how you might create such a collection in code and add three points to it:

```
Point3DCollection ptcoll = new Point3DCollection();
ptcoll.Add(new Point3D(2.55, 1.5, -2));
ptcoll.Add(new Point3D(0, 2.5, 7));
ptcoll.Add(new Point3D(1, 1, -3));
```

The *Point3DCollection* behaves just like other .NET collection classes: As you add elements to the collection, it automatically reallocates memory space if necessary to store the items. A *Clear* method clears all items from the collection; a *Count* property tells you how many items are in the collection; and an indexer allows you to refer to specific *Point3D* objects by indexing the collection object; for example, *ptcoll[1]* refers to the second item in the collection. The *Point3DCollection* class defines a constructor that lets you create a collection based on an existing *Point3D* array, and a *CopyTo* method that copies the collection into an array of type *Point3D*.

In XAML, you define a collection of 3D points just by listing them in a string:

```
"2.55 1.5 -2, 0 2.5 7, 1 1 -3"
```

I like to use commas to separate the points, but spaces are sufficient as well.

Besides *Point3DCollection*, in this chapter you'll also encounter the similar *Int32Collection* (defined in the *System.Windows.Media* namespace), which stores 32-bit integers. Both *Point3DCollection* and *Int32Collection* derive from a class named *Freezable*. Perhaps a better name for this class would have been *Notifiable*, because the class implements an event named *Changed* that is triggered whenever something about the object changes. (The name *Freezable* comes from the *Freeze* method defined by the class that causes the object to become unmodifiable.) The *Point3DCollection* and *Int32Collection* classes fire the *Changed* event whenever the collection changes, such as when an item in the collection is replaced. This little fact has *extremely* powerful implications: Classes that define properties based on these collections can respond dynamically to changes in the collections to implement animations.

The *System.Windows.Media.Media3D* namespace includes a structure named *Size3D* that encapsulates a three-dimensional size with three properties also named *X*, *Y*, and *Z*. These properties must be non-negative or an *ArgumentException* is raised. A *Size3D* object with *X*, *Y*, and *Z* all equal to zero is considered to be "empty." *Size3D* defines a get-only Boolean property named *IsEmpty* and a static get-only property named *Size3D.Empty* that returns an empty *Size3D* structure. The *Size3D* parameterless constructor also returns an empty *Size3D* structure.

The *Rect3D* structure defines a rectangle in 3D space as a combination of a *Point3D* object and a *Size3D* object, which are exposed by *Rect3D* as the properties *Location* and *Size*. The *Location* property is considered to be the origin of the rectangle, and the *Size* property its dimensions. Because the three components of the *Size* property must be non-negative, the *Location* property is always the lower-left-rear corner of the rectangle. *Rect3D* also defines properties *X*, *Y*, and *Z*, which are the same as the *X*, *Y*, and *Z* properties of the *Point3D* object referenced by its *Location* property, and *SizeX*, *SizeY*, and *SizeZ* that correspond to the *X*, *Y*, and *Z* properties of its *Size* property. Like *Size3D*, *Rect3D* defines a Boolean *IsEmpty* property and a static *Empty* property.

In actual practice, the *Size3D* and *Rect3D* structures are rarely used. Some classes in the *System.Windows.Media.Media3D* namespace define a read-only *Bounds* property of type *Rect3D*, but that's about it.

Introduction to Vectors

In WPF 3D programming, you find that you use the *Vector3D* structure almost as much as *Point3D*. I'll discuss some basic concepts of vectors in this chapter, but I'll be introducing progressively more and more vector-related mathematics throughout this book.

A vector encapsulates a magnitude and a direction, and is generally pictured in 3D space like so:

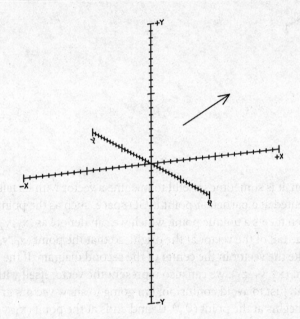

AxesWithVector.xaml

The magnitude of the vector is symbolized by its length; the direction is symbolized by the arrow. Showing a vector occupying a specific location in 3D space is somewhat deceptive, however. Vectors have no physical location, much like a weight or a length. All the vectors in the following diagram are the same because they all have the same magnitude and direction:

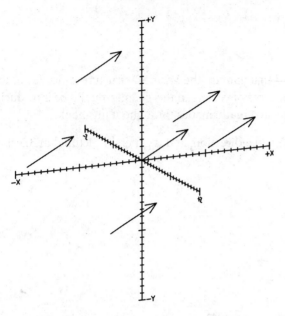

AxesWithVectors.xaml

Although vectors have no location, it is sometimes useful to imagine a vector with its tail—the end without the arrowhead—oriented at a particular point in 3D space, such as the point (x_0, y_0, z_0). The head of the vector then meets a unique point, which we can denote as (x_1, y_1, z_1). It's most illuminating to orient the tail of the vector at the origin, so that the point (x_0, y_0, z_0) is really the point $(0, 0, 0)$, just like the vector in the center of the second diagram. If the head of the vector then meets the point (x_1, y_1, z_1), we can also represent the vector itself with the same three numbers as that point. Just to avoid confusion, I'm going to show vectors in boldface: A vector oriented so that it begins at the point $(0, 0, 0)$ and ends at the point (x_1, y_1, z_1) is the vector $(\mathbf{x_1}, \mathbf{y_1}, \mathbf{z_1})$.

Generalizing, a vector can be calculated by subtracting the X, Y, and Z components of one point from another. The vector with its tail at (x_0, y_0, z_0) and its head at (x_1, y_1, z_1) is $(\mathbf{x_1 - x_0},$ $\mathbf{y_1 - y_0}, \mathbf{z_1 - z_0})$. In other words, the vector $(\mathbf{x_1 - x_0}, \mathbf{y_1 - y_0}, \mathbf{z_1 - z_0})$ points in the direction from (x_0, y_0, z_0) to (x_1, y_1, z_1). Or, analyzed from another perspective, suppose you have a vector $(\mathbf{x_v}, \mathbf{y_v}, \mathbf{z_v})$. If that vector is oriented with its tail at the point (x_0, y_0, z_0), its head is at the point $(x_0 + x_v, y_0 + y_v, z_0 + z_v)$.

We might even be so bold as to write arithmetic statements that combine points and vectors. This statement shows the calculation of a vector that begins at (x_0, y_0, z_0) and ends at (x_1, y_1, z_1):

$$(x_1, y_1, z_1) - (x_0, y_0, z_0) = (\mathbf{x_1 - x_0}, \mathbf{y_1 - y_0}, \mathbf{z_1 - z_0})$$

Normally, subtracting one point from another doesn't make any sense, but if we define the operation as a subtraction of the X, Y, and Z components separately, the resultant vector is a good physical representation of the difference between the points. Even with vectors it doesn't make sense to *add* two points together, however. Instead, you can add a vector to a point to get another point:

$$(x_0, y_0, z_0) + (\mathbf{x_v}, \mathbf{y_v}, \mathbf{z_v}) = (x_0 + x_v, y_0 + y_v, z_0 + z_v)$$

You can add two vectors like so:

$$(\mathbf{x_1, y_1, z_1}) + (\mathbf{x_2, y_2, z_2}) = (\mathbf{x_1 + x_2, y_1 + y_2, z_1 + z_2})$$

Vector addition has an interesting physical interpretation. In the following diagrams, **V1** and **V2** are vectors. Adding two vectors is equivalent to orienting the head of the first vector with the tail of the second. The sum is the vector from the tail of the first to the head of the second:

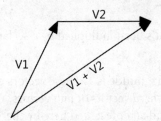

Since the addition is commutative, you can switch the two vectors and the result is the same, but the sum is now clearly the diagonal of the parallelogram formed by the two vectors:

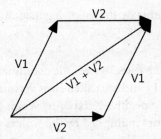

For vector $(\mathbf{x_v}, \mathbf{y_v}, \mathbf{z_v})$, the direction of the vector is the direction from the origin $(0, 0, 0)$ to the point (x_v, y_v, z_v). The magnitude of the vector is the square root of the sum of the squares of the three components:

$$\sqrt{x_v^2 + y_v^2 + z_v^2}$$

If this is not immediately obvious, consider a vector from (x_0, y_0, z_0) to (x_1, y_1, z_1). The magnitude of the vector is the distance between the points, which can be calculated by the three-dimensional form of the Pythagorean Theorem:

$$\sqrt{(x_1 - x_0)^2 + (y_1 - y_0)^2 + (z_1 - z_0)^2}$$

You can multiply a vector by a number, often called a *scalar*, and the result is equivalent to each of the individual components multiplied by that scalar:

$$k \times (x_v, y_v, z_v) = (k \times x_v, k \times y_v, k \times z_v)$$

For example, multiplying a vector by 2 doubles the magnitude of the vector without changing its direction. Similarly, you can divide a vector by a scalar.

If you multiply or divide a vector by a negative scalar, the direction of the vector is reversed. In particular, multiplying by −1 produces a vector of the same magnitude but the opposite direction:

$$-1 \times (x_v, y_v, z_v) = (-x_v, -y_v, -z_v)$$

For that reason, you can subtract a vector from a point:

$$(x_0, y_0, z_0) - (x_v, y_v, z_v) = (x_0 - x_v, y_0 - y_v, z_0 - z_v)$$

The result is the same as adding the point to a vector that's been multiplied by a scalar of −1. It makes no sense to subtract a point from a vector.

Sometimes it's convenient to work with vectors whose magnitude is 1. These vectors essentially encapsulate only a direction. These are called *normalized* vectors or *unit* vectors. You can normalize an existing vector by dividing it by its magnitude (represented here by the scalar M):

$$(x_v, y_v, z_v) / M$$

This is the same as dividing each of the vector's components by the following magnitude:

$$(x_v / M, y_v / M, z_v / M)$$

Three very special unit vectors point in the direction of the three axes of the coordinate system. These are the vectors $(1, 0, 0)$, $(0, 1, 0)$, and $(0, 0, 1)$ and are called *basis* vectors. The vector $(1, 0, 0)$, for example, points in the direction of the positive X axis. Any vector (x_v, y_v, z_v) can be represented as the sum of the three basis vectors multiplied by the scalars x_v, y_v, and z_v:

$$x_v \times (1, 0, 0) + y_v \times (0, 1, 0) + z_v \times (0, 0, 1)$$

The *Vector3D* structure defines *X*, *Y*, and *Z* properties just like *Point3D* and *Size3D*. All three structures define conversions between themselves and the other two structures, so you can use explicit casts to convert objects among the three types.

The *Vector3D* structure also defines a *Length* property that provides the magnitude of the vector. Another property named *LengthSquared* sounds like it's the *Length* property squared, but it's actually calculated as *X* squared plus *Y* squared plus *Z* squared without the square root, so it's slightly faster than calling the *Length* property and might be preferred if you're simply comparing the magnitudes of various vectors.

Both the *Point3D* structure and the *Vector3D* structure overload the addition and subtraction operators to provide the results that I've described. In the following C# code examples, all variables that begin with the prefix *point* are instances of the *Point3D* structure, and variables that begin with *vector* are instances of the *Vector3D* structure. The *Point3D* structure provides the following operations. The first operand is always a *Point3D* instance:

```
point2 = point1 + vector;
vector = point2 - point1;
point1 = point2 - vector;
```

The *Vector3D* structure defines operations where a *Vector3D* instance is the first operand. Some of these are simply commutative variations of the operations defined by *Point3D*:

```
point2 = vector + point1;
vector3 = vector1 + vector2;
point2 = vector - point1;
vector3 = vector1 - vector2;
```

The third of those four operations is an oddity I earlier classified as something that "makes no sense," and seems to imply that a vector is the sum of two points, but there it is if you ever need it.

The *Vector3D* structure also overloads the negation operator:

```
vector2 = -vector1;
```

The resultant vector has the same magnitude but points in the opposite direction. The *Vector3D* structure also overrides the multiplication and division operators for applications of scalars. In the following examples, *D* is a *double*:

```
vector2 = D * vector1;
vector2 = vector1 * D;
vector2 = vector1 / D;
```

The *Vector3D* structure also defines two types of multiplication between vectors, called the *dot product* and the *cross product*, but these are topics that we won't tackle until Chapter 4, "Light and Shading."

Defining the 3D Figure

Traditionally in 3D computer graphics, the surfaces of three-dimensional figures are defined by a polygon *mesh*, which is a collection of 3D coordinate points arranged to form polygons. For figures with flat surfaces, generally only a few polygons are needed, but curved surfaces require many polygons to approximate the curvature of the figure.

In WPF 3D, the simplest form of polygon—the triangle—is used for this mesh. Triangles are very useful in 3D graphics. Any three non-coincident and non-collinear points define a triangle and, in effect, a plane, so that triangles are always flat. You know you're spending a lot of time with 3D programming when you begin seeing everything in the real world in terms of triangles.

In WPF 3D, the simplest 3D figure consists of a single triangle, such as this one on the YZ plane with its three vertices conveniently labeled:

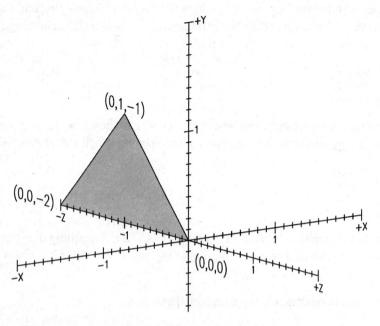

TriangleOnAxes.xaml

When you first set up a 3D scene, it's usually easiest to put the figure you'll be creating somewhere in the region of the origin. You can center it on the origin, or put one corner at the origin, or whatever's convenient. The units of 3D space have no physical meaning. Everything is relative. It's customary to give the figure small coordinates, and the more you can use numbers such as 0, 1, and −1, the happier you'll generally be. Often you'll put figures in the back half of 3D space, and the camera will be in the front half of 3D space pointed in the negative Z direction.

You specify the vertices of the figure and the triangles that connect these vertices with an object of type *MeshGeometry3D*. The two essential properties of *MeshGeometry3D* are *Positions* and *TriangleIndices*, both of which are collections. The *Positions* property contains the vertices of the figure and *TriangleIndices* describes how those vertices connect to form triangles.

I'm going to show this first example entirely in XAML, and then I'll show an equivalent (and somewhat enhanced) program entirely in C#.

The *Positions* property is of type *Point3DCollection* and contains one *Point3D* object for every vertex in the 3D figure. For a figure containing only a single triangle, that's three points. The following markup shows the three vertices of this triangle separated by commas:

```
<MeshGeometry3D Positions="0 0 0, 0 1 -1, 0 0 -2" ... />
```

Each of these *Point3D* objects now has a zero-based index within the *Positions* collection. The three points in this particular *Positions* collection have indices of 0, 1, and 2.

The *TriangleIndices* property of the *MeshGeometry3D* object is of type *Int32Collection*, and contains three integers for every triangle in the figure. These integers are indices of the points in the *Positions* collection, so for a figure that consists of one triangle, the complete *MeshGeometry3D* object with the *TriangleIndices* property might be defined like so:

```
<MeshGeometry3D Positions="0 0 0, 0 1 -1, 0 0 -2"
                TriangleIndices="0 1 2" />
```

This *TriangleIndices* collection defines a single triangle that consists of the first, second, and third points in the *Positions* collection.

It might seem as if *MeshGeometry3D* is more complicated than it needs to be. Why not use just one collection to list three vertices for each triangle that comprises the figure? That approach would certainly be feasible, but in the general case, the same vertex might be shared by several triangles, so the use of separate collections of points and indices is ultimately most convenient.

The order of the three integers in the *TriangleIndices* collection makes a difference in how the figure appears. Although this triangle is flat, it exists in three-dimensional space and it has a front and a back. You might want the front and the back to be different colors, which means you must distinguish between them in some way. In the preceding diagram, one side of the triangle faces left (toward the negative X axis) and the other faces right, and you might want those sides to be considered the front and the back, respectively. When the triangle is viewed from the front, the three indices in the *TriangleIndices* collection must refer to the vertices of the triangle in a counterclockwise direction.

In this example, a *TriangleIndices* collection of "1 2 0" or "2 0 1" is exactly the same as "0 1 2" because in all cases the three indices reference the vertices of the triangle in a counterclockwise direction when the triangle is viewed from the front.

On the other hand, if you had specified "0 2 1" or "2 1 0" or "1 0 2," the side of the triangle facing the position X axis would be considered the front, and the side that we can see in the diagram would be considered the back.

The *MeshGeometry3D* object defines the geometry of the figure. You also need to indicate how the surfaces of the figure are colored. For this job you use an object of type *Material*, which is an abstract class from which several classes derive, including the simplest, which is *DiffuseMaterial*. The *DiffuseMaterial* class is intended to give the figure a plain, matte-like finish. The most important property of this class is *Brush*, which is of type *Brush*, the abstract base class for the various two-dimensional brushes offered by the WPF and described in Chapters 2 and 31 of my book *Applications = Code + Markup* (Microsoft Press, 2006). As you'll discover in Chapter 5, "Texture and Materials," you can cover a 3D figure with brushes displaying gradients, images, drawings, and visuals, but for this chapter, I want to stick to solid colors. That means you can simply set the *Brush* property of *DiffuseMaterial* to one of the static read-only properties of the *Brushes* class:

```
<DiffuseMaterial Brush="Cyan" />
```

For defining simple scenes and when experimenting, I generally start by using a cyan brush for coloring the fronts of figures and a red brush for coloring the backs. As you start to create solid objects, often the backs of triangles won't be visible because they're inside the figure, but I still like to include a material for the backs so I can tell if I've defined the *MeshGeometry3D* correctly. If I see some red, I know I did something wrong. After everything has been debugged, I remove the materials for any invisible surfaces to improve performance.

The *MeshGeometry3D* and two *Material* objects come together in an object of type *Geometry-Model3D*, which has three essential properties: The *Geometry* property is assigned a *Mesh-Geometry3D*, and the *Material* and *BackMaterial* properties are assigned objects of type *Material*:

```
<GeometryModel3D>
    <GeometryModel3D.Geometry>
        <MeshGeometry3D Positions="0 0 0, 0 1 -1, 0 0 -2"
                        TriangleIndices="0 1 2" />
    </GeometryModel3D.Geometry>

    <GeometryModel3D.Material>
        <DiffuseMaterial Brush="Cyan"/>
    </GeometryModel3D.Material>

    <GeometryModel3D.BackMaterial>
        <DiffuseMaterial Brush="Red"/>
    </GeometryModel3D.BackMaterial>
</GeometryModel3D>
```

In the Windows Presentation Foundation, the term *geometry* usually refers to an abstract mathematical definition of a shape. In 2D graphics, a geometry consists solely of coordinate points; in 3D graphics, it's necessary to supplement these coordinate points with information describing how they are organized into a three-dimensional surface.

The term *model* is used in the WPF 3D to indicate an object that contains rendering information. As you'll see, what actually appears on the screen is known as a *visual*. Visuals use models for determining what they display.

Class names in WPF 3D often consist of two words: an adjective followed by a noun. A *GeometryModel3D* is a certain type of model. A *DiffuseMaterial* is a certain type of *Material*.

Lights and Camera

A 3D scene usually requires some light. If you don't have any light in a 3D scene, you'll still be able to see the figures you've created, but they won't have any color, and the only reason you'll see them is because they're usually displayed against a white background. Different types of light are available in WPF 3D, but for this first program, I'll stick to the simplest, which is a class named *AmbientLight*:

```
<AmbientLight Color="White" />
```

The *AmbientLight* class inherits the *Color* property from the abstract *Light* class, and it's white by default, so if you want white light you don't even have to include the attribute:

```
<AmbientLight />
```

Early in this chapter I described the three types of WPF 3D cameras. For this first example, I want to use a *PerspectiveCamera*, which is similar to the way that the human eye and a conventional camera both work. Objects farther from the camera appear smaller.

The camera must be located in a specific position in 3D space, which you indicate by setting the *Position* property to an object of type *Point3D*. Generally you'll position the camera somewhere in the positive Z half of 3D space. For simple scenes, the camera often sits right on the positive Z axis, which means that the X and Y coordinates are set to zero. For this example, I want to place the camera a little off-center and to the left of the Z axis:

```
<PerspectiveCamera Position="-2 0 5" ... />
```

You also need to specify a direction in which the camera is pointed. This is called the *Look-Direction* and because it's a direction, it's a *Vector3D* object. Generally you'll assemble your figures in the back half of 3D space, so you want the camera to be pointed roughly in the direction of the negative Z axis. The simplest vector you can use is one pointed in a direction parallel to the negative Z axis, which is the vector $(0, 0, -1)$:

```
<PerspectiveCamera Position="-2 0 5"
                   LookDirection="0 0 -1" ... />
```

The *LookDirection* vector does not need to be normalized, but only the direction is used and not the magnitude. Substituting $(0, 0, -2)$, $(0, 0, -3)$, and so forth will work the same way. Not coincidentally, $(0, 0, -1)$ is the default value of *LookDirection*, so you don't even have to explicitly include this property if you want your camera pointing straight back. The default value of *Position*, however, is the point $(0, 0, 0)$, and that is a less useful default unless your figures are further behind the XY plane.

If you think you're finished with the *PerspectiveCamera* by defining the *Position* and *Look-Direction*, you're partially right, but only because I'll be using the default values of two other properties. The *UpDirection* property·is another *Vector3D* property that indicates how the camera is oriented. The default is the vector **(0, 1, 0)**, which points upward and indicates that the camera is held so that the top is pointed in the positive Y direction.

The fourth important property of *PerspectiveCamera* is *FieldOfView*, which is an angle that you specify in degrees. The default is 45 degrees, and that's also what I want to use here:

```
<PerspectiveCamera Position="-2 0 5"
                   LookDirection="0 0 -1"
                   UpDirection="0 1 0"
                   FieldOfView="45" />
```

A low *FieldOfView* value is like a telephoto lens: You're narrowing the view so figures appear larger. A high *FieldOfView* is like a wide-angle lens: You get more visuals within the frame, but everything is smaller.

Let's look at the pinhole camera again, or rather, three different pinhole cameras all custom-built for different focal lengths. These cameras are all 36 millimeters wide, which is just wide enough to fit a single frame of 35mm photographic film. (Of course, you're free to imagine that you've actually equipped your pinhole camera with a charge-coupled device rather than film to get a digital image.) The focal length of the camera is the distance between the pinhole and the film. A standard focal length for 35mm cameras—and their modern digital equivalents—is 50 millimeters, which means that the pinhole (or lens) is 50 millimeters from the film. Here's the camera in actual size viewed from above with the film at the left and camera pointed to the right:

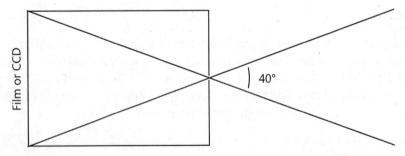

50mmFocalLength.xaml

Based on the width of the film and the distance of the pinhole from the film, the field of view is about 40 degrees. That's calculated by taking half the width of the film (18 millimeters), dividing by the focal length (50 millimeters), taking the inverse tangent, and then doubling. (I'll show the basis for this calculation later in this chapter.) The film is 24 millimeters high, so the vertical field of view is only about 27 degrees, but as you'll see, the field of view in WPF 3D is based on width rather than height, so the 40-degree horizontal field of view associated with a standard 50 millimeter lens is about the same as the 45-degree default *FieldOfView* property for the *PerspectiveCamera* class.

A moderate telephoto lens of 100 millimeters looks like this:

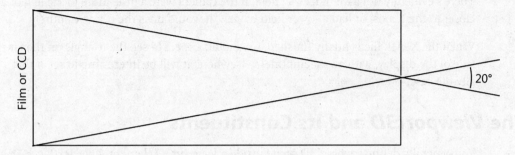

100mmFocalLength.xaml

The field of view is narrower. A wide-angle lens might have a focal length of about 25 millimeters: the field of view is wider:

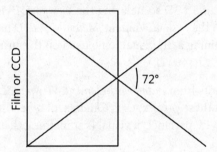

25mmFocalLength.xaml

In the 3D scene I've been assembling, the triangle sits on the Z axis with Z coordinates that range from 0 to −2. I've positioned the camera at the point (−2, 0, 5) pointed in the negative Z direction with a field of view of 45 degrees. An aerial view of this setup looks something like this:

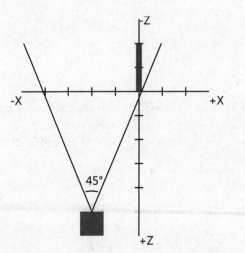

TriangleAerialView.xaml

The gray box is the camera. The triangle is represented by the thicker gray line on the Z axis. There's evidently not a lot of leeway here: If the camera were a little more to the left, or a little closer to the X axis, or had a lower field of view, it would miss the triangle entirely.

When the XAML file is finally finished, we should expect to see the triangle on the far right side of the display, with a vast emptiness elsewhere. It will be interesting to see if that's actually the case.

The *Viewport3D* and Its Constituents

You generally define a whole 3D scene inside a *Viewport3D* element. Like *TextBlock*, *Image*, *Page*, *Panel*, and *Control*, *Viewport3D* derives from *FrameworkElement*, which means that it can be a part of a larger layout of elements, and it can receive mouse, keyboard, and stylus input. Although most 3D classes are defined in the *System.Windows.Media.Media3D* namespace, *Viewport3D* appears in the *System.Windows.Controls* namespace along with other common elements and controls. (It is also possible to define a 3D scene using the *Viewport3DVisual* class, which derives from *Visual* and is found in the *System.Windows.Media.Media3D* namespace, but this class is generally used when defining a 3D visual to be used on the surface of a two-dimensional brush, as I'll demonstrate in Chapter 5.)

Besides all the properties that *Viewport3D* inherits from *FrameworkElement*, *Viewport3D* also defines a few properties of its own. One of these properties is *Children*, of type *Visual3D-Collection*, a collection of *Visual3D* objects. In WPF parlance, a visual is something that has a graphical representation and can render itself.

Visual3D is an abstract class and has only one descendent, named *ModelVisual3D*. This is a crucial class because it's a visual, which means that it can render itself, but it contains content that is a model, which is a description of what the visual renders. *ModelVisual3D* has a property named *Content* of type *Model3D*. Within a *Viewport3D* you'll almost always see at least one piece of markup that looks like this:

```
<ModelVisual3D>
    <ModelVisual3D.Content>
        . . .
    </ModelVisual3D.Content>
</ModelVisual3D>
```

What is that *Content*? It's an object of type *Model3D*. *Model3D* is also abstract, but it has two important descendents: *GeometryModel3D*—which, as you've seen, combines a *MeshGeometry3D* and *Material* objects for coloring the surfaces—and *Light*, from which all the various light classes descend, including *AmbientLight*.

Viewport3D also defines a *Camera* property, so the general structure of a simple *Viewport3D* usually looks something like this:

```
<Viewport3D>
    <ModelVisual3D>
        <ModelVisual3D.Content>
            <GeometryModel3D>
                ...
            </GeometryModel3D>
        </ModelVisual3D.Content>
    </ModelVisual3D>

    <ModelVisual3D>
        <ModelVisual3D.Content>
            <AmbientLight ... />
        </ModelVisual3D.Content>
    </ModelVisual3D>

    <Viewport3D.Camera>
        <PerspectiveCamera ... />
    </Viewport3D.Camera>
</Viewport3D>
```

Viewport3D doesn't need an explicit property element for its *Children* property because *Children* is defined as the element's content property. Just nest all the *ModelVisual3D* children within the *Viewport3D* tags.

In addition, I usually like to put my markup inside a *Page* element, which lets me give it a *WindowTitle* property (which appears in the title bar when you view the content directly in Windows Vista or .NET 3.0) and a *Title* property, which appears in the browser navigation stack. In the following XAML file I've also put the *Viewport3D* in a *Border* element so that the following screenshot shows where the triangle is displayed within the total width of the *Viewport3D*. At this point, everything in this XAML file should look familiar.

Simple3DScene.xaml
```
<!-- =============================================
        Simple3DScene.xaml (c) 2007 by Charles Petzold
     ============================================= -->
<Page xmlns="http://schemas.microsoft.com/winfx/2006/xaml/presentation"
      xmlns:x="http://schemas.microsoft.com/winfx/2006/xaml"
      WindowTitle="Simple 3D Scene"
      Title="Simple 3D Scene">
    <Border BorderThickness="1" BorderBrush="Black">
        <Viewport3D>
            <ModelVisual3D>
                <ModelVisual3D.Content>
                    <GeometryModel3D>
                        <GeometryModel3D.Geometry>
                            <MeshGeometry3D Positions="0 0 0, 0 1 -1, 0 0 -2"
                                            TriangleIndices="0 1 2" />
                        </GeometryModel3D.Geometry>
```

```
                            <GeometryModel3D.Material>
                                <DiffuseMaterial Brush="Cyan"/>
                            </GeometryModel3D.Material>

                            <GeometryModel3D.BackMaterial>
                                <DiffuseMaterial Brush="Red" />
                            </GeometryModel3D.BackMaterial>
                        </GeometryModel3D>
                    </ModelVisual3D.Content>
                </ModelVisual3D>

                <ModelVisual3D>
                    <ModelVisual3D.Content>
                        <AmbientLight Color="White" />
                    </ModelVisual3D.Content>
                </ModelVisual3D>

                <Viewport3D.Camera>
                    <PerspectiveCamera Position="-2 0 5"
                                       LookDirection="0 0 -1"
                                       UpDirection="0 1 0"
                                       FieldOfView="45" />
                </Viewport3D.Camera>
            </Viewport3D>
        </Border>
    </Page>
```

If you're running Windows Vista or the .NET Framework 3.0, you can type this file into Windows Notepad and launch it as if it were an executable, and it will run in Internet Explorer. Or, you can create the file in a XAML-editing program such as XAMLPad (available with the .NET Framework 3.0 Software Development Kit) or my XamlCruncher program (available on my Web site at *www.charlespetzold.com/wpf*).

And yes indeed, the triangle is way over at the right.

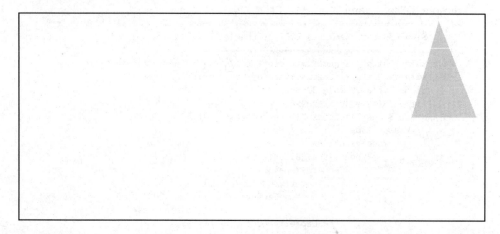

As you make the window wider or narrower, the triangle changes proportionally in size, but it stays at the right edge. As you make the window taller or shorter, the triangle does *not* change in size, but the bottom of the triangle stays vertically centered. That's because the camera is oriented evenly with the baseline of the triangle.

Although the triangle is isosceles, the left edge looks a little shorter than the right edge because it's farther from the camera. Try changing the camera's *Position* property from (−2, 0, 5) to (2, 0, 5). Now the triangle jumps to the left of the screen and you can see the reverse side in red. If you set the *Position* property to (0, 0, 5) so that the camera sits on the Z axis, you won't see anything because the triangle has zero width and sits on the YZ plane, and you're looking straight at the edge.

How can you set the camera properties so that the coordinate origin—the point (0, 0, 0)—is in the center of the display? You need to set the *LookDirection* property to a vector that points from the *Position* property to the point (0, 0, 0). If the *Position* property is (−2, 0, 5), the calculation is

$$(0, 0, 0) - (-2, 0, 5) = \mathbf{(2, 0, -5)}$$

The calculation yields a *LookDirection* vector that is simply the negation of the *CameraPosition*. In general, you can always set *LookDirection* to the negation of *CameraPosition* to make the origin appear in the center of the display. It's also possible to calculate *LookDirection* so that the center of the triangle appears in the center of the display. The center of the triangle is the point (0, 0.5, −1), so subtract the *CameraPosition* point from that:

$$(0, 0.5, -1) - (-2, 0, 5) = \mathbf{(2, 0.5, -6)}$$

Set the *LookDirection* vector to **(2, 0.5, −6)**.

You might also try experimenting with the *Position* and *FieldOfView* properties to get different effects. As you increase *FieldOfView*, the triangle gets smaller and moves toward the center of the display. You can also experiment with *UpDirection*. Change it to the vector **(1, 0, 0)**, which orients the top of the camera to point in the positive X direction, and the triangle will appear at the top of the display.

Variations in Code and Markup

Although most of the simpler demonstrations of 3D in this book will be done in XAML, you can also do everything in code using your favorite .NET-compliant language. The following program is an enhanced version of Simple3DScene written in C#.

Simple3DSceneInCode.cs
```
//----------------------------------------------------
// Simple3DSceneInCode.cs (c) 2007 by Charles Petzold
//----------------------------------------------------
using System;
using System.Windows;
```

```
using System.Windows.Controls;
using System.Windows.Controls.Primitives;
using System.Windows.Media;
using System.Windows.Media.Media3D;

namespace Petzold.Simple3DSceneInCode
{
    public class Simple3DSceneInCode : Window
    {
        PerspectiveCamera cam;

        [STAThread]
        public static void Main()
        {
            Application app = new Application();
            app.Run(new Simple3DSceneInCode());
        }

        public Simple3DSceneInCode()
        {
            Title = "Simple 3D Scene in Code";

            // Make DockPanel content of window.
            DockPanel dock = new DockPanel();
            Content = dock;

            // Create Scrollbar for moving camera.
            ScrollBar scroll = new ScrollBar();
            scroll.Orientation = Orientation.Horizontal;
            scroll.Value = -2;
            scroll.Minimum = -2;
            scroll.Maximum = 2;
            scroll.ValueChanged += ScrollBarOnValueChanged;
            dock.Children.Add(scroll);
            DockPanel.SetDock(scroll, Dock.Bottom);

            // Create Viewport3D for 3D scene.
            Viewport3D viewport = new Viewport3D();
            dock.Children.Add(viewport);

            // Define the MeshGeometry3D.
            MeshGeometry3D mesh = new MeshGeometry3D();
            mesh.Positions.Add(new Point3D(0, 0, 0));
            mesh.Positions.Add(new Point3D(0, 1, -1));
            mesh.Positions.Add(new Point3D(0, 0, -2));
            mesh.TriangleIndices = new Int32Collection(new int[] { 0, 1, 2 });

            // Define the GeometryModel3D.
            GeometryModel3D geomod = new GeometryModel3D();
            geomod.Geometry = mesh;
            geomod.Material = new DiffuseMaterial(Brushes.Cyan);
            geomod.BackMaterial = new DiffuseMaterial(Brushes.Red);
```

```
                    // Create ModelVisual3D for GeometryModel3D.
                    ModelVisual3D modvis = new ModelVisual3D();
                    modvis.Content = geomod;
                    viewport.Children.Add(modvis);

                    // Create another ModelVisual3D for light.
                    modvis = new ModelVisual3D();
                    modvis.Content = new AmbientLight(Colors.White);
                    viewport.Children.Add(modvis);

                    // Create the camera.
                    cam = new PerspectiveCamera(new Point3D(-2, 0, 5),
                                new Vector3D(0, 0, -1), new Vector3D(0, 1, 0), 45);
                    viewport.Camera = cam;
                }
                void ScrollBarOnValueChanged(object sender,
                                RoutedPropertyChangedEventArgs<double> args)
                {
                    cam.Position = new Point3D(args.NewValue, 0, 5);
                }
            }
        }
```

This program creates a *Window* rather than a *Page* and uses a *DockPanel* to host both the *Viewport3D* element and a *ScrollBar*, which is docked at the bottom of the window. Notice how the *TriangleIndices* collection is set from an array of the three integers, which is somewhat easier than three separate *Add* calls.

The *ScrollBar* value ranges between –2 and 2, and the *ValueChanged* event handler uses that value to define a new *Position* property for the camera. Thus, you can dynamically shift the camera between the points (–2, 0, 5) and (2, 0, 5). *Position*—like many properties of classes in the *System.Windows.Media.Media3D* namespace—is backed by a dependency property so that the *PerspectiveCamera* object is notified whenever the property changes.

Can you include a *ScrollBar* in the XAML file to move the camera? Well, yes and no. The C# program uses an event handler, which certainly *could* be added to the XAML file as a block of C# code, but then the XAML file wouldn't run in Internet Explorer or XAMLPad or anything except a compiled program. Very often you can use data bindings in XAML to link two properties of two different elements, but such a binding would have to be defined between the *Value* property of the *ScrollBar* and the *X* property of the *Position* property of the *Perspective-Camera*, which would be represented in the binding syntax as the path *Position.X*. If you gave the *PerspectiveCamera* the name *cam*, the binding in the *ScrollBar* control would look like this:

```
Value="{Binding ElementName=cam, Path=Position.X, Mode=OneWayToSource}"
```

The problem is that *X* is not backed by a dependency property, and *X* can't be backed by a dependency property unless *Point3D* derives from *DependencyObject*, and *Point3D* isn't even a class. *Point3D* is a structure, and this structure doesn't implement any notification protocol when its properties change. What happens with this binding is that the *X* property of *Position* is actually changed by the *ScrollBar*, but nobody knows about it, so nothing gets updated.

You *can* move the camera with a *ScrollBar* entirely in XAML, but it involves 3D graphics transforms, and that's a subject to which I've devoted all of the next two chapters.

I'd like to make a little change in the overall structure of Simple3DScene.xaml and use this revised structure for many of the simpler XAML files I'll be showing you in this chapter and the chapters ahead. In Simple3DScene.xaml, the *Viewport3D* element has two children of type *ModelVisual3D*, each of which has a *Content* property of type *Model3D*. The first of these *Content* properties is the *GeometryModel3D* that defines the actual figure. The other is the *AmbientLight* object.

It's possible to combine the geometry and light into one *ModelVisual3D* by making the *Content* property an object of type *Model3DGroup*, which can then have multiple children of type *Model3D*. This results in slightly more nested markup, but a rather shorter overall length, as the following file demonstrates. I've also removed the *Border* element.

Simple3DSceneShortened.xaml

```
<!-- ======================================================
        Simple3DSceneShortened.xaml (c) 2007 by Charles Petzold
     ====================================================== -->
<Page xmlns="http://schemas.microsoft.com/winfx/2006/xaml/presentation"
      xmlns:x="http://schemas.microsoft.com/winfx/2006/xaml"
      WindowTitle="Simple 3D Scene (Shortened)"
      Title="Simple 3D Scene (Shortened)">
    <Viewport3D>
        <ModelVisual3D>
            <ModelVisual3D.Content>
                <Model3DGroup>
                    <GeometryModel3D>
                        <GeometryModel3D.Geometry>
                            <MeshGeometry3D Positions="0 0 0, 0 1 -1, 0 0 -2"
                                            TriangleIndices="0 1 2" />
                        </GeometryModel3D.Geometry>

                        <GeometryModel3D.Material>
                            <DiffuseMaterial Brush="Cyan"/>
                        </GeometryModel3D.Material>

                        <GeometryModel3D.BackMaterial>
                            <DiffuseMaterial Brush="Red" />
                        </GeometryModel3D.BackMaterial>
                    </GeometryModel3D>

                    <AmbientLight Color="White" />

                </Model3DGroup>
            </ModelVisual3D.Content>
        </ModelVisual3D>
```

```
        <Viewport3D.Camera>
            <PerspectiveCamera Position="-2 0 5"
                               LookDirection="0 0 -1"
                               UpDirection="0 1 0"
                               FieldOfView="45" />
        </Viewport3D.Camera>
    </Viewport3D>
</Page>
```

Fields of View

If you have experience with two-dimensional graphics, you're probably familiar with drawing in units of pixels, millimeters, or—in the Windows Presentation Foundation—"device-independent units" of 1/96 inch. In the WPF 3D you're dealing entirely with relative units, so you may initially be confused by how big something will be on the screen and what you can actually see.

Programmers will often use small numbers for points within a *Viewport3D*, but it's not a requirement. If you change one of the programs shown so far by increasing all the *Point3D* coordinates by a factor of 100 in the *Positions* collection of the *MeshGeometry3D* and the *Position* property of the *PerspectiveCamera*, everything will look the same.

You've already noted that when you make the width of the window narrower or wider, you'll see the figure contract and expand proportionally. Adjusting the height of the window has no effect, and will even clip the figure if the height isn't sufficient to fit the whole figure. Thus, the size of the figures in the 3D scene certainly depend (in part) on the width of the *Viewport3D*.

The *Viewport3D* itself always has a specific width and height, which is available from the get-only properties *ActualWidth* and *ActualHeight*. How large these dimensions are depends on how the *Viewport3D* is hosted. In the examples you've seen so far, the *Viewport3D* is as large as the interior of the *Border* or *Window* or *Page* in which it appears. The *Viewport3D* element occupies the entire interior of its parent because its default *HorizontalAlignment* and *VerticalAlignment* properties are both set to *Stretch*. However, *Viewport3D* is not like *Button*, which can automatically size itself to a dimension adequate to display its content. For example, try doing this in either of the two XAML files shown so far:

```
<Viewport3D HorizontalAlignment="Center">
```

This setting causes the *Viewport3D* to shrink down to a width of 0, and nothing will be displayed. In essence, the *Viewport3D* doesn't know how much screen space it needs to display the 3D scene you've defined. Instead, it displays this scene based on its *ActualWidth* and *ActualHeight* properties.

You can run into problems if you put a *Viewport3D* in a *StackPanel*. A vertical *StackPanel*, for example, only offers its children the minimum height requested by the child. The *Viewport3D* normally requests a height of zero, so that's what it gets.

You can wrest control of the size of the *Viewport3D* element from the WPF layout system and avoid problems like these by assigning the *Width* and *Height* properties explicitly. (The default values are *Double.NaN*.) For example, try this:

```
<Viewport3D Width="4in">
```

Now the *Viewport3D* always has a width of four inches, and it is centered within its host. You can move the *Viewport3D* to the left or right side of its host by setting the *HorizontalAlignment* property of the *Viewport3D* to *Left* or *Right*. If you make the window narrower than four inches, it won't be large enough for the fixed width of the *Viewport3D*. The triangle will begin to be obscured and eventually disappear.

You can also set the *Height* property, but it's often less useful than *Width*, and sometimes might cause problems. Try this:

```
<Viewport3D Width="4in" Height="1in">
```

Now the top of the triangle is lopped off because the overall size of the triangle is governed by the width of the *Viewport3D*, and the height is no longer sufficient to display the entire figure. However, if you want to make the *Viewport3D* smaller than its host and align it at the top or bottom by setting the *VerticalAlignment* property, you need to indicate a *Height* property. You'll also need an explicit *Height* property if you're putting the *Viewport3D* in a vertical *Stack-Panel*, and you'll almost definitely pair that with a *Width* property so that the *Viewport3D* doesn't get so wide that vertical clipping of the display occurs.

In many of the XAML files used to generate illustrations in this book, I've explicitly set a *Width* property in *Viewport3D* to enforce a specific metrical size on the images. This helps me reproduce images of the same size if I need to do some tweaking.

An alternative to setting *Width* and *Height* is setting *MinWidth* and *MinHeight*, which have default values of zero. For example:

```
<Viewport3D MinWidth="4in">
```

Now the *Viewport3D* will expand to fill a parent wider than four inches but doesn't get narrower than four inches. If you make the parent narrower than four inches, the triangle will be clipped. *MinWidth* is good if you're displaying something that doesn't make visual sense at small sizes, but which is fine at much larger sizes. To avoid truncation when the parent gets narrower than *MinWidth*, you might consider putting the *Viewport3D* inside a *ScrollViewer*. (Remember to set the *HorizontalScrollBarVisibility* property of *ScrollViewer* to *Auto* or *Visible*, because the property is *Hidden* by default.)

You can also set *MaxWidth* and *MaxHeight* to impose maximums. I've sometimes found *Max-Width* useful when defining a complex 3D animation. (I'll start showing animations in the next chapter.) As animated figures get larger, they eat up more processing time, and sometimes the animation degrades and becomes jerky. Imposing a *MaxWidth* keeps the figures down to a reasonable size, but lets the user make them even smaller if desired.

Now you've seen how *Viewport3D* gets an actual size—a size that is always available from the get-only *ActualWidth* and *ActualHeight* properties. What you see within those dimensions depends on the coordinates of the *MeshGeometry3D*, and the various properties of the *Camera* object you're using. Theoretically, the *FieldOfView* property defines a cone, and if you were to look through such a cone, you'd see a circular view. The WPF 3D bases its display on the width of that view, which you can imagine as a horizontal line of length *ActualWidth* across the center of the *Viewport3D*.

Let's quantify some of this: Suppose your camera is on the Z axis, which means that the *Position* property is (0, 0, *D*), where *D* stands for *Distance* from the XY plane. The *LookDirection* is **(0, 0, -1)**, which is straight back along the Z axis. The *UpDirection* is **(0, 1, 0)** or straight up. The *FieldOfView* property is set to *F*. How much of the *X* axis can you see? Let's call that amount *W*, for *Width*. Here's the aerial view:

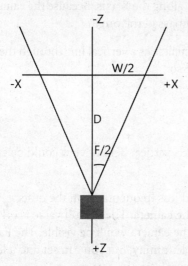

PerspectiveAerialView.xaml

With these labels, the simple trigonometric relationship can be written like so:

$$\tan\left(\frac{F}{2}\right) = \frac{W/2}{D}$$

And just solve for *W*:

$$W = 2D \cdot \tan\left(\frac{F}{2}\right)$$

You can move the camera left or right, and the visible width of the X axis will remain the same, but the origin won't be in the center.

Here's a little table with some common values. For the orientation shown in the diagram, the table shows the approximate width of the X axis that is visible.

Camera Distance	Field of View					
	15°	30°	45°	60°	75°	90°
1	0.26	0.54	0.83	1.15	1.53	2.0
2	0.53	1.07	1.65	2.3	3.1	4.0
3	0.79	1.61	2.5	3.5	4.6	6.0
4	1.05	2.1	3.3	4.6	6.1	8.0
5	1.32	2.7	4.1	5.8	7.7	10.0

The Simple3DScene.xaml file had a *FieldOfView* of 45 degrees and a camera distance of 5, which meant that you could see a width of about 4.1 along the X axis. Because the camera was positioned as an X coordinate of −2, it barely encompassed the origin.

The actual vertical field of view—which you might visualize as a vertical line through the center of the *Viewport3D*—can be calculated in degrees like so:

$$\frac{ActualHeight}{ActualWidth} \times FieldOfView$$

Depending on the aspect ratio of the *Viewport3D*, this vertical field of view could be greater than or less than the horizontal field of view.

Two other properties of PerspectiveCamera are used less frequently than the others. NearPlaneDistance eliminates figures too close to the camera. The default value is 0.125, which means that anything 0.125 units in front of the camera won't be visible. The FarPlaneDistance property has a default value of Double.Infinity, but you can set it to a lesser value to eliminate all objects beyond a certain distance from the camera.

In particularly complex animated 3D scenes, the various transforms that WPF 3D applies might create situations where figures that are different distances from the camera are mapped to the same plane. To avoid this problem, the programmer can narrow the depth of the 3D scene by explicitly setting the *NearPlaneDistance* and *FarPlaneDistance* properties.

Defining Flat Rectangles

One step up from the triangle on the *MeshGeometry3D* complexity ladder is the rectangle. As with the triangle, I want to put the rectangle on the negative Z axis with the following vertices:

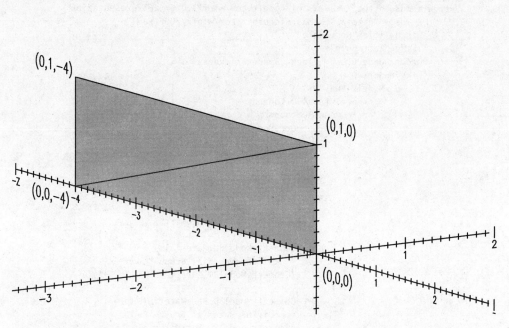

RectangleOnAxes.xaml

The *Positions* property of the *MeshGeometry3D* might be defined like so:

```
<MeshGeometry3D Positions="0 1 -4, 0 0 -4, 0 1 0, 0 0 0" ... />
```

The order of the points in this collection doesn't matter except when it comes time to define the *TriangleIndices* collection. A line drawn through the preceding rectangle shows how it can be divided into two triangles. The *TriangleIndices* collection consists of two triplets, or a total of six integers. If the side of the rectangle we can see in the diagram is considered the front, the *TrianglesIndices* collection contains the indices 0, 1, and 2 in that order (for the top-left triangle), and 1, 3, and 2 in that order. Here's the complete *MeshGeometry3D* object:

```
<MeshGeometry3D  Positions="0 1 -4, 0 0 -4, 0 1 0, 0 0 0"
                TriangleIndices="0 1 2, 1 3 2" />
```

The two triangles share two vertices. The complete XAML file follows.

Rectangle.xaml

```xml
<!-- ==========================================
        Rectangle.xaml (c) 2007 by Charles Petzold
     ========================================== -->
<Page xmlns="http://schemas.microsoft.com/winfx/2006/xaml/presentation"
      xmlns:x="http://schemas.microsoft.com/winfx/2006/xaml"
      WindowTitle="Rectangle"
      Title="Rectangle">
    <Border BorderBrush="Black" BorderThickness="1">
        <Viewport3D>
            <ModelVisual3D>
                <ModelVisual3D.Content>
                    <Model3DGroup>
                        <GeometryModel3D>
                            <GeometryModel3D.Geometry>

                                <!-- Rectangle. -->
                                <MeshGeometry3D
                                    Positions="0 1 -4, 0 0 -4, 0 1 0, 0 0 0"
                                    TriangleIndices=" 0 1 2, 1 3 2" />
                            </GeometryModel3D.Geometry>

                            <GeometryModel3D.Material>
                                <DiffuseMaterial Brush="Cyan" />
                            </GeometryModel3D.Material>

                            <GeometryModel3D.BackMaterial>
                                <DiffuseMaterial Brush="Red" />
                            </GeometryModel3D.BackMaterial>
                        </GeometryModel3D>

                        <!-- Light source. -->
                        <AmbientLight Color="White" />

                    </Model3DGroup>
                </ModelVisual3D.Content>
            </ModelVisual3D>

            <!-- Camera. -->
            <Viewport3D.Camera>
                <PerspectiveCamera Position="-1 0.5 4"
                                   LookDirection="0 0 -1"
                                   UpDirection="0 1 0"
                                   FieldOfView="45" />
            </Viewport3D.Camera>
        </Viewport3D>
    </Border>
</Page>
```

Notice that the camera still points straight back along the negative Z axis but it's not quite as far from the X axis as in the triangle example, and not quite as far to the left of the Z axis either. Also, the Y coordinate of the camera *Position* property is 0.5, putting the camera even with the vertical center of the rectangle. The foreshortening effect is clearly visible:

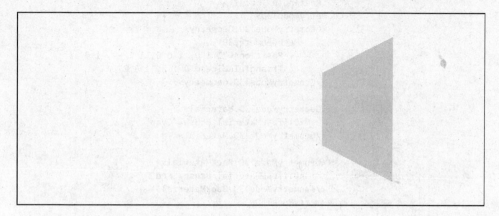

The following XAML file contains two *GeometryModel3D* elements to define two rectangles. The first rectangle is defined the same way as in Rectangle.xaml. The second is parallel to it and one unit farther to the right on the X axis.

TwoRectangles.xaml
```
<!-- =============================================
     TwoRectangles.xaml (c) 2007 by Charles Petzold
     ============================================= -->
<Page xmlns="http://schemas.microsoft.com/winfx/2006/xaml/presentation"
      xmlns:x="http://schemas.microsoft.com/winfx/2006/xaml"
      WindowTitle="Two Rectangles"
      Title="Two Rectangles">
    <Viewport3D>
        <ModelVisual3D>
            <ModelVisual3D.Content>
                <Model3DGroup>

                    <!-- Rectangle One. -->
                    <GeometryModel3D>
                        <GeometryModel3D.Geometry>
                            <MeshGeometry3D
                                Positions="0 1 -4, 0 0 -4, 0 1 0, 0 0 0"
                                TriangleIndices="0 1 2, 1 3 2" />
                        </GeometryModel3D.Geometry>

                        <GeometryModel3D.Material>
                            <DiffuseMaterial Brush="Cyan" />
                        </GeometryModel3D.Material>

                        <GeometryModel3D.BackMaterial>
                            <DiffuseMaterial Brush="Red" />
                        </GeometryModel3D.BackMaterial>
                    </GeometryModel3D>
```

```
                <!-- Rectangle Two. -->
                <GeometryModel3D>
                    <GeometryModel3D.Geometry>
                        <MeshGeometry3D
                            Positions="1 1 0, 1 0 0, 1 1 -4, 1 0 -4"
                            TriangleIndices="0 1 2, 1 3 2" />
                    </GeometryModel3D.Geometry>

                    <GeometryModel3D.Material>
                        <DiffuseMaterial Brush="Cyan" />
                    </GeometryModel3D.Material>

                    <GeometryModel3D.BackMaterial>
                        <DiffuseMaterial Brush="Red" />
                    </GeometryModel3D.BackMaterial>
                </GeometryModel3D>

                <!-- Light source. -->
                <AmbientLight Color="White" />

            </Model3DGroup>
        </ModelVisual3D.Content>
    </ModelVisual3D>

    <!-- Camera. -->
    <Viewport3D.Camera>
        <PerspectiveCamera Position="-2 2 4"
                           LookDirection="2 -1 -4"
                           UpDirection="0 1 0"
                           FieldOfView="45" />
    </Viewport3D.Camera>
  </Viewport3D>
</Page>
```

I've also defined the camera *Position* and *LookDirection* properties so that the figure appears roughly in the center of the *Viewport3D*. Because the second rectangle is designed so that the front faces the positive X axis, we're actually viewing the reverse side, which is red. (In this gray-shade image, red appears as a darker gray than the gray representing cyan.)

We're starting to get more of a 3D effect here because one of the figures obscures part of the second.

In the TwoRectangles.xaml file, I've defined the rectangles with wholly separate *Geometry-Model3D* elements. You need to do this if the two figures have different *Material* or *Back-Material* properties. In this case, however, the *Material* and *BackMaterial* properties are the same, and you can replace the two *GeometryModel3D* elements with a single one that combines the two rectangles in one *MeshGeometry3D*:

```
<GeometryModel3D>
    <GeometryModel3D.Geometry>
        <MeshGeometry3D Positions="0 1 -4, 0 0 -4, 0 1 0, 0 0 0,
                                   1 1 0, 1 0 0, 1 1 -4, 1 0 -4"
                    TriangleIndices="0 1 2, 1 3 2,
                                     4 5 6, 5 7 6" />
    </GeometryModel3D.Geometry>

    <GeometryModel3D.Material>
        <DiffuseMaterial Brush="Cyan" />
    </GeometryModel3D.Material>

    <GeometryModel3D.BackMaterial>
        <DiffuseMaterial Brush="Red" />
    </GeometryModel3D.BackMaterial>
</GeometryModel3D>
```

The first four points in the *Positions* collection define the coordinates of the leftmost rectangle, and the first six *TriangleIndices* items refer to those coordinates. The second four points are for the second rectangle, and the last six *TriangleIndices* items refer to those four coordinates.

Defining "Solid" Figures

Let's ascend the *MeshGeometry3D* complexity ladder again and try constructing a solid figure, which is simply a matter of defining triangles that aren't in the same plane. A cube, for example, is simply six squares, each of which consists of two triangles, and it only looks like a cube because the corners and sides of the six squares meet. I put the word "solid" in quotation marks in the heading to this section because these figures only appear to be solid. A cube is defined as a collection of six squares, and the cube is actually hollow inside.

Rather than a cube, I want to construct a square cuboid such as the ones I showed toward the beginning of this chapter. Like the cube, the square cuboid consist of six sides, which we can conveniently label as front, left, top, right, bottom, and rear. The left and right sides have the same positions and dimensions as the two rectangles in TwoRectangles.xaml.

The following *MeshGeometry3D* markup is really just an expansion of the one in the alternative markup for TwoRectangles.xaml. The six faces of the figure are defined in a single *Mesh-Geometry3D*, but they are otherwise independent. The first four points in the *Positions* collection are the vertices for the front side, and the first six integers in the *TriangleIndices* collection refer to those points. The next four items in the *Positions* collection are vertices for the left side, and the next six integers in the *TriangleIndices* collection refer to those four points. This may seem wasteful because the *Positions* collection ends up containing 24 points when it really need contain only 8, but you'll see shortly why I chose to do it this way.

```
WashedOutSquareCuboid.xaml
<!-- =======================================================
        WashedOutSquareCuboid.xaml (c) 2007 by Charles Petzold
     ======================================================= -->
<Page xmlns="http://schemas.microsoft.com/winfx/2006/xaml/presentation"
      xmlns:x="http://schemas.microsoft.com/winfx/2006/xaml"
      WindowTitle="Washed-Out Square Cuboid"
      Title="Washed-Out Square Cuboid">
    <Viewport3D>
        <ModelVisual3D>
            <ModelVisual3D.Content>
                <Model3DGroup>
                    <GeometryModel3D>
                        <GeometryModel3D.Geometry>

                            <!-- Square cuboid sides in order:
                                   front, left, top, right, bottom, rear. -->
                            <MeshGeometry3D
                                Positions="0 1  0, 0 0  0, 1 1  0, 1 0  0,
                                           0 1 -4, 0 0 -4, 0 1  0, 0 0  0,
                                           1 1 -4, 0 1 -4, 1 1  0, 0 1  0,
                                           1 1  0, 1 0  0, 1 1 -4, 1 0 -4,
                                           1 0  0, 0 0  0, 1 0 -4, 0 0 -4,
                                           1 1 -4, 1 0 -4, 0 1 -4, 0 0 -4"

                                TriangleIndices=" 0  1  2,  1  3  2,
                                                  4  5  6,  5  7  6,
                                                  8  9 10,  9 11 10,
                                                 12 13 14, 13 15 14,
                                                 16 17 18, 17 19 18,
                                                 20 21 22, 21 23 22" />
                        </GeometryModel3D.Geometry>

                        <GeometryModel3D.Material>
                            <DiffuseMaterial Brush="Cyan" />
                        </GeometryModel3D.Material>

                        <GeometryModel3D.BackMaterial>
                            <DiffuseMaterial Brush="Red" />
                        </GeometryModel3D.BackMaterial>
                    </GeometryModel3D>

                    <!-- Light source. -->
                    <AmbientLight Color="White" />

                </Model3DGroup>
            </ModelVisual3D.Content>
        </ModelVisual3D>
```

```
        <!-- Camera. -->
        <Viewport3D.Camera>
            <PerspectiveCamera Position="-2 2 4"
                               LookDirection="2 -1 -4"
                               UpDirection="0 1 0"
                               FieldOfView="45" />
        </Viewport3D.Camera>
    </Viewport3D>
</Page>
```

If you run this program, you'll see why I called it WashedOutSquareCuboid. The front, top, and left sides are visible, but it's hard to tell where one face ends and the next begins. There are no edges and everything is colored uniformly.

What exactly is the problem here? It's not the figure itself, and it's not the camera. It's actually the lighting. The light source in this file is an object of type *AmbientLight*, which illuminates all surfaces uniformly, meaning that all the surfaces are colored the same way, and that's why they seamlessly blend with each other.

Balancing Light Sources

AmbientLight resembles the outdoors on a very overcast day—the type of day where you know the sun is up there somewhere, but that's about it. You can still see things around you, but everything is illuminated equally and there are no shadows. We experience ambient light because the molecules in our atmosphere bounce available light among themselves.

AmbientLight defines no public properties on its own but inherits a *Color* property, which is the only property defined by the abstract *Light* class. The *Color* property is white by default.

You can set the *Color* property of *AmbientLight* to any of the 141 static read-only properties defined by the *Colors* class. (The transparency channel of the *Color* property is ignored, so the *Transparent* member of the *Colors* class is the same as *White*.) For example:

```
<AmbientLight Color="Cyan" />
```

That change will have no effect on cyan surfaces because the surfaces are only reflecting cyan anyway. But try something like this:

```
<AmbientLight Color="Green" />
```

Now the ambient light is green, so the cyan surface reflects only green light, and the surface appears green. Perhaps the ambient light is entirely red:

```
<AmbientLight Color="Red" />
```

The cyan brush has no red in it, so no light will be reflected, and the surface appears black.

You can also specify the RGB values of the color in hexadecimal:

```
<AmbientLight Color="#000080" />
```

That's a dark blue, so a figure colored with a cyan brush will appear dark blue with such ambient lighting. In these simple examples, the figure's color is a combination of the figure's brush color and the *AmbientLight* color. If you take each of the three red, green, and blue primaries separately, you can calculate a reflected value based on the *Brush* color used for the *Diffuse-Material* and the *Color* property of the *AmbientLight*:

Reflected Value = (Material Brush Value × Ambient Light Value) / 255

This is actually rather simplified, because I'm treating the *Material* as just a simple color. In reality, the *DiffuseMaterial* class defines an *AmbientColor* property that indicates how much of the ambient light is reflected by the brush. The property is white by default, which means that the brush reflects all the ambient light that corresponds with its own color. This is a matter I'll take up in more detail in Chapter 4.

You can set the ambient light color as medium gray:

```
<AmbientLight Color="Gray" />
```

This is the same as:

```
<AmbientLight Color="#808080" />
```

That's half the amount of light as white, and figures colored with a cyan brush will appear dark cyan.

You can have more than one light source, and for many purposes you'll want to combine some ambient light with some directional light, specifically an object of type *DirectionalLight*. Like *AmbientLight*, *DirectionalLight* inherits the *Color* property from the abstract *Light* class, but it also defines a *Direction* vector. The default is $(0, 0, -1)$, which is the same default as the camera *LookDirection* property—that is, pointing straight back along the negative Z axis. *DirectionalLight* is assumed to come from an infinite location, much like the apparent location of the sun for small regions on earth.

Directional light strikes surfaces at a particular angle. The amount of reflected light is proportional to the sine of the angle that the light makes with the surface. (This is rather simplified; the detailed version is actually much messier; I will allude to it briefly toward the end of this chapter and discuss it more in Chapter 4.) All planes parallel to each other reflect the same amount of directional light, with no attenuation effect and no shadows.

The default *Direction* property of *DirectionalLight* points in the direction of the negative Z axis. I think it makes more sense for directional light to come from above, but I wouldn't set the *Direction* property to the high noon vector $(0, -1, 0)$. That setting would maximally illuminate the top sides of surfaces parallel to the XZ plane, but provide no illumination of surfaces parallel to the XY plane or YZ plane. Nor would I choose $(1, -1, 0)$, which makes the light come from the upper left. Now the light is at the same 45-degree angle to the XZ plane and the YZ plane, and the XY plane isn't illuminated at all. With $(1, -1, -1)$ the light comes from behind the viewer, but then the XY, XZ, and YZ planes are illuminated equally.

If a figure has sides parallel to the XY, XZ, and YZ planes (as the square cuboid does), you probably want all three visible sides to get some illumination, but different degrees of illumination. This means that the *Direction* vector for *DirectionalLight* must have three different values, such as $(2, -3, -1)$. This is light that comes from the upper left and behind the viewer, but it's higher than it is leftwards, and more leftwards than it is behind.

If the individual primary values of the *Color* properties of *AmbientLight* and *DirectionalLight* add up to more than 255, sides that might not be parallel to each other may be fully illuminated. It's probably better to fully illuminate only those surfaces perpendicular to the *DirectionalLight* vector, which means that the primary color values of *AmbientLight* and *DirectionalLight* should add up to 255, or perhaps 256 for calculational convenience.

You might want to use *Gray* (or equivalently, "#808080") for both *AmbientLight* and *DirectionalLight*, or you might want to go even further in emphasizing *DirectionalLight*. The next file is basically the same markup as WashedOutSquareCuboid.xaml except that the *AmbientLight* color is set to "#404040", and a new *DirectionalLight* element has a *Color* value of "#C0C0C0". Total light is split between 25 percent ambient light and 75 percent directional light.

PerspectiveSquareCuboid.xaml

```
<!-- =======================================================
     PerspectiveSquareCuboid.xaml (c) 2007 by Charles Petzold
     ======================================================= -->
<Page xmlns="http://schemas.microsoft.com/winfx/2006/xaml/presentation"
      xmlns:x="http://schemas.microsoft.com/winfx/2006/xaml"
      WindowTitle="Perspective Square Cuboid"
      Title="Perspective Square Cuboid">
    <Viewport3D>
        <ModelVisual3D>
            <ModelVisual3D.Content>
                <Model3DGroup>
                    <GeometryModel3D>
                        <GeometryModel3D.Geometry>
```

```xml
                    <!-- Square cuboid sides in order:
                            front, left, top, right, bottom, rear. -->
                    <MeshGeometry3D
                        Positions="0 1 0, 0 0 0, 1 1 0, 1 0 0,
                                   0 1 -4, 0 0 -4, 0 1 0, 0 0 0,
                                   1 1 -4, 0 1 -4, 1 1 0, 0 1 0,
                                   1 1 0, 1 0 0, 1 1 -4, 1 0 -4,
                                   1 0 0, 0 0 0, 1 0 -4, 0 0 -4,
                                   1 1 -4, 1 0 -4, 0 1 -4, 0 0 -4"

                        TriangleIndices=" 0  1  2,  1  3  2,
                                          4  5  6,  5  7  6,
                                          8  9 10,  9 11 10,
                                         12 13 14, 13 15 14,
                                         16 17 18, 17 19 18,
                                         20 21 22, 21 23 22" />
                </GeometryModel3D.Geometry>

                <GeometryModel3D.Material>
                    <DiffuseMaterial Brush="Cyan" />
                </GeometryModel3D.Material>

                <GeometryModel3D.BackMaterial>
                    <DiffuseMaterial Brush="Red" />
                </GeometryModel3D.BackMaterial>

            </GeometryModel3D>

            <!-- Light sources. -->
            <AmbientLight Color="#404040" />
            <DirectionalLight Color="#C0C0C0" Direction="2 -3 -1" />

        </Model3DGroup>
      </ModelVisual3D.Content>
    </ModelVisual3D>

    <!-- Camera. -->
    <Viewport3D.Camera>
        <PerspectiveCamera Position="-2 2 4"
                           LookDirection="2 -1 -4"
                           UpDirection="0 1 0"
                           FieldOfView="45" />
    </Viewport3D.Camera>
  </Viewport3D>
</Page>
```

And this does the trick, as you can see.

All three visible sides are illuminated differently, and now it looks much more like a 3D figure. The two light sources I've used in PerspectiveSquareCuboid.xaml are my favorites and you'll see them in many XAML files in this book.

The Orthographic Projection

The alternative to *PerspectiveCamera* is *OrthographicCamera*. (There's also a *MatrixCamera*, but it requires you to define your own pair of 4×4 matrices that define the projection, and that's a rather advanced topic awaiting us in Chapter 7.) *PerspectiveCamera* and *OrthographicCamera* both derive from *ProjectionCamera*, which defines the *Position*, *LookDirection*, *UpDirection*, *NearPlaneDistance*, and *FarPlaneDistance* properties. *PerspectiveCamera* defines only one public property itself, *FieldOfView*. *OrthographicCamera* also defines a single public property, *Width*, and gives it a default setting of 2.

The *OrthographicCamera* effectively defines a projection plane, the center of which is located at the *Position* property. The projection plane is perpendicular to the *LookDirection* vector and oriented in accordance with the *UpDirection* property. It is *Width* units wide.

If the *Position* property is any point on the positive Z axis, and the *LookDirection* vector points in the direction of the negative Z axis, and the *UpDirection* vector points up, the horizontal width of the *Viewport3D* will show everything between X coordinates of −*Width* / 2 to *Width* / 2, as the following diagram demonstrates.

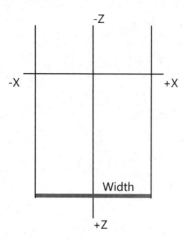

OrthographicAerialView.xaml

Everything within this viewing swatch is then scaled to the *ActualWidth* dimension of the *Viewport3D*.

The following XAML file is identical to the previous one except that it includes an *Orthographic-Camera* rather than a *PerspectiveCamera*.

```
OrthographicSquareCuboid.xaml
<!-- =========================================================
      OrthographicSquareCuboid.xaml (c) 2007 by Charles Petzold
     ========================================================= -->
<Page xmlns="http://schemas.microsoft.com/winfx/2006/xaml/presentation"
      xmlns:x="http://schemas.microsoft.com/winfx/2006/xaml"
      WindowTitle="Orthographic Square Cuboid"
      Title="Orthographic Square Cuboid">
    <Viewport3D>
        <ModelVisual3D>
            <ModelVisual3D.Content>
                <Model3DGroup>
                    <GeometryModel3D>
                        <GeometryModel3D.Geometry>

                            <!-- Square cuboid sides in order:
                                 front, left, top, right, bottom, rear. -->
                            <MeshGeometry3D
                                Positions="0 1  0, 0 0  0, 1 1  0, 1 0  0,
                                           0 1 -4, 0 0 -4, 0 1  0, 0 0  0,
                                           1 1 -4, 0 1 -4, 1 1  0, 0 1  0,
                                           1 1  0, 1 0  0, 1 1 -4, 1 0 -4,
                                           1 0  0, 0 0  0, 1 0 -4, 0 0 -4,
                                           1 1 -4, 1 0 -4, 0 1 -4, 0 0 -4"

                                TriangleIndices=" 0  1  2,  1  3  2,
                                                  4  5  6,  5  7  6,
                                                  8  9 10,  9 11 10,
```

```
                                   12 13 14, 13 15 14,
                                   16 17 18, 17 19 18,
                                   20 21 22, 21 23 22" />
            </GeometryModel3D.Geometry>

            <GeometryModel3D.Material>
                <DiffuseMaterial Brush="Cyan" />
            </GeometryModel3D.Material>

            <GeometryModel3D.BackMaterial>
                <DiffuseMaterial Brush="Red" />
            </GeometryModel3D.BackMaterial>

        </GeometryModel3D>

        <!-- Light sources. -->
        <AmbientLight Color="#404040" />
        <DirectionalLight Color="#C0C0C0" Direction="2 -3 -1" />

      </Model3DGroup>
    </ModelVisual3D.Content>
  </ModelVisual3D>

  <!-- Camera. -->
  <Viewport3D.Camera>
      <OrthographicCamera Position="-2 2 4"
                          LookDirection="2 -1 -4"
                          UpDirection="0 1 0"
                          Width="5" />
  </Viewport3D.Camera>
 </Viewport3D>
</Page>
```

The resultant image has a back end that is the same size as the front end.

And if you think the back looks larger than the front, it's an optical illusion. Measure it!

Why Not Share the Vertices?

The three XAML files that display a square cuboid all define the six faces of the image independently. This results in a *Positions* collection that has 24 points rather than just 8 points for the 8 vertices of the figure. Why not just put 8 points in the *Positions* collection and share the vertices among the faces?

Don't fall into the trap of thinking you'll get better performance with 8 points in the *Positions* collection rather than 24. The rendering of 3D objects is triangle-driven and not vertex-driven. But let's try it. The following XAML file has only eight points in the *Positions* collection and defines the *TriangleVertices* collection appropriately.

```
SharedVerticesSquareCuboid.xaml
<!-- ============================================================
        SharedVerticesSquareCuboid.xaml (c) 2007 by Charles Petzold
     ============================================================ -->
<Page xmlns="http://schemas.microsoft.com/winfx/2006/xaml/presentation"
      xmlns:x="http://schemas.microsoft.com/winfx/2006/xaml"
      WindowTitle="Shared Vertices Square Cuboid"
      Title="Shared Vertices Square Cuboid">
    <Viewport3D>
        <ModelVisual3D>
            <ModelVisual3D.Content>
                <Model3DGroup>
                    <GeometryModel3D>
                        <GeometryModel3D.Geometry>

                            <!-- Square cuboid shared vertices. -->
                            <MeshGeometry3D
                                Positions="0 1 0, 0 0 0, 1 1 0, 1 0 0,
                                           1 1 -4, 1 0 -4, 0 1 -4, 0 0 -4"

                                TriangleIndices="0 1 2, 1 3 2,
                                                 6 7 0, 7 1 0,
                                                 4 6 2, 6 1 2,
                                                 2 3 4, 3 5 4,
                                                 3 1 5, 1 7 5,
                                                 4 5 6, 5 7 6" />
                        </GeometryModel3D.Geometry>

                        <GeometryModel3D.Material>
                            <DiffuseMaterial Brush="Cyan" />
                        </GeometryModel3D.Material>

                        <GeometryModel3D.BackMaterial>
                            <DiffuseMaterial Brush="Red" />
                        </GeometryModel3D.BackMaterial>
                    </GeometryModel3D>

                    <!-- Light sources. -->
                    <AmbientLight Color="#404040" />
                    <DirectionalLight Color="#C0C0C0" Direction="2 -3 -1" />
```

```
            </Model3DGroup>
          </ModelVisual3D.Content>
        </ModelVisual3D>

        <!-- Camera. -->
        <Viewport3D.Camera>
            <PerspectiveCamera Position="-2 2 4"
                               LookDirection="2 -1 -4"
                               UpDirection="0 1 0"
                               FieldOfView="45" />
        </Viewport3D.Camera>
      </Viewport3D>
    </Page>
```

The result is rather shocking. Although the light sources are the same as those in the previous two XAML files, the faces of the figure are no longer distinct colors. Instead, each face seems to have oddly gradiated shades of cyan.

What has happened here?

Earlier I discussed how triangles reflect *DirectionalLight* based on the angle that the *Direction* vector makes with the surface. This was a rather simplified explanation. In reality, the calculations going on behind the scenes are rather more complex. The calculations actually involve each *vertex* of the figure rather than the faces. The percentage of light reflected at each vertex is calculated based on the average of all the triangles that meet at that vertex. If the vertices for each face are discrete—as they are in the previous XAML files that displayed square cuboids—the one or two triangles that meet at each vertex are parallel to each other, and the light reflected from that vertex is based on that shared plane.

In the SharedVerticesSquareCuboid.xaml file, vertices are shared among multiple triangles that meet at angles. The amount of light reflected at that vertex is based on an average of the angles that these individual triangles make with the light source. Then, the light reflected within each triangle is an interpolation of the value of light reflected at each of the vertices. This has the effect of smoothing out edges. This smoothing effect is entirely appropriate if you are using triangles to approximate curved surfaces, but it doesn't work well at all if you want your surfaces to look flat and distinct.

The simple rule is this: Don't share vertices of triangles that meet at an angle unless you want edges to be smoothed.

Transparency

In the PerspectiveSquareCuboid.xaml file, remove the markup that defines the *Material* property, or set the *Brush* property of the first *DiffuseMaterial* element to *Transparent*. Here's what you'll see:

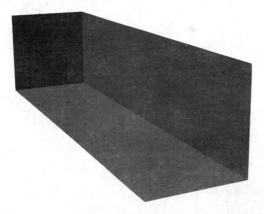

PerspectiveSquareCuboidNoMaterial.xaml

You're actually peering inside the figure. Although the orientation is visually ambiguous, the darker square part is actually the inside rear of the figure. Because the *Material* property is now gone or set to a transparent brush, any triangle viewed from the front is invisible. Because the *BackMaterial* still exists, any triangle viewed from the rear is red. Consequently, the top, left, and front faces of the square cuboid are completely invisible from the front, and you're actually looking at the backs of the right, bottom, and rear faces.

One interesting effect is to set the *DiffuseMaterial* brush to a semi-transparent color, or perhaps for both the *Material* and *BackMaterial* properties, as in this program.

```
SixSquaresInSearchOfACube.xaml
<!-- ============================================================
     SixSquaresInSearchOfACube.xaml (c) 2007 by Charles Petzold
     ============================================================ -->
<Page xmlns="http://schemas.microsoft.com/winfx/2006/xaml/presentation"
      xmlns:x="http://schemas.microsoft.com/winfx/2006/xaml"
      WindowTitle="Six Squares in Search of a Cube"
      Title="Six Squares in Search of a Cube">
```

```xml
<Viewport3D>
    <ModelVisual3D>
        <ModelVisual3D.Content>
            <Model3DGroup>
                <GeometryModel3D>
                    <GeometryModel3D.Geometry>

                        <!-- Square sides in order:
                                front, left, top, right, bottom, rear. -->
                        <MeshGeometry3D
                            Positions=
                                "0 2 -0.5, 0 0 -0.5, 2 2 -0.5, 2 0 -0.5,
                                 0.5 2 -2, 0.5 0 -2, 0.5 2  0, 0.5 0  0,
                                 2 1.5 -2, 0 1.5 -2, 2 1.5  0, 0 1.5  0,
                                 1.5 2  0, 1.5 0  0, 1.5 2 -2, 1.5 0 -2,
                                 2 0.5  0, 0 0.5  0, 2 0.5 -2, 0 0.5 -2,
                                 2 2 -1.5, 2 0 -1.5, 0 2 -1.5, 0 0 -1.5"

                            TriangleIndices=" 0  1  2,  1  3  2,
                                              4  5  6,  5  7  6,
                                              8  9 10,  9 11 10,
                                             12 13 14, 13 15 14,
                                             16 17 18, 17 19 18,
                                             20 21 22, 21 23 22" />
                    </GeometryModel3D.Geometry>

                    <GeometryModel3D.Material>
                        <DiffuseMaterial Brush="#8000FFFF" />
                    </GeometryModel3D.Material>

                    <GeometryModel3D.BackMaterial>
                        <DiffuseMaterial Brush="#80FF0000" />
                    </GeometryModel3D.BackMaterial>
                </GeometryModel3D>

                <!-- Light sources -->
                <AmbientLight Color="#404040" />
                <DirectionalLight Color="#C0C0C0" Direction="2 -3 -1" />

            </Model3DGroup>
        </ModelVisual3D.Content>
    </ModelVisual3D>

    <!-- Camera -->
    <Viewport3D.Camera>
        <OrthographicCamera Position="-2.5 2.5 4"
                            LookDirection="2.7 -1 -4"
                            UpDirection="0 1 0"
                            Width="5" />
    </Viewport3D.Camera>
</Viewport3D>
</Page>
```

The program displays six squares with semi-transparent *DiffuseMaterial* brushes, and arranges them in somewhat of a cube, but intersecting each other. WPF 3D has no collision detection: Any figures that occupy that same space simply meld into and through each other, often creating some interesting effects.

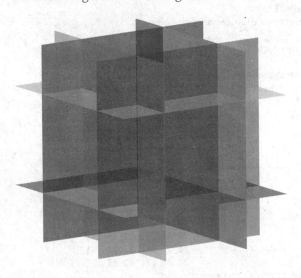

Sorting Out the Classes

Partially because of the differentiation between visuals and models, the class hierarchy in the *System.Windows.Media.Media3D* namespace can be a bit confusing. To conclude this chapter, I want to take a stab at sorting out those class hierarchies that you've encountered in this chapter. More class hierarchies will follow in the next several chapters.

You assemble 3D scenes in an element of type *Viewport3D*, a class that derives directly from *FrameworkElement* through this long class hierarchy:

Object
    DispatcherObject (abstract)
        DependencyObject
            Visual (abstract)
                UIElement
                    FrameworkElement
                        Viewport3D

Viewport3D defines two crucial properties: *Camera* (of type *Camera*) and *Children*, of type *Visual3DCollection*. The *Children* property is the content property of *Viewport3D*, so it usually doesn't explicitly appear in markup.

The complete class hierarchy surrounding *Camera* is:

Object
    DispatcherObject (abstract)
        DependencyObject
            Freezable (abstract)
                Animatable (abstract)
                    Camera (abstract)
                        ProjectionCamera (abstract)
                            PerspectiveCamera (sealed)
                            OrthographicCamera (sealed)
                        MatrixCamera (sealed)

A *Viewport3D* contains one object of type *Camera* and multiple child objects of type *Visual3D*. In WPF parlance, a visual is something that has a visual appearance and can render itself on the screen. *Visual3D* is actually abstract and has one descendent:

Object
    DispatcherObject (abstract)
        DependencyObject
            Visual3D (abstract)
                ModelVisual3D

Like *Viewport3D*, *ModelVisual3D* also has a *Children* property of type *Visual3DCollection*, but it's not used as much as its *Content* property. The *Content* property is of type *Model3D*. In WPF 3D parlance, a model is information for rendering something on the screen. As you can see from this class hierarchy, a WPF 3D model is either a 3D figure (of type *GeometryModel3D*) or a derivative of the *Light* class.

Object
    DispatcherObject (abstract)
        DependencyObject
            Freezable (abstract)
                Animatable (abstract)
                  Model3D (abstract)
                    GeometryModel3D (sealed)
                    Light (abstract)
                    ...
                  Model3DGroup (sealed)

I'll discuss the classes that descend from *Light* in Chapter 4. So far you've seen *AmbientLight* and *DirectionalLight*.

The *GeometryModel3D* class has three properties: *Geometry* of type *Geometry3D*, and *Material* and *BackMaterial*, both of type *Material*.

I'll discuss the *Material* class and its derivatives in Chapter 5. The *Geometry3D* class is abstract and has just one descendent:

Object
        DispatcherObject (abstract)
                DependencyObject
                        Freezable (abstract)
                                Animatable (abstract)
                                        Geometry3D (abstract)
                                                MeshGeometry3D (sealed)

The *MeshGeometry3D* class defines the *Positions* and *TriangleIndices* collections that you've already seen, plus two other collections named *Normals* and *TextureCoordinates* that you'll encounter in Chapters 4 and 5, respectively.

Any *Viewport3D* object has only one camera. If you want to present multiple simultaneous views of a scene, you need multiple *Viewport3D* elements. You might overlay them (perhaps in a single *Grid* cell) or put them side-by-side. Also, all the light sources of a *Viewport3D* illuminate all the 3D figures. If you want some figures illuminated by the light sources, but others illuminated by other light sources, again you need more than one *Viewport3D*.

By taking advantage of defaults—and by being aware that the absence of a light source causes objects to be rendered as black—you can actually create a functional 3D scene in just 14 lines of XAML (not counting the comments). The following file might be assumed to qualify as the tiniest 3D program.

```
Tiniest3D.xaml
<!-- =========================================
        Tiniest3D.xaml (c) 2007 by Charles Petzold
     ========================================= -->
<Viewport3D xmlns="http://schemas.microsoft.com/winfx/2006/xaml/presentation">
    <ModelVisual3D>
        <ModelVisual3D.Content>
            <GeometryModel3D>
                <GeometryModel3D.Geometry>
                    <MeshGeometry3D Positions="-1 0 -8, 1 0 -8, 0 1 -8" />
                </GeometryModel3D.Geometry>
                <GeometryModel3D.Material>
                    <DiffuseMaterial Brush="Red" />
                </GeometryModel3D.Material>
            </GeometryModel3D>
        </ModelVisual3D.Content>
    </ModelVisual3D>
</Viewport3D>
```

But is it really the tiniest? After I posted that markup in my blog (originally including a *PerspectiveCamera*, which turned out to be created by default), Nathan Dunlap of *designerslove.net* showed how to use resources to make it even tinier:

```
<Viewport3D xmlns="http://schemas.microsoft.com/winfx/2006/xaml/presentation"
            xmlns:x="http://schemas.microsoft.com/winfx/2006/xaml">
    <Viewport3D.Resources>
        <MeshGeometry3D x:Key="mesh" Positions="-1 0 -8, 1 0 -8, 0 1 -8" />
        <DiffuseMaterial x:Key="mat" Brush="Red" />
        <GeometryModel3D x:Key="model"
                         Geometry="{StaticResource mesh}"
                         Material="{StaticResource mat}" />
    </Viewport3D.Resources>
    <ModelVisual3D Content="{StaticResource model}" />
</Viewport3D>
```

As you'll see in Chapter 2, "Transforms and Animation," resources are essential to reusing models and other objects, particularly in combination with transforms. But I'm afraid that nothing else in this book will be quite as simple as these tiniest 3D programs.

Chapter 2
Transforms and Animation

Three-dimensional figures on the computer screen are usually more satisfying when they move. In the grand scheme of things, both 3D and animation are considered somewhat "advanced" graphics techniques, so it's probably not surprising that they often seem to be used together. Animation helps 3D figures demonstrate their extra dimensionality and reveal parts previously hidden from view. Animation brings 3D figures to life.

The Windows Presentation Foundation has a versatile animation system largely defined in the *System.Windows.Media.Animation* namespace and most conveniently accessed in XAML. Whenever possible, you'll probably want to use one of the many classes that derive from *AnimationTimeline* for defining simple animations. (Chapter 30 of my book *Applications = Code + Markup* is an 80-page overview of these classes as they apply to two-dimensional graphics animation.) The animation classes that derive from *AnimationTimeline* are all devoted to animating properties of various data types. For example, to animate properties of type *Double*, you use *DoubleAnimation*, *DoubleAnimationUsingKeyFrames*, or *DoubleAnimationUsingPath*. The classes particularly well-suited for 3D graphics are those that animate properties of type *Double*, *Color*, *Point3D*, *Vector3D*, *Rotation3D*, and *Quaternion*.

For example, the *Point3DAnimation* and *Point3DAnimationUsingKeyFrames* classes can animate properties of type *Point3D*, such as the *Position* property defined by *ProjectionCamera*. Properties targeted by these animation classes must be backed by dependency properties; virtually all properties defined by the 3D classes fit that criterion. For example, the *Position* property defined by *ProjectionCamera* is associated with a static field of type *Dependency-Property* named *PositionProperty*. As I'll demonstrate shortly, you can easily define an animation that targets the *Position* property of *PerspectiveCamera* and seems to move the camera within the three-dimensional coordinate space.

Although you can change the position of a camera relative to a 3D figure, changing the location of the 3D figure itself is not quite as easy. The *Positions* property defined by *MeshGeometry3D* is an object of type *Point3DCollection* and contains the points that define the figure's vertices. Although *Positions* is backed by the dependency property *PositionsProperty*, no predefined class animates a property of type *Point3DCollection*. Nor is it possible to use the *Point3DAnimation* class to target a particular element of the *Positions* collection. A different strategy is required.

One approach to changing the *Positions* collection that I'll demonstrate in this chapter involves accessing the individual elements of the *Positions* collection directly, perhaps initiated by a *DispatcherTimer* or *CompositionTarget* event, or in response to user input. Because *Point3DCollection* is derived from the *Freezable* class and includes a *Changed* event, the *MeshGeometry3D* object that contains that collection can respond to any change to the *Positions* object. In turn, this change ripples up through the *GeometryModel3D* object that contains that mesh geometry, the *ModelVisual3D* that contains that model, and the *Viewport3D* that contains that visual.

Another approach to altering a 3D figure is through the use of graphics transforms. Used in their simplest way, transforms let you change a figure's location or size, or let you rotate the figure around an axis. Generally you'll define a particular transform, and then animate properties of that transform. You can apply transforms to models (that is, to lights and meshes), to visuals (specifically, the *ModelVisual3D* class) and to the camera. Animating a transform is perhaps the most common technique for basic 3D animation.

Transforms also help you to share and reuse objects of type *MeshGeometry3D* or *GeometryModel3D*. You can define one basic form (for example, a cube centered on the origin with one-unit sides) and then use transforms to display multiple cubes with different locations, sizes, and orientations.

One warning: Animation looks much better when you enable anti-aliasing. Without anti-aliasing, the jaggedness of the animated 3D figures often changes in distracting ways. Having the proper video board for Tier 2 graphics rendering makes a big difference in the appearance of the animated graphics. In your own applications, you might even consider limiting 3D animation when the program is running on a computer that is not capable of Tier 2 rendering.

Animation Without Transforms

The standard WPF animation classes are those that derive from the *AnimationTimeline* class in the *System.Windows.Media.Animation* namespace. These classes allow animating properties of several data types found in the common 3D classes. You can animate properties of the following types:

- *Point3D* (the *Position* property of *ProjectionCamera*)

- *Vector3D* (the *LookDirection* and *UpDirection* properties of *ProjectionCamera*, or the *Direction* property of *DirectionalLight*)

- *Double* (the *FieldOfView* property of *PerspectiveCamera* or the *Width* property of *OrthographicCamera*)

Animating properties of type *Double* also comes into play when animating 3D transforms. More complex rotation transforms can make use of the *Vector3D*, *Rotation3D*, and *Quaternion* animation classes. Because of their complexity, I won't be discussing quaternions until Chapter 8.

The first chapter of this book began by displaying a triangle. The XAML version of this program required you to manually change the *Position* property of the *PerspectiveCamera* to view the figure from different viewpoints; the C# version of the program let you change that *Position* property by manipulating a *ScrollBar*. If I wanted to overload you with information at the beginning of Chapter 1, "Lights! Camera! Mesh Geometries!" I could have shown you how to animate the *Position* property, as the following XAML file does. The object it displays is a *unit cube*—that is, a cube with sides of one unit in length—that I'll use for many examples in this chapter. The cube is centered on the origin.

```
BackAndForth1.xaml
<!-- =============================================
        BackAndForth1.xaml (c) 2007 by Charles Petzold
     ============================================= -->
<Page xmlns="http://schemas.microsoft.com/winfx/2006/xaml/presentation"
    xmlns:x="http://schemas.microsoft.com/winfx/2006/xaml"
    WindowTitle="Back and Forth #1"
    Title="Back and Forth #1">
    <Viewport3D>
        <ModelVisual3D>
            <ModelVisual3D.Content>
                <Model3DGroup>
                    <GeometryModel3D>
                        <GeometryModel3D.Geometry>

                            <!-- Unit cube: front, back, left,
                                            right, top, bottom. -->
                            <MeshGeometry3D
                                Positions="-0.5  0.5  0.5,   0.5  0.5  0.5,
                                           -0.5 -0.5  0.5,   0.5 -0.5  0.5,

                                            0.5  0.5 -0.5,  -0.5  0.5 -0.5,
                                            0.5 -0.5 -0.5,  -0.5 -0.5 -0.5,

                                           -0.5  0.5 -0.5,  -0.5  0.5  0.5,
                                           -0.5 -0.5 -0.5,  -0.5 -0.5  0.5,

                                            0.5  0.5  0.5,   0.5  0.5 -0.5,
                                            0.5 -0.5  0.5,   0.5 -0.5 -0.5,
```

```
                                        -0.5  0.5 -0.5,   0.5  0.5 -0.5,
                                        -0.5  0.5  0.5,   0.5  0.5  0.5,

                                         0.5 -0.5 -0.5,  -0.5 -0.5 -0.5,
                                         0.5 -0.5  0.5,  -0.5 -0.5  0.5"

                          TriangleIndices=" 0  2  1,  1  2  3
                                            4  6  5,  5  6  7,
                                            8 10  9,  9 10 11,
                                           12 14 13, 13 14 15
                                           16 18 17, 17 18 19
                                           20 22 21, 21 22 23" />
                </GeometryModel3D.Geometry>

                <GeometryModel3D.Material>
                    <DiffuseMaterial Brush="Cyan" />
                </GeometryModel3D.Material>
            </GeometryModel3D>

            <!-- Light sources. -->
            <AmbientLight Color="#404040" />
            <DirectionalLight Color="#C0C0C0" Direction="2 -3 -1" />
        </Model3DGroup>
      </ModelVisual3D.Content>
    </ModelVisual3D>

    <Viewport3D.Camera>
        <PerspectiveCamera x:Name="cam"
                           Position="0 1 6"
                           LookDirection="0 -1 -6"
                           UpDirection="0 1 0"
                           FieldOfView="45" />
    </Viewport3D.Camera>
  </Viewport3D>

  <!-- Animation. -->
  <Page.Triggers>
    <EventTrigger RoutedEvent="Page.Loaded">
        <BeginStoryboard>
            <Storyboard TargetName="cam" TargetProperty="Position">
                <Point3DAnimation From="-2 1 6" To="2 1 6"
                                  Duration="0:0:2" AutoReverse="True"
                                  RepeatBehavior="Forever" />
            </Storyboard>
        </BeginStoryboard>
    </EventTrigger>
  </Page.Triggers>
</Page>
```

The *PerspectiveCamera* is given the name "cam" so that it can be a target of the animation. The animation is defined at the bottom of the XAML file. It is triggered by the *Loaded* event of the *Page* class, which occurs when the page is first laid out and rendered on the screen. The target property of the animation is the *Position* property, which is of type *Point3D*. The *Point3DAnimation* class changes the *Position* property from (−2, 1, 6) to (2, 1, 6) over the course of two seconds, and then reverses the animation and repeats it "forever" or until you get bored or the power grid fails.

The change in the *Position* property of the camera from (−2, 1, 6) to (2, 1, 6) seems to make the cube move from the right to left side of the *Viewport3D*. Judging solely from the visuals and without any other landmarks, you'd be hard-pressed to determine whether the figure or the camera is really moving. Regardless, the change in perspective is quite satisfying.

The following program is similar to the first, except that the camera swings from (−10, 1, 6) to (10, 1, 6). That wide range would normally cause the figure to disappear from the *Viewport3D*, except that the program also uses a *Vector3DAnimation* to animate the *LookDirection* property of *PerspectiveCamera* from **(10, −1, −6)** to **(−10, −1, −6)**—that is, the negative of the *Position* property. Much of the file is the same as BackAndForth.xaml.

```
BackAndForth2.xaml
<!-- =============================================
     BackAndForth2.xaml (c) 2007 by Charles Petzold
     ============================================= -->
<Page xmlns="http://schemas.microsoft.com/winfx/2006/xaml/presentation"
      xmlns:x="http://schemas.microsoft.com/winfx/2006/xaml"
      WindowTitle="Back and Forth #2"
      Title="Back and Forth #2">

    ...

    <!-- Animations. -->
    <Page.Triggers>
        <EventTrigger RoutedEvent="Page.Loaded">
            <BeginStoryboard>
                <Storyboard TargetName="cam">
                    <Point3DAnimation Storyboard.TargetProperty="Position"
                                      From="-10 1 6" To="10 1 6"
                                      Duration="0:0:2" AutoReverse="True"
                                      RepeatBehavior="Forever" />

                    <Vector3DAnimation Storyboard.TargetProperty="LookDirection"
                                       From="10 -1 -6" To="-10 -1 -6"
                                       Duration="0:0:2" AutoReverse="True"
                                       RepeatBehavior="Forever" />
                </Storyboard>
            </BeginStoryboard>
        </EventTrigger>
    </Page.Triggers>
</Page>
```

Imagine yourself shooting a movie: You've mounted the camera on a dolly, which is a platform on wheels that usually runs along a straight track. As the dolly moves back and forth on this track, you direct the camera operator to swivel the camera to always point at the cube. The result is that the center of the cube remains in the center of the *Viewport3D*. At the extreme camera positions, the cube seems to become smaller, but that's only because the camera is moving in a straight line and has receded from the cube.

You can compensate for the change in size of the cube by manipulating the camera zoom. As you recede from the cube, you can zoom in (that is, you can reduce the *FieldOfView* property), and as you approach the cube, you can zoom out. The BackAndForth3.xaml file uses a *DoubleAnimationUsingKeyFrames* object to change the *FieldOfView* property between 20 degrees and the default 45 degrees.

BackAndForth3.xaml

```xml
<!-- ===============================================
        BackAndForth3.xaml (c) 2007 by Charles Petzold
     =============================================== -->
<Page xmlns="http://schemas.microsoft.com/winfx/2006/xaml/presentation"
      xmlns:x="http://schemas.microsoft.com/winfx/2006/xaml"
      WindowTitle="Back and Forth #3"
      Title="Back and Forth #3">

    . . .

    <!-- Animations. -->
    <Page.Triggers>
        <EventTrigger RoutedEvent="Page.Loaded">
            <BeginStoryboard>
                <Storyboard TargetName="cam">
                    <Point3DAnimation Storyboard.TargetProperty="Position"
                                      From="-10 1 6" To="10 1 6"
                                      Duration="0:0:2" AutoReverse="True"
                                      RepeatBehavior="Forever" />

                    <Vector3DAnimation Storyboard.TargetProperty="LookDirection"
                                       From="10 -1 -6" To="-10 -1 -6"
                                       Duration="0:0:2" AutoReverse="True"
                                       RepeatBehavior="Forever" />

                    <DoubleAnimationUsingKeyFrames
                                Storyboard.TargetProperty="FieldOfView"
                                AutoReverse="True"
                                RepeatBehavior="Forever">
                        <LinearDoubleKeyFrame KeyTime="0:0:0" Value="20" />
                        <LinearDoubleKeyFrame KeyTime="0:0:1" Value="45" />
                        <LinearDoubleKeyFrame KeyTime="0:0:2" Value="20" />
                    </DoubleAnimationUsingKeyFrames>
                </Storyboard>
            </BeginStoryboard>
        </EventTrigger>
    </Page.Triggers>
</Page>
```

Now the cube stays *approximately* the same size as it twists back and forth and changes perspective. A simple animation like this can't maintain the exact size of the cube because the relationship between the field of view, the camera distance, and the apparent size of figures is not linear—it's based on a trigonometric tangent.

Keeping foreground objects the same size while zooming the camera is a movie trick often known as the *Vertigo* effect, referring to the 1958 Alfred Hitchcock movie in which the effect was first used. My blog entry *http://www.charlespetzold.com/blog/2007/03/070716.html* has a description of the *Vertigo* effect and a sample 3D program to illustrate it. The program uses a *DrawingBrush* in connection with *DiffuseMaterial*, which is something I won't be discussing in this book until Chapter 5, "Texture and Materials."

You can also animate the *Direction* property of *DirectionalLight*, which is another *Vector3D* property. The following XAML file attempts to simulate sunrise and sunset over a square cuboid.

SunriseSunset.xaml

```
<!-- ================================================
    SunriseSunset.xaml (c) 2007 by Charles Petzold
    ================================================ -->
<Page xmlns="http://schemas.microsoft.com/winfx/2006/xaml/presentation"
    xmlns:x="http://schemas.microsoft.com/winfx/2006/xaml"
    WindowTitle="Sunrise/Sunset"
    Title="Sunrise/Sunset">
    <Viewport3D>
        <ModelVisual3D>
            <ModelVisual3D.Content>
                <Model3DGroup>
                    <GeometryModel3D>
                        <GeometryModel3D.Geometry>

                            <!-- Square cuboid. -->
                            <MeshGeometry3D
                                Positions="0 1  0,  0 0  0,  1 1  0,  1 0  0,
                                           0 1 -4,  0 0 -4,  0 1  0,  0 0  0,
                                           1 1 -4,  0 1 -4,  1 1  0,  0 1  0,
                                           1 1  0,  1 0  0,  1 1 -4,  1 0 -4,
                                           1 0  0,  0 0  0,  1 0 -4,  0 0 -4,
                                           1 1 -4,  1 0 -4,  0 1 -4,  0 0 -4"

                                TriangleIndices=" 0  1  2,  1  3  2,
                                                  4  5  6,  5  7  6,
                                                  8  9 10,  9 11 10,
                                                 12 13 14, 13 15 14,
                                                 16 17 18, 17 19 18,
                                                 20 21 22, 21 23 22" />
                        </GeometryModel3D.Geometry>
```

```
                    <GeometryModel3D.Material>
                        <DiffuseMaterial Brush="Cyan" />
                    </GeometryModel3D.Material>
                </GeometryModel3D>

                <!-- Light. -->
                <DirectionalLight x:Name="light" />
            </Model3DGroup>
        </ModelVisual3D.Content>
    </ModelVisual3D>

    <!-- Camera. -->
    <Viewport3D.Camera>
        <PerspectiveCamera Position="-2 2 4"
                           LookDirection="2 -1 -4"
                           UpDirection="0 1 0"
                           FieldOfView="45" />
    </Viewport3D.Camera>
</Viewport3D>

<!-- Animations. -->
<Page.Triggers>
    <EventTrigger RoutedEvent="Page.Loaded">
        <BeginStoryboard>
            <Storyboard TargetName="light">
                <Vector3DAnimationUsingKeyFrames
                        Storyboard.TargetProperty="Direction">
                    <LinearVector3DKeyFrame KeyTime="0:0:0" Value="2 0 -1"/>
                    <LinearVector3DKeyFrame KeyTime="0:0:10" Value="0 -1 0"/>
                    <LinearVector3DKeyFrame KeyTime="0:0:20" Value="-2 0 -1"/>
                </Vector3DAnimationUsingKeyFrames>

                <ColorAnimationUsingKeyFrames
                        Storyboard.TargetProperty="Color">
                    <LinearColorKeyFrame KeyTime="0:0:0" Value="Black" />
                    <LinearColorKeyFrame KeyTime="0:0:3" Value="White" />
                    <LinearColorKeyFrame KeyTime="0:0:17" Value="White" />
                    <LinearColorKeyFrame KeyTime="0:0:20" Value="Black" />
                </ColorAnimationUsingKeyFrames>
            </Storyboard>
        </BeginStoryboard>
    </EventTrigger>
</Page.Triggers>
</Page>
```

The animation lasts 20 seconds and does not repeat. The *Vector3DAnimationUsingKeyFrames* object animates the *Direction* property of the *DirectionalLight* object beginning at $(2, 0, -1)$, which simulates the light on the horizon, but points somewhat back as well to illuminate the front of the square cuboid. The *Direction* value goes to $(0, -1, 0)$, which is straight down, and then to $(-2, 0, -1)$ at sunset. A second animation controls the *Color* property of the

DirectionalLight, going from *Black* to *White* during the first three seconds, and then from *White* to *Black* over the last three seconds.

Manipulating Collections

The *Positions* collection defined by *MeshGeometry3D* is of type *Point3DCollection*, which derives from the *Freezable* class and includes an event named *Changed*, all of which implies that any change to the *Positions* collection—including changes to individual elements of the collection—triggers this event and causes the change to be recognized in the visual appearance of the object.

Dynamically manipulating collections such as *Positions* is a powerful technique, and I will use it in various ways in future chapters of this book. It is not too early to learn about making this process as efficient as possible, however.

Suppose *mesh* is an object of type *MeshGeometry3D* and a *Viewport3D* is currently displaying a figure based on this object. It's possible for some code (probably in an event handler of some sort) to dynamically add points to the collection:

```
mesh.Positions.Add(new Point3D(1.5, 0, 1.5));
```

Or you can remove points from the collection:

```
mesh.Positions.RemoveAt(i);
```

In either case, just the act of altering the collection is sufficient to notify the *GeometryModel3D* that something has changed, and for this change to be registered throughout the *Viewport3D*, and for the figure to change appearance. In reality, you'll probably also alter the *TriangleIndices* collection if you change *Positions* in this way.

Perhaps more commonly, you can change individual members of the *Positions* collection simply by indexing the collection like an array and assigning an object of type *Point3D*:

```
mesh.Positions[i] = new Point3D(0.5, 1, -0.25);
```

That code is sufficient to alter the visual appearance of the figure.

Don't try to change individual properties of existing items in the collection, such as one of the properties of a *Point3D* object. The C# compiler won't let you do it, and even if you could, the *Point3D* structure has no notification mechanism to inform the collection that it has changed. To dynamically change the *Positions* collection, you must replace entire *Point3D* objects and not simply alter *Point3D* properties already in the collection.

The following file might look like a standalone XAML file, but it's not, for two reasons: First, the root element is *Window*. Second, the *Window* tag contains an *x:Class* attribute that indicates the namespace and name of the class derived from *Window* defined in this XAML file.

CubeDeformation.xaml

```
<!-- ================================================
        CubeDeformation.xaml (c) 2007 by Charles Petzold
     ================================================ -->
<Window xmlns="http://schemas.microsoft.com/winfx/2006/xaml/presentation"
        xmlns:x="http://schemas.microsoft.com/winfx/2006/xaml"
        x:Class="Petzold.CubeDeformation.CubeDeformation"
        Title="Cube Deformation">
    <Viewport3D>
        <ModelVisual3D>
            <ModelVisual3D.Content>
                <Model3DGroup>
                    <GeometryModel3D>
                        <GeometryModel3D.Geometry>

                            <!-- Unit cube. -->
                            <MeshGeometry3D x:Name="cube"
                                Positions="-0.5  0.5  0.5,   0.5  0.5  0.5,
                                           -0.5 -0.5  0.5,   0.5 -0.5  0.5,
                                            0.5  0.5 -0.5,  -0.5  0.5 -0.5,
                                            0.5 -0.5 -0.5,  -0.5 -0.5 -0.5,
                                           -0.5  0.5 -0.5,  -0.5  0.5  0.5,
                                           -0.5 -0.5 -0.5,  -0.5 -0.5  0.5,
                                            0.5  0.5  0.5,   0.5  0.5 -0.5,
                                            0.5 -0.5  0.5,   0.5 -0.5 -0.5,
                                           -0.5  0.5 -0.5,   0.5  0.5 -0.5,
                                           -0.5  0.5  0.5,   0.5  0.5  0.5,
                                            0.5 -0.5 -0.5,  -0.5 -0.5 -0.5,
                                            0.5 -0.5  0.5,  -0.5 -0.5  0.5"

                                TriangleIndices=" 0  2  1,   1  2  3
                                                  4  6  5,   5  6  7,
                                                  8 10  9,   9 10 11,
                                                 12 14 13,  13 14 15,
                                                 16 18 17,  17 18 19,
                                                 20 22 21,  21 22 23" />
                        </GeometryModel3D.Geometry>

                        <GeometryModel3D.Material>
                            <DiffuseMaterial Brush="Cyan" />
                        </GeometryModel3D.Material>
                    </GeometryModel3D>
```

```
                     <!-- Light sources. -->
                     <AmbientLight Color="#404040" />
                     <DirectionalLight Color="#C0C0C0" Direction="2, -3 -1" />
                 </Model3DGroup>
             </ModelVisual3D.Content>
         </ModelVisual3D>

         <!-- Camera. -->
         <Viewport3D.Camera>
             <PerspectiveCamera Position="2 3 4"
                                LookDirection="-2 -3 -4"
                                UpDirection="0 1 0"
                                FieldOfView="45" />
         </Viewport3D.Camera>
     </Viewport3D>
 </Window>
```

Although this is not a standalone XAML file, the contents should look fairly familiar by now. The file contains a *Viewport3D* that displays the unit cube. One change from previous XAML files is that the *MeshGeometry3D* is given the name "cube" so that it can be referenced in code.

The CubeDeformation project is completed with the following CubeDeformation.cs file. The C# code sets a timer to randomly change the eight vertices of the cube to turn the cube into a continually changing hexahedron.

This job requires a little preparatory work. Each of the eight vertices of the cube appears three times in the *Positions* collection, once for each of the three faces that meet at that vertex. I wanted to animate these three vertices in the same way so that the figure remained a solid and didn't split up into six unconnected quadrilaterals. The constructor handles the preparatory work by filling two arrays named *vertices* and *indices*. The *vertices* array contains the eight unique vertices of the cube; the *indices* array indicates the indices within the *Positions* collection of the three appearances of every unique vertex. (This *indices* array is unrelated to the *TriangleIndices* collection of the *MeshGeometry3D*, which remains unchanged.)

CubeDeformation.cs
```
//-------------------------------------------------
// CubeDeformation.cs (c) 2007 by Charles Petzold
//-------------------------------------------------
using System;
using System.Windows;
using System.Windows.Media.Media3D;
using System.Windows.Threading;
```

```
namespace Petzold.CubeDeformation
{
    public partial class CubeDeformation : Window
    {
        // Animation parameters.
        static readonly TimeSpan interval = TimeSpan.FromSeconds(0.1);
        const int changeDirection = 10;
        const double vectorFactor = 0.005;

        // Fields used in timer event handler.
        MeshGeometry3D mesh;
        Point3D[] vertices = new Point3D[8];
        int[,] indices = new int[8,3];
        Random rand = new Random();
        Vector3D[] vectors = new Vector3D[8];

        [STAThread]
        public static void Main()
        {
            Application app = new Application();
            app.Run(new CubeDeformation());
        }

        // Constructor.
        public CubeDeformation()
        {
            // Initialize XAML file.
            InitializeComponent();

            // Find the MeshGeometry3D object in the XAML file.
            mesh = FindName("cube") as MeshGeometry3D;

            // Find all the unique vertices; store in 'vertices' field.
            // For each vertex, find the three indices of the Positions
            //   collection where that vertex is found; store in 'indices' field.
            int verticesFound = 0;
            int[] indicesFound = new int[8];

            for (int i = 0; i < mesh.Positions.Count; i++)
            {
                Point3D point = mesh.Positions[i];
                int j;

                for (j = 0; j < verticesFound; j++)
                    if (point == vertices[j])
                    {
                        indices[j, indicesFound[j]++] = i;
                        break;
                    }
```

```
                    if (j == verticesFound)
                    {
                        vertices[verticesFound] = point;
                        indices[verticesFound++, indicesFound[j]++] = i;
                    }
                }

            // Set up the timer for the animation.
            DispatcherTimer tmr = new DispatcherTimer();
            tmr.Interval = interval;
            tmr.Tick += TimerOnTick;
            tmr.Start();
        }

        void TimerOnTick(object sender, EventArgs args)
        {
            // Detach the Positions collection from the MeshGeometry3D.
            Point3DCollection coll = mesh.Positions;
            mesh.Positions = null;

            // Look through the 8 unique vertices.
            for (int i = 0; i < 8; i++)
            {
                // For each vertex, possibly change the animation
                //  direction stored in the 'vectors' array.
                if (rand.Next(changeDirection) == 0)
                {
                    Vector3D vector = new Vector3D(rand.NextDouble() - 0.5,
                                                  rand.NextDouble() - 0.5,
                                                  rand.NextDouble() - 0.5);
                    vector.Normalize();
                    vectors[i] = vector;
                }

                // Regardless, change the vertex based on the vector.
                vertices[i] += vectorFactor * vectors[i];

                // Change all three copies of the vertex in the collection.
                for (int j = 0; j < 3; j++)
                    coll[indices[i, j]] = vertices[i];
            }
            // Reattach the collection to the MeshGeometry3D.
            mesh.Positions = coll;
        }
    }
}
```

The *DispatcherTimer* is set for an interval of a tenth of a second, so the *TimerOnTick* event handler is called every 100 milliseconds. You'll notice two statements at the beginning of this method and one at the end that reference the *MeshGeometry3D* object. Without these statements, consider what happens: Each time this event handler is invoked, it changes each of the 24 members of the *Positions* collection of the *MeshGeometry3D*. Each time this event handler changes a member of the *Positions* collection, the collection object fires a *Changed* event so that the figure can be redrawn with the new point.

But changing a member of the *Positions* collection 24 times in a row and generating 24 events within a very short period of time makes no sense at all! It's wickedly inefficient! Fortunately, avoiding all of these superfluous events is very simple, as *TimerOnTick* demonstrates. You begin by getting a reference to the *Positions* collection of the *MeshGeometry3D* object (stored as the field *mesh*) and setting the *Positions* property to *null*:

```
Point3DCollection coll = mesh.Positions;
mesh.Positions = null;
```

Both statements are required: Within the *TimerOnTick* event handler, all changes are made to the *coll* variable, but if you don't set the *Positions* property to *null*, any changes you make to *coll* will also affect the *Positions* property because *coll* is a reference to the same collection. When you set the *Positions* property to *null*, the *MeshGeometry3D* detaches its event handler from the *Changed* event of *Point3DCollection*, so that nobody's taking heed of any changes to the collection. After the *TimerOnTick* event handler has completed modifying the collection, it reattaches the collection to the *MeshGeometry3D*:

```
mesh.Positions = coll;
```

Now the new collection of points is taken into account and the visual figure is updated.

Positions is backed by a dependency property in *MeshGeometry3D*, so it has its own notification system, which is fired twice during *TimerOnTick*—once when *null* is assigned to the property and again when the modified collection is reassigned. You might consider cutting down these notifications even further by initially making a copy of the *Point3DCollection*:

```
Point3DCollection coll = mesh.Positions.Clone();
```

You could then modify the *coll* collection and assign that to the *Positions* property at the end of the event handler:

```
mesh.Positions = coll;
```

But this approach is *not* a good idea. The problem is that the *Clone* method implicitly uses a *new* expression to create a new object of type *Point3DCollection*, and then copies objects from one collection to another. When this new collection is assigned to the *Positions* property, the old collection becomes eligible for garbage collection. If the animation continues for awhile, these frequent memory allocations might accumulate to a point where memory becomes low and the .NET garbage collector kicks into action, probably disrupting the animation.

If at all possible, an event handler that executes continuously multiple times per second should not perform any memory allocations or contain any explicit or implicit *new* instructions that instantiate classes. You'll notice a *new* instruction in *TimerOnTick*, but it refers to *Vector3D*, which is a structure rather than a class. This is fine because instances of structures are stored on the stack and no allocation from the heap is required.

The actual random alteration of the points in the *Positions* collection by the *TimerOnTick* handler is rather straightforward: Each of the eight vertices of the cube is associated with a *Vector3D* object stored in the *vectors* array. This vector indicates a direction that the vertex changes. Normally the vertex changes by an amount equal to the constant *vectorFactor* field multiplied by the *Vector3D*. However, if a random number between zero and *changeDirection* equals zero, the *Vector3D* in the *vectors* array is set to a new random value. Here's a typical view of a randomly deformed cube:

The program has no logic to prevent a vertex from crashing through one of the faces, so eventually you might see something like this:

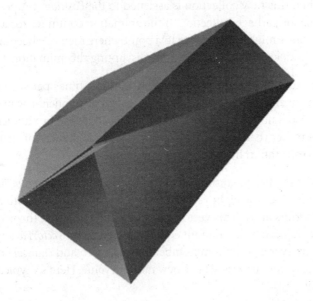

The movement of each vertex qualifies as a mathematical "random walk." The vertices will tend to stray from the original positions, but not very quickly.

The timer in the CubeDeformation program is set for 100 milliseconds. If you find yourself working with faster timers—perhaps with a period of 20 milliseconds or so—you're getting close to the vertical refresh rate of the video display, which is probably in the 60 to 85 Hz region (corresponding to periods of about 12 to 17 milliseconds) but might be as high as 120 Hz (a period of about 8 milliseconds).

It doesn't make sense for an animation to be faster than the vertical refresh rate of the display. At these speeds, you might want to abandon *DispatcherTimer* and instead use *Composition-Target*, which has a static event member named *Rendering*. You can define a handler for this event in accordance with the *EventHandler* delegate:

```
void OnRender(object sender, EventArgs args)
{
    ...
}
```

You then attach this handler to the *Rendering* event like so:

```
CompositionTarget.Rendering += OnRender;
```

Now the *OnRender* method is called with a frequency equal to the vertical scan rate of the video display. Animation and layout have already been performed when the handler is called, but the visual objects have not yet been rendered. This is your ideal opportunity to change anything that may affect rendering.

The *Transform3D* Class

Transforms are a generalized and systematic approach to modifying coordinate points (and perhaps vectors as well) of a particular graphical object. A transform is basically a mathematical formula that is generally applied to each point in a collection, such as the *Positions* collection of a *MeshGeometry3D* object. The actual points in the *Positions* collection do not change, but the transform modifies the points used to render the object.

When you use the native Windows Win32 API to program two-dimensional graphics, the graphics transform is a characteristic of the device context, which essentially represents a display surface such as the screen. All objects drawn on that device context are subject to the current transform in effect at the time the object is drawn. Similarly, in Windows Forms, the transform is a property of the *Graphics* class, which is the encapsulation of a drawing surface.

The Windows Presentation Foundation is different: Transforms are always applied to objects themselves rather than to the drawing surface. (This is true of two-dimensional WPF graphics as well.) In other words, you don't do anything to *Viewport3D* to set 3D transforms. This may be a little confusing because the *Viewport3D* has *RenderTransform* and *LayoutTransform* properties of type *Transform*. But *Viewport3D* inherits these properties from *FrameworkElement*. These are two-dimensional transforms of type *Transform* and govern the location, size, and rotation of the *Viewport3D* itself in relation to its parent element and sibling elements.

For three-dimensional transforms, you make use of classes that derive from the abstract *Transform3D* class. Exactly three classes in the *System.Windows.Media.Media3D* namespace define *Transform* properties of type *Transform3D*:

- *Camera*
- *Model3D*
- *ModelVisual3D*

Camera is the abstract class that is parent to all the camera classes, including *PerspectiveCamera* and *OrthographicCamera*.

Model3D is the abstract parent class to *GeometryModel3D*, *Light*, and *Model3DGroup*. The *Transform* property lets you apply a transform to a single figure or light source, as well as to a collection of *Model3D* objects.

ModelVisual3D is the only class that derives from the abstract *Visual3D* class. By setting the *Transform* property of *ModelVisual3D*, you can apply the transform to everything within *ModelVisual3D*, which might be a single figure, a collection of figures, or figures together with light sources, and also might include child objects of type *ModelVisual3D*.

The *Transform3D* class shows up in the following class hierarchy:

Object
>   *DispatcherObject* (abstract)
>>   *DependencyObject*
>>>   *Freezable* (abstract)
>>>>   *Animatable* (abstract)
>>>>>   *Transform3D* (abstract)
>>>>>>   *AffineTransform3D* (abstract)
>>>>>>>   *TranslateTransform3D* (sealed)
>>>>>>>   *ScaleTransform3D* (sealed)
>>>>>>>   *RotateTransform3D* (sealed)
>>>>>>   *MatrixTransform3D* (sealed)
>>>>>>   *Transform3DGroup* (sealed)

This chapter will focus on the *TranslateTransform3D* and *ScaleTransform3D* classes, as well as the *Transform3DGroup* class that lets you assemble composite transforms. *Transform3DGroup* has a property named *Children* of type *Transform3DGroupCollection*, a collection of *Transform3D* objects. *RotateTransform3D* is the subject of Chapter 3, "Axis/Angle Rotation," and *MatrixTransform3D* is covered in Chapter 7, "Matrix Transforms."

You can imagine a transform as changing a point (x, y, z) to a point (x', y', z'):

$$(x, y, z) \rightarrow (x', y', z')$$

The transform can be represented as a series of formulas that calculate x', y', and z' from x, y, and z. A *linear* transform is one in which these formulas involve only constants applied to the coordinates. In the following generalized linear transform formulas, the K_i values are constants dependent on the transform:

$x' = K_1 x + K_2 y + K_3 z$
$y' = K_4 x + K_5 y + K_6 z$
$z' = K_7 x + K_8 y + K_9 z$

An *affine* transform is a superset of the linear transform where another constant is added:

$x' = K_1 x + K_2 y + K_3 z + C_1$
$y' = K_4 x + K_5 y + K_6 z + C_2$
$z' = K_7 x + K_8 y + K_9 z + C_3$

The three standard types of transforms—called translation, scaling, and rotation—are all affine transforms, as the class hierarchy suggests. In an affine transform, straight lines are always transformed to straight lines, and lines that are parallel remain parallel.

WPF 3D also allows non-affine transforms, where parallelism is not preserved. In fact, the perspective projection itself is a non-affine projection because three-dimensional figures are displayed on a two-dimensional surface in a way that does not preserve parallel lines. Objects are tapered as they recede from the camera. The orthographic projection, on the other hand, is an affine transformation.

In this chapter, I will not discuss non-affine transforms, the *MatrixTransform3D* class, or the *Matrix3D* structure. Those are subjects for Chapter 7, which has a fuller mathematical analysis of transforms.

For this chapter and the next, I'll stick to the three standard types of transforms:

- Translation: Moving the location of a figure
- Scaling: Changing the size of a figure
- Rotation: Rotating a figure around an axis.

One warning before we begin: When you hand-code XAML, it is very easy to forget to type a "3D" in the element name. You might type *TranslateTransform* rather than *Translate-Transform3D*, or *TransformGroup* rather than *Transform3DGroup*. This is a mistake I make all the time. Sometimes the error is unclear because *TranslateTransform* and *TransformGroup* are actual classes in the Windows Presentation Foundation, but they are two-dimensional graphics classes rather than 3D classes.

The Translation Transform

Translation is the type of transform that simply moves a figure to another location without changing its size or orientation. The *TranslateTransform3D* class defines three properties of type *double* with default values of 0: *OffsetX*, *OffsetY*, and *OffsetZ*. You might want to apply a *TranslateTransform3D* to a *GeometryModel3D* element, for example. This requires property element syntax for the *Transform* property of *GeometryModel3D* to enclose the *Translate-Transform3D* element:

```
<GeometryModel3D>
    ...
    <GeometryModel3D.Transform>
        <TranslateTransform3D OffsetX="2" OffsetY="0" OffsetZ="-1" />
    </GeometryModel3D.Transform>
</GeometryModel3D>
```

The figure described by the *GeometryModel3D* is effectively transposed as if you had added 2 to the X coordinates and −1 to the Z coordinates of all the points in the *Positions* collection of the *MeshGeometry3D* associated with the figure.

In general, a transform calculates a point (x', y', z') from a point (x, y, z). The *TranslateTransform3D* class involves the following formulas:

$x' = x + OffsetX$
$y' = y + OffsetY$
$z' = z + OffsetZ$

The TranslateTransformExperimenter.xaml program lets you experiment with translation. The program draws a simple ramp-like figure that looks like this:

It is one unit high, two units wide, and three units deep. The front left corner sits on the origin.

The program has three scrollbars on the top to change the *OffsetX*, *OffsetY*, and *OffsetZ* properties of a *TranslateTransform3D* applied to the *GeometryModel3D*. Three scrollbars on the bottom change the same properties of a *TranslateTransform3D* applied to the *PerspectiveCamera*.

TranslateTransformExperimenter.xaml

```
<!-- ================================================================
        TranslateTransformExperimenter.xaml (c) 2007 by Charles Petzold
     ================================================================ -->
<Page xmlns="http://schemas.microsoft.com/winfx/2006/xaml/presentation"
      xmlns:x="http://schemas.microsoft.com/winfx/2006/xaml"
      WindowTitle="TranslateTransform3D Experimenter"
      Title="TranslateTransform3D Experimenter">
    <DockPanel>
        <ScrollBar Name="xMod" DockPanel.Dock="Top" Orientation="Horizontal"
                   Minimum="-5" Maximum="5" Value="0" ToolTip="Model X" />

        <ScrollBar Name="yMod" DockPanel.Dock="Top" Orientation="Horizontal"
                   Minimum="-5" Maximum="5" Value="0" ToolTip="Model Y" />

        <ScrollBar Name="zMod" DockPanel.Dock="Top" Orientation="Horizontal"
                   Minimum="-5" Maximum="5" Value="0" ToolTip="Model Z" />

        <ScrollBar Name="zCam" DockPanel.Dock="Bottom" Orientation="Horizontal"
                   Minimum="-5" Maximum="5" Value="0" ToolTip="Camera Z" />

        <ScrollBar Name="yCam" DockPanel.Dock="Bottom" Orientation="Horizontal"
                   Minimum="-5" Maximum="5" Value="0" ToolTip="Camera Y" />

        <ScrollBar Name="xCam" DockPanel.Dock="Bottom" Orientation="Horizontal"
                   Minimum="-5" Maximum="5" Value="0" ToolTip="Camera X" />
```

```
<Viewport3D>
    <ModelVisual3D>
        <ModelVisual3D.Content>
            <Model3DGroup>
                <GeometryModel3D>
                    <GeometryModel3D.Geometry>

                        <!-- Front, rear, top, right, bottom. -->
                        <MeshGeometry3D
                            Positions="0 0  0, 2 0  0, 2 1  0,
                                       0 0 -3, 2 0 -3, 2 1 -3,
                                       2 1 -3, 0 0 -3, 2 1  0, 0 0  0,
                                       2 1  0, 2 0  0, 2 1 -3, 2 0 -3,
                                       2 0  0, 0 0  0, 2 0 -3, 0 0 -3"

                            TriangleIndices=" 0  1  2,
                                              3  5  4,
                                              6  7  8,  7  9  8,
                                             10 11 12, 11 13 12,
                                             14 15 16, 15 17 16" />
                    </GeometryModel3D.Geometry>

                    <GeometryModel3D.Material>
                        <DiffuseMaterial Brush="Cyan" />
                    </GeometryModel3D.Material>

                    <GeometryModel3D.Transform>
                        <Transform3DGroup>
                            <TranslateTransform3D
                                OffsetX="{Binding ElementName=xMod,
                                                  Path=Value}"
                                OffsetY="{Binding ElementName=yMod,
                                                  Path=Value}"
                                OffsetZ="{Binding ElementName=zMod,
                                                  Path=Value}" />
                        </Transform3DGroup>
                    </GeometryModel3D.Transform>
                </GeometryModel3D>

                <!-- Light sources. -->
                <AmbientLight Color="#404040" />

                <DirectionalLight Color="#C0C0C0" Direction="2 -3 -1">
                    <DirectionalLight.Transform>
                        <Transform3DGroup>
                            <!-- Placeholder for light transform. -->
                        </Transform3DGroup>
                    </DirectionalLight.Transform>
                </DirectionalLight>
```

```
                        <Model3DGroup.Transform>
                            <Transform3DGroup>
                                <!-- Placeholder for group transform. -->
                            </Transform3DGroup>
                        </Model3DGroup.Transform>
                    </Model3DGroup>
                </ModelVisual3D.Content>

                <ModelVisual3D.Transform>
                    <Transform3DGroup>
                        <!-- Placeholder for visual transform. -->
                    </Transform3DGroup>
                </ModelVisual3D.Transform>
            </ModelVisual3D>

            <!-- Camera. -->
            <Viewport3D.Camera>
                <PerspectiveCamera Position="-2 2 4"
                                   LookDirection="2 -1 -4"
                                   UpDirection="0 1 0"
                                   FieldOfView="45">
                    <PerspectiveCamera.Transform>
                        <Transform3DGroup>
                            <TranslateTransform3D
                                OffsetX="{Binding ElementName=xCam,
                                                  Path=Value}"
                                OffsetY="{Binding ElementName=yCam,
                                                  Path=Value}"
                                OffsetZ="{Binding ElementName=zCam,
                                                  Path=Value}" />
                        </Transform3DGroup>
                    </PerspectiveCamera.Transform>
                </PerspectiveCamera>
            </Viewport3D.Camera>
        </Viewport3D>
    </DockPanel>
</Page>
```

The *Viewport3D* here occupies the center of a *DockPanel*. Docked at the top are three *ScrollBar* controls, and docked on the bottom are three more. The six *ScrollBar* controls all have ranges from −5 to 5. The three at the top have the names "xMod", "yMod", and "zMod", referring to a *GeometryModel3D*, which has a transform set like so:

```
<GeometryModel3D.Transform>
    <Transform3DGroup>
        <TranslateTransform3D
            OffsetX="{Binding ElementName=xMod, Path=Value}"
            OffsetY="{Binding ElementName=yMod, Path=Value}"
            OffsetZ="{Binding ElementName=zMod, Path=Value}" />
    </Transform3DGroup>
</GeometryModel3D.Transform>
```

The *TranslateTransform3D* here has its *OffsetX*, *OffsetY*, and *OffsetZ* properties set to data bindings referencing the *Value* properties of the three scrollbars at the top of the page. A transform applied to a *GeometryModel3D* affects all the points in the *Positions* collection defined by the *MeshGeometry3D*. As you move the topmost *ScrollBar* to the right, the figure slides right along the X axis. You can also set negative values to *OffsetX* by moving the *ScrollBar* to the left. Similarly, positive values of *OffsetY* move the figure up, and positive values of *OffsetZ* move the figure closer to the viewer.

In the markup following the *GeometryModel3D.Transform* tag, the *Transform3DGroup* tags are not required because they enclose only one transform. However, in a few paragraphs I'm going to instruct you to remove that *TranslateTransform3D* element from the markup. That won't cause a problem because a *Transform3DGroup* element can be empty. However, if those *Transform3DGroup* tags were not present, removing the *TranslateTransform3D* would result in an error, because *GeometryModel3D.Transform* tags must always enclose some content of type *Transform3D*.

The scrollbars on the bottom of the page are bound to a *TranslateTransform3D* applied to the camera:

```
<PerspectiveCamera.Transform>
    <Transform3DGroup>
        <TranslateTransform3D
            OffsetX="{Binding ElementName=xCam, Path=Value}"
            OffsetY="{Binding ElementName=yCam, Path=Value}"
            OffsetZ="{Binding ElementName=zCam, Path=Value}" />
    </Transform3DGroup>
</PerspectiveCamera.Transform>
```

This transform affects the *Position* property of the camera. As you move the top *ScrollBar* of those bottom three to the right, the camera effectively moves to the right and the figure seems to move to the left. In general, a transform applied to a camera performs the inverse effect of the same transform applied to a 3D figure. (But sometimes that inverse effect might be a little surprising, as you'll soon see.)

In TranslateTransformExperimenter.xaml, you'll notice three additional sets of *Transform-3DGroup* tags enclosing XML comments identified as "placeholders." These are the other places in this file where a transform can appear. Move the first *TranslateTransform3D* element (applied to the *GeometryModel3D*) right after the comment "Placeholder for light transform." Now the scrollbars are applied to the *DirectionalLight*, and they now have no effect. Translation does not affect *DirectionalLight*. (However, translation does affect *PointLight* and *SpotLight*, which I'll cover in Chapter 4, "Light and Shading.")

Now move the *TranslateTransform3D* element to the second placeholder with the comment "Placeholder for group transform." This is a transform applied to the *Model3DGroup* that contains both the *GeometryModel3D* and the lights. In theory, the scrollbars now affect both the *GeometryModel3D* and the lights, but only the *GeometryModel3D* responds. You'll get a similar effect when you move the *TranslateTransform3D* element to the third placeholder with the comment "Placeholder for visual transform." Now the transform affects the entire *ModelVisual3D*.

Move that first *TranslateTransform3D* element back to its original position within the *Geometry-Model3D*. Move the second *TranslateTransform3D* (currently associated with the camera) to either the *Model3DGroup* or the *ModelVisual3D*. Now both sets of scrollbars affect the location of the figure. The two transforms are compounded: The actual location of the figure is governed by its *Positions* collection translated by the sum of the *Scrollbar* settings. Although it doesn't make a difference in this example, transforms are applied starting from the innermost element. The transform on the *GeometryModel3D* is applied first, then the transform on the *Model3DGroup* (if any), then the *ModelVisual3D*. After those transforms have been applied, the whole 3D scene is affected by the transform set on the camera.

Generally, animating a *TranslateTransform3D* requires separate animation objects for the *OffsetX*, *OffsetY*, and *OffsetZ* properties. Here's a program that animates just the *OffsetX* and *OffsetZ* properties to make a cube move back and forth and, in a slower cycle, nearer and further away from the viewer.

ZigZag.xaml

```xml
<!-- ======================================
     ZigZag.xaml (c) 2007 by Charles Petzold
     ====================================== -->
<Page xmlns="http://schemas.microsoft.com/winfx/2006/xaml/presentation"
      xmlns:x="http://schemas.microsoft.com/winfx/2006/xaml"
      WindowTitle="Zig-Zag"
      Title="Zig-Zag">
    <Viewport3D>
        <ModelVisual3D>
            <ModelVisual3D.Content>
                <Model3DGroup>
                    <GeometryModel3D>
                        <GeometryModel3D.Geometry>

                            <!-- Unit cube. -->
                            <MeshGeometry3D
                                Positions="-0.5  0.5  0.5,   0.5  0.5  0.5,
                                           -0.5 -0.5  0.5,   0.5 -0.5  0.5,
                                            0.5  0.5 -0.5,  -0.5  0.5 -0.5,
                                            0.5 -0.5 -0.5,  -0.5 -0.5 -0.5,
                                           -0.5  0.5 -0.5,  -0.5  0.5  0.5,
                                           -0.5 -0.5 -0.5,  -0.5 -0.5  0.5,
                                            0.5  0.5  0.5,   0.5  0.5 -0.5,
                                            0.5 -0.5  0.5,   0.5 -0.5 -0.5,
                                           -0.5  0.5 -0.5,   0.5  0.5 -0.5,
                                           -0.5  0.5  0.5,   0.5  0.5  0.5,
                                            0.5 -0.5 -0.5,  -0.5 -0.5 -0.5,
                                            0.5 -0.5  0.5,  -0.5 -0.5  0.5"
```

```
                                    TriangleIndices=" 0  2  1,  1  2  3
                                                      4  6  5,  5  6  7,
                                                      8 10  9,  9 10 11,
                                                     12 14 13, 13 14 15
                                                     16 18 17, 17 18 19
                                                     20 22 21, 21 22 23" />
                    </GeometryModel3D.Geometry>

                    <GeometryModel3D.Material>
                        <DiffuseMaterial Brush="Cyan" />
                    </GeometryModel3D.Material>

                    <GeometryModel3D.Transform>
                        <TranslateTransform3D x:Name="translate" />
                    </GeometryModel3D.Transform>
                </GeometryModel3D>

                <!-- Light sources. -->
                <AmbientLight Color="#404040" />
                <DirectionalLight Color="#C0C0C0" Direction="2 -3 -1" />

            </Model3DGroup>
        </ModelVisual3D.Content>
    </ModelVisual3D>

    <Viewport3D.Camera>
        <PerspectiveCamera Position="0 2 6"
                           LookDirection="0 -2 -6"
                           UpDirection="0 1 0"
                           FieldOfView="45" />
    </Viewport3D.Camera>
</Viewport3D>

<!-- Animations. -->
<Page.Triggers>
    <EventTrigger RoutedEvent="Page.Loaded">
        <BeginStoryboard>
            <Storyboard TargetName="translate">
                <DoubleAnimation Storyboard.TargetProperty="OffsetX"
                                 From="-2" To="2" Duration="0:0:0.5"
                                 AutoReverse="True" RepeatBehavior="Forever" />

                <DoubleAnimation Storyboard.TargetProperty="OffsetZ"
                                 From="0" To="-20" Duration="0:0:10"
                                 AutoReverse="True" RepeatBehavior="Forever" />

            </Storyboard>
        </BeginStoryboard>
    </EventTrigger>
</Page.Triggers>
</Page>
```

The *TranslateTransform3D* element is given the name "translate", which becomes the *Target-Name* of the *Storyboard*. It's possible to give other elements names and adjust the animation properties accordingly. For example, you can give the *GeometryModel* a name:

```
<GeometryModel3D x:Name="model">
```

Now the *TargetName* of the *Storyboard* can be "model" but *TargetProperty* must now reference a path from the *GeometryModel3D* to the *OffsetX* and *OffsetY* properties of the transforms. You do this by setting *TargetProperty* to "Transform.OffsetX" and "Transform.OffsetZ."

Or, you can give a name to the *ModelVisual3D* element:

```
<ModelVisual3D x:Name="visual">
```

You can use that as the *TargetName* of the *Storyboard*, but now you must set the *TargetProperty* to the complete property path, which is "Content.Children[0].Transform.OffsetX" and "Content.Children[0].Transform.OffsetZ." The *Children[0]* part of this path indicates the first child of the *Model3DGroup*, which is the *GeometryModel3D*.

Shareable Models

The classes in the *System.Windows.Media.Media3D* namespace distinguish between *visuals* and *models*. The only instantiable visual class is *ModelVisual3D*, which has a *Content* property of type *Model3D*. The *Model3D* class is the parent of *GeometryModel3D* and *Light*, which is parent to all the classes that provide lighting in your 3D scenes. For purposes of this discussion, the *Camera* classes, the *Material* classes, and the *Transform3D* classes can also be considered models.

A visual is something that has a visual appearance and can actually be rendered on the screen. The model provides information to the visual that the visual uses to render itself.

One crucial difference between visuals and models is that models can be shared among multiple visuals. For example, you can define one *GeometryModel3D* object that you use as the *Content* property in multiple *ModelVisual3D* objects. However, visuals cannot be shared. The same *ModelVisual3D* cannot appear multiple times in the same *Viewport3D* or different *Viewport3D* elements. A *ModelVisual3D* can have only one parent in the visual tree.

How do you share models? In code, you can simply create an object of type *GeometryModel3D*, or one of the classes that derive from *Light*, and reuse that same object when creating *ModelVisual3D* objects. In XAML, you can define the *GeometryModel3D* or the light object as a resource, and then reference that resource later in the XAML file.

A resources section can appear in a XAML file as a property element in the *Viewport3D*, or in a parent class to the *Viewport3D* (generally *Page* or *Window*), or in the *Application* element in an application definition file, if any. In the XAML files in this chapter, I'll often define a

Resources section in the *Page* element. The example shown here includes a resource of type *GeometryModel3D*:

```
<Page ... >
    <Page.Resources>
        <GeometryModel3D x:Key="geomodel">
            ...
        </GeometryModel3D>
        ...
    </Page.Resources>
    ...
</Page>
```

That *GeometryModel3D* object can then be referenced later in the XAML file like this:

```
<ModelVisual3D Content="{StaticResource geomodel}" />
```

A resource is always just a single instance, so if the resource is referred to again in the XAML file, the same object is shared. The following classes are good candidates for defining as resources and sharing among multiple visuals in a XAML file:

- *MeshGeometry3D*
- Classes that derive from *Material*, including *MaterialGroup*
- *GeometryModel3D*
- Classes that derive from *Light*
- *Model3DGroup*
- Classes that derive from *Camera*
- Classes that derive from *Transform3D*, including *Transform3DGroup*

You can also define simple *Point3D* or *Vector3D* resources, or a resource based on one of the collection classes, such as *Point3DCollection*. The class that you probably won't *ever* see defined as a resource is *ModelVisual3D*. Nothing prevents you from defining a *ModelVisual3D* as a resource, but you can only use it once as a child of a *Viewport3D*, so why bother? If you try to reuse a *ModelVisual3D* as a child of a *Viewport3D*, you'll get the error message: "'ModelVisual3D' object cannot be added to 'Viewport3D'. Specified Visual is already the child of another Visual or the root of a CompositionTarget."

Sharing models becomes particularly compelling when you add transforms to the mix. You create one model and use it multiple times with different transforms. The following XAML file offers you a little taste of this. This file contains a Resources section containing just one item: a complete *GeometryModel3D* object with the key name "pyramid" that defines a four-sided pyramid centered around the origin and colored gray. (To keep it simple, the bottom of the pyramid is not included in the *MeshGeometry3D* definition.)

LandOfThePyramids1.xaml

```xml
<!-- ==================================================
        LandOfThePyramids1.xaml (c) 2007 by Charles Petzold
     ================================================== -->
<Page xmlns="http://schemas.microsoft.com/winfx/2006/xaml/presentation"
      xmlns:x="http://schemas.microsoft.com/winfx/2006/xaml"
      WindowTitle="Land of the Pyramids #1"
      Title="Land of the Pyramids #1"
      Background="SkyBlue">

    <Page.Resources>
        <GeometryModel3D x:Key="pyramid">
            <GeometryModel3D.Geometry>

                <!-- Pyramid: Front, back, left, right. -->
                <MeshGeometry3D
                    Positions="0 1 0, -0.5 0  0.5,  0.5 0  0.5,
                               0 1 0,  0.5 0 -0.5, -0.5 0 -0.5,
                               0 1 0, -0.5 0 -0.5, -0.5 0  0.5,
                               0 1 0,  0.5 0  0.5,  0.5 0 -0.5"
                    TriangleIndices="0 1 2, 3 4 5, 6 7 8, 9 10 11" />
            </GeometryModel3D.Geometry>

            <GeometryModel3D.Material>
                <DiffuseMaterial Brush="Gray" />
            </GeometryModel3D.Material>
        </GeometryModel3D>
    </Page.Resources>

    <Viewport3D>

        <!-- Golden sand.-->
        <ModelVisual3D>
            <ModelVisual3D.Content>
                <GeometryModel3D>
                    <GeometryModel3D.Geometry>
                        <MeshGeometry3D
                            Positions="-1000 0    5, 1000 0     5,
                                       -1000 0 -1000, 1000 0 -1000"
                            TriangleIndices="0 1 2, 1 3 2" />
                    </GeometryModel3D.Geometry>

                    <GeometryModel3D.Material>
                        <DiffuseMaterial Brush="Gold" />
                    </GeometryModel3D.Material>
                </GeometryModel3D>
            </ModelVisual3D.Content>
        </ModelVisual3D>

        <!-- The six pyramids. -->
        <ModelVisual3D Content="{StaticResource pyramid}" />
```

```
        <ModelVisual3D Content="{StaticResource pyramid}">
            <ModelVisual3D.Transform>
                <TranslateTransform3D OffsetX="-1" OffsetZ="-5" />
            </ModelVisual3D.Transform>
        </ModelVisual3D>

        <ModelVisual3D Content="{StaticResource pyramid}">
            <ModelVisual3D.Transform>
                <TranslateTransform3D OffsetX="1.5" OffsetZ="-10" />
            </ModelVisual3D.Transform>
        </ModelVisual3D>

        <ModelVisual3D Content="{StaticResource pyramid}">
            <ModelVisual3D.Transform>
                <TranslateTransform3D OffsetX="3" OffsetZ="-3" />
            </ModelVisual3D.Transform>
        </ModelVisual3D>

        <ModelVisual3D Content="{StaticResource pyramid}">
            <ModelVisual3D.Transform>
                <TranslateTransform3D OffsetX="10" OffsetZ="-25" />
            </ModelVisual3D.Transform>
        </ModelVisual3D>

        <ModelVisual3D Content="{StaticResource pyramid}">
            <ModelVisual3D.Transform>
                <TranslateTransform3D OffsetX="0" OffsetZ="-50" />
            </ModelVisual3D.Transform>
        </ModelVisual3D>

        <!-- Light sources. -->
        <ModelVisual3D>
            <ModelVisual3D.Content>
                <Model3DGroup>
                    <AmbientLight Color="#404040" />
                    <DirectionalLight Color="#C0C0C0" Direction="2 -3 -1" />
                </Model3DGroup>
            </ModelVisual3D.Content>
        </ModelVisual3D>

        <!-- Camera. -->
        <Viewport3D.Camera>
            <PerspectiveCamera Position="-1 2 4"
                               LookDirection="1 -1 -4"
                               UpDirection="0 1 0"
                               FieldOfView="45" />
        </Viewport3D.Camera>
    </Viewport3D>
</Page>
```

The *Viewport3D* that follows the Resources section contains eight child *ModelVisual3D* elements. The first defines a flat area for the sands of the desert; the last includes the typical

AmbientLight and *DirectionalLight* elements. The middle six *ModelVisual3D* elements display six pyramids. Each of these *ModelVisual3D* elements has its *Content* property set to the *GeometryModel3D* resource. With the exception of the first pyramid, a *TranslateTransform3D* is applied to the *ModelVisual3D* that places the pyramid in a particular location:

```
<ModelVisual3D Content="{StaticResource pyramid}">
    <ModelVisual3D.Transform>
        <TranslateTransform3D OffsetX="-1" OffsetZ="-5" />
    </ModelVisual3D.Transform>
</ModelVisual3D>
```

The composite *Viewport3D* displays a landscape of six pyramids:

The blue sky, by the way, is not part of the *Viewport3D*. It is instead the *Background* property of the *Page*, and shows through the top of the *Viewport3D* because the *Viewport3D* is transparent in the absence of visuals. If you try to make another *ModelVisual3D* for the sky and give it a color of *SkyBlue*, it will look too dark because it's illuminated like everything else in the *Viewport3D*. Sky should really be illuminated a little differently, and I'll discuss alternate solutions to this problem in Chapters 4 and 5.

Many of the previous XAML files in this book have contained a *Viewport3D* element structured like this:

```
<Viewport3D>
    <ModelVisual3D>
        <ModelVisual3D.Content>
            <Model3DGroup>
                <!-- Multiple Model3D objects go here,
                     including GeometryModel3D and lights.  -->
            </Model3DGroup>
        </ModelVisual3D.Content>
    </ModelVisual3D>
</Viewport3D>
```

```
    <Viewport3D.Camera>
        <!-- Camera goes here. -->
    </Viewport3D.Camera>
</Viewport3D>
```

When you define a *GeometryModel3D* as a resource, this structure becomes a little awkward, and that's why I switched to a structure in LandOfThePyramids1.xaml that defined a separate *ModelVisual3D* for each *GeometryModel3D*. It's somewhat problematic to have a single *ModelVisual3D* with *GeometryModel3D* resources. The problem might not be so obvious until you try to do it. Look at it this way: The string "{StaticResource pyramid}" that accesses the *GeometryModel3D* resource has to be assigned to a property of type *Model3D*. The only property that satisfies that criterion is the *Content* property of *ModelVisual3D*. With a structure based on a single *ModelVisual3D* element, that property is already assigned to *Model3DGroup* object. To include the *GeometryModel3D* resource in this *Model3DGroup*, you need to resort to the object-element syntax for *StaticResource*:

```
<Viewport3D>
    <ModelVisual3D>
        <ModelVisual3D.Content>
            <Model3DGroup>
                <StaticResource ResourceKey="pyramid" />
                ...
            </Model3DGroup>
        </ModelVisual3D.Content>
    </ModelVisual3D>
    ...
</Viewport3D>
```

That's not too vile in itself, but you'd need multiple identical *StaticResource* elements in this *Model3DGroup* for the multiple pyramids, and you can't apply separate transforms to these elements. The syntax doesn't allow it, and that's not even the worst problem: You're only dealing with one object of type *GeometryModel3D* for all the pyramids, and that object can have only one transform applied to its *Transform* property.

To make this work with a single *ModelVisual3D*, you need to have nested *Model3DGroup* elements for each *GeometryModel3D* that you want transformed, and you'd need to apply the transform to this nested *Model3DGroup*:

```
<Viewport3D>
    <ModelVisual3D>
        <ModelVisual3D.Content>
            <Model3DGroup>
                <!-- Pyramid with no transform. -->
                <StaticResource ResourceKey="pyramid" />

                <!-- Pyramid with transform. -->
                <Model3DGroup>
                    <StaticResource ResourceKey="pyramid" />
                    <Model3DGroup.Transform>
                        <TranslateTransform3D OffsetX="-1" OffsetZ="-5" />
                    </Model3DGroup.Transform>
                </Model3DGroup>
```

```
        <!-- Other pyramids. -->
        ...
      </Model3DGroup>
    </ModelVisual3D.Content>
  </ModelVisual3D>
  ...
</Viewport3D>
```

This is probably getting a little more complicated than you find comfortable.

On the other hand, you might prefer instead to define the *MeshGeometry3D* and the *Diffuse-Material* as resources, and then create *GeometryModel3D* objects in the body of the XAML files that reference these resources. To position each of the six pyramids, you could apply the transform to this *GeometryModel3D*. With this scheme, it becomes easy to use a single *ModelVisual3D* for all the pyramids, as the following program demonstrates.

```
LandOfThePyramids2.xaml
<!-- ====================================================
     LandOfThePyramids2.xaml (c) 2007 by Charles Petzold
     ==================================================== -->
<Page xmlns="http://schemas.microsoft.com/winfx/2006/xaml/presentation"
      xmlns:x="http://schemas.microsoft.com/winfx/2006/xaml"
      WindowTitle="Land of the Pyramids #2"
      Title="Land of the Pyramids #2"
      Background="SkyBlue">

    <Page.Resources>

        <!-- Pyramid: Front, back, left, right. -->
        <MeshGeometry3D x:Key="mesh"
            Positions="0 1 0, -0.5 0  0.5,  0.5 0  0.5,
                       0 1 0,  0.5 0 -0.5, -0.5 0 -0.5,
                       0 1 0, -0.5 0 -0.5, -0.5 0  0.5,
                       0 1 0,  0.5 0  0.5,  0.5 0 -0.5"
            TriangleIndices="0 1 2, 3 4 5, 6 7 8, 9 10 11" />

        <!-- Gray material for pyramids. -->
        <DiffuseMaterial x:Key="mat" Brush="Gray" />
    </Page.Resources>

    <Viewport3D>

        <!-- Golden sand.-->
        <ModelVisual3D>
            <ModelVisual3D.Content>
                <GeometryModel3D>
                    <GeometryModel3D.Geometry>
                        <MeshGeometry3D
                            Positions="-1000 0     5, 1000 0     5,
                                       -1000 0 -1000, 1000 0 -1000"
                            TriangleIndices="0 1 2, 1 3 2" />
                    </GeometryModel3D.Geometry>
```

```xml
                <GeometryModel3D.Material>
                    <DiffuseMaterial Brush="Gold" />
                </GeometryModel3D.Material>
            </GeometryModel3D>
        </ModelVisual3D.Content>
</ModelVisual3D>

<!-- The six pyramids. -->
<ModelVisual3D>
    <ModelVisual3D.Content>
        <Model3DGroup>
            <GeometryModel3D Geometry="{StaticResource mesh}"
                            Material="{StaticResource mat}" />

            <GeometryModel3D Geometry="{StaticResource mesh}"
                            Material="{StaticResource mat}">
                <GeometryModel3D.Transform>
                    <TranslateTransform3D OffsetX="-1" OffsetZ="-5" />
                </GeometryModel3D.Transform>
            </GeometryModel3D>

            <GeometryModel3D Geometry="{StaticResource mesh}"
                            Material="{StaticResource mat}">
                <GeometryModel3D.Transform>
                    <TranslateTransform3D OffsetX="1.5" OffsetZ="-10" />
                </GeometryModel3D.Transform>
            </GeometryModel3D>

            <GeometryModel3D Geometry="{StaticResource mesh}"
                            Material="{StaticResource mat}">
                <GeometryModel3D.Transform>
                    <TranslateTransform3D OffsetX="3" OffsetZ="-3" />
                </GeometryModel3D.Transform>
            </GeometryModel3D>

            <GeometryModel3D Geometry="{StaticResource mesh}"
                            Material="{StaticResource mat}">
                <GeometryModel3D.Transform>
                    <TranslateTransform3D OffsetX="10" OffsetZ="-25" />
                </GeometryModel3D.Transform>
            </GeometryModel3D>

            <GeometryModel3D Geometry="{StaticResource mesh}"
                            Material="{StaticResource mat}">
                <GeometryModel3D.Transform>
                    <TranslateTransform3D OffsetX="0" OffsetZ="-50" />
                </GeometryModel3D.Transform>
            </GeometryModel3D>
        </Model3DGroup>
    </ModelVisual3D.Content>
</ModelVisual3D>
```

```
              <!-- Light sources. -->
              <ModelVisual3D>
                  <ModelVisual3D.Content>
                      <Model3DGroup>
                          <AmbientLight Color="#404040" />
                          <DirectionalLight Color="#C0C0C0" Direction="2 -3 -1" />
                      </Model3DGroup>
                  </ModelVisual3D.Content>
              </ModelVisual3D>

              <!-- Camera. -->
              <Viewport3D.Camera>
                  <PerspectiveCamera Position="-1 2 4"
                                     LookDirection="1 -1 -4"
                                     UpDirection="0 1 0"
                                     FieldOfView="45" />
              </Viewport3D.Camera>
          </Viewport3D>
      </Page>
```

Of course, even if you define the *MeshGeometry3D* and *DiffuseMaterial* objects as resources, you don't need to share all the pyramids in one *ModelVisual3D*. You could easily have a visual for each pyramid:

```
<ModelVisual3D>
    <ModelVisual3D.Content>
        <GeometryModel3D Geometry="{StaticResource mesh}"
                         Material="{StaticResource mat}">
            <GeometryModel3D.Transform>
                <TranslateTransform3D OffsetX="-1" OffsetZ="-5" />
            </GeometryModel3D.Transform>
        </GeometryModel3D>
    </ModelVisual3D.Content>
</ModelVisual3D>
```

Regardless of how you structure the XAML file, separating the *MeshGeometry3D* and the *DiffuseMaterial* as resources makes things easier if you want to color a particular pyramid differently:

```
<GeometryModel3D Geometry="{StaticResource mesh}">
    <GeometryModel3D.Material>
        <DiffuseMaterial Brush="Silver" />
    </GeometryModel3D.Material>
    <GeometryModel3D.Transform>
        <TranslateTransform3D OffsetX="-1" OffsetZ="-5" />
    </GeometryModel3D.Transform>
</GeometryModel3D>
```

Or, suppose you want pyramids of just two different colors. You could define the two *Diffuse-Material* objects as resources:

```
<DiffuseMaterial x:Key="matRed" Brush="Red" />
<DiffuseMaterial x:Key="matBlue" Brush="Blue" />
```

You could then reference one of those in the *GeometryModel3D* markup:

```
<ModelVisual3D>
    <ModelVisual3D.Content>
        <GeometryModel3D Geometry="{StaticResource mesh}"
                         Material="{StaticResource matRed}" />
    </ModelVisual3D.Content>
</ModelVisual3D>
```

Or, you could define the two different *GeometryModel3D* objects as resources that reference previously defined resources:

```
<GeometryModel3D x:Key="pyramidRed"
                 Geometry="{StaticResource mesh}"
                 Material="{StaticResource matRed}" />

<GeometryModel3D x:Key="pyramidBlue"
                 Geometry="{StaticResource mesh}"
                 Material="{StaticResource matBlue}" />
```

Then, referencing the *GeometryModel3D* resource in markup is the same as in the LandOfThePyramids1.xaml file.

One last example: Suppose you've defined an entire *GeometryModel3D* as a resource, and that's fine for all your pyramids except one, which you'd like to make red. You can use a binding to reference just the *Geometry* property—that is, the object of type *MeshGeometry3D*—from the *GeometryModel3D* resource, and then redefine the *Material* property:

```
<GeometryModel3D Geometry="{Binding Source={StaticResource pyramid},
                                    Path=Geometry}">
    <GeometryModel3D.Material>
        <DiffuseMaterial Brush="Red" />
    </GeometryModel3D.Material>
</GeometryModel3D>
```

You have lots of options and different ways you can structure your *Viewport3D* elements. The intention of the developers of WPF 3D was for the individual figures in a 3D scene to be mostly individual *ModelVisual3D* objects, and whenever possible, these visuals would share reusable models. In other words, LandOfThePyramids1.xaml is preferable to LandOfThe-Pyramids2.xaml. This is not because the resource is of type *GeometryModel3D*, but because it defines a separate *ModelVisual3D* for each pyramid.

Having separate *ModelVisual3D* objects for each figure becomes crucial when using methods defined by the *VisualTreeHelper* class, and in particular, when hit-testing—that is, determining what object in a 3D scene the user is clicking with the mouse. As you'll see a bit toward the end of Chapter 3 and more in Chapter 9, this hit-testing logic is based around visuals. When you specify a particular two-dimensional coordinate to be hit-tested, the callback method implemented for WPF 3D returns the topmost *ModelVisual3D* at that coordinate point. You are also provided with the particular *GeometryModel3D* involved, and even the triangle within the particular *MeshGeometry3D*. But you might not be interested in that particular topmost *ModelVisual3D*. You might instead want to know about the next deepest *ModelVisual3D* at the mouse coordinates. You can do this, but what you *can't* do is find the next deepest model within the same *ModelVisual3D*. If all your 3D figures are in the same *ModelVisual3D*, you can't easily get an idea of how these figures overlap at a particular two-dimensional coordinate point. (In a very real sense, the importance of using separate *ModelVisual3D* elements for each figure in the scene is implied by the options of an enumeration called *HitTestResultBehavior*.)

Even so, you might want to group a few figures together in the same *ModelVisual3D* so you can treat them as a unit for either applying transforms or when hit-testing.

In the TranslateTransformExperimenter.xaml file, you got a little taste of how you can compound transforms. You can apply a transform to a *GeometryModel3D*, to a *Model3DGroup* that contains that *GeometryModel3D*, and to the *ModelVisual3D* whose content is that *Model3DGroup*. The transforms are applied starting at the lowest level (that is, the *GeometryModel3D*) and working up to the *ModelVisual3D*.

But this nesting of transforms can go much deeper than the simple explanation implies: A *Model3DGroup* can contain other *Model3DGroup* children. *ModelVisual3D* also has a *Children* property of type *Visual3DCollection*. In other words, a *ModelVisual3D* can have children of type *ModelVisual3D*, which can themselves have children of type *ModelVisual3D*, and so forth. The purpose for this conceivably extensive hierarchy is to allow the complex nesting of transforms. Each figure in a scene can have its own transform, and then you can group figures (either in a *Model3DGroup* or a *ModelVisual3D*) and apply a transform to that group as a whole. You might then combine that group with other groups (again, either in a *Model3DGroup* or a *ModelVisual3D*) and apply another transform. And then all the *ModelVisual3D* objects are subject to the transform defined for the camera.

Schemes such as this don't have a clear cutoff point where you stop grouping models and start grouping visuals. Just keep in mind two guidelines: If you want it to be reusable and shareable, it's got to be a model. If you want to use visual services (such as hit-testing), separate visuals are usually more convenient.

The Scale Transform

The *ScaleTransform3D* makes a figure larger or smaller by multiplying its *X*, *Y*, and *Z* coordinates by properties named *ScaleX*, *ScaleY*, and *ScaleZ*, all of which have default values of 1. Here's how the *ScaleTransform3D* might appear in markup to transform a *GeometryModel3D*:

```
<GeometryModel3D>
    ...
    <GeometryModel3D.Transform>
        <ScaleTransform3D ScaleX="3" ScaleY="1" ScaleZ="2" />
    </GeometryModel3D.Transform>
</GeometryModel3D>
```

The figure is effectively widened by a factor of 3 and doubled in size along the Z axis. The *ScaleY* attribute set the value to its default and can be removed. The scale transform formulas are:

x' = *ScaleX* * x
y' = *ScaleY* * y
z' = *ScaleZ* * z

The ScaleTransformExperimenter.xaml program (not shown here because it's quite similar to TranslateTransformExperimenter.xaml) lets you experiment with the *ScaleTransform3D* in the same ways.

Notice that the initial values of the scrollbars are all set at 1, which is the default value of the *ScaleX*, *ScaleY*, and *ScaleZ* properties of the transform. As you move the topmost *ScrollBar* to the right, the width of the figure gets larger. The left-front corner of the figure at the coordinate origin remains anchored, however.

You can also decrease *ScaleX* below 1 and narrow the figure. At 0 the figure collapses into a plane, but at values less than 0, it extends toward the left. All the X coordinates are scaled by a negative value, so the figure is effectively flipped around the YZ plane. Similarly, increasing and decreasing the second and third *ScrollBar* affects the figure's height and depth. By independently changing the scaling factor along the three axes, you can turn a figure into something that's certainly related to the original but seems quite different. Here's what you'll see when you set *ScaleX* to 0.125, *ScaleY* to 0.25, and *ScaleZ* to 4:

Notice that as you change the height or width of the figure, the color of the sloped top part changes somewhat because changing the dimensions of the figure also changes the angle that the face makes with the *DirectionalLight*.

The scaling of a figure occurs with reference to a point called the "center," which by default is the origin—the point (0, 0, 0). That's why the front-left corner of the figure remains planted in the same spot during all scaling operations. That the point (0, 0, 0) is unaffected by scaling is obvious from the scaling transform formulas:

x' = *ScaleX* * x
y' = *ScaleY* * y
z' = *ScaleZ* * z

However, these are not the *complete* scaling formulas. You can change the center point of the transform by altering three properties of *ScaleTransform3D* named *CenterX*, *CenterY*, and *CenterZ*, all of which have default values of 0. The complete scale transform formulas are actually:

x' = *ScaleX* * (x − *CenterX*) + *CenterX*
y' = *ScaleY* * (y − *CenterY*) + *CenterY*
z' = *ScaleZ* * (z − *CenterZ*) + *CenterZ*

Let's take an example: Suppose a 3D object has a side whose X values range from 0 to 2. If *ScaleX* is 2, these transformed values will range from 0 to 4. Simple enough. But if *CenterX* is set to 1, the original X value of 0 is lessened by 1 to be −1, then multiplied by 2 to be −2, and then *CenterX* is added to be −1. The X value of 2 is lessened by *CenterX* to be 1, multiplied by 2 to be 2, and then *CenterX* is added again to be 3. The transformed object now extends along the X axis from −1 to 3. It's still doubled in size, but that part of the object where X equals the *CenterX* value of 1 has remained anchored in place.

You can add the following attributes to the first *ScaleTransform3D* element in the XAML file:

```
CenterX="1" CenterY="0.5" CenterZ="-1.5"
```

Now the figure is expanded and compressed around its center.

The unit cube used in many of the XAML files in this chapter has X, Y, and Z coordinates of −0.5 and 0.5, so the cube is already centered around the origin. Defining the cube in this way is often convenient when applying transforms.

In the discussion of the translation transform, I said that transforms applied to the camera have the inverse effect of transforms applied to 3D figures. For the scale transform, that means that the coordinates of the figure effectively get *divided* by the *ScaleX*, *ScaleY*, and *ScaleZ* factors. You can manipulate the bottom three scrollbars to see what I mean. As you increase the top *ScrollBar* of those bottom three, the *ScaleX* property of the transform applied to the camera increases, but the figure gets smaller. If you decrease the *ScrollBar* below 1, the figure gets larger until the *ScrollBar* hits a value of zero. At that point, the figure is (theoretically) infinitely wide, and as you move the *ScrollBar* below zero, the figure flips around to become negatively infinitely wide, and for further negative values, the figure decreases in size. The *CenterX*, *CenterY*, and *CenterZ* properties affect the camera transform in the same way they affect the transform applied to the *GeometryModel3D*.

In the ScaleTransformExperimenter.xaml file, try moving the first *ScaleTransform3D* element to the *DirectionalLight* placeholder. The *ScaleTransform3D* changes the direction of the light by effectively multiplying the three elements of the *Direction* vector by *ScaleX*, *ScaleY*, and *ScaleZ*. As you increase the first *ScrollBar*, the direction of the light tends more toward the positive X axis. As you increase the second *ScrollBar*, the direction of the light becomes more accentuated in the negative Y direction. Increasing the third *ScrollBar* moves the light in a direction to the negative Z axis. The *CenterX*, *CenterY*, and *CenterZ* properties have no effect when you apply a *ScaleTransform3D* to *DirectionalLight*.

If you move the transform to the *Model3DGroup* or the *ModelVisual3D*, the transform affects both the size of the figure and the orientation of the light. It is actually the inverse of this transform that is performed when you apply a scale transform to the camera. (I am not so sure that this implementation of scaling is theoretically the correct behavior: When applying a scale transform to the camera or to the composite figure and light, I would expect illumination of the figure to remain constant. That would require the directional vector of the light to be divided by the scaling factors.)

When scale transforms are applied to both the *GeometryModel3D* and the *Model3DGroup*, or to the *GeometryModel3D* and the *ModelVisual3D*, the corresponding scale factors are effectively multiplied for the composite transform.

Combining Translation and Scaling

It is common to apply multiple transforms to the same model or visual. To do this, you need to define the transform to be a *Transform3DGroup*:

```
<GeometryModel3D.Transform>
    <Transform3DGroup>
        ...
    </Transform3DGroup>
</GeometryModel3D.Transform>
```

This *Transform3DGroup* can have multiple children. You might know now (or you'll discover in Chapter 7) that combining transforms is equivalent to matrix multiplication, and in general, matrix multiplication is not commutative. The order that the transforms appear in the *Transform3DGroup* makes a difference.

For multiple transforms of the type *TranslateTransform3D*, this is not a problem. The composite effect is simply the sum of the *OffsetX*, *OffsetY*, and *OffsetZ* properties. If you actually have a *Transform3DGroup* containing multiple consecutive *TranslateTransform3D* elements with explicit values, you can generally improve performance by combining them into one. However, if a particular *TranslateTransform3D* is affected by a data binding or animation, you probably won't be able to combine it with other transforms.

Similarly, if the *CenterX*, *CenterY*, and *CenterZ* properties of several *ScaleTransform3D* elements are all set to their default values of zero, multiple *ScaleTransform3D* elements simply produce a composite effect equivalent to a transform containing a product of the *ScaleX*, *ScaleY*, and *ScaleZ* properties.

But combine a *TranslateTransform3D* and a *ScaleTransform3D*, or multiple scale transforms with non-default centers, and you really need to know what you're doing.

Let's examine the case of combining a single *TranslateTransform3D* and a single *Scale-Transform3D* with default centering. If the *TranslateTransform3D* comes first, the first transform formulas are:

x' = x + *OffsetX*
y' = y + *OffsetY*
z' = z + *OffsetZ*

The *ScaleTransform3D* (with default center properties) is then applied to that sum:

x" = *ScaleX* * x' = *ScaleX* * (x + *OffsetX*)
y" = *ScaleY* * y' = *ScaleY* * (y + *OffsetY*)
z" = *ScaleZ* * z' = *ScaleZ* * (z + *OffsetZ*)

Now let's try the other order. Apply the *ScaleTransform3D* first:

x' = *ScaleX* * x
y' = *ScaleY* * y
z' = *ScaleZ* * z

And now apply the *TranslateTransform3D*:

x" = x' + *OffsetX* = *ScaleX* * x + *OffsetX*
y" = y' + *OffsetY* = *ScaleY* * y + *OffsetY*
z" = z' + *OffsetZ* = *ScaleZ* * z + *OffsetZ*

When the *TranslateTransform3D* comes first, any translation factors are effectively multiplied by the *ScaleTransform3D*. When the *ScaleTransform3D* comes first, this doesn't happen. This second approach is probably how you imagine a composite translation and scaling. In general, you'll probably be happier combining the transforms with the *ScaleTransform3D* first, followed by *TranslateTransform3D*.

Applying a *TranslateTransform3D* before a *ScaleTransform3D* isn't always a bad idea if you properly anticipate the results. In fact, the *CenterX*, *CenterY*, and *CenterZ* properties of the *ScaleTransform3D* can be visualized as a composite transform where a translation is performed before and after the scaling operation. Here's a scale transform with all its properties set to symbolic values:

```
<ScaleTransform3D ScaleX="SX" ScaleY="SY" ScaleZ="SZ"
                  CenterX="CX" CenterY="CY" CenterZ="CZ" />
```

That's equivalent to:

```
<TranslateTransform3D OffsetX="-CX" OffsetY="-CY" OffsetZ="-CZ" />
<ScaleTransform3D ScaleX="SX" ScaleY="SY" ScaleZ="SZ" />
<TranslateTransform3D OffsetX="CX" OffsetY="CY" OffsetZ="CZ" />
```

It's also equivalent to:

```
<ScaleTransform3D ScaleX="SX" ScaleY="SY" ScaleZ="SZ" />
<TranslateTransform3D OffsetX="CX(1-SX)" OffsetY="CY(1-SY)" OffsetZ="CZ(1-SZ)" />
```

Or:

```
<TranslateTransform3D OffsetX="CX/SZ-CX" OffsetY="CY/SY-CY" OffsetZ="CZ/SZ-CZ" />
<ScaleTransform3D ScaleX="SX" ScaleY="SY" ScaleZ="SZ" />
```

In some cases, you might be able to fiddle with a combination of a *ScaleTransform3D* and *TranslateTransform3D* in ways that reduce the total number of transforms. Whenever any single transform in a group changes as a result of an animation or data binding, WPF 3D needs to recalculate the entire composite transform, and this is obviously faster if the transform group has fewer members. I'll have some examples of transform reduction in the next section.

Suppose you go back to LandOfThePyramids2.xaml with the intent to double the size of the pyramids. You might consider adding the following markup to the end of the *ModelVisual3D* element containing the pyramids:

```
<ModelVisual3D.Transform>
    <ScaleTransform3D ScaleX="2" ScaleY="2" ScaleZ="2" />
</ModelVisual3D.Transform>
```

That definitely makes all the pyramids double in size, but this transform is applied after the translate transforms on the individual *GeometryModel3D* objects, so what also doubles in size are the coordinate locations of all the pyramids (except for the one sitting at the origin). If you wanted to double the size of the pyramids while keeping them in the same locations, you'd need to add a *ScaleTransform3D* element to each *GeometryModel3D*. This *ScaleTransform3D* element would go before the *TranslateTransform3D* element, and both transforms would need to be children of a *Transform3DGroup*.

Making a global change like this is much easier in the LandOfThePyramids1.xaml file. All you need to do is insert the following markup at the end of the *GeometryModel3D* object defined as a resource:

```
<GeometryModel3D.Transform>
    <ScaleTransform3D ScaleX="2" ScaleY="2" ScaleZ="2" />
</GeometryModel3D.Transform>
```

Now this scaling transform is applied before the translate transforms that appear in the individual *ModelVisual3D* elements.

How to Build a Chair

Suppose you need to populate a virtual auditorium with a bunch of chairs. These chairs are identical in size and color. The only difference between the chairs is their location on the auditorium floor—in other words, a *TranslateTransform3D*.

You'll probably want the entire chair to be defined as a resource so that you can simply set it to the *Content* property of a *ModelVisual3D* and then set the *Transform* property to move the chair to its proper location:

```
<ModelVisual3D Content="{StaticResource chair}">
    <ModelVisual3D.Transform>
        <TranslateTransform3D OffsetX="-3" OffsetZ="2" />
    </ModelVisual3D.Transform>
</ModelVisual3D>
```

That resource must be a type that descends from *Model3D*. You might assume it's a *GeometryModel3D*, where the geometry of the entire chair is defined in a single *MeshGeometry3D* object, but that doesn't seem like the best approach to me. Instead, the resource named "chair" will be an object of type *Model3DGroup*, and its children will be the various parts of the chair: its legs, the seat, and the back.

I want to construct this entire chair from cubes. The Resources section of the XAML file will contain a *MeshGeometry3D* object named "cube" that defines a unit cube centered on the origin. I also want a resource of type *DiffuseMaterial* named "wood."

The "chair" resource looks like this:

```
<Model3DGroup x:Key="chair">
    ...
</Model3DGroup>
```

Every child of this *Model3DGroup* is an object of type *GeometryModel3D* and defines one part of the chair. Approximately one unit of 3D space will be equivalent to one foot of reality, so the seat of the chair will be 1.5 units off the ground. The chair will be constructed so that the bottoms of the legs sit on the XZ plane (the floor), and the center of the chair is aligned with the Y axis. The two front legs will have positive Z coordinates and the two right legs will have positive X coordinates.

Here, for example, is the *GeometryModel3D* element for the right front leg of the chair:

```
<GeometryModel3D Geometry="{StaticResource cube}"
                 Material="{StaticResource wood}">
    <GeometryModel3D.Transform>
        <Transform3DGroup>
            <ScaleTransform3D ScaleX="0.1" ScaleY="1.5" ScaleZ="0.1" />
            <TranslateTransform3D OffsetX="0.5" OffsetY="0.75" OffsetZ="0.5" />
        </Transform3DGroup>
    </GeometryModel3D.Transform>
</GeometryModel3D>
```

This object references the "cube" and "wood" resources but the remainder is devoted to a composite transform. Remember that we're starting out with a unit cube. The *ScaleTransform3D* scales the X and Z coordinates by 0.1, which means that the leg will be 0.1 units wide and deep. The *ScaleY* property is 1.5, so the leg becomes 1.5 units tall.

However, following the *ScaleTransform3D*, this leg is still centered on the origin, which means that it extends 0.75 units along the negative Y axis and 0.75 units along the positive Y axis. The *TranslateTransform3D* that follows needs to raise the leg up so it sits on the XZ plane (that's accomplished by the *OffsetY* property) and move the leg to its proper horizontal position 0.5 units from the center of the chair along both the X and Z axes. The left leg is identical except that the *OffsetX* property is −0.5.

You might instead be more comfortable developing a series of transforms that performed these operations in a slightly different order. Here's an example:

```
<TranslateTransform3D OffsetY="0.5" />
<ScaleTransform3D ScaleX="0.1" ScaleY="1.5" ScaleZ="0.1" />
<TranslateTransform3D OffsetX="0.5" OffsetZ="0.5" />
```

The first *TranslateTransform3D* simply elevates the unit cube so that it's already sitting on the top of the XZ plane. The *ScaleTransform3D* is the same as before, but the *TranslateTransform3D* that follows just needs to put the leg in its proper position relative to the center of the chair.

The seat of the chair looks like this:

```
<GeometryModel3D Geometry="{StaticResource cube}"
                 Material="{StaticResource wood}">
    <GeometryModel3D.Transform>
        <Transform3DGroup>
            <ScaleTransform3D ScaleX="1.25" ScaleY="0.1" ScaleZ="1.25" />
            <TranslateTransform3D OffsetY="1.55" />
        </Transform3DGroup>
    </GeometryModel3D.Transform>
</GeometryModel3D>
```

Here the *ScaleTransform3D* makes the width and depth of the seat 1.25 units, but the height of the seat is only 0.1 units. The *TranslateTransform3D* is the tricky one: Because the seat is still centered on the origin, it now extends 0.05 units on the positive and negative Y axis. It needs to be elevated 0.05 units to sit on the XZ plane, and another 1.5 units to sit on the top of the chair legs. Again, it might be more comprehensible if the *TranslateTransform3D* were split into two parts:

```
<TranslateTransform3D OffsetY="0.5" />
<ScaleTransform3D ScaleX="1.25" ScaleY="0.1" ScaleZ="1.25" />
<TranslateTransform3D OffsetY="1.5" />
```

The BuildChair.xaml file is rather lengthy so it's not shown here.

Eight chairs are positioned on the green linoleum floor of the auditorium, and the result looks like this:

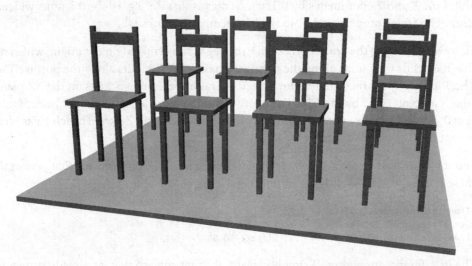

It's possible to modularize the resource even further. Both front legs are identical in everything but location. (The back legs are longer because they become part of the back of the chair.) You could begin by defining a "frontleg" resource like this:

```
<GeometryModel3D x:Key="frontleg"
                 Geometry="{StaticResource cube}"
                 Material="{StaticResource wood}">
    <GeometryModel3D.Transform>
        <ScaleTransform3D CenterY="-1.5" ScaleX="0.1" ScaleY="1.5" ScaleZ="0.1" />
    </GeometryModel3D.Transform>
</GeometryModel3D>
```

This markup contains a little cleverness. The *CenterY* property of the *ScaleTransform3D* is set to −1.5. What could that mean? Normally we think of the center properties as indicating that point in the figure that remains rooted by the scaling. But it's all just arithmetic. The complete scale transform formula for the Y coordinates is:

$y' = ScaleY * (y − CenterY) + CenterY$

Or, with the values I've indicated:

$y' = 1.5 * (y + 1.5) − 1.5$

The bottom of the unit cube has a Y coordinate of −0.5, so that's transformed to 0. The top of the unit cube has a Y coordinate of 0.5, which is transformed to 1.5. Thus, the chair leg is raised above the XZ plane without an additional *TranslateTransform3D*.

Within the *Model3DGroup* for the complete chair, the right and left legs require only a *TranslateTransform3D* to move them into position:

```
<Model3DGroup x:Key="chair">
    <!-- Right front leg. -->
    <Model3DGroup>
        <StaticResource ResourceKey="frontleg" />
        <Model3DGroup.Transform>
            <TranslateTransform3D OffsetX="0.5" OffsetZ="0.5" />
        </Model3DGroup.Transform>
    </Model3DGroup>

    <!-- Left front leg. -->
    <Model3DGroup>
        <StaticResource ResourceKey="frontleg" />
        <Model3DGroup.Transform>
            <TranslateTransform3D OffsetX="-0.5" OffsetZ="0.5" />
        </Model3DGroup.Transform>
    </Model3DGroup>
    ...
</Model3DGroup>
```

This approach results in slightly less markup, but probably not enough to justify using it. But I'll make use of this type of modularization for the four legs of a table coming up in the next chapter.

The construction of the 3D chair shows a clear distinction between visuals and models. Each visual chair is a separate *ModelVisual3D*, yet all these visuals share the same model. As a program in the next chapter demonstrates, you can implement hit-testing so that a program can determine exactly which chair the user is clicking. Yet, the user can click any part of the chair. The chair is treated as an entire entity for transforms or hit-testing.

Of course, it's always possible that you'll assemble a program like this and then your boss or a client (or your own inner gremlin) will say "Now I want to see a chair fall apart into its constituent pieces" or "I want to allow the user to assemble a chair from its parts using the mouse." At that point, you have to rethink the entire structure of the program. You would need to define each of the pieces as a separate resource. Perhaps most chairs could be a single *ModelVisual3D*, but a disassembled chair would probably be multiple *ModelVisual3D* elements.

And then, if a second request comes in that says "Now I want to see the legs of the chair break in half as the chair falls apart," you might be dividing the chair into ever finer resources. Some people are never satisfied.

Chapter 3
Axis/Angle Rotation

The third of the three standard types of 3D transforms is the rotation. Both conceptually and syntactically, the rotation is quite a bit more complex than translation or scaling, and it's no use trying to persuade you otherwise. Combinations of rotations in several planes can be so complex that a special mathematical tool called the *quaternion* exists solely for working with them. Yet, the quaternion itself is so complex that I'm going to delay discussing it until Chapter 8, "Quaternions."

The Rotation Transform

The *RotateTransform3D* class defines just four properties. Like *ScaleTransform3D*, *RotateTransform3D* defines *CenterX*, *CenterY*, and *CenterZ* properties that are 0 by default. These indicate a point that remains in the same place when the rotation occurs. But the only other property defined by *RotateTransform3D* is named *Rotation*. You set this property to an object of type *Rotation3D*, which is an abstract class as shown in the following hierarchy:

```
Object
        DispatcherObject (abstract)
                DependencyObject
                        Freezable (abstract)
                                Animatable (abstract)
                                        Rotation3D (abstract)
                                                AxisAngleRotation3D (sealed)
                                                QuaternionRotation3D (sealed)
```

The markup for a *RotationTransform3D* is wordier than the other transforms because a property element tag is generally required for the *Rotation* property:

```
<RotateTransform3D ... >
    <RotateTransform3D.Rotation>
        <AxisAngleRotation3D ... />
```

```
        </RotateTransform3D.Rotation>
    </RotateTransform3D>
```

You can avoid this property element if the *Rotation3D* object is defined by a resource or controlled by a *Rotation3DAnimation*.

Within the *RotateTransform3D.Rotation* tag you specify either an *AxisAngleRotation3D* or a *QuaternionRotation3D*, but I'll focus solely on the former in this chapter. As the name suggests, *AxisAngleRotation3D* rotates a figure around an axis by a specified number of degrees.

AxisAngleRotation3D defines just two properties. The *Axis* property is of type *Vector3D* and has a default value of $(0, 1, 0)$, which is a vector in the direction of the positive Y axis. Rotation occurs around an axis parallel to that vector. You also indicate an *Angle* property, which is the angle of rotation.

If you leave the *CenterX*, *CenterY*, and *CenterZ* properties defined by *RotateTransform3D* at their default settings of 0, the default *Axis* value of $(0, 1, 0)$ causes a figure to rotate around the Y axis. For non-default center values and an *Axis* value of $(0, 1, 0)$, the rotation occurs around a line parallel to the Y axis. You can determine where that line is actually located from the *CenterX* and *CenterZ* properties of the *RotateTransform3D* object. All points of the form $(CenterX, y, CenterZ)$ remain in the same place during the rotation. Similarly, if the *Axis* value is $(1, 0, 0)$, all points of the form $(x, CenterY, CenterZ)$ remain in the same place. If the *Axis* value is $(0, 0, 1)$, all points of the form $(CenterX, CenterY, z)$ remain unchanged.

You can also specify an *Axis* value not parallel to the X, Y, or Z axis, for example, $(1, 1, 0)$. That's a vector that points toward the upper right. Find the point $(CenterX, CenterY, CenterZ)$, and orient the vector with its tail at that point. That's the axis around which the figure rotates.

Rotation around any particular axis can be one of two ways. In a two-dimensional coordinate system, it is convenient to refer to clockwise rotation and counterclockwise rotation, but those terms become a little awkward when dealing with arbitrary axes in three-dimensional space. Instead, we call upon the right-hand rule to decipher rotation direction: If you point the thumb of your right hand in the direction of the *Axis* vector, the curves of your other fingers indicate the direction of rotation for positive *Angle* values.

For example, suppose the *Axis* value is $(0, 0, 1)$, and the *CenterX*, *CenterY*, and *CenterZ* haven't been changed from their defaults. Rotation occurs around the Z axis. Positive *Angle* values cause points on the positive X axis to move toward the positive Y axis, and points on the positive Y axis to move toward the negative X axis, and so forth. Here's a rotation of 30 degrees:

If you'd prefer that rotation occur in the opposite direction, either use the negative of the *Axis* vector—for example, $(0, 0, -1)$—or use negative *Angle* values. Here's a rotation around $(0, 0, -1)$ of 30 degrees, or a rotation around $(0, 0, 1)$ of −30 degrees:

The following program lets you experiment with axis rotations.

AxisRotationExperimenter.xaml

```
<!-- =========================================================
        AxisRotationExperimenter.xaml (c) 2007 by Charles Petzold
     ========================================================= -->
<Page xmlns="http://schemas.microsoft.com/winfx/2006/xaml/presentation"
      xmlns:x="http://schemas.microsoft.com/winfx/2006/xaml"
      WindowTitle="AxisAngleRotation3D Experimenter"
      Title="AxisAngleRotation3D Experimenter">
    <DockPanel>
        <ScrollBar Name="xMod" DockPanel.Dock="Top" Orientation="Horizontal"
                   Minimum="-100" Maximum="180" LargeChange="10" Value="1"
                   ToolTip="X Model" />
```

```
        <ScrollBar Name="yMod" DockPanel.Dock="Top" Orientation="Horizontal"
                  Minimum="-180" Maximum="180" LargeChange="10" Value="1"
                  ToolTip="Y Model" />

        <ScrollBar Name="zMod" DockPanel.Dock="Top" Orientation="Horizontal"
                  Minimum="-180" Maximum="180" LargeChange="10" Value="1"
                  ToolTip="Z Model" />

        <ScrollBar Name="zCam" DockPanel.Dock="Bottom" Orientation="Horizontal"
                  Minimum="-180" Maximum="180" LargeChange="10" Value="1"
                  ToolTip="Z Camera" />

        <ScrollBar Name="yCam" DockPanel.Dock="Bottom" Orientation="Horizontal"
                  Minimum="-180" Maximum="180" LargeChange="10" Value="1"
                  ToolTip="Y Camera" />

        <ScrollBar Name="xCam" DockPanel.Dock="Bottom" Orientation="Horizontal"
                  Minimum="-180" Maximum="180" LargeChange="10" Value="1"
                  ToolTip="X Camera" />
<Viewport3D>
    <ModelVisual3D>
        <ModelVisual3D.Content>
            <Model3DGroup>
                <GeometryModel3D>
                    <GeometryModel3D.Geometry>

                        <!-- Front, rear, top, right, bottom. -->
                        <MeshGeometry3D
                            Positions="0 0  0, 2 0  0, 2 1  0,
                                       0 0 -3, 2 0 -3, 2 1 -3,
                                       2 1 -3, 0 0 -3, 2 1  0, 0 0  0,
                                       2 1  0, 2 0  0, 2 1 -3, 2 0 -3,
                                       2 0  0, 0 0  0, 2 0 -3, 0 0 -3"

                            TriangleIndices=" 0  1  2,
                                              3  5  4,
                                              6  7  8,  7  9  8,
                                             10 11 12, 11 13 12,
                                             14 15 16, 15 17 16" />
                    </GeometryModel3D.Geometry>

                    <GeometryModel3D.Material>
                        <DiffuseMaterial Brush="Cyan" />
                    </GeometryModel3D.Material>

                    <GeometryModel3D.Transform>
                        <Transform3DGroup>
                            <RotateTransform3D>
                                <RotateTransform3D.Rotation>
                                    <AxisAngleRotation3D Axis="1 0 0"
                                        Angle="{Binding ElementName=xMod,
                                                        Path=Value}" />
                                </RotateTransform3D.Rotation>
                            </RotateTransform3D>
                        </Transform3DGroup>
                    </GeometryModel3D.Transform>
```

```xml
                    <RotateTransform3D>
                        <RotateTransform3D.Rotation>
                            <AxisAngleRotation3D Axis="0 1 0"
                                Angle="{Binding ElementName=yMod,
                                                Path=Value}" />
                        </RotateTransform3D.Rotation>
                    </RotateTransform3D>

                    <RotateTransform3D>
                        <RotateTransform3D.Rotation>
                            <AxisAngleRotation3D Axis="0 0 1"
                                Angle="{Binding ElementName=zMod,
                                                Path=Value}" />
                        </RotateTransform3D.Rotation>
                    </RotateTransform3D>
                </Transform3DGroup>
            </GeometryModel3D.Transform>
        </GeometryModel3D>

        <!-- Light sources. -->
        <AmbientLight Color="#404040" />

        <DirectionalLight Color="#C0C0C0" Direction="2 -3 -1">
                <DirectionalLight.Transform>
                    <Transform3DGroup>
                        <!-- Placeholder for light transform. -->
                    </Transform3DGroup>
                </DirectionalLight.Transform>
        </DirectionalLight>

        <Model3DGroup.Transform>
            <Transform3DGroup>
                <!-- Placeholder for group transform. -->
            </Transform3DGroup>
        </Model3DGroup.Transform>
    </Model3DGroup>
</ModelVisual3D.Content>

<ModelVisual3D.Transform>
    <Transform3DGroup>
        <!-- Placeholder for visual transform. -->
    </Transform3DGroup>
</ModelVisual3D.Transform>
</ModelVisual3D>

<!-- Camera. -->
<Viewport3D.Camera>
    <PerspectiveCamera Position="-2 2 4"
                       LookDirection="2 -1 -4"
                       UpDirection="0 1 0"
                       FieldOfView="45">
        <PerspectiveCamera.Transform>
            <Transform3DGroup>
                <RotateTransform3D>
```

```
                              <RotateTransform3D.Rotation>
                                  <AxisAngleRotation3D Axis="1 0 0"
                                      Angle="{Binding ElementName=xCam,
                                                       Path=Value}" />
                              </RotateTransform3D.Rotation>
                          </RotateTransform3D>

                          <RotateTransform3D>
                              <RotateTransform3D.Rotation>
                                  <AxisAngleRotation3D Axis="0 1 0"
                                      Angle="{Binding ElementName=yCam,
                                                       Path=Value}" />
                              </RotateTransform3D.Rotation>
                          </RotateTransform3D>

                          <RotateTransform3D>
                              <RotateTransform3D.Rotation>
                                  <AxisAngleRotation3D Axis="0 0 1"
                                      Angle="{Binding ElementName=zCam,
                                                       Path=Value}" />
                              </RotateTransform3D.Rotation>
                          </RotateTransform3D>
                      </Transform3DGroup>
                  </PerspectiveCamera.Transform>
              </PerspectiveCamera>
          </Viewport3D.Camera>
      </Viewport3D>
    </DockPanel>
  </Page>
```

Each of the three scrollbars at the top is linked to an *Angle* property of a different *AxisAngleRotation3D* element that's part of a *RotateTransform3D* element. The three *AxisAngleRotation3D* elements have their *Axis* properties set to (1, 0, 0), (0, 1, 0), and (0, 0, 1), so the three scrollbars rotate the figure around the X, Y, and Z axes, respectively. Moving each scrollbar to the right increases the *Angle* from 0 to 180 degrees; moving each scrollbar to the left makes the *Angle* property negative to −180 degrees.

Regardless of the rotation, the left-front corner of the figure remains anchored at the origin. You can change the three *RotateTransform3D* elements applied to the *GeometryModel3D* to the following:

```
<RotateTransform3D CenterX="1" CenterY="0.5" CenterZ="-1.5">
```

Now the center of the figure remains anchored. Setting a *CenterX* property isn't required for rotation around the X axis, because all X values remain the same anyway. Similar rules apply to the *CenterY* and *CenterZ* properties.

The three scrollbars at the bottom of the page control rotations applied to the camera. As you can see, the effect of the rotation is reversed because conceptually the camera is being rotated rather than the figure. The camera rotates around the point (*CenterX, CenterY, CenterZ*). You can imagine the camera tethered to that point by a rope. The length of the rope is governed by the relationship of the camera's *Position* properties to *CenterX, CenterY,* and *CenterZ*. As the camera rotates around that point, the *LookDirection* vector is rotated similarly, in effect so it makes the same angle with the tethering rope.

In the second of the three rotations applied to the camera, change the *RotateTransform3D* element to the following:

```
<RotateTransform3D CenterX="1" CenterZ="-10">
```

Now manipulate the second of the three scrollbars at the bottom of the page. You can effectively swing the camera around the figure and view it from the back but at a further distance.

Move the first set of three *RotateTransform3D* elements to the light. Now you can use the scrollbars on the top to rotate the *Direction* vector of *DirectionalLight*. The experimentation here might be a little clearer if you change the initial value of the *Direction* vector to (0, −1, 0)—that is, straight down. It is tempting to imagine that the source of the light (that is, the imaginary sun at the base of the *Direction* vector) is rotating around the origin. But that's not so: Instead, the *Direction* vector rotates around the imaginary sun. When you increase the first *ScrollBar*, the *Direction* vector rotates around a line parallel to the X axis so that it's pointing more in the negative Z direction. When you increase the third *ScrollBar*, the *Direction* vector rotates around a line parallel to the Z axis so that it points more in the positive X direction. The *CenterX, CenterY,* and *CenterZ* properties have no effect on a *RotateTransform3D* applied to a *DirectionalLight*.

Move the three *RotateTransform3D* elements to either the *Model3DGroup* or the *ModelVisual3D* where they affect the figure and the light together. Now as the figure rotates, the light rotates with it, and the illumination of the sides of the figure remains constant.

The generalized transform formulas for rotation are quite complex, but they are considerably simpler when rotation is around the X, Y, or Z axis. Here are the formulas for rotation around the Y axis, where α is the *Angle* property:

$$x' = x \cdot \cos(\alpha) + z \cdot \sin(\alpha)$$
$$y' = y$$
$$z' = z \cdot \cos(\alpha) - x \cdot \sin(\alpha)$$

When α is zero, there is no rotation. When α is 90 degrees, $\sin(\alpha)$ is 1, and $\cos(\alpha)$ is 0. The point (1, 0, 0) on the X axis is rotated to the point (0, 0, −1) on the negative Z axis, and the point (0, 0, −1) is rotated to the point (−1, 0, 0), which in turn is rotated to the point (0, 0, 1), just as we would predict.

In the following markup, the *CenterX*, *CenterY*, and *CenterZ* properties have symbolic values of CX, CY, and CZ:

```
<RotateTransform3D CenterX="CX" CenterY="CY" CenterZ="CZ">
    ...
</RotateTransform3D>
```

That transform is equivalent to translating the point (CX, CY, CZ) to the origin, then rotating, and then translating the point at the origin back to (CX, CY, CZ):

```
<TranslateTransform3D OffsetX="-CX" OffsetY="-CY" OffsetZ="-CZ" />
<RotateTransform3D>
    ...
</RotateTransform3D>
<TranslateTransform3D OffsetX="CX" OffsetY="CY" OffsetZ="CZ" />
```

The simplest type of animated rotation involves defining a *RotateTransform3D* with fixed *CenterX*, *CenterY*, and *CenterZ* properties and an *AxisAngleRotation3D* with a fixed *Axis* property, and then animating the *Angle* property. Such is the case in the following program, which creates a dodecahedron (a 12-sided regular polyhedron with pentagonal faces) with translucent sides and then spins it slowly around the axis (**1, 2, 0**), which points approximately in the direction of one o'clock.

```
RotatingDodecahedron.xaml
<!-- =================================================
         RotatingDodecahedron.xaml (c) 2007 by Charles Petzold
     ================================================= -->
<Page xmlns="http://schemas.microsoft.com/winfx/2006/xaml/presentation"
      xmlns:x="http://schemas.microsoft.com/winfx/2006/xaml"
      WindowTitle="Rotating Dodecahedron"
      Title="Rotating Dodecahedron">

    <Viewport3D>
        <ModelVisual3D>
            <ModelVisual3D.Content>
                <Model3DGroup>
                    <GeometryModel3D>
                        <GeometryModel3D.Geometry>
                            <MeshGeometry3D
                                Positions=

"1.171 -0.724 0, 1 -1 -1, 1.618 0 -0.618, 1.618 0  0.618, 1 -1  1, 0.618 -1.618 0,
 -1.171 -0.724 0,-1 -1  1,-1.618 0  0.618,-1.618 0 -0.618,-1 -1 -1,-0.618 -1.618 0,
 -1.171  0.724 0,-1  1 -1,-1.618 0 -0.618,-1.618 0  0.618,-1  1  1,-0.618  1.618 0,
  1.171  0.724 0, 1  1  1, 1.618 0  0.618, 1.618 0 -0.618, 1  1 -1, 0.618  1.618 0,
 -0.724 0 -1.171,-1  1 -1,0  0.618 -1.618,0 -0.618 -1.618,-1 -1 -1,-1.618 0 -0.618,
 -0.724 0  1.171,-1 -1  1,0 -0.618  1.618,0  0.618  1.618,-1  1  1,-1.618 0  0.618,
  0.724 0 -1.171, 1 -1 -1,0 -0.618 -1.618,0  0.618 -1.618, 1  1 -1, 1.618 0 -0.618,
  0.724 0  1.171, 1  1  1,0  0.618  1.618,0 -0.618  1.618, 1 -1  1, 1.618 0  0.618,
 0 -1.171 -0.724, 1 -1 -1, 0.618 -1.618 0,-0.618 -1.618 0,-1 -1 -1,0 -0.618 -1.618,
 0  1.171 -0.724,-1  1 -1,-0.618  1.618 0, 0.618  1.618 0, 1  1 -1,0  0.618 -1.618,
```

```
0 -1.171  0.724,-1 -1  1,-0.618 -1.618 0, 0.618 -1.618 0, 1 -1  1,0 -0.618  1.618,
0  1.171  0.724, 1  1  1, 0.618  1.618 0,-0.618  1.618 0,-1  1  1,0  0.618  1.618"

                    TriangleIndices=
        " 0  1  2,  0  2  3,  0  3  4,  0  4  5,  0  5  1,
          6  7  8,  6  8  9,  6  9 10,  6 10 11,  6 11  7,
         12 13 14, 12 14 15, 12 15 16, 12 16 17, 12 17 13,
         18 19 20, 18 20 21, 18 21 22, 18 22 23, 18 23 19,

         24 25 26, 24 26 27, 24 27 28, 24 28 29, 24 29 25,
         30 31 32, 30 32 33, 30 33 34, 30 34 35, 30 35 31,
         36 37 38, 36 38 39, 36 39 40, 36 40 41, 36 41 37,
         42 43 44, 42 44 45, 42 45 46, 42 46 47, 42 47 43,

         48 49 50, 48 50 51, 48 51 52, 48 52 53, 48 53 49,
         54 55 56, 54 56 57, 54 57 58, 54 58 59, 54 59 55,
         60 61 62, 60 62 63, 60 63 64, 60 64 65, 60 65 61,
         66 67 68, 66 68 69, 66 69 70, 66 70 71, 66 71 67" />

            </GeometryModel3D.Geometry>

            <!-- Semi-transparent brushes. -->
            <GeometryModel3D.Material>
                <DiffuseMaterial Brush="#A00000FF" />
            </GeometryModel3D.Material>

            <GeometryModel3D.BackMaterial>
                <DiffuseMaterial Brush="#A0FF0000" />
            </GeometryModel3D.BackMaterial>

            <!-- Transform for animated rotation. -->
            <GeometryModel3D.Transform>
                <RotateTransform3D>
                    <RotateTransform3D.Rotation>
                        <AxisAngleRotation3D x:Name="rotate"
                                             Axis="1 2 0" />
                    </RotateTransform3D.Rotation>
                </RotateTransform3D>
            </GeometryModel3D.Transform>
        </GeometryModel3D>

        <!-- Light sources. -->
        <AmbientLight Color="Gray" />
        <DirectionalLight Color="Gray" Direction="1, -3 -2" />

    </Model3DGroup>
  </ModelVisual3D.Content>
</ModelVisual3D>

<Viewport3D.Camera>
    <PerspectiveCamera Position="0 0 5"
                       LookDirection="0 0 -5"
                       UpDirection="0 1 0"
                       FieldOfView="45" />
```

```
            </Viewport3D.Camera>
        </Viewport3D>

        <!-- Animation. -->
        <Page.Triggers>
            <EventTrigger RoutedEvent="Page.Loaded">
                <BeginStoryboard>
                    <Storyboard TargetName="rotate" TargetProperty="Angle">
                        <DoubleAnimation To="360" Duration="0:0:30"
                                         RepeatBehavior="Forever" />
                    </Storyboard>
                </BeginStoryboard>
            </EventTrigger>
        </Page.Triggers>
    </Page>
```

In the definition of the *Positions* collection in the XAML file, each line is one pentagon. The first point is the center, and the numbers that show up repeatedly are equal to $(\sqrt{5} + 5) / 10$ and $(3\sqrt{5} + 5) / 10$. The other points in each line are the vertices of the pentagon, and the recurrent numbers are equal to $(1 + \sqrt{5}) / 2$ (also known as the golden ratio), and $2 / (1 + \sqrt{5})$, the inverse of the golden ratio, also equal to the golden ratio minus one. (That relationship is what makes the ratio "golden.")

It is possible to rotate an object around multiple axes at the same time, but the results might be somewhat unpredictable. The most predictable results come when the rotations are much different in speed—for example, if you rotate an object very quickly around the X axis and also much slower around the Y axis. You can probably visualize such a composite rotation in your head. However, if the object is rotating at similar speeds around two or more axes, the resultant movement might be quite confounding, as this program demonstrates.

ThreeRotations.xaml
```
<!-- ================================================
     ThreeRotations.xaml (c) 2007 by Charles Petzold
     ================================================ -->
<Page xmlns="http://schemas.microsoft.com/winfx/2006/xaml/presentation"
      xmlns:x="http://schemas.microsoft.com/winfx/2006/xaml"
      WindowTitle="Three Rotations"
      Title="Three Rotations">
    <Viewport3D>
        <ModelVisual3D>
            <ModelVisual3D.Content>
                <GeometryModel3D>
                    <GeometryModel3D.Geometry>
                        <!-- Unit cube. -->
                        <MeshGeometry3D
                            Positions="-0.5  0.5  0.5,   0.5  0.5  0.5,
                                       -0.5 -0.5  0.5,   0.5 -0.5  0.5,
                                        0.5  0.5 -0.5,  -0.5  0.5 -0.5,
                                        0.5 -0.5 -0.5,  -0.5 -0.5 -0.5,
```

```
                                    -0.5  0.5 -0.5,  -0.5  0.5  0.5,
                                    -0.5 -0.5 -0.5,  -0.5 -0.5  0.5,
                                     0.5  0.5  0.5,   0.5  0.5 -0.5,
                                     0.5 -0.5  0.5,   0.5 -0.5 -0.5,
                                    -0.5  0.5 -0.5,   0.5  0.5 -0.5,
                                    -0.5  0.5  0.5,   0.5  0.5  0.5,
                                     0.5 -0.5 -0.5,  -0.5 -0.5 -0.5,
                                     0.5 -0.5  0.5,  -0.5 -0.5  0.5"

                    TriangleIndices=" 0  2  1,   1  2  3
                                      4  6  5,   5  6  7,
                                      8 10  9,   9 10 11,
                                     12 14 13, 13 14 15
                                     16 18 17, 17 18 19
                                     20 22 21, 21 22 23" />
            </GeometryModel3D.Geometry>

            <GeometryModel3D.Material>
                <DiffuseMaterial Brush="cyan" />
            </GeometryModel3D.Material>

            <GeometryModel3D.Transform>
                <Transform3DGroup>
                    <RotateTransform3D>
                        <RotateTransform3D.Rotation>
                            <AxisAngleRotation3D x:Name="rotateX"
                                                 Axis="1 0 0" />
                        </RotateTransform3D.Rotation>
                    </RotateTransform3D>

                    <RotateTransform3D>
                        <RotateTransform3D.Rotation>
                            <AxisAngleRotation3D x:Name="rotateY"
                                                 Axis="0 1 0" />
                        </RotateTransform3D.Rotation>
                    </RotateTransform3D>

                    <RotateTransform3D>
                        <RotateTransform3D.Rotation>
                            <AxisAngleRotation3D x:Name="rotateZ"
                                                 Axis="0 0 1" />
                        </RotateTransform3D.Rotation>
                    </RotateTransform3D>
                </Transform3DGroup>
            </GeometryModel3D.Transform>
        </GeometryModel3D>
    </ModelVisual3D.Content>
</ModelVisual3D>

<!-- Light sources. -->
<ModelVisual3D>
    <ModelVisual3D.Content>
        <Model3DGroup>
            <AmbientLight Color="#404040" />
```

```
                    <DirectionalLight Color="#C0C0C0" Direction="2 -3 -1" />
                </Model3DGroup>
            </ModelVisual3D.Content>
        </ModelVisual3D>

        <!-- Camera. -->
        <Viewport3D.Camera>
            <PerspectiveCamera Position="0 0 4"
                               LookDirection="0 0 -4"
                               UpDirection="0 1 0"
                               FieldOfView="45" />
        </Viewport3D.Camera>
    </Viewport3D>

    <!-- Animations. -->
    <Page.Triggers>
        <EventTrigger RoutedEvent="Page.Loaded">
            <BeginStoryboard>
                <Storyboard TargetProperty="Angle">
                    <DoubleAnimation Storyboard.TargetName="rotateX"
                                     From="0" To="360" Duration="0:0:3"
                                     RepeatBehavior="Forever" />

                    <DoubleAnimation Storyboard.TargetName="rotateY"
                                     From="0" To="360" Duration="0:0:3"
                                     RepeatBehavior="Forever" />

                    <DoubleAnimation Storyboard.TargetName="rotateZ"
                                     From="0" To="360" Duration="0:0:3"
                                     RepeatBehavior="Forever" />
                </Storyboard>
            </BeginStoryboard>
        </EventTrigger>
    </Page.Triggers>
</Page>
```

This program simply rotates a cube around the X, Y, and Z axes, and each rotation is three seconds per cycle. But the composite movement of the object is very odd. At times it seems to tumble, but then it slows down and wiggles a bit from side to side.

According to a famous rotation theorem by Leonhard Euler (1707–1783), successive rotations around the X, Y, and Z axes are equivalent to a single composite rotation around a particular axis. Similarly, any rotation around a particular axis can be decomposed into successive rotations around the X, Y, and Z axes. However, if the angles of these individual rotations are constantly changing (as they certainly are in this demonstration), the composite axis of rotation is constantly changing as well.

If complex composite three-dimensional rotations interest you, you might get a kick out of the advanced coverage of rotation and quaternions in Chapter 7, "Matrix Transforms," and Chapter 8.

Combining Rotation and Other Transforms

If you keep all *CenterX*, *CenterY*, and *CenterZ* properties set to their default values of 0, and you define a *ScaleTransform3D* with equal *ScaleX*, *ScaleY*, and *ScaleZ* properties, you can combine that *ScaleTransform3D* and a *RotateTransform3D* in a *Transform3DGroup*, and the ordering doesn't matter. If the *ScaleTransform3D* scales differently in different dimensions, you need to decide whether the scaling takes place along non-rotated or rotated axes. Introduce a *TranslateTransform3D* into the mix and the order of the transforms makes a big difference. This difference is most dramatically illustrated in the following program.

RotationAndRevolution.xaml

```
<!-- =======================================================
       RotationAndRevolution.xaml (c) 2007 by Charles Petzold
     ======================================================= -->
<Page xmlns="http://schemas.microsoft.com/winfx/2006/xaml/presentation"
      xmlns:x="http://schemas.microsoft.com/winfx/2006/xaml"
      WindowTitle="Rotation &amp; Revolution"
      Title="Rotation &amp; Revolution">

    <Page.Resources>
        <!-- Unit cube: front, back, left, right, top, bottom. -->
        <MeshGeometry3D x:Key="cube"
            Positions="-0.5  0.5  0.5,  0.5  0.5  0.5,
                       -0.5 -0.5  0.5,  0.5 -0.5  0.5,
                        0.5  0.5 -0.5, -0.5  0.5 -0.5,
                        0.5 -0.5 -0.5, -0.5 -0.5 -0.5,
                       -0.5  0.5 -0.5, -0.5  0.5  0.5,
                       -0.5 -0.5 -0.5, -0.5 -0.5  0.5,
                        0.5  0.5  0.5,  0.5  0.5 -0.5,
                        0.5 -0.5  0.5,  0.5 -0.5 -0.5,
                       -0.5  0.5 -0.5,  0.5  0.5 -0.5,
                       -0.5  0.5  0.5,  0.5  0.5  0.5,
                        0.5 -0.5 -0.5, -0.5 -0.5 -0.5,
                        0.5 -0.5  0.5, -0.5 -0.5  0.5"

            TriangleIndices=" 0  2  1,  1  2  3
                              4  6  5,  5  6  7,
                              8 10  9,  9 10 11,
                             12 14 13, 13 14 15
                             16 18 17, 17 18 19
                             20 22 21, 21 22 23" />
    </Page.Resources>

    <Viewport3D>
        <ModelVisual3D>
            <ModelVisual3D.Content>
                <Model3DGroup>

                    <!-- Gray cube: No transform. -->
                    <GeometryModel3D Geometry="{StaticResource cube}">
                        <GeometryModel3D.Material>
                            <DiffuseMaterial Brush="LightGray" />
```

```xml
                    </GeometryModel3D.Material>
                </GeometryModel3D>

                <!-- Cyan cube: Rotate before translate. -->
                <GeometryModel3D Geometry="{StaticResource cube}">
                    <GeometryModel3D.Material>
                        <DiffuseMaterial Brush="Cyan" />
                    </GeometryModel3D.Material>
                    <GeometryModel3D.Transform>
                        <Transform3DGroup>
                            <RotateTransform3D>
                                <RotateTransform3D.Rotation>
                                    <AxisAngleRotation3D x:Name="rotate1" />
                                </RotateTransform3D.Rotation>
                            </RotateTransform3D>
                            <TranslateTransform3D OffsetX="3" />
                        </Transform3DGroup>
                    </GeometryModel3D.Transform>
                </GeometryModel3D>

                <!-- Pink cube: Translate before rotate. -->
                <GeometryModel3D Geometry="{StaticResource cube}">
                    <GeometryModel3D.Material>
                        <DiffuseMaterial Brush="Pink" />
                    </GeometryModel3D.Material>
                    <GeometryModel3D.Transform>
                        <Transform3DGroup>
                            <TranslateTransform3D OffsetX="3" />
                            <RotateTransform3D>
                                <RotateTransform3D.Rotation>
                                    <AxisAngleRotation3D x:Name="rotate2" />
                                </RotateTransform3D.Rotation>
                            </RotateTransform3D>
                        </Transform3DGroup>
                    </GeometryModel3D.Transform>
                </GeometryModel3D>

                <!-- Light sources. -->
                <AmbientLight Color="#404040" />
                <DirectionalLight Color="#C0C0C0" Direction="2, -3 -1" />

            </Model3DGroup>
        </ModelVisual3D.Content>
    </ModelVisual3D>

    <Viewport3D.Camera>
        <PerspectiveCamera Position="-1 2 10"
                           LookDirection="1 -2 -10"
                           UpDirection="0 1 0"
                           FieldOfView="45" />
    </Viewport3D.Camera>
</Viewport3D>
```

```
    <Page.Triggers>
        <EventTrigger RoutedEvent="Page.Loaded">
            <BeginStoryboard>
                <Storyboard TargetProperty="Angle">
                    <DoubleAnimation Storyboard.TargetName="rotate1"
                                     From="0" To="360" Duration="0:0:3"
                                     RepeatBehavior="Forever" />

                    <DoubleAnimation Storyboard.TargetName="rotate2"
                                     From="0" To="360" Duration="0:0:3"
                                     RepeatBehavior="Forever" />

                </Storyboard>
            </BeginStoryboard>
        </EventTrigger>
    </Page.Triggers>
</Page>
```

The program creates three figures based on the unit cube. The first, colored gray, has no transforms. It simply sits on the origin in the center of the screen. The second, colored cyan, is given a *RotateTransform3D* followed by a *TranslateTransform3D* to move it three units on the X axis. The third cube, colored pink, gets the same transforms but in reverse order. Both rotations are animated around the Y axis.

If you think this through, you should be able to anticipate what you'll see: The cyan cube is subjected first to a rotation, which rotates the cube in place around the origin. The translation transform moves that rotating cube to the point (3, 0, 0). The pink cube, however, is moved first to the point (3, 0, 0) and then rotated. That rotation is centered at the point (0, 0, 0), so the cube actually moves in a circle around the point (0, 0, 0).

When discussing celestial bodies like the sun, earth, and moon, it's common to use the word *rotation* to describe the movement of an object as it spins on its axis, and the word *revolution* to describe how an object moves in an orbit around another. The difference between rotation and revolution is the difference between applying the *RotateTransform3D* before or after the *TranslateTransform3D*.

To make the rotating cyan cube behave like the revolving pink cube, you can change the *RotateTransform3D* tag applied to the cyan cube to this:

```
<RotateTransform3D CenterX=" 3" />
```

As you'll recall, setting the *CenterX* property on *RotateTransform3D* is the same as preceding and following the rotation with a translation:

```
<TranslateTransform3D CenterX="3" />
<RotateTransform3D>
   ...
</RotateTransform3D>
<TranslateTransform3D CenterX="-3" />
```

That last implicit *TranslateTransform3D* is cancelled out by the explicit *TranslateTransform3D* in the composite transform for the cyan cube, making the composite transform the same as the pink cube.

To make the revolving pink cube behave like the rotating cyan cube, try this:

```
<RotateTransform3D CenterX="3" />
```

That puts the center of rotation in the center of the translated cube. This *RotateTransform3D* is equivalent to:

```
<TranslateTransform3D CenterX="-3" />
<RotateTransform3D>
   ...
</RotateTransform3D>
<TranslateTransform3D CenterX="3" />
```

The first implicit *TranslateTransform3D* is cancelled out by the explicit *TranslateTransform3D* for the pink cube, and the composite result is the same as the original cyan cube.

As the pink cube revolves around the gray cube in the center, for each revolution it also makes one rotation. A single side of the pink cube always faces toward the gray cube. What does that remind you of? The moon, perhaps?

Let's try to mimic the sun, earth, and moon with a combination of *TranslateTransform3D*, *ScaleTransform3D*, and *RotateTransform3D*. Unfortunately, it's almost impossible to portray these three celestial bodies with proper proportions. If the moon is the size of one pixel (that is, 1/96th inch under standard display options), the earth is about 4 pixels in size, and the two bodies would be separated by 100 pixels of space. That's not too bad until the sun enters the picture. The sun would be about 400 pixels in size and located about 40,000 pixels from the earth. That's a little more than most monitors are capable of these days.

Besides, we're working with cubes, so it's not going to look very realistic anyway.

CelestialBodies.xaml

```xml
<!-- ===============================================
     CelestialBodies.xaml (c) 2007 by Charles Petzold
     =============================================== -->
<Page xmlns="http://schemas.microsoft.com/winfx/2006/xaml/presentation"
      xmlns:x="http://schemas.microsoft.com/winfx/2006/xaml"
      WindowTitle="Celestial Bodies"
      Title="Celestial Bodies"
      Background="Black">

    <Page.Resources>
        <!-- Unit cube: front, back, left, right, top, bottom. -->
        <MeshGeometry3D x:Key="cube"
            Positions="-0.5  0.5  0.5,  0.5  0.5  0.5,
                       -0.5 -0.5  0.5,  0.5 -0.5  0.5,
                        0.5  0.5 -0.5, -0.5  0.5 -0.5,
                        0.5 -0.5 -0.5, -0.5 -0.5 -0.5,
                       -0.5  0.5 -0.5, -0.5  0.5  0.5,
                       -0.5 -0.5 -0.5, -0.5 -0.5  0.5,
                        0.5  0.5  0.5,  0.5  0.5 -0.5,
                        0.5 -0.5  0.5,  0.5 -0.5 -0.5,
                       -0.5  0.5 -0.5,  0.5  0.5 -0.5,
                       -0.5  0.5  0.5,  0.5  0.5  0.5,
                        0.5 -0.5 -0.5, -0.5 -0.5 -0.5,
                        0.5 -0.5  0.5, -0.5 -0.5  0.5"

            TriangleIndices=" 0  2  1,  1  2  3
                              4  6  5,  5  6  7,
                              8 10  9,  9 10 11,
                             12 14 13, 13 14 15
                             16 18 17, 17 18 19
                             20 22 21, 21 22 23" />
    </Page.Resources>

    <Viewport3D>
        <!-- The yellow sun. -->
        <ModelVisual3D>
            <ModelVisual3D.Content>
                <GeometryModel3D Geometry="{StaticResource cube}">
                    <GeometryModel3D.Material>
                        <DiffuseMaterial Brush="Yellow" />
                    </GeometryModel3D.Material>
                    <GeometryModel3D.Transform>
                        <Transform3DGroup>
                            <ScaleTransform3D
                                ScaleX="3" ScaleY="3" ScaleZ="3" />
                            <RotateTransform3D>
                                <RotateTransform3D.Rotation>
                                    <AxisAngleRotation3D x:Name="rotateSun" />
                                </RotateTransform3D.Rotation>
                            </RotateTransform3D>
                        </Transform3DGroup>
                    </GeometryModel3D.Transform>
                </GeometryModel3D>
            </ModelVisual3D.Content>
        </ModelVisual3D>
```

```xml
        <!-- The earth/moon combination. -->
    <ModelVisual3D>
        <ModelVisual3D.Content>
            <Model3DGroup>

                <!-- The green/blue earth. -->
                <GeometryModel3D Geometry="{StaticResource cube}">
                    <GeometryModel3D.Material>
                        <DiffuseMaterial Brush="Cyan" />
                    </GeometryModel3D.Material>
                    <GeometryModel3D.Transform>
                        <RotateTransform3D>
                            <RotateTransform3D.Rotation>
                                <AxisAngleRotation3D x:Name="rotateEarth" />
                            </RotateTransform3D.Rotation>
                        </RotateTransform3D>
                    </GeometryModel3D.Transform>
                </GeometryModel3D>

                <!-- The rocky gray moon. -->
                <GeometryModel3D Geometry="{StaticResource cube}">
                    <GeometryModel3D.Material>
                        <DiffuseMaterial Brush="LightGray" />
                    </GeometryModel3D.Material>
                    <GeometryModel3D.Transform>
                        <Transform3DGroup>
                            <ScaleTransform3D
                                ScaleX="0.3" ScaleY="0.3" ScaleZ="0.3" />
                            <TranslateTransform3D OffsetX="2" />

                            <RotateTransform3D>
                                <RotateTransform3D.Rotation>
                                    <AxisAngleRotation3D
                                        x:Name="revolveMoon" />
                                </RotateTransform3D.Rotation>
                            </RotateTransform3D>
                        </Transform3DGroup>
                    </GeometryModel3D.Transform>
                </GeometryModel3D>

            </Model3DGroup>
        </ModelVisual3D.Content>

        <!-- Transform applied to earth/moon combination. -->
        <ModelVisual3D.Transform>
            <Transform3DGroup>
                <TranslateTransform3D OffsetX="10" />
                <RotateTransform3D>
                    <RotateTransform3D.Rotation>
                        <AxisAngleRotation3D x:Name="revolveEarth" />
                    </RotateTransform3D.Rotation>
                </RotateTransform3D>
            </Transform3DGroup>
        </ModelVisual3D.Transform>
    </ModelVisual3D>
```

```
        <!-- Light sources. -->
        <ModelVisual3D>
            <ModelVisual3D.Content>
                <Model3DGroup>
                    <AmbientLight Color="#404040" />
                    <DirectionalLight Color="#C0C0C0" Direction="2 -3 -1" />
                </Model3DGroup>
            </ModelVisual3D.Content>
        </ModelVisual3D>

        <!-- Camera. -->
        <Viewport3D.Camera>
            <PerspectiveCamera Position="-5 15 25"
                               LookDirection="5 -15 -25"
                               UpDirection="0 1 0"
                               FieldOfView="45" />
        </Viewport3D.Camera>
    </Viewport3D>

    <!-- Animations. -->
    <Page.Triggers>
        <EventTrigger RoutedEvent="Page.Loaded">
            <BeginStoryboard>
                <Storyboard TargetProperty="Angle">
                    <DoubleAnimation Storyboard.TargetName="rotateSun"
                                     From="0" To="360" Duration="0:0:25"
                                     RepeatBehavior="Forever" />

                    <DoubleAnimation Storyboard.TargetName="rotateEarth"
                                     From="0" To="360" Duration="0:0:1"
                                     RepeatBehavior="Forever" />

                    <DoubleAnimation Storyboard.TargetName="revolveMoon"
                                     From="0" To="360" Duration="0:0:27"
                                     RepeatBehavior="Forever" />

                    <DoubleAnimation Storyboard.TargetName="revolveEarth"
                                     From="0" To="360" Duration="0:6:5"
                                     RepeatBehavior="Forever" />
                </Storyboard>
            </BeginStoryboard>
        </EventTrigger>
    </Page.Triggers>
</Page>
```

And here's what it looks like with the background not set to *Black* as it is in the XAML file:

Of course, another silly part of this program is that all three objects are illuminated by *AmbientLight* and *DirectionalLight*, whereas all the illumination should really be coming from the sun. But that type of illumination won't be possible until Chapter 5, "Texture and Materials."

The animations are set so that one second is equivalent to approximately one day of reality. The sun rotates on its axis approximately once every 25 days. The moon revolves around the earth about every 27 days. The earth rotates on its axis approximately every 24 hours. (You might think the earth rotates on its axis *exactly* every 24 hours, but that's not entirely correct. The period of rotation with respect to the stars is called the sidereal day, and is equal to 23 hours, 56 minutes, and about 4 seconds. The day appears to have a length of 24 hours because this rotation is combined with a revolution around the sun, so the sun doesn't occupy the same position in the sky until about 4 minutes following the end of the sidereal day. The period of 24 hours is called a *mean* solar day, and it's only an average: The earth revolves around the sun in an ellipse; it moves faster in the revolution when it's closer to the sun. The actual solar day—the time between two consecutive appearances of the sun highest in the sky at noon—can vary from 24 hours by almost half a minute. But this is much more information than required for this silly program.) Finally, the earth and moon revolve around the sun approximately every 365 days, which translates to six minutes and five seconds.

The important aspect of this program is the treatment of the earth and moon. The second *ModelVisual3D* element in the XAML file contains as content two *GeometryModel3D* objects for the earth and moon. The earth is the only one of these three celestial bodies that is not scaled, but it has a *RotateTransform3D* for the rotation of the earth on its axis. The *Geometry-Model3D* for the moon has a *ScaleTransform3D* to scale it to size, and a *RotateTransform3D* to make the moon revolve around the earth. Another *RotateTransform3D* is applied to the *Model-Visual3D* itself, and hence to the earth and moon in combination. This is the rotation transform that causes the earth and moon to revolve around the sun.

The next program is a 3D animation of something you might see at a magic show. The program begins with the six sides of a box opened up so that you can see that there's nothing inside:

During the entire course of the program, the box spins around its center. The sides of the box slowly rise:

When all the sides are up, the top begins to close:

When the box is closed, the top then begins opening from the other side:

And slowly, something not previously seen arises from the box, as if by magic:

It's only a cube, but it could very well be a rabbit. After the cube reaches a certain height, it descends back into the box, and the sides unfold in reverse to reveal that the box is truly empty. When the box is totally unfolded, the animation begins from the beginning and repeats "forever."

Here's the program.

MagicBox.xaml

```
<!-- =======================================
     MagicBox.xaml (c) 2007 by Charles Petzold
     ======================================= -->
<Page xmlns="http://schemas.microsoft.com/winfx/2006/xaml/presentation"
      xmlns:x="http://schemas.microsoft.com/winfx/2006/xaml"
      WindowTitle="Magic Box"
      Title="Magic Box"
      Background="#000040">
```

```xml
<Page.Resources>
    <!-- Materials for box sides. -->
    <DiffuseMaterial x:Key="mat" Brush="Yellow" />
    <DiffuseMaterial x:Key="backmat" Brush="Red" />

    <!-- Side of box. -->
    <GeometryModel3D x:Key="side"
                    Material="{StaticResource mat}"
                    BackMaterial="{StaticResource backmat}" >
        <GeometryModel3D.Geometry>
            <MeshGeometry3D Positions="-1 0 1, -1 0 -1, 1 0 -1, 1 0 1"
                        TriangleIndices="0 1 2, 0 2 3" />
        </GeometryModel3D.Geometry>
    </GeometryModel3D>

</Page.Resources>
<Viewport3D>
    <!-- Main ModelVisual3D is continuously rotated. -->
    <ModelVisual3D>

        <!-- Child ModelVisual3D elements are sides of box. -->

        <!-- Box bottom: No transform. -->
        <ModelVisual3D Content="{StaticResource side}" />

        <!-- Box left side. -->
        <ModelVisual3D Content="{StaticResource side}">
            <ModelVisual3D.Transform>
                <Transform3DGroup>
                    <TranslateTransform3D OffsetX="-2" />
                    <RotateTransform3D CenterX="-1">
                        <RotateTransform3D.Rotation>
                            <AxisAngleRotation3D x:Name="boxleft"
                                                Axis="0 0 -1" />
                        </RotateTransform3D.Rotation>
                    </RotateTransform3D>
                </Transform3DGroup>
            </ModelVisual3D.Transform>
        </ModelVisual3D>

        <!-- Box right side. -->
        <ModelVisual3D Content="{StaticResource side}">
            <ModelVisual3D.Transform>
                <Transform3DGroup>
                    <TranslateTransform3D OffsetX="2" />
                    <RotateTransform3D CenterX="1">
                        <RotateTransform3D.Rotation>
                            <AxisAngleRotation3D x:Name="boxright"
                                                Axis="0 0 1" />
                        </RotateTransform3D.Rotation>
                    </RotateTransform3D>
                </Transform3DGroup>
            </ModelVisual3D.Transform>
        </ModelVisual3D>
```

```
<!-- Box front. -->
<ModelVisual3D Content="{StaticResource side}">
    <ModelVisual3D.Transform>
        <Transform3DGroup>
            <TranslateTransform3D OffsetZ="2" />
            <RotateTransform3D CenterZ="1">
                <RotateTransform3D.Rotation>
                    <AxisAngleRotation3D x:Name="boxfront"
                                         Axis="-1 0 0" />
                </RotateTransform3D.Rotation>
            </RotateTransform3D>
        </Transform3DGroup>
    </ModelVisual3D.Transform>
</ModelVisual3D>

<!-- Box rear. -->
<ModelVisual3D Content="{StaticResource side}">
    <ModelVisual3D.Transform>
        <Transform3DGroup>
            <TranslateTransform3D OffsetZ="-2" />
            <RotateTransform3D CenterZ="-1">
                <RotateTransform3D.Rotation>
                    <AxisAngleRotation3D x:Name="boxrear"
                                         Axis="1 0 0" />
                </RotateTransform3D.Rotation>
            </RotateTransform3D>
        </Transform3DGroup>
    </ModelVisual3D.Transform>
</ModelVisual3D>

<!-- Box top. -->
<ModelVisual3D Content="{StaticResource side}">
    <ModelVisual3D.Transform>
        <Transform3DGroup>
            <RotateTransform3D CenterY="-2" CenterZ="1">
                <RotateTransform3D.Rotation>
                    <AxisAngleRotation3D Axis="1 0 0" Angle="90" />
                </RotateTransform3D.Rotation>
            </RotateTransform3D>

            <RotateTransform3D CenterZ="1">
                <RotateTransform3D.Rotation>
                    <AxisAngleRotation3D x:Name="boxtop1"
                                         Axis="-1 0 0" />
                </RotateTransform3D.Rotation>
            </RotateTransform3D>

            <RotateTransform3D CenterY="2" CenterZ="1">
                <RotateTransform3D.Rotation>
                    <AxisAngleRotation3D x:Name="boxtop2"
                                         Axis="-1 0 0" />
                </RotateTransform3D.Rotation>
            </RotateTransform3D>
```

```xml
                    <RotateTransform3D CenterY="2" CenterZ="-1">
                        <RotateTransform3D.Rotation>
                            <AxisAngleRotation3D x:Name="boxtop3"
                                             Axis="-1 0 0" />
                        </RotateTransform3D.Rotation>
                    </RotateTransform3D>
                </Transform3DGroup>
            </ModelVisual3D.Transform>
        </ModelVisual3D>

        <ModelVisual3D.Content>

            <!-- The cube inside the box. -->
            <GeometryModel3D>
                <GeometryModel3D.Geometry>
                    <MeshGeometry3D
                        Positions="-0.5  0.5  0.5,  0.5  0.5  0.5,
                                   -0.5 -0.5  0.5,  0.5 -0.5  0.5,
                                    0.5  0.5 -0.5, -0.5  0.5 -0.5,
                                    0.5 -0.5 -0.5, -0.5 -0.5 -0.5,
                                   -0.5  0.5 -0.5, -0.5  0.5  0.5,
                                   -0.5 -0.5 -0.5, -0.5 -0.5  0.5,
                                    0.5  0.5  0.5,  0.5  0.5 -0.5,
                                    0.5 -0.5  0.5,  0.5 -0.5 -0.5,
                                   -0.5  0.5 -0.5,  0.5  0.5 -0.5,
                                   -0.5  0.5  0.5,  0.5  0.5  0.5,
                                    0.5 -0.5 -0.5, -0.5 -0.5 -0.5,
                                    0.5 -0.5  0.5, -0.5 -0.5  0.5"

                        TriangleIndices=" 0  2  1,  1  2  3
                                          4  6  5,  5  6  7,
                                          8 10  9,  9 10 11,
                                         12 14 13, 13 14 15
                                         16 18 17, 17 18 19
                                         20 22 21, 21 22 23" />
                </GeometryModel3D.Geometry>

                <GeometryModel3D.Material>
                    <DiffuseMaterial Brush="Gold" />
                </GeometryModel3D.Material>

                <GeometryModel3D.Transform>
                    <TranslateTransform3D x:Name="cubexform"
                                      OffsetY="-100" OffsetZ="0" />
                </GeometryModel3D.Transform>
            </GeometryModel3D>
        </ModelVisual3D.Content>

        <!-- Transform applied to entire ModelVisual3D. -->
        <ModelVisual3D.Transform>
            <RotateTransform3D>
                <RotateTransform3D.Rotation>
                    <AxisAngleRotation3D x:Name="model"
                                     Axis="0 1 0" Angle="30" />
```

```
                        </RotateTransform3D.Rotation>
                    </RotateTransform3D>
                </ModelVisual3D.Transform>
            </ModelVisual3D>

            <!-- Lights in a separate Model3DGroup so not subjected to rotation. -->
            <ModelVisual3D>
                <ModelVisual3D.Content>
                    <Model3DGroup>
                        <AmbientLight Color="#606060" />
                        <DirectionalLight Color="#A0A0A0" Direction="1, -3 -2" />
                    </Model3DGroup>
                </ModelVisual3D.Content>
            </ModelVisual3D>

            <Viewport3D.Camera>
                <PerspectiveCamera Position="0 6 20"
                                   LookDirection="0 -2 -10"
                                   UpDirection="0 1 0"
                                   FieldOfView="30" />
            </Viewport3D.Camera>
        </Viewport3D>

        <Page.Triggers>
            <EventTrigger RoutedEvent="Page.Loaded">
                <BeginStoryboard>
                    <Storyboard SpeedRatio="1.5" RepeatBehavior="Forever">

                        <!-- Constant rotation. -->
                        <DoubleAnimation Storyboard.TargetName="model"
                                    Storyboard.TargetProperty="Angle"
                                    From="0" To="360" Duration="0:0:20"
                                    RepeatBehavior="8x" />

                        <!-- Other animations are reversed. -->
                        <ParallelTimeline Duration="0:1:20" AutoReverse="True">
                            <DoubleAnimation Storyboard.TargetName="boxleft"
                                        Storyboard.TargetProperty="Angle"
                                        From="0" To="90" Duration="0:0:30" />

                            <DoubleAnimation Storyboard.TargetName="boxright"
                                        Storyboard.TargetProperty="Angle"
                                        From="0" To="90" Duration="0:0:30" />

                            <DoubleAnimation Storyboard.TargetName="boxfront"
                                        Storyboard.TargetProperty="Angle"
                                        From="0" To="90" Duration="0:0:30" />

                            <DoubleAnimation Storyboard.TargetName="boxrear"
                                        Storyboard.TargetProperty="Angle"
                                        From="0" To="90" Duration="0:0:30" />

                            <DoubleAnimation Storyboard.TargetName="boxtop1"
                                        Storyboard.TargetProperty="Angle"
                                        From="0" To="90" Duration="0:0:30" />
```

```
                       <DoubleAnimation Storyboard.TargetName="boxtop2"
                                        Storyboard.TargetProperty="Angle"
                                        BeginTime="0:0:30"
                                        From="0" To="180" Duration="0:0:15"  />

                       <DoubleAnimation Storyboard.TargetName="boxtop3"
                                        Storyboard.TargetProperty="Angle"
                                        BeginTime="0:0:45"
                                        From="0" To="90" Duration="0:0:15"  />

                       <DoubleAnimation Storyboard.TargetName="cubexform"
                                        Storyboard.TargetProperty="OffsetY"
                                        BeginTime="0:0:45"
                                        From="0.5" To="6" Duration="0:0:35" />
                 </ParallelTimeline>
              </Storyboard>
           </BeginStoryboard>
        </EventTrigger>
    </Page.Triggers>
 </Page>
```

All six sides of the box are based on a single *GeometryModel3D* object defined as a resource. It's just two triangles arranged to form a square with a width and depth of two units. The *MeshGeometry3D* coordinates in the resource are appropriate for the bottom of the box; in the body of the program, the *ModelVisual3D* element for the bottom of the box is the only piece of this scene that doesn't require its own transform:

```
<ModelVisual3D Content="{StaticResource side}" />
```

The other five sides of the box require transforms to position them in their initial locations and to animate them. Here, for example, is the *ModelVisual3D* for the left side of the box:

```
<ModelVisual3D Content="{StaticResource side}">
    <ModelVisual3D.Transform>
        <Transform3DGroup>
            <TranslateTransform3D OffsetX="-2" />
            <RotateTransform3D CenterX="-1">
                <RotateTransform3D.Rotation>
                    <AxisAngleRotation3D x:Name="boxleft" Axis="0 0 -1" />
                </RotateTransform3D.Rotation>
            </RotateTransform3D>
        </Transform3DGroup>
    </ModelVisual3D.Transform>
</ModelVisual3D>
```

The *TranslateTransform3D* shifts the side two units to the left so that its initial position is in the same plane as the bottom of the box, but next to it. The bottom and left sides of the box seem to join at the line that extends from $(-1, 0 -1)$ to $(-1, 0, 1)$. The rotation of the left side of the box must be parallel to the Z axis and have a *CenterX* property of -1. That's what the *RotateTransform3D* specifies. The *AxisAngleRotation3D* element is given a name of "boxleft" that is referred to in a *DoubleAnimation* that changes the *Angle* property from 0 degrees to 90 degrees.

The top of the box is more complex, and the *ModelVisual3D* element includes four *RotateTransform3D* objects. The first one moves the object to its initial position—seemingly attached to the front side of the box but hanging down. The rotation is around the X axis, and the *CenterY* and *CenterZ* properties are set so that the front edge of the *GeometryModel3D* extending from (−1, 0, 1) to (1, 0, 1) will end up at (−1, −2, 3) to (1, −2, 3). The rear edge of the *GeometryModel3D* at (−1, 0, −1) to (1, 0, −1) ends up at (−1, 0, 3) to (1, 0, 3).

```
<RotateTransform3D CenterY="-2" CenterZ="1">
    <RotateTransform3D.Rotation>
        <AxisAngleRotation3D Axis="1 0 0" Angle="90" />
    </RotateTransform3D.Rotation>
</RotateTransform3D>
```

The other three *RotateTransform3D* objects are for the animation of the top of the box. The first mimics the animation of the front of the box so the two sides move together. Then, the box top has a second animation to close, and a third to open up again.

All six sides of the box are child *ModelVisual3D* elements of a parent *ModelVisual3D* that has its own transform to be rotated continuously around the Y axis. The content of the parent *ModelVisual3D* is the cube that emerges from the box. A *TranslateTransform3D* element gives the box an initial location with an *OffsetY* value of −100, which is very much off the screen. When the final animation begins, that *OffsetY* value is set to 0.5, putting the cube inside the box, and then animated to a value of 6, lifting the cube out of the box to be displayed to the incredulous audience.

Introduction to Hit-Testing

At times you'll want to allow the user to interact with 3D objects using the mouse. The first step is a job called *hit-testing*. Your program obtains the two-dimensional point of the mouse and determines the object under that point. Specifically, when working with 3D visuals, your program obtains the *ModelVisual3D* at the mouse coordinates. More than one visual may be overlapped at that point, so you can obtain first the *ModelVisual3D* on the foreground at the mouse coordinates, and then the *ModelVisual3D* objects farther in the background. With the specific *ModelVisual3D*, you also obtain the *GeometryModel3D*, the *MeshGeometry3D*, the coordinates of the particular triangle, and weights that indicate the precise point within that triangle.

Notice that this 3D hit-testing is based entirely on *ModelVisual3D* objects. If the user clicks the mouse over an area of a *Viewport3D* where no figure is located, your program is not notified. Also, there is no generalized translation between the 2D points of the *Viewport3D* and the 3D points of the scene displayed by that *Viewport3D*. Part of the problem is that every 2D point corresponds to an infinite number of 3D points. The conversion in the other direction—from 3D to 2D—is theoretically straightforward, but in practice requires obtaining the two matrix transforms associated with the camera. This is a job I'll discuss in Chapter 7 and apply in Chapter 9, "Applications and Curiosa."

The following file might look like a standalone XAML program, but it's not, because it contains an *x:Class* attribute in the root element. (The rest of the *TableForFour* class is in the Table-ForFour.cs file.) The Resources section of this file defines a chair in the same way as the earlier BuildChair.xaml file, and also defines a table by first defining a *GeometryModel3D* for the table leg. Both the table and four chairs sit on a green linoleum floor.

TableForFour.xaml

```
<!-- ===============================================
        TableForFour.xaml (c) 2007 by Charles Petzold
     =============================================== -->
<Page xmlns="http://schemas.microsoft.com/winfx/2006/xaml/presentation"
      xmlns:x="http://schemas.microsoft.com/winfx/2006/xaml"
      x:Class="Petzold.TableForFour.TableForFour"
      WindowTitle="Table for Four"
      Title="Table for Four">

    <Page.Resources>

        <!-- Unit cube: front, back, left, right, top, bottom. -->
        <MeshGeometry3D x:Key="cube"
                     Positions="-0.5  0.5  0.5,   0.5  0.5  0.5,
                                -0.5 -0.5  0.5,   0.5 -0.5  0.5,
                                 0.5  0.5 -0.5,  -0.5  0.5 -0.5,
                                 0.5 -0.5 -0.5,  -0.5 -0.5 -0.5,
                                -0.5  0.5 -0.5,  -0.5  0.5  0.5,
                                -0.5 -0.5 -0.5,  -0.5 -0.5  0.5,
                                 0.5  0.5  0.5,   0.5  0.5 -0.5,
                                 0.5 -0.5  0.5,   0.5 -0.5 -0.5,
                                -0.5  0.5 -0.5,   0.5  0.5 -0.5,
                                -0.5  0.5  0.5,   0.5  0.5  0.5,
                                 0.5 -0.5 -0.5,  -0.5 -0.5 -0.5,
                                 0.5 -0.5  0.5,  -0.5 -0.5  0.5"

                  TriangleIndices=" 0  2  1,   1  2  3
                                    4  6  5,   5  6  7,
                                    8 10  9,   9 10 11,
                                   12 14 13,  13 14 15
                                   16 18 17,  17 18 19
                                   20 22 21,  21 22 23" />

        <DiffuseMaterial x:Key="wood" Brush="BurlyWood" />

        <!-- Table leg. -->
        <GeometryModel3D x:Key="tableLeg"
                      Geometry="{StaticResource cube}"
                      Material="{StaticResource wood}">
            <GeometryModel3D.Transform>
                <ScaleTransform3D CenterY="-1" ScaleX="0.1"
                                  ScaleY="2" ScaleZ="0.1" />
```

```
                    </GeometryModel3D.Transform>
            </GeometryModel3D>


            <!-- Table. -->
            <Model3DGroup x:Key="table">

                <!-- Four table legs. -->
                <Model3DGroup>
                    <StaticResource ResourceKey="tableLeg" />
                    <Model3DGroup.Transform>
                        <TranslateTransform3D OffsetX="-1" OffsetZ="-1" />
                    </Model3DGroup.Transform>
                </Model3DGroup>

                <Model3DGroup>
                    <StaticResource ResourceKey="tableLeg" />
                    <Model3DGroup.Transform>
                        <TranslateTransform3D OffsetX="1" OffsetZ="-1" />
                    </Model3DGroup.Transform>
                </Model3DGroup>

                <Model3DGroup>
                    <StaticResource ResourceKey="tableLeg" />
                    <Model3DGroup.Transform>
                        <TranslateTransform3D OffsetX="-1" OffsetZ="1" />
                    </Model3DGroup.Transform>
                </Model3DGroup>

                <Model3DGroup>
                    <StaticResource ResourceKey="tableLeg" />
                    <Model3DGroup.Transform>
                        <TranslateTransform3D OffsetX="1" OffsetZ="1" />
                    </Model3DGroup.Transform>
                </Model3DGroup>

                <!-- Table top. -->
                <GeometryModel3D Geometry="{StaticResource cube}"
                                 Material="{StaticResource wood}">
                    <GeometryModel3D.Transform>
                        <Transform3DGroup>
                            <ScaleTransform3D
                                ScaleX="2.5" ScaleZ="2.5" ScaleY="0.1" />
                            <TranslateTransform3D OffsetY="2.05" />
                        </Transform3DGroup>
                    </GeometryModel3D.Transform>
                </GeometryModel3D>
            </Model3DGroup>


            <!-- Chair. -->
            <Model3DGroup x:Key="chair">

                <!-- Front right leg. -->
                <GeometryModel3D Geometry="{StaticResource cube}"
                                 Material="{StaticResource wood}">
```

```
        <GeometryModel3D.Transform>
            <Transform3DGroup>
                <ScaleTransform3D
                    ScaleX="0.1" ScaleY="1.5" ScaleZ="0.1" />
                <TranslateTransform3D
                    OffsetX="0.5" OffsetY="0.75" OffsetZ="0.5" />
            </Transform3DGroup>
        </GeometryModel3D.Transform>
</GeometryModel3D>

<!-- Front left leg. -->
<GeometryModel3D Geometry="{StaticResource cube}"
                 Material="{StaticResource wood}">
    <GeometryModel3D.Transform>
        <Transform3DGroup>
            <ScaleTransform3D
                ScaleX="0.1" ScaleY="1.5" ScaleZ="0.1" />
            <TranslateTransform3D
                OffsetX="-0.5" OffsetY="0.75" OffsetZ="0.5" />
        </Transform3DGroup>
    </GeometryModel3D.Transform>
</GeometryModel3D>

<!-- Back right leg. -->
<GeometryModel3D Geometry="{StaticResource cube}"
                 Material="{StaticResource wood}">
    <GeometryModel3D.Transform>
        <Transform3DGroup>
            <ScaleTransform3D
                ScaleX="0.1" ScaleY="3.0" ScaleZ="0.1" />
            <TranslateTransform3D
                OffsetX="0.5" OffsetY="1.5" OffsetZ="-0.5" />
        </Transform3DGroup>
    </GeometryModel3D.Transform>
</GeometryModel3D>

<!-- Back left leg. -->
<GeometryModel3D Geometry="{StaticResource cube}"
                 Material="{StaticResource wood}">
    <GeometryModel3D.Transform>
        <Transform3DGroup>
            <ScaleTransform3D
                ScaleX="0.1" ScaleY="3.0" ScaleZ="0.1" />
            <TranslateTransform3D
                OffsetX="-0.5" OffsetY="1.5" OffsetZ="-0.5" />
        </Transform3DGroup>
    </GeometryModel3D.Transform>
</GeometryModel3D>

<!-- Chair seat. -->
<GeometryModel3D Geometry="{StaticResource cube}"
                 Material="{StaticResource wood}">
    <GeometryModel3D.Transform>
        <Transform3DGroup>
```

```xml
                  <ScaleTransform3D
                      ScaleX="1.25" ScaleY="0.1" ScaleZ="1.25" />
                  <TranslateTransform3D OffsetY="1.55" />
              </Transform3DGroup>
          </GeometryModel3D.Transform>
      </GeometryModel3D>

      <!-- Back brace. -->
      <GeometryModel3D Geometry="{StaticResource cube}"
                       Material="{StaticResource wood}">
          <GeometryModel3D.Transform>
              <Transform3DGroup>
                  <ScaleTransform3D
                      ScaleX="0.9" ScaleY="0.25" ScaleZ="0.1" />
                  <TranslateTransform3D OffsetZ="-0.5" OffsetY="2.75" />
              </Transform3DGroup>
          </GeometryModel3D.Transform>
      </GeometryModel3D>
    </Model3DGroup>
</Page.Resources>

<Viewport3D Name="viewport3d">

    <!-- Green linoleum floor. -->
    <ModelVisual3D x:Name="floor">
        <ModelVisual3D.Content>
            <GeometryModel3D Geometry="{StaticResource cube}">
                <GeometryModel3D.Material>
                    <DiffuseMaterial Brush="Lime" />
                </GeometryModel3D.Material>
            </GeometryModel3D>
        </ModelVisual3D.Content>

        <ModelVisual3D.Transform>
            <Transform3DGroup>
                <ScaleTransform3D ScaleX="8" ScaleY="0.1" ScaleZ="8" />
                <TranslateTransform3D OffsetY="-0.05" />
            </Transform3DGroup>
        </ModelVisual3D.Transform>
    </ModelVisual3D>

    <!-- Table in the middle. -->
    <ModelVisual3D x:Name="table" Content="{StaticResource table}">
        <ModelVisual3D.Transform>
            <Transform3DGroup>
                <TranslateTransform3D x:Name="translate" />
                <RotateTransform3D>
                    <RotateTransform3D.Rotation>
                        <AxisAngleRotation3D x:Name="rotate" />
                    </RotateTransform3D.Rotation>
                </RotateTransform3D>
            </Transform3DGroup>
        </ModelVisual3D.Transform>
    </ModelVisual3D>
```

```xml
<!-- Four chairs. -->
<ModelVisual3D Content="{StaticResource chair}">
    <ModelVisual3D.Transform>
        <Transform3DGroup>
            <RotateTransform3D>
                <RotateTransform3D.Rotation>
                    <AxisAngleRotation3D Angle="-90" />
                </RotateTransform3D.Rotation>
            </RotateTransform3D>
            <TranslateTransform3D OffsetX="2.5" />
        </Transform3DGroup>
    </ModelVisual3D.Transform>
</ModelVisual3D>

<ModelVisual3D Content="{StaticResource chair}">
    <ModelVisual3D.Transform>
        <Transform3DGroup>
            <RotateTransform3D>
                <RotateTransform3D.Rotation>
                    <AxisAngleRotation3D Angle="180" />
                </RotateTransform3D.Rotation>
            </RotateTransform3D>
            <TranslateTransform3D OffsetZ="2.5" />
        </Transform3DGroup>
    </ModelVisual3D.Transform>
</ModelVisual3D>

<ModelVisual3D Content="{StaticResource chair}">
    <ModelVisual3D.Transform>
        <Transform3DGroup>
            <RotateTransform3D>
                <RotateTransform3D.Rotation>
                    <AxisAngleRotation3D Angle="90" />
                </RotateTransform3D.Rotation>
            </RotateTransform3D>
            <TranslateTransform3D OffsetX="-2.5" />
        </Transform3DGroup>
    </ModelVisual3D.Transform>
</ModelVisual3D>

<ModelVisual3D Content="{StaticResource chair}">
    <ModelVisual3D.Transform>
        <Transform3DGroup>
            <RotateTransform3D>
                <RotateTransform3D.Rotation>
                    <AxisAngleRotation3D Angle="0" />
                </RotateTransform3D.Rotation>
            </RotateTransform3D>
            <TranslateTransform3D OffsetZ="-2.5" />
        </Transform3DGroup>
    </ModelVisual3D.Transform>
</ModelVisual3D>
```

```
        <!-- Light sources. -->
        <ModelVisual3D>
            <ModelVisual3D.Content>
                <Model3DGroup>
                    <AmbientLight Color="#404040" />
                    <DirectionalLight Color="#C0C0C0" Direction="2, -3 -1" />
                </Model3DGroup>
            </ModelVisual3D.Content>
        </ModelVisual3D>

        <!-- Camera. -->
        <Viewport3D.Camera>
            <PerspectiveCamera Position="3 4 12"
                               LookDirection="-1.5 -1.5 -5"
                               UpDirection="0 1 0"
                               FieldOfView="45" />
        </Viewport3D.Camera>
    </Viewport3D>
</Page>
```

Three of the chairs require a *RotateTransform3D*; otherwise they'd all face the same direction and it would be difficult to carry on a conversation.

The scene responds to clicks of any mouse button. Click the floor and it changes to a random color. Click a chair, and it pulls into the table. Click it again and it pulls out. If you click the table, it rises, turns 90 degrees counterclockwise, and comes back down, which is probably easier than having everyone at the table move one seat to the right.

If you examine the XAML file closely, you'll see that it contains several elements and *x:Name* attributes not used elsewhere in the file. The *ModelVisual3D* elements for the floor and table have *x:Name* attributes of "floor" and "table," respectively. The table has a *TranslateTransform3D* and an *AxisAngleRotation3D* with names of "translate" and "rotate," but both transforms are set to default values.

The C# portion of the *TableForFour* class implements the hit-testing and animation logic.

TableForFour.cs

```
//---------------------------------------------
// TableForFour.cs (c) 2007 by Charles Petzold
//---------------------------------------------
using System;
using System.Windows;
using System.Windows.Input;
using System.Windows.Media;
using System.Windows.Media.Animation;
using System.Windows.Media.Media3D;

namespace Petzold.TableForFour
{
    public partial class TableForFour
    {
        // Constructor.
        public TableForFour()
        {
            InitializeComponent();
        }

        // OnMouseDown handler.
        protected override void OnMouseDown(MouseButtonEventArgs args)
        {
            Point pt = args.GetPosition(viewport3d);

            // Obtain the Visual3D objects under the mouse pointer.
            VisualTreeHelper.HitTest(viewport3d, null, HitTestDown,
                                new PointHitTestParameters(pt));
        }

        // Callback for VisualTreeHelp.HitTest.
        HitTestResultBehavior HitTestDown(HitTestResult result)
        {
            // Cast result parameter to RayMeshGeometry3DHitTestResult.
            RayMeshGeometry3DHitTestResult resultMesh =
                                result as RayMeshGeometry3DHitTestResult;

            // This should not happen, but play it safe anyway.
            if (resultMesh == null)
                return HitTestResultBehavior.Continue;

            // Obtain clicked ModelVisual3D.
            ModelVisual3D vis = resultMesh.VisualHit as ModelVisual3D;

            // This should not happen, but play it safe anyway.
            if (vis == null)
                return HitTestResultBehavior.Continue;
```

```
                // If the user clicks the floor, set a new color.
                if (vis == (viewport3d.FindName("floor") as ModelVisual3D))
                {
                    GeometryModel3D model = resultMesh.ModelHit as GeometryModel3D;
                    DiffuseMaterial mat = model.Material as DiffuseMaterial;

                    Random rand = new Random();
                    mat.Brush = new SolidColorBrush(
                                        Color.FromRgb((byte)rand.Next(256),
                                                      (byte)rand.Next(256),
                                                      (byte)rand.Next(256)));

                    return HitTestResultBehavior.Stop;
                }

                // If the user clicks the table, rotate it.
                if (vis == (viewport3d.FindName("table") as ModelVisual3D))
                {
                    // Create a Storyboard for the animations.
                    Storyboard storybrd = new Storyboard();

                    // Define a DoubleAnimation to lift the table.
                    DoubleAnimation animaDouble = new DoubleAnimation();
                    animaDouble.From=0;
                    animaDouble.To=3;
                    Storyboard.SetTargetName(animaDouble, "translate");
                    Storyboard.SetTargetProperty(animaDouble,
                            new PropertyPath(TranslateTransform3D.OffsetYProperty));
                    storybrd.Children.Add(animaDouble);

                    // Another animation turns the table.
                    animaDouble = new DoubleAnimation();
                    animaDouble.From=0;
                    animaDouble.To=90;
                    animaDouble.BeginTime=TimeSpan.FromSeconds(1);
                    Storyboard.SetTargetName(animaDouble, "rotate");
                    Storyboard.SetTargetProperty(animaDouble,
                            new PropertyPath(AxisAngleRotation3D.AngleProperty));
                    storybrd.Children.Add(animaDouble);

                    // A third animation sets the table back down.
                    animaDouble = new DoubleAnimation();
                    animaDouble.From=3;
                    animaDouble.To=0;
                    animaDouble.BeginTime=TimeSpan.FromSeconds(2);
                    Storyboard.SetTargetName(animaDouble, "translate");
                    Storyboard.SetTargetProperty(animaDouble,
                            new PropertyPath(TranslateTransform3D.OffsetYProperty));
                    storybrd.Children.Add(animaDouble);

                    // Start the Storyboard.
                    storybrd.Begin(this);

                    return HitTestResultBehavior.Stop;
                }
```

```
        // Otherwise it's a chair. Get the Transform3DGroup.
        Transform3DGroup xformgrp = vis.Transform as Transform3DGroup;

        // This should not happen, but play it safe anyway.
        if (xformgrp == null)
            return HitTestResultBehavior.Stop;

        // Loop through the child tranforms.
        for (int i = 0; i < xformgrp.Children.Count; i++)
        {
            // Find the TranslateTransform3D.
            TranslateTransform3D trans =
                        xformgrp.Children[i] as TranslateTransform3D;

            if (trans != null)
            {
                // Define an animation for the transform.
                DoubleAnimation anima = new DoubleAnimation();
                DependencyProperty prop = null;

                if (trans.OffsetZ == 0)
                {
                    prop = TranslateTransform3D.OffsetXProperty;

                    if (Math.Abs(trans.OffsetX) < 2)
                        anima.To = 2.5 * Math.Sign(trans.OffsetX);
                    else
                        anima.To = 1.25 * Math.Sign(trans.OffsetX);
                }
                else
                {
                    prop = TranslateTransform3D.OffsetZProperty;

                    if (Math.Abs(trans.OffsetZ) < 2)
                        anima.To = 2.5 * Math.Sign(trans.OffsetZ);
                    else
                        anima.To = 1.25 * Math.Sign(trans.OffsetZ);
                }

                // Start the animation and stop the hit-testing.
                trans.BeginAnimation(prop, anima);
                return HitTestResultBehavior.Stop;
            }
        }
        return HitTestResultBehavior.Continue;
    }
  }
}
```

To perform hit-testing on a *Viewport3D*, you make use of the static *VisualTreeHelper.HitTest* method. This is not specifically a 3D graphics method. You can use this method for hit-testing on two-dimensional visual objects as well. When using this method with 3D, you'll probably set the first argument to the *Viewport3D* object, but you might set it to something else if you want to begin the hit-test at a higher level in the visual tree and involve non-3D visuals as well.

The second argument to the *VisualTreeHelper.HitTest* overload I've used is an optional callback method for filtering results. You can use this method to ignore whole parts of a visual tree. The code above sets this argument to *null*. The third argument to *VisualTreeHelper.HitTest* is a callback method for results, and this argument cannot be *null* because it's the entire point of the exercise. The fourth argument is an object of type *HitTestParameters*, which is an abstract class that has two descendents. You use *PointHitTestParameters* to test a particular two-dimensional point, and *GeometryHitTextParameters* to test a two-dimensional geometry. When using *VisualTreeHelper.HitTest* with a *Viewport3D*, you can alternatively set this argument to an object of type *RayHitTestParameters*, which allows the hit-test to be performed along a ray—which is a *Point3D* and a *Vector3D* that originates at that point.

The TableForFour.cs file calls *VisualTreeHelper.HitTest* based on the mouse pointer position relative to the *Viewport3D*:

```
protected override void OnMouseDown(MouseButtonEventArgs args)
{
    Point pt = args.GetPosition(viewport3d);

    // Obtain the Visual3D objects under the mouse pointer.
    VisualTreeHelper.HitTest(viewport3d, null, HitTestDown,
                        new PointHitTestParameters(pt));
}
```

The callback method—here called *HitTestDown*—is documented as having an argument of type *HitTestResult*. However, when performing hit-testing on a *Viewport3D*, the argument is of type *RayMeshGeometry3DHitTestResult*, which has properties *VisualHit*, *ModelHit*, and *MeshHit* (and others) that let you get information about which figure—and what part of that figure— is being clicked.

The *HitTestDown* method in TableForFour.cs does something different depending on whether the user clicks the floor or the table. If something's been clicked and it's not the floor or table, it must be one of the chairs.

For the floor, the *HitTestDown* method obtains the *GeometryModel3D* being clicked and changes the *Brush* property of the *DiffuseMaterial* object associated with that model to a random color.

When the user clicks the table, *HitTestDown* assembles a *Storyboard* containing three animations. Each of the three animations refers specifically to one of the named elements in the *Transform3DGroup* associated with the *ModelVisual3D* for the table, and each has a different *BeginTime* property so that they play in sequence. Putting all three animations in a single *Storyboard* is the easiest way to handle multiple animations like these.

For the chairs, however, a different strategy is used. There are four chairs, and none of them has a name, and none of the transforms has a name. The code instead searches through the *Transform3DGroup* associated with the *ModelVisual3D* looking for a *TranslateTransform3D*. It then sets up an animation on this *TranslateTransform3D* depending on the setting of the *OffsetX* and *OffsetY* properties.

The callback method is required to return a value of type *HitTestResultBehavior*, which is an enumeration that has two members named *Continue* and *Stop*. If the method returns *HitTestResultBehavior.Continue*, the method is possibly called again with the next visual at that particular point. Returning *HitTestResultBehavior.Stop* halts further calls to the callback method. The *HitTestDown* method in TableForFour.cs returns *HitTestResultBehavior.Stop* whenever it does something in response to the mouse click and returns *HitTestResultBehavior.Continue* when it does not, which in this particular method generally indicates some kind of unexpected result, such as an object being null when it really shouldn't be.

Try changing the penultimate return value—the one that concludes animating the individual chairs—to *HitTestResultBehavior.Continue* and recompile. Now if you happen to click a spot where one chair overlaps another, both chairs will respond.

An application definition file completes the TableForFour project:

TableForFourApp.xaml

```
<!-- =============================================
        TableForFourApp.xaml (c) 2007 by Charles Petzold
     ============================================= -->
<Application xmlns="http://schemas.microsoft.com/winfx/2006/xaml/presentation"
             StartupUri="TableForFour.xaml" />
```

If you'd like your 3D scene to respond to mouse clicks but you don't need to determine which visual is being clicked with the mouse, you can simply trigger an animation based on the *MouseDown* event. That's what the following XAML file does. Although the program can't determine which figure is being clicked, the user must click one of the figures for the program to respond.

SlidingBox.xaml

```
<!-- =========================================
        SlidingBox.xaml (c) 2007 by Charles Petzold
     ========================================= -->
<Page xmlns="http://schemas.microsoft.com/winfx/2006/xaml/presentation"
      xmlns:x="http://schemas.microsoft.com/winfx/2006/xaml"
      WindowTitle="Sliding Box"
      Title="Sliding Box">

    <Page.Resources>

        <!-- Unit cube: front, back, left, right, top, bottom. -->
```

```
<MeshGeometry3D x:Key="cube"
                Positions="-0.5  0.5  0.5,   0.5  0.5  0.5,
                          -0.5 -0.5  0.5,   0.5 -0.5  0.5,
                           0.5  0.5 -0.5,  -0.5  0.5 -0.5,
                           0.5 -0.5 -0.5,  -0.5 -0.5 -0.5,
                          -0.5  0.5 -0.5,  -0.5  0.5  0.5,
                          -0.5 -0.5 -0.5,  -0.5 -0.5  0.5,
                           0.5  0.5  0.5,   0.5  0.5 -0.5,
                           0.5 -0.5  0.5,   0.5 -0.5 -0.5,
                          -0.5  0.5 -0.5,   0.5  0.5 -0.5,
                          -0.5  0.5  0.5,   0.5  0.5  0.5,
                           0.5 -0.5 -0.5,  -0.5 -0.5 -0.5,
                           0.5 -0.5  0.5,  -0.5 -0.5  0.5"

                TriangleIndices=" 0  2  1,  1  2  3
                                  4  6  5,  5  6  7,
                                  8 10  9,  9 10 11,
                                 12 14 13, 13 14 15
                                 16 18 17, 17 18 19
                                 20 22 21, 21 22 23" />

<DiffuseMaterial x:Key="wood" Brush="BurlyWood" />

<!-- Table leg. -->
<GeometryModel3D x:Key="tableLeg"
                 Geometry="{StaticResource cube}"
                 Material="{StaticResource wood}">
    <GeometryModel3D.Transform>
        <ScaleTransform3D CenterY="-1" ScaleX="0.1"
                          ScaleY="2" ScaleZ="0.1" />
    </GeometryModel3D.Transform>
</GeometryModel3D>

<!-- Table. -->
<Model3DGroup x:Key="table">
    <Model3DGroup>
        <StaticResource ResourceKey="tableLeg" />
        <Model3DGroup.Transform>
            <TranslateTransform3D OffsetX="-1" OffsetZ="-1" />
        </Model3DGroup.Transform>
    </Model3DGroup>

    <Model3DGroup>
        <StaticResource ResourceKey="tableLeg" />
        <Model3DGroup.Transform>
            <TranslateTransform3D OffsetX="1" OffsetZ="-1" />
        </Model3DGroup.Transform>
    </Model3DGroup>

    <Model3DGroup>
        <StaticResource ResourceKey="tableLeg" />
        <Model3DGroup.Transform>
            <TranslateTransform3D OffsetX="-1" OffsetZ="1" />
        </Model3DGroup.Transform>
    </Model3DGroup>
```

```
            <Model3DGroup>
                <StaticResource ResourceKey="tableLeg" />
                <Model3DGroup.Transform>
                    <TranslateTransform3D OffsetX="1" OffsetZ="1" />
                </Model3DGroup.Transform>
            </Model3DGroup>

            <GeometryModel3D Geometry="{StaticResource cube}"
                            Material="{StaticResource wood}">
                <GeometryModel3D.Transform>
                    <Transform3DGroup>
                        <ScaleTransform3D
                            ScaleX="2.5" ScaleZ="2.5" ScaleY="0.1" />
                        <TranslateTransform3D OffsetY="2.05" />
                    </Transform3DGroup>
                </GeometryModel3D.Transform>
            </GeometryModel3D>
        </Model3DGroup>
    </Page.Resources>

    <Viewport3D>
        <!-- Green linoleum floor. -->
        <ModelVisual3D>
            <ModelVisual3D.Content>
                <GeometryModel3D Geometry="{StaticResource cube}">
                    <GeometryModel3D.Material>
                        <DiffuseMaterial Brush="Lime" />
                    </GeometryModel3D.Material>
                </GeometryModel3D>
            </ModelVisual3D.Content>

            <ModelVisual3D.Transform>
                    <ScaleTransform3D CenterY="-0.05" ScaleX="6"
                                    ScaleY="0.1" ScaleZ="4" />
            </ModelVisual3D.Transform>
        </ModelVisual3D>

        <!-- This ModelVisual3D defines the table. -->
        <ModelVisual3D Content="{StaticResource table}">
            <ModelVisual3D.Transform>
                <RotateTransform3D CenterX="1.05">
                    <RotateTransform3D.Rotation>
                        <AxisAngleRotation3D x:Name="rotateTable"
                                            Axis="0 0 -1" />
                    </RotateTransform3D.Rotation>
                </RotateTransform3D>
            </ModelVisual3D.Transform>
        </ModelVisual3D>

        <!-- The box on the table. -->
        <ModelVisual3D>
            <ModelVisual3D.Content>
                <GeometryModel3D Geometry="{StaticResource cube}">
                    <GeometryModel3D.Material>
```

```xml
                    <DiffuseMaterial Brush="Blue" />
                </GeometryModel3D.Material>
                <GeometryModel3D.Transform>
                    <Transform3DGroup>
                        <ScaleTransform3D
                            ScaleX="0.5" ScaleY="0.5" ScaleZ="0.5" />

                        <RotateTransform3D x:Name="rotateBox1"
                                           CenterY="-0.5">
                            <RotateTransform3D.Rotation>
                                <AxisAngleRotation3D Axis="0 0 -1" />
                            </RotateTransform3D.Rotation>
                        </RotateTransform3D>

                        <TranslateTransform3D x:Name="translateBox"
                                              OffsetY="2.35" />

                        <RotateTransform3D x:Name="rotateBox2"
                                           CenterX="1.05">
                            <RotateTransform3D.Rotation>
                                <AxisAngleRotation3D Axis="0 0 -1" />
                            </RotateTransform3D.Rotation>
                        </RotateTransform3D>
                    </Transform3DGroup>
                </GeometryModel3D.Transform>
            </GeometryModel3D>
        </ModelVisual3D.Content>
    </ModelVisual3D>

    <!-- Light sources. -->
    <ModelVisual3D>
        <ModelVisual3D.Content>
            <Model3DGroup>
                <AmbientLight Color="#404040" />
                <DirectionalLight Color="#C0C0C0" Direction="2, -3 -1" />
            </Model3DGroup>
        </ModelVisual3D.Content>
    </ModelVisual3D>

    <Viewport3D.Camera>
        <PerspectiveCamera Position="2 4 8"
                           LookDirection="-1.5 -2.25 -5"
                           UpDirection="0 1 0"
                           FieldOfView="45" />
    </Viewport3D.Camera>
</Viewport3D>

<Page.Triggers>
    <EventTrigger RoutedEvent="Page.MouseDown">
        <BeginStoryboard>
            <Storyboard>
                <DoubleAnimationUsingKeyFrames
                        Storyboard.TargetName="rotateTable"
                        Storyboard.TargetProperty="Angle">
```

```xml
                <DiscreteDoubleKeyFrame KeyTime="0:0:0" Value="0" />
                <LinearDoubleKeyFrame KeyTime="0:0:1" Value="10" />
                <DiscreteDoubleKeyFrame KeyTime="0:0:3" Value="10" />
                <LinearDoubleKeyFrame KeyTime="0:0:4" Value="0" />
            </DoubleAnimationUsingKeyFrames>

            <DoubleAnimationUsingKeyFrames
                    Storyboard.TargetName="rotateBox2"
                    Storyboard.TargetProperty="Rotation.Angle">
                <DiscreteDoubleKeyFrame KeyTime="0:0:0" Value="0" />
                <LinearDoubleKeyFrame KeyTime="0:0:1" Value="10" />
            </DoubleAnimationUsingKeyFrames>

            <DoubleAnimationUsingKeyFrames
                    Storyboard.TargetName="translateBox"
                    Storyboard.TargetProperty="OffsetX">
                <DiscreteDoubleKeyFrame KeyTime="0:0:0" Value="0" />
                <SplineDoubleKeyFrame KeyTime="0:0:3" Value="1.25"
                                        KeySpline="0.25 0 0.6 0.2" />
                <LinearDoubleKeyFrame KeyTime="0:0:4" Value="1.5" />
            </DoubleAnimationUsingKeyFrames>

            <DoubleAnimationUsingKeyFrames
                    Storyboard.TargetName="rotateBox1"
                    Storyboard.TargetProperty="Rotation.Angle">
                <DiscreteDoubleKeyFrame KeyTime="0:0:0" Value="0" />
                <DiscreteDoubleKeyFrame KeyTime="0:0:3" Value="0" />
                <LinearDoubleKeyFrame KeyTime="0:0:4" Value="80" />
            </DoubleAnimationUsingKeyFrames>

            <DoubleAnimationUsingKeyFrames
                    Storyboard.TargetName="translateBox"
                    Storyboard.TargetProperty="OffsetY">
                <DiscreteDoubleKeyFrame KeyTime="0" Value="2.35" />
                <DiscreteDoubleKeyFrame KeyTime="0:0:3.1" Value="2.35" />
                <SplineDoubleKeyFrame KeyTime="0:0:4" Value="0.83"
                                        KeySpline="0.25 0 0.6 0.2" />
            </DoubleAnimationUsingKeyFrames>
        </Storyboard>
      </BeginStoryboard>
    </EventTrigger>
  </Page.Triggers>
</Page>
```

This program defines a table and again sets it on a green linoleum floor. On the table is a box. If you click the floor, the table, or the box, the table tilts up and the box slides off and falls on the floor. Here it is in mid-action:

Setting the scene should be a snap at this point. The tricky part of this program is certainly the animations. The first two animations rotate both the table and the box around the Z axis with a *CenterY* property of 0.5. That makes the center of the rotation the bottom of the two right-most legs of the table. (This rotation of the box is governed by an *AxisAngleRotation3D* element with a name of "rotateBox2," but the number indicates the placement of the rotation transform rather than the order of animation.) At the same time, an animated *TranslateTransform3D* moves the box to the end of the able. A *SplineDoubleKeyFrame* element ensures that the movement starts off slowly but picks up speed.

The other animations of the box make this whole program rather more complex. After the box reaches a point where it's hanging half off the table, another rotation kicks in with the target name of "rotateBox1." The first rotation accounted for 10 degrees. This rotation adds another 90 degrees. Another *DoubleAnimationUsingKeyFrames* then translates the box down to the floor.

So far, I've shown two programs with resources defining a chair, and two programs with resources defining a table. For purposes of clarity and to avoid distractions, I've shown these separate programs containing the same resource markup. In reality, you'd probably want to put those chair and table definitions into their own files and then reference them when needed. This is entirely possible, and the technique is illustrated on pages 542 to 544 of my book *Applications = Code + Markup*. Basically you put the resources you want to share among applications into separate files with root elements of *ResourceDictionary*. The resource section of the application definition file then contains a resources section like so:

```
<Application.Resources>
    <ResourceDictionary>
        <ResourceDictionary.MergedDictionaries>
            <ResourceDictionary Source="MyResources1.xaml" />
            <ResourceDictionary Source="MyResources2.xaml" />
            ...
        <ResourceDictionary.MergedDictionaries>
    </ResourceDictionary>
</Application.Resources>
```

I'll use this technique for the *Slider3D* class in Chapter 9.

Animating the Axis

Often when you're animating a rotation around an axis, you want to keep the center properties constant, and the *Axis* property constant, and animate the *Angle* property. However, you can also animate the *Axis* property using a *Vector3DAnimation* object while keeping everything else constant. The following program demonstrates this technique with a single square figure.

AnimatingTheAxis.xaml
```
<!-- ================================================
        AnimatingTheAxis.xaml (c) 2007 by Charles Petzold
     ================================================ -->
<Page xmlns="http://schemas.microsoft.com/winfx/2006/xaml/presentation"
      xmlns:x="http://schemas.microsoft.com/winfx/2006/xaml"
      WindowTitle="Animating the Axis"
      Title="Animating the Axis">
    <Viewport3D>
        <ModelVisual3D>
            <ModelVisual3D.Content>
                <Model3DGroup>
                    <GeometryModel3D>
                        <GeometryModel3D.Geometry>
                            <MeshGeometry3D
                                Positions="-0.5  0.5  0,  0.5  0.5  0,
                                           -0.5 -0.5  0,  0.5 -0.5  0"

                                TriangleIndices="0 2 1, 1 2 3" />
                        </GeometryModel3D.Geometry>

                        <GeometryModel3D.Material>
                            <DiffuseMaterial Brush="Cyan" />
                        </GeometryModel3D.Material>

                        <GeometryModel3D.Transform>
                            <RotateTransform3D>
                                <RotateTransform3D.Rotation>
                                    <AxisAngleRotation3D x:Name="rotate"
                                                         Angle="60" />
                                </RotateTransform3D.Rotation>
                            </RotateTransform3D>
                        </GeometryModel3D.Transform>
```

```
            </GeometryModel3D>

            <!-- Light sources. -->
            <AmbientLight Color="#404040" />
            <DirectionalLight Color="#C0C0C0" Direction="2, -3 -1" />

        </Model3DGroup>
      </ModelVisual3D.Content>
    </ModelVisual3D>

    <Viewport3D.Camera>
      <PerspectiveCamera Position="0 0 3"
                         LookDirection="0 0 -1"
                         UpDirection="0 1 0"
                         FieldOfView="45" />
    </Viewport3D.Camera>
  </Viewport3D>

  <Page.Triggers>
    <EventTrigger RoutedEvent="Page.Loaded">
      <BeginStoryboard>
        <Storyboard TargetName="rotate" TargetProperty="Axis">
          <Vector3DAnimationUsingKeyFrames RepeatBehavior="Forever">
            <LinearVector3DKeyFrame KeyTime="0:0:0" Value="-1 0 0" />
            <LinearVector3DKeyFrame KeyTime="0:0:1" Value="0 -1 0" />
            <LinearVector3DKeyFrame KeyTime="0:0:2" Value="1 0 0" />
            <LinearVector3DKeyFrame KeyTime="0:0:3" Value="0 1 0" />
            <LinearVector3DKeyFrame KeyTime="0:0:4" Value="-1 0 0" />
          </Vector3DAnimationUsingKeyFrames>
        </Storyboard>
      </BeginStoryboard>
    </EventTrigger>
  </Page.Triggers>
</Page>
```

This animation basically keeps the square positioned at a constant angle from the viewer, but rotated around a different axis. As you watch this animation, it might appear to slow down as the *Axis* nears $(1, 0, 0)$ or $(0, 1, 0)$ or the negatives of those axes, and then speed up afterward. This is not an illusion, and it's based on simple trigonometry. The animation of the *Vector3D* involves linear interpolation. As it changes from $(1, 0, 0)$ to $(0, 1, 0)$, for example, the vector makes a certain angle with the X axis that doesn't have a linear relationship with the changing vector. The following table shows some sample values:

Axis Vector	Angle to X Axis
(1, 0, 0)	0°
(0.75, 0.25, 0)	18°
(0.5, 0.5, 0)	45°
(0.25, 0.75, 0)	72°
(0, 1, 0)	90°

That angle is the inverse tangent of the Y value of the *Vector3D* divided by the X value. That angle changes less from $(1, 0, 0)$ to $(0.75, 0.25, 0)$ than it does from $(0.75, 0.25, 0)$ to $(0.5, 0.5, 0)$. I'll have another version of this program in Chapter 8 to show the difference when you use quaternions for the rotation.

At this point, you might be eager to move on from rectangles, pyramids, cubes, and square cuboids, and start working with 3D figures with actual rounded surfaces and curves, but I need to delay that gratification for just two more chapters. It is important first to learn about light shading in more detail, and how to cover a 3D figure with the many varieties of two-dimensional brushes.

Chapter 4
Light and Shading

Several factors contribute to a successful three-dimensional scene. Getting the geometry correct is certainly important, and it's often desirable to use transforms or other means to animate the 3D figures. But a successful 3D scene also depends on lighting, particularly the interaction of the light with the surfaces (or texture) of figures—an effect called *shading*.

I'll begin this chapter establishing how light illuminates surfaces in WPF 3D. I'll show how vector mathematics contribute to the calculation of lighting, and I'll conclude the chapter with demonstrations of two derivatives of the abstract *Light* class that I haven't yet discussed—*PointLight* and *SpotLight*.

In real life, light sources such as the sun and incandescent bulbs emit photons. Some of these photons are dispersed when they strike molecules in the air. Some photons strike surfaces of solid objects; some pass through (if the object is transparent or translucent), some are absorbed, and others are reflected, whereupon they might strike other objects. Some of these photons eventually end up entering the human eye—quite possibly after a long, circuitous path—where they stimulate the retina.

It is possible to write computer software to simulate the complex trajectories of photons. This is a technique called *ray tracing*. However, ray tracing is very *expensive*, which in "computer talk" means that it's algorithmically complex and very time consuming. If ray tracing were implemented in WPF 3D, you'd need to wait for 3D scenes to be rendered, and real-time animation would be impossible.

Instead, WPF 3D implements a time-honored illumination model first described by French computer scientist Henri Gouraud (b. 1944) in 1971 and called *Gouraud shading*. Gouraud shading gives maximum 3D bang for the computing buck.

Throughout this chapter, you're probably going to be looking at pixels on the video display and wondering what color they are. You shouldn't have to guess, so I've written a WPF program called WhatColor that uses the Win32 API to access pixels anywhere on the screen and display their RGB values. I adapted WhatColor from the WHATCLR program in the

5th edition of *Programming Windows* (Microsoft Press, 1999). Because the code is not 3D specific, I won't show it in the pages of this book, but you can find the program among the other downloadable source code for this chapter.

WhatColor's little client area displays three lines of information: The first line shows the X and Y coordinates of the video display where the mouse cursor is positioned. These coordinates are in units of pixels, not the device-independent units used in the WPF! The second line shows the RGB color value of that pixel in hexadecimal. The third line shows the RGB color value in decimal. The program remains on top of other windows on the desktop, but it can be minimized.

In this chapter, I'll be referring to colors using their hexadecimal RGB values, such as 00-FF-FF for cyan. When I'm specifically referring to an RGB color that might appear in XAML, I'll use the text syntax, such as "#00FFFF".

Lessons in Illumination

Here's a program that displays one-quarter of a tube based on a hexadecagon (a 16-sided polygon). The partial tube consists of four rectangles divided into two triangles each. If the tube were whole, it would be centered on the Z axis. The length extends along the Z axis from 0 to −4.

```
ConvexSurface.xaml
<!-- ============================================
     ConvexSurface.xaml (c) 2007 by Charles Petzold
     ============================================ -->
<Page xmlns="http://schemas.microsoft.com/winfx/2006/xaml/presentation"
      xmlns:x="http://schemas.microsoft.com/winfx/2006/xaml"
      WindowTitle="Convex Surface"
      Title="Convex Surface">
    <DockPanel>
        <ScrollBar Name="vert" DockPanel.Dock="Right" Orientation="Vertical"
                   Minimum="-180" Maximum="180"
                   LargeChange="10" SmallChange="1" />

        <Viewport3D>
            <ModelVisual3D>
                <ModelVisual3D.Content>
                    <Model3DGroup>
                        <GeometryModel3D>
                            <GeometryModel3D.Geometry>
                                <MeshGeometry3D
                                    Positions=
                    "0.707 0.707 -4,  0.707 0.707 0,  0.383 0.924 -4,  0.383 0.924 0,
                     0.383 0.924 -4,  0.383 0.924 0,  0.000 1.000 -4,  0.000 1.000 0,
                     0.000 1.000 -4,  0.000 1.000 0, -0.383 0.934 -4, -0.383 0.924 0,
                    -0.383 0.934 -4, -0.383 0.924 0, -0.707 0.707 -4, -0.707 0.707 0"
```

```
                                  TriangleIndices=" 0  2  1,  1  2  3
                                                    4  6  5,  5  6  7,
                                                    8 10  9,  9 10 11,
                                                   12 14 13, 13 14 15" />
                </GeometryModel3D.Geometry>

                <GeometryModel3D.Material>
                    <DiffuseMaterial Brush="Cyan" />
                </GeometryModel3D.Material>

                <GeometryModel3D.BackMaterial>
                    <DiffuseMaterial Brush="Pink" />
                </GeometryModel3D.BackMaterial>

                <GeometryModel3D.Transform>
                    <RotateTransform3D CenterZ="-2">
                        <RotateTransform3D.Rotation>
                            <AxisAngleRotation3D Axis="1 0 0"
                                Angle="{Binding ElementName=vert,
                                                Path=Value}" />
                        </RotateTransform3D.Rotation>
                    </RotateTransform3D>
                </GeometryModel3D.Transform>
            </GeometryModel3D>

            <AmbientLight Color="#404040" />
            <DirectionalLight Color="#C0C0C0" Direction="2 -3 1" />
        </Model3DGroup>
      </ModelVisual3D.Content>
    </ModelVisual3D>

        <Viewport3D.Camera>
            <PerspectiveCamera Position="-2 4 4"
                               LookDirection="0.4 -0.55 -1"
                               UpDirection="0 1 0"
                               FieldOfView="30" />
        </Viewport3D.Camera>
    </Viewport3D>
  </DockPanel>
</Page>
```

Each line in the *Positions* collection is a rectangle. If the figure is viewed from above with the positive Z axis to the right, the vertices are in the following order: upper-left, upper-right, lower-left, and lower-right. The X coordinates are the cosines of 45, 67.5, 90, 112.5, and 135 degrees, and the Y coordinates are the sines of those angles. If you copied the four lines in the *Positions* collection three times and changed the signs of some of these values appropriately, you could complete the tube. For now just the top quarter of the tube will be sufficient. A vertical *ScrollBar* lets you view the figure from the top or bottom. The outside of the tube is colored cyan, and the inside is colored pink.

Here's the figure:

As you can see, the four rectangles are clearly delimited and the figure has a faceted appearance. Each rectangle has a different angle to *DirectionalLight*, so each rectangle is shaded based on that angle. You can verify with WhatColor that each rectangle is uniformly colored over its entire surface, with the possible exception of a little anti-aliasing at the edges depending on your graphics hardware and operating system.

Without the WhatColor program, you might actually doubt that each of the four rectangles is uniformly colored. If you look closely—not so much on the printed page but at the actual program running under Windows—you might swear that each rectangle has a slightly different shade near the border where it meets the next rectangle. For example, the right edge of the second rectangle from the left seems a little lighter than the rest of the rectangle; similarly, the left edge of the third rectangle seems a little darker than the rest of it.

This is an optical illusion called a *Mach band*, named after Austrian physicist Ernst Mach (1838–1916). In reality, the only gradation of color at the edges is a result of anti-aliasing. The eye—or more precisely, the human nervous system devoted to visual perception—tends to exaggerate gradations in shading. Mach bands often occur at borders where color changes from one shade to another. Mach bands can also occur when color changes gradually over a surface. A sudden change in the rate of change—mathematically speaking, a discontinuity in the first derivative of the color change—can create a Mach band.

I mention Mach bands now because they tend to be a characteristic artifact of Gouraud shading, and you'll be seeing Mach bands throughout this chapter. But you don't need Gouraud shading to generate Mach bands, as the ConvexSurface.xaml program demonstrates.

The surfaces in ConvexSurface.xaml are just like most of the surfaces you've seen so far in this book. The shading of the surface is governed by the angle that the *DirectionalLight* source makes with the surface. This shading is the same regardless of how the surfaces are viewed. For example, if you were to change the *Position* property of the camera somewhat, the shading wouldn't change. But change the *Direction* property of the *DirectionalLight* source—or rotate the figure in relation to the light—and the shading changes.

This behavior is the result of covering the surfaces of the figure with a *DiffuseMaterial* object, which is intended to simulate a surface that reflects light equally in all directions. The shading of the surface is independent of the location of the camera (or viewer). The most diffuse surfaces you probably encounter in real life are woven fabrics such as cotton or wool. Plastic, metal, or other smooth flat surfaces are not diffuse materials because you tend to see a reflection of the light source that is dependent on the viewing angle.

The shading algorithms implemented in WPF 3D involve vectors called *normals*. Normal vectors shouldn't be confused with *normalized* vectors, which are vectors that have a magnitude equal to one. Normal vectors are vectors that are perpendicular to a plane, such as the surface of a triangle:

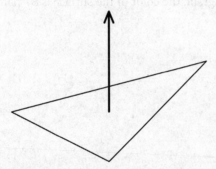

SurfaceNormal.xaml

The normal vector shown in this diagram is called a *surface normal* because it is perpendicular to the surface. The normal is what determines how the surface reflects directional light. The normal and the direction vector of the light form an angle:

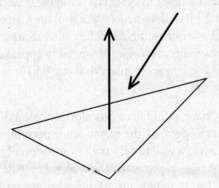

SurfaceNormalWithLight.xaml

Although the angle between those two vectors appears to be about 30 degrees, it's actually more like 150 degrees because the two vectors are going in opposite directions. If you're more comfortable thinking of the angle as 30 degrees rather than 150 degrees, that's fine. The mathematics work out the same.

Diffuse surfaces obey a shading model known as Lambert's Cosine Law, named after German mathematician and physicist Johann Heinrich Lambert (1728–1777). The percentage of reflected light from a diffuse surface is equal to the negative cosine of the angle between the surface normal and the light vector. The negative cosine of 150 degrees (which is the same as the positive cosine of 30 degrees, if that's how you prefer to look at it) is about 0.87, which means that the surface reflects 87 percent of the directional light.

For example, suppose that the *DiffuseMaterial* used for a surface is associated with a cyan brush that has an RGB color of 00-FF-FF. The only light illuminating the surface is a *DirectionalLight* with a color of *White*. If the light *Direction* vector is perpendicular to the surface, the cosine of the angle is one, and the color of the surface is 00-FF-FF. If the light is 30 degrees from the perpendicular as in the preceding diagram, the color of the surface is 87 percent of that, or 00-DE-DE.

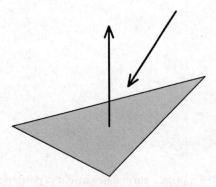

SurfaceNormalWithShading.xaml

That's how the shading for each of eight triangles in the ConvexSurface.xaml file is calculated. If your goal is to write a XAML file to create a tube based on a hexadecagon, the ConvexSurface.xaml file is a good start. But you could have different goals: The ConvexSurface.xaml file could be a little experiment to determine how many rectangles you need to approximate a curved surface, and you're starting to wonder if you'll need so many that you'll have to resort to writing some C# code to generate all the points.

Because each of the rectangles in the ConvexSurface.xaml figure is uniformly colored, it is very clear where the rectangles meet. These sharp edges are the major factor preventing the figure from looking like a curved surface. If you had a way to *vary* the illumination of these rectangles from one edge to another, it might be possible to make them blend in with each other. But how? Each rectangle is composed of two triangles, and triangles are always flat, so the whole surface of a triangle has to reflect the same amount of light. Even if you were to angle the two triangles in each rectangle a little differently, you'd still see obvious edges. This is a drawback of geometry—a limitation of straight lines and flat triangles.

Enter Gouraud shading, which overcomes this apparent geometrical limitation. With Gouraud shading, all the triangles in the mesh remain flat, but different areas of each triangle are made to reflect light differently. This creates the illusion that different areas are indeed angled differently to the light source. The result is that the triangles are *not* uniformly colored, so you can make the shading of adjacent triangles blend and appear continuous.

At first it might seem like an overwhelming job to specify how different parts of the triangle reflect different percentages of light, but it actually doesn't involve a whole lot of information. When using Gouraud shading, you specify three different normal vectors at each of the vertices of the triangle:

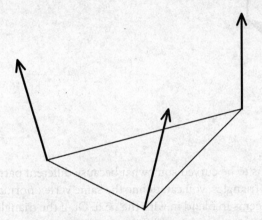

VertexNormals.xaml

These are called *vertex normals* because they apply to vertices rather than to a surface. Each of these normals potentially makes a different angle with the direction vector of the light:

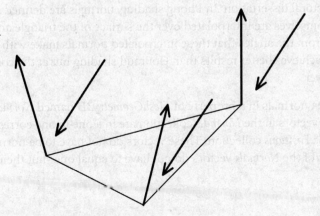

VertexNormalsWithLight.xaml

I've drawn the direction vector of the light as three separate vectors, but these vectors are all parallel, so it's really just the same vector. For each vertex, WPF 3D calculates the negative cosine of the angle between the normal and the light direction vector: That's the fraction of light reflected at the vertex. The illumination of any point within the triangle can then be calculated by interpolation, which is a fairly easy calculation: Points along the borders of the triangle are calculated by interpolating between two vertices; points within the triangle are calculated by interpolating between two points on the border.

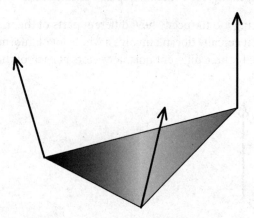

VertexNormalsWithShading.xaml

Although the triangle is still flat, it seems to be curved somewhat because different parts are shaded differently. If you have multiple triangles, you can define the same vertex normals for adjoining vertices so that one triangle seems to blend in with the next. Or, if the triangles are supposed to meet at a non-rounded edge, you can define different vertex normals at that point.

Gouraud shading has the benefit of being simple and fast. An alternative shading algorithm is called Phong shading, described by Vietnamese-born computer scientist Bui Tuong Phong (1942-1975) in his 1973 doctoral dissertation. In Phong shading, normals are defined at the vertices, but the normals themselves are interpolated over the surface of the triangle and the cosines are then calculated from the angles that these interpolated normals make with the light vector. Phong shading achieves better results than Gouraud shading but at the cost of more calculational horsepower.

In WPF 3D, you define vertex normals in a property of *MeshGeometry3D* named *Normals*, of type *Vector3DCollection*. The vectors in the *Normals* collection are in a one-to-one correspondence with the vertices in the *Positions* collection. These vectors do not have to be normalized—that is, the magnitudes of the *Normals* vectors do not have to equal one—but their magnitudes are ignored.

Let's try a simple example first. This XAML file displays a rectangle composed of two triangles. The *Positions* collection contains four *Point3D* items, and the *Normals* collection contains four vectors corresponding to those four points.

```
FourNormals.xaml
<!-- ==========================================
        FourNormals.xaml (c) 2007 by Charles Petzold
     ========================================== -->
<Page xmlns="http://schemas.microsoft.com/winfx/2006/xaml/presentation"
      xmlns:x="http://schemas.microsoft.com/winfx/2006/xaml"
      WindowTitle="Four Normals"
      Title="Four Normals">
    <Viewport3D>
        <ModelVisual3D>
            <ModelVisual3D.Content>
                <Model3DGroup>
                    <GeometryModel3D>
                        <GeometryModel3D.Geometry>
                            <!-- Rectangle. -->
                            <MeshGeometry3D x:Name="rect"
                                Positions="0 1 0, 1 0 0, 0 -1 0, -1 0 0"
                                TriangleIndices="0 2 1, 0 3 2"
                                Normals="0 0 1, 0 1.11 1, 0 2.85 1, 1 0 0" />
                        </GeometryModel3D.Geometry>

                        <GeometryModel3D.Material>
                            <DiffuseMaterial Brush="Cyan" />
                        </GeometryModel3D.Material>
                    </GeometryModel3D>

                    <!-- Light source. -->
                    <DirectionalLight Color="White" Direction="0 0 -1" />

                </Model3DGroup>
            </ModelVisual3D.Content>
        </ModelVisual3D>

        <Viewport3D.Camera>
            <PerspectiveCamera Position="0 0 5"
                               LookDirection="0 0 -1"
                               UpDirection="0 1 0"
                               FieldOfView="45" />
        </Viewport3D.Camera>
    </Viewport3D>
</Page>
```

To keep this example simple, I've restricted the lighting to just a *DirectionalLight* and I've set the *Direction* vector to shoot straight back along the negative Z axis and be perpendicular to the figure. If the *MeshGeometry3D* did not include a *Normals* collection, the entire figure would be fully illuminated and have an RGB color value of 00-FF-FF corresponding to the cyan brush. But the vectors in the *Normals* collection prevent that from happening, as you can easily see:

I deliberately chose the four vectors in the *Normals* collection so that the four vertices reflected specific fractions of light. The vertex normal on the top corner is **(0, 0, 1)**, which means it's exactly opposite to the *Direction* vector of the light. The angle is 180 degrees, the cosine is one, and the vertex reflects all light. Using WhatColor, you can verify that the RGB color at the top corner is 00-FF-FF.

The corner on the right has a vertex normal of **(0, 1.11, 1)**. The angle between that vector and the *Direction* vector of the light is 132 degrees. (Where did this number come from? If you don't know, I'll discuss vector mathematics in the next section.) The negative cosine is 0.67 or two-thirds of the maximum color, or 00-AA-AA.

The corner on the bottom has a vertex normal of **(0, 2.85, 1)**, which makes an angle of 109 degrees with the light, so the negative cosine is 0.33, and the color is 00-55-55.

The corner on the left has a vertex normal of **(1, 0, 0)**, which is at right angles to the light. The negative cosine is zero, and the color is black.

You'll notice a vertical bright line running down the center. That's a Mach band. The color of the point in the center of the rectangle is the average of the top and bottom, or 00-AA-AA. The interpolation is dependent on the way the two triangles are defined. If you change the *TriangleIndices* collection to "0 3 1, 1 3 2", the point in the center is now the average of the left and right, or 00-55-55.

Let's introduce a *Normals* collection into the *MeshGeometry3D* element defining the quarter hexadecagonal tube. What should these vertex normals be?

The vertices of the figure in ConvexSurface.xaml were defined so that the complete tube would be centered on the Z axis. If we want the tube to appear circular, each vertex normal should be a vector from the Z axis through the vertex. This makes it easy: The *Normals* collection is exactly the same as the *Positions* collection except that the Z coordinates of the vectors are always zero. In other words, if a particular point in the *Positions* collection is (x, y, z), the normal should be a vector that ends at that point but begins on the Z axis in the center of the tube. That point on the Z axis is $(0, 0, z)$. The normal is (x, y, z) minus $(0, 0, z)$ or **(x, y, 0)**. Most of the file is the same as ConvexSurface.xaml.

```
ConvexSurfaceWithNormals.xaml
<!-- =========================================================
        ConvexSurfaceWithNormals.xaml (c) 2007 by Charles Petzold
     ========================================================= -->

  . . .
                    <GeometryModel3D.Geometry>
                        <MeshGeometry3D
                            Positions=
            "0.707 0.707 -4,  0.707 0.707 0,  0.383 0.924 -4,  0.383 0.924 0,
             0.383 0.924 -4,  0.383 0.924 0,  0.000 1.000 -4,  0.000 1.000 0,
             0.000 1.000 -4,  0.000 1.000 0, -0.383 0.934 -4, -0.383 0.924 0,
            -0.383 0.934 -4, -0.383 0.924 0, -0.707 0.707 -4, -0.707 0.707 0"

                            TriangleIndices=" 0  2  1,  1  2  3
                                              4  6  5,  5  6  7,
                                              8 10  9,  9 10 11,
                                             12 14 13, 13 14 15"
                            Normals=
            "0.707 0.707 0,  0.707 0.707 0,  0.383 0.924 0,  0.383 0.924 0,
             0.383 0.924 0,  0.383 0.924 0,  0.000 1.000 0,  0.000 1.000 0,
             0.000 1.000 0,  0.000 1.000 0, -0.383 0.934 0, -0.383 0.924 0,
            -0.383 0.934 0, -0.383 0.924 0, -0.707 0.707 0, -0.707 0.707 0" />
                    </GeometryModel3D.Geometry>

  . . .
```

And here it is:

Aside from the faint Mach bands, it works. The surface appears rounded, and only at the two ends can you see that it's really just four flat surfaces.

If you don't explicitly provide a *Normals* collection, WPF 3D will calculate a set of vertex normals for you. WPF 3D calculates a normal at each vertex by averaging the surface normals of all the triangles that share that vertex. For purposes of this calculation, a particular *Point3D* object in the *Positions* collection is considered to be shared if and only if it's referenced from multiple indices from the *TriangleIndices* collection. If the same *Point3D* object shows up multiple times in the *Positions* collection, but only one triangle references each of those vertices, the vertex is not considered to be shared.

For example, if a particular vertex in the *Positions* collection is referenced three times in the *TriangleIndices* collection, that vertex is shared by three triangles. The vertex normal is assumed to be the average of the three surface normals of the three triangles.

For most of the examples in this book, I've defined the *Positions* collections so that only triangles in the same plane share vertices. For example, in the ConvexSurface.xaml file, each vertex is shared by two triangles at most, but those two triangles form a flat rectangle. The two triangles have the same surface normals, so the vertex normal is the same as the surface normal. That's why the surfaces appear flat and distinct.

However, you might recall the SharedVerticesSquareCuboid.xaml program from Chapter 1, "Lights! Camera! Mesh Geometries!" As the name indicates, that program displayed a square cuboid with shared vertices, and it looked like this:

WPF 3D calculated normals at each vertex based on the triangles sharing that vertex, and this gave the figure a smoother appearance at the edges. At the time I rejected this approach because the initial goal was to define figures that appeared to have flat edges. Now let's try the same technique with the partial tube. In the following file, the *Positions* collection has been reduced to just the unique vertices, and there is no *Normals* collection. Most of the file is the same as ConvexSurface.xaml.

ConvexSurfaceWithSharedVertices.xaml

```
<!-- =============================================================
        ConvexSurfaceWithSharedVertices.xaml (c) 2007 by Charles Petzold
     ============================================================= -->

    . . .

                    <GeometryModel3D.Geometry>
                      <MeshGeometry3D
                        Positions=" 0.707 0.707 -4,  0.707 0.707 0,
                                    0.383 0.924 -4,  0.383 0.924 0,
                                    0.000 1.000 -4,  0.000 1.000 0,
                                   -0.383 0.934 -4, -0.383 0.924 0,
                                   -0.707 0.707 -4, -0.707 0.707 0"

                        TriangleIndices="0 2 1, 1 2 3,
                                         2 4 3, 3 4 5,
                                         4 6 5, 5 6 7,
                                         6 8 7, 7 8 9" />
                    </GeometryModel3D.Geometry>

    . . .
```

The resultant image looks good:

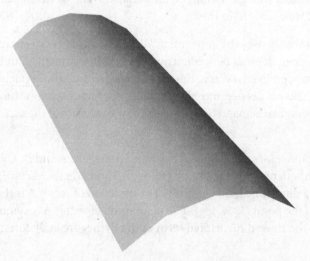

Based on the convenience of not specifying the *Normals* collection, you might not even care that it's not exactly correct. Here's the problem: Three triangles meet at each vertex (except for the four vertices on the outer edges). Two of these three triangles are always in the same plane, and the third is not. This skews the average toward the surface normal of the two triangles in the same plane.

You might prefer another approach to defining the vertices so that each triangle has a slightly different angle, rather than each pair of triangles making up a flat rectangle. If you were defining a whole tube, you might calculate the vertices at one end of the tube based on angles of 0 degrees, 22.5 degrees, 45 degrees, 67.5 degrees, and so forth, and vertices at the other end of the tube based on angles of 11.25 degrees, 33.75 degrees, 56.25 degrees, and so forth. Each triangle would then be in a separate plane, each vertex would be shared by three triangles, and the normals calculated by WPF 3D would be theoretically correct.

Of course, there's nothing preventing you from explicitly including a *Normals* collection even if you share vertices among surfaces, and that's probably what you want to do, if only to improve the rendering efficiency.

Try to follow this general rule: Determine early on whether you want flat faceted surfaces with distinct edges, or smooth edges and apparently curved surfaces. If you want flat surfaces, share vertices among triangles only in the same plane and do not include a *Normals* collection. If you want smooth edges and curved surfaces, share vertices among all triangles that you want blended at a particular vertex, and supply an explicit *Normals* collection. The calculation of the *Positions* and *Normals* collections is generally easier if you're generating mesh geometries algorithmically in code, which is the subject of Chapter 6, "Algorithmic Mesh Geometries."

Vector Mathematics

When determining how a particular triangle should be illuminated, WPF 3D must calculate an angle between two vectors. How does it do this?

The simple answer is that it probably uses the convenient *Vector3D.AngleBetween* static method, which returns the angle in degrees between its two *Vector3D* arguments. But I hope you're not satisfied with that answer! Even if you're not very curious about how to calculate an angle between two vectors, as you get deeper into 3D graphics programming, you should try to become more fluent with vector mathematics and at least know the basics of these concepts and calculations.

In this section, I'll be referring to vectors using boldface capital letters, like **A** and **B**. These vectors consist of X, Y, and Z components: **A** is the vector (x_a, y_a, z_a) and **B** is the vector (x_b, y_b, z_b). Each vector encapsulates a direction and magnitude. The direction of vector **A** is the direction from the point $(0, 0, 0)$ to the point (x_a, y_a, z_a). The magnitude of vector **A** is symbolized as $|A|$ and is calculated from the three-dimensional form of the Pythagorean Theorem:

$$|A| = \sqrt{x_a^2 + y_a^2 + z_a^2}$$

You can divide a vector by its magnitude to create a normalized vector, also called a unit vector. A unit vector has a magnitude of one. For example, the vector $(2, -3, 6)$ has a magnitude of 7. The unit vector of $(2/7, -3/7, 6/7)$ has a magnitude of 1. The *Normalize* method of the *Vector3D* structure normalizes an existing vector.

Three very special unit vectors point in the direction of the three axes of the coordinate system. These are called *basis vectors* or *Cartesian unit vectors* or *fundamental unit vectors*. These three vectors are given the names **i**, **j**, and **k**, and are defined like this:

i = (1, 0, 0)
j = (0, 1, 0)
k = (0, 0, 1)

A vector such as **A** equal to (x_a, y_a, z_a) can also be written as a sum of these fundamental unit vectors multiplied by the three components of the vector:

$$\mathbf{A} = x_a\mathbf{i} + y_a\mathbf{j} + z_a\mathbf{k}$$

To calculate the angle between two vectors, it's convenient to recall a technique from trigonometry called the Law of Cosines. For any triangle, it is possible to calculate any interior angle knowing the lengths of the three sides, or any side knowing the length of two sides and the angle between them. Here's such a triangle.

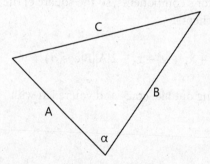

LawOfCosines.xaml

The Law of Cosines says that:

$$C^2 = A^2 + B^2 - 2AB\cos(\alpha)$$

If α is a right angle, the cosine is zero, and the Law of Cosines reduces to the Pythagorean Theorem.

Now let's apply this same concept to vectors. If we want to know the angle between two vectors **A** and **B**, we can orient the two vectors with their tails together. The vector from one head to the other is the difference between the two vectors, or **B** − **A**, as shown next.

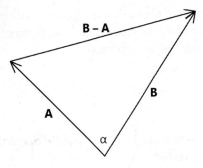

LawOfCosinesForVectors.xaml

The Law of Cosines is applied to the magnitude of these three vectors:

$$|\mathbf{B}-\mathbf{A}|^2 = |\mathbf{A}|^2 + |\mathbf{B}|^2 - 2|\mathbf{A}||\mathbf{B}|\cos(\alpha)$$

Notice that three vector magnitudes in the equation are squared. The vector magnitude is the square root of the sum of the squares of the vector's components, so the square of the magnitude is just the sum of the squares of the components:

$$(x_b - x_a)^2 + (y_b - y_a)^2 + (z_b - z_a)^2 = x_a^2 + y_a^2 + z_a^2 + x_b^2 + y_b^2 + z_b^2 - 2|\mathbf{A}||\mathbf{B}|\cos(\alpha)$$

If you expand these squares, terms start dropping out like crazy and you're left with:

$$|\mathbf{A}||\mathbf{B}|\cos(\alpha) = x_a x_b + y_a y_b + z_a z_b$$

Or:

$$\cos(\alpha) = \frac{x_a x_b + y_a y_b + z_a z_b}{|\mathbf{A}||\mathbf{B}|}$$

The angle between two vectors **A** and **B** is just the inverse cosine of the right side of that equation. However, if all you need is the cosine of an angle—which is the case when WPF 3D applies Lambert's Cosine Law to normals and light directions—only the right side of the equation need be calculated.

The angle between two vectors is not only something that might be needed on its own. It also shows up in vector multiplication. Just to make things fun, two types of multiplication are defined for vectors: the *dot product* and the *cross product*, referring to the symbol used to represent the multiplication. The *Vector3D* structure includes static methods named *DotProduct* and *CrossProduct* that perform these two operations.

It is probably not intuitively obvious what should happen when two vectors are multiplied, and the definitions of the dot product and cross product might at first appear to be somewhat arbitrary. However, these two products have proven themselves time and time again to be useful in various applications in mathematics and physics. (For some of the rationale behind vector mathematics, see the book *About Vectors* by Banesh Hoffmann, published by Prentice-Hall in 1966, republished by Dover Publications in 1975, and still available in an inexpensive paperback.)

A little thought might convince you that a multiplication of two vectors should somehow take the vector magnitudes into account, and indeed, both the dot product and cross product involve a multiplication of the magnitudes of the two vectors. But vector multiplication should also somehow take into account the relationship between the directions of the two vectors. Both the dot product and the cross product involve a trigonometric function of the angle between the two vectors.

Both the dot product and the cross product are distributive over addition, an operation that's commonly expressed with normal scalar multiplication like this:

$$A(B+C) = AB + AC$$

In practical use of vectors, the distributive law turns out to be much more important than commutativity. Commutativity is the operation commonly expressed with normal scalar multiplication like this:

$$AB = BA$$

Many mathematical operations, such as subtraction and division, are not commutative. The dot product is commutative; the cross product is not. Neither the dot product nor the cross product obeys the associative law, expressed with normal scalar multiplication like this:

$$A(BC) = (AB)C$$

The dot product is also called the *inner product*, or the *scalar product* because the result of a dot product is a scalar rather than another vector. (In the very first full-length book published on vector mathematics—*Vector Analysis: A Text-Book for the Use of Students of Mathematics and Physics, Founded upon the Lectures of J. Willard Gibbs* by Edwin Bidwell Wilson, published in 1901—the term *direct product* is used.)

The dot product is symbolized with a dot, and is defined like this:

$$\mathbf{A} \bullet \mathbf{B} = |\mathbf{A}||\mathbf{B}|\cos(\alpha)$$

That expression on the right involving the two magnitudes and the cosine should look familiar because it also showed up in the determination of the angle between two vectors. If the two vectors are both normalized, the dot product is just the cosine of the angle between them.

If two vectors are parallel, the angle between them is zero, the cosine is one, and the dot product is equal to the product of the magnitudes of the vectors. The dot product of a vector and itself is the magnitude squared:

$$A \bullet A = |A|^2$$

This seems like a reasonable and desirable result. The dot product of two vectors in opposite directions is the negative of the product of their magnitudes. Perpendicular vectors form an angle of 90 degrees: The cosine of 90 degrees is zero, so the dot product is zero. You can use the dot product to test for perpendicularity of two vectors: A zero dot product implies the vectors are perpendicular. The following formulas show the results when you apply the dot product to the fundamental unit vectors.

$$i \bullet i = j \bullet j = k \bullet k = 1$$

$$i \bullet j = j \bullet k = k \bullet i = 0$$

That second batch of dot products all result in zero because the fundamental unit vectors are perpendicular to each other. Because the dot product is commutative, these products are also zero:

$$j \bullet i = k \bullet j = i \bullet k = 0$$

Earlier, when I showed you how to use the Law of Cosines to derive the angle between two vectors, one equation that turned up was this:

$$|A||B|\cos(\alpha) = x_a x_b + y_a y_b + z_a z_b$$

The left side of that equation is the definition of the dot product, so you can easily calculate the dot product without any trigonometry simply by multiplying corresponding elements of the two vectors and summing them:

$$A \bullet B = x_a x_b + y_a y_b + z_a z_b$$

Because the formula doesn't involve any trigonometry, this is the probably the fastest way to calculate a dot product. You can derive this non-trigonometric formula for the dot product simply by assuming that the dot product is distributive over addition, that the dot product of a unit vector with itself is one, and the dot product of perpendicular vectors is zero. First represent the two vectors involved in the dot product using the fundamental unit vectors:

$$\mathbf{A} \bullet \mathbf{B} = (x_a\mathbf{i} + y_a\mathbf{j} + z_a\mathbf{k}) \bullet (x_b\mathbf{i} + y_b\mathbf{j} + z_b\mathbf{k})$$

Now carry out all the cross multiplications. Here's where you need to know that the dot product is distributive over addition:

$$\begin{aligned}
\mathbf{A} \bullet \mathbf{B} = {}& x_a x_b \mathbf{i} \bullet \mathbf{i} + x_a y_b \mathbf{i} \bullet \mathbf{j} + x_a z_b \mathbf{i} \bullet \mathbf{k} + \\
& y_a x_b \mathbf{j} \bullet \mathbf{i} + y_a y_b \mathbf{j} \bullet \mathbf{j} + y_a z_b \mathbf{j} \bullet \mathbf{k} + \\
& z_a x_b \mathbf{k} \bullet \mathbf{i} + z_a y_b \mathbf{k} \bullet \mathbf{j} + z_a z_b \mathbf{k} \bullet \mathbf{k}
\end{aligned}$$

The dot product of any vector with itself is one. The dot product of perpendicular vectors is zero. So,

$$\mathbf{A} \bullet \mathbf{B} = x_a x_b + y_a y_b + z_a z_b$$

I wouldn't be surprised if the *Vector3D.DotProduct* method were defined like this:

```
public static double DotProduct(Vector3D v1, Vector3D v2)
{
    return v1.X * v2.X + v1.Y * v2.Y + v1.Z * v2.Z;
}
```

Nor would I be surprised to learn that the static *Vector3D.AngleBetween* method builds upon this calculation:

```
public static double AngleBetween(Vector3D v1, Vector3D v2)
{
    return 180 / Math.PI * Math.ACos(Vector3D.DotProduct(v1, v2) /
                        (v1.Length * v2.Length));
}
```

Earlier, I said that WPF 3D possibly determines the angle between the surface normal and the lighting direction by calling the *Vector3D.AngleBetween* method. Because WPF 3D needs only the cosine of that angle rather than the angle itself, it might very well achieve a little more efficiency by calling the *DotProduct* method and dividing the result by the magnitudes of the two vectors.

The dot product has a graphical representation. If both **A** and **B** are both normalized, the dot product is the cosine of the angle between the vectors, or the projection of one vector on another.

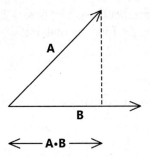

VectorProjection.xaml

The dot product is commutative, so it will be the same regardless of which normalized vector is projected on the other.

For vector **A** that equals (x_a, y_a, z_a), what is the angle between the vector and the X, Y, and Z axes? Let's examine just the case for the X axis: The angle between the vector and the X axis is θ_x ("theta sub x"). The dot product between the vector and the X axis can be written in two ways:

$$\mathbf{A} \bullet \mathbf{i} = |\mathbf{A}||\mathbf{i}|\cos(\theta_x) = x_a \cdot 1 + y_a \cdot 0 + z_a \cdot 0$$

So,

$$\cos(\theta_x) = \frac{x_a}{|\mathbf{A}|}$$

and similarly for the other two axes. If **A** is normalized, the cosine of the angle between **A** and the X axis is the X component of the vector.

The second form of vector multiplication is called the cross product, or the *outer product*, or the *vector product* because the result is another vector. (E. B. Wilson's 1901 book on *Vector Analysis* calls this the *skew product*.) The cross product is symbolized by a multiplication symbol:

$$\mathbf{A} \times \mathbf{B}$$

The result is another vector whose magnitude is calculated like this:

$$|\mathbf{A} \times \mathbf{B}| = |\mathbf{A}||\mathbf{B}|\sin(\alpha)$$

Notice that this is a sine rather than the cosine that shows up in the dot product. If **A** and **B** are parallel (that is, if **A** and **B** have the same direction), the angle between them is zero and the magnitude of the cross product is also zero. If **A** and **B** are perpendicular, the magnitude of the cross product is the product of the magnitudes of **A** and **B**. In general, the magnitude of the cross product can be graphically represented as the area of the parallelogram formed by the two vectors:

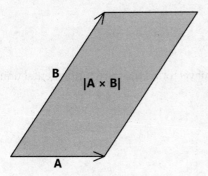

CrossProductMagnitude.xaml

The direction of the cross product is perpendicular to both **A** and **B**, which means that it's perpendicular to the plane formed from vectors **A** and **B**:

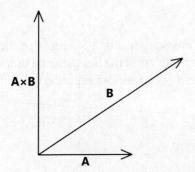

CrossProductDirection.xaml

To determine the direction of the cross product, use the right hand rule: Curve the fingers of your right hand to sweep from **A** to **B**. Your thumb points in the direction of the vector result of the cross product.

Although the cross product is not commutative, a relationship certainly exists between the two different results when you switch the arguments:

$$\mathbf{A} \times \mathbf{B} = -\mathbf{B} \times \mathbf{A}$$

The magnitude is the same but the direction is opposite.

The cross products of the fundamental unit vectors are interesting. The cross products of each unit vector by itself is zero:

$$\mathbf{i} \times \mathbf{i} = 0$$
$$\mathbf{j} \times \mathbf{j} = 0$$
$$\mathbf{k} \times \mathbf{k} = 0$$

The cross product of each pair of fundamental unit vectors is the third fundamental unit vector:

$$\mathbf{i} \times \mathbf{j} = \mathbf{k}$$
$$\mathbf{j} \times \mathbf{k} = \mathbf{i}$$
$$\mathbf{k} \times \mathbf{i} = \mathbf{j}$$

But if you switch the order, the results are negative:

$$\mathbf{j} \times \mathbf{i} = -\mathbf{k}$$
$$\mathbf{k} \times \mathbf{j} = -\mathbf{i}$$
$$\mathbf{i} \times \mathbf{k} = -\mathbf{j}$$

It is possible to derive a numeric calculation of the cross product by assuming that the operation is distributive over addition, and that the cross products of the fundamental unit vectors obey the rules shown above. Here's the cross product of two vectors expressed with the fundamental unit vectors:

$$\mathbf{A} \times \mathbf{B} = (x_a\mathbf{i} + y_a\mathbf{j} + z_a\mathbf{k}) \times (x_b\mathbf{i} + y_b\mathbf{j} + z_b\mathbf{k})$$

Just as you did with the dot product, multiply all the factors by each other:

$$\mathbf{A} \times \mathbf{B} = x_a x_b \mathbf{i} \times \mathbf{i} + x_a y_b \mathbf{i} \times \mathbf{j} + x_a z_b \mathbf{i} \times \mathbf{k} +$$
$$y_a x_b \mathbf{j} \times \mathbf{i} + y_a y_b \mathbf{j} \times \mathbf{j} + y_a z_b \mathbf{j} \times \mathbf{k} +$$
$$z_a x_b \mathbf{k} \times \mathbf{i} + z_a y_b \mathbf{k} \times \mathbf{j} + z_a z_b \mathbf{k} \times \mathbf{k}$$

Now apply the rules. The cross product of a vector with itself is zero, but the cross product of two fundamental unit vectors is the positive or negative third fundamental unit vector, depending on the order. Here's the eventual result:

$$\mathbf{A} \times \mathbf{B} = (y_a z_b - z_a y_b)\mathbf{i} + (z_a x_b - x_a z_b)\mathbf{j} + (x_a y_b - y_a x_b)\mathbf{k}$$

It is very likely that the *Vector3D.CrossProduct* method is implemented much like this:

```
public static Vector3D CrossProduct(Vector3D v1, Vector3D v2)
{
    return new Vector3D(v1.Y * v2.Z - v1.Z * v2.Y,
                        v1.Z * v2.X - v1.X * v2.Z,
                        v1.X * v2.Y - v1.Y * v2.X);
}
```

The cross product turns out to be very useful, and we've already encountered an internal use of the cross product in WPF 3D: to determine surface normals. Suppose a particular *MeshGeometry3D* named *mesh* is being processed. A particular triangle encoded in the *TriangleIndices* collection has integer indices *i1*, *i2*, and *i3*. The 3D points corresponding to those indices are *mesh.Positions[i0]*, *mesh.Positions[i1]*, and *mesh.Positions[i2]*. Each pair of those points forms a vector.

The surface normal is:

```
Vector3D vectSurfaceNormal =
    Vector3D.CrossProduct(mesh.Positions[i1] - mesh.Positions[i0],
                          mesh.Positions[i2] - mesh.Positions[i0]);
```

This formula implicitly assumes that triangle indices are specified in a counterclockwise order when the triangle is viewed from the front, which is the same direction as the surface normal.

Sometimes you'll encounter a job in which one vector must be rotated so that it becomes parallel with another vector. This sounds like a scary job in 3D, but you can calculate the angle of rotation from the dot product, and you can calculate the axis of rotation from the cross product.

DiffuseMaterial and Its Properties

When I introduced the *DiffuseMaterial* class in Chapter 1, I focused almost exclusively on its *Brush* property. The *Brush* property is *null* by default and without it *DiffuseMaterial* is entirely transparent, so obviously *Brush* is the most important of the class's properties.

DiffuseMaterial actually defines two additional properties named *Color* and *AmbientColor*, both of type *Color* and both with default values of *White*. Together with the *Brush* property and the angle of the *DirectionalLight* source, these two properties govern the extent to which the material reflects light. The *Color* property indicates the amount of reflected light from a *DirectionalLight* source, and the *AmbientColor* property indicates the amount of reflected light from an *AmbientLight* source. The default settings of these properties essentially indicate that the material reflects *all* light, but, of course, the resultant shading of the figure is subject to the color of the brush and the lighting angle. It is convenient to imagine the *Color* and *Ambient-Color* properties as indicating what light the figure reflects, but to think of the *Brush* property as a kind of filter that lets colors through or blocks them.

At first you might find the *Color* property somewhat redundant. Why set the *Color* property when you could instead set the color of the brush? As you'll see in the next chapter, brushes don't have to be solid colors. The *Color* property of *DiffuseMaterial* is a single color that applies to the entire surface; the brush can be a bitmap or drawing that consists of many different colors.

Let's look at a few examples involving a single triangle. A *DirectionalLight* source with a *Color* property of "#4080C0" points straight at the triangle. The triangle surface is covered with a *DiffuseMaterial* object with a *Color* property of "#808080" (gray) and a *SolidColorBrush* of "#00C0FF." Examine the three red, green, and blue color primaries separately:

For the red primary, the light value is 0x40. The *Color* property of the *DiffuseMaterial* indicates that only half of that will be reflected, or 0x20, but the *Brush* property has no red, so the result is zero.

For the green primary, the light value is 0x80, the *DiffuseMaterial* reflects half of that, or 0x40, and the *Brush* property lets three-quarters of that through, or 0x30.

For the blue primary, the light value is 0xC0, the material reflects half of that, or 0x60, and the brush lets all of that through.

The resultant color of the triangle is 00-30-60.

If you set the *Color* property of *DiffuseMaterial* to *Black*, the material reflects no directional light regardless of the setting of the *Brush* property. If the *Color* property is set to *White* (the default), all directional light is reflected, and the color of the figure is dependent on *Brush*.

Just as the *Color* property of *DiffuseMaterial* indicates the amount of directional light reflected from the surface, the *AmbientColor* property indicates the amount of reflected ambient light. If you set the *AmbientColor* property to "#808080" (gray), only half the ambient light is reflected from the figure. (Some 3D programming systems such as DirectX define a material that might be called *AmbientMaterial* in WPF 3D. WPF 3D has no *AmbientMaterial* object but compensates with the *AmbientColor* property of *DiffuseMaterial*. You can simulate an *AmbientMaterial* by setting *Color* to 00-00-00.)

You can have multiple *AmbientLight* and *DirectionalLight* objects illuminating a figure. The final color of a figure is the sum of the *DirectionalLight* colors attenuated by the *Color* property of *DiffuseMaterial* (and a factor for the cosine of the angle of directional light), and the sum of *AmbientLight* color attenuated by the *AmbientColor* property of *DiffuseMaterial*, all subjected to the *Brush* property. This calculation occurs for each primary separately. The following formula symbolically shows the calculation of the red component of a particular figure for one *DirectionalLight*, one *AmbientLight*, and a *DiffuseMaterial* based on a *SolidColorBrush*. To simplify the formula, I've assumed color values between 0 and 1 rather than 0 and 255. Otherwise, the formula requires some divisions by 255. The *NormalFactor* is a number between 0 and 1 calculated from the *Direction* property of *DirectionalLight* and the normals of the vertices triangle, and interpolated over the surface of the triangle:

Red = [*DirectionalLight.Color.R* * *DiffuseMaterial.Color.R* * *NormalFactor* +
    AmbientLight.Color.R * *DiffuseMaterial.AmbientColor.R*] *
    DiffuseMaterial.Brush.Color.R

Because each pixel of the figure could potentially have a different *NormalFactor*, each pixel could be shaded a little differently. If you had multiple *DirectionalLight* objects, each *Directional-Light* could have a different *Direction* vector, which would result in different vertex normals and different *NormalFactor* values, so obviously this formula represents a very simple case.

I could have used the *AmbientColor* property to help me out of a jam with the LandOfThe-Pyramids1.xaml program from Chapter 2, "Transforms and Animation." I originally wrote that program so that the sky was another rectangle covered with *DiffuseMaterial* with a *Solid-ColorBrush* of *SkyBlue*. However, the sky turned out to be considerably darker than the color I wanted because it was getting a combination of *DirectionalLight* and *AmbientLight.* I eventually eliminated that rectangle as part of the 3D scene and made the *Page* have a background of *Sky-Blue.* However, another solution involves the *AmbientColor* property. I could have changed *AmbientLight* so that the color was "#FFFFFF" rather than "#404040." Then, for every *Diffuse-Material* except for the sky, I could have set *AmbientColor* to #404040." Everything would be the same, except the sky would be fully illuminated by the *AmbientLight.*

The WPF 3D developers at Microsoft refer to the *Color* and *AmbientColor* properties of *Diffuse-Material* as "color knobs" because you can use them to dial down the reflected colors of the material. (See the WPF 3D blog entry at *http://blogs.msdn.com/wpf3d/archive/2006/12/08/material-color-knobs.aspx* for some background.) This facility is particularly useful when the *Brush* property is not a *SolidColorBrush* but a type of brush without a uniform color.

The application of the *Color* and *AmbientColor* properties occurs during the stage of processing known as *vertex processing,* when the normals are evaluated and the amount of reflected directional light is determined for the vertices. The application of the *Brush* property occurs later, during the stage known as *pixel processing.* In the preceding formula, vertex processing is the part of the calculation within the square brackets.

Depending upon the *Color* properties of *DirectionalLight* and *AmbientLight,* the vertex processing inside the square brackets can result in a value greater than 1, which corresponds to a color value greater than 255. If that happens, the color value is *clamped,* or maximized, at 255. This means that the brush can never make the figure lighter in color. The brush can only make the figure darker than the color value determined during vertex processing.

This behavior is certainly contrary to real-life experience. If you shine more and more light on a real-life object, the color gets more washed out and it will appear lighter and lighter. Of course, you're never going to mimic "blinding white light" on a computer monitor anyway, because the maximum color value of a pixel is FF-FF-FF, but you can trick the system into making objects lighter with multiple light sources.

Consider a 3D scene with two similar figures colored with the two different *DiffuseMaterial* objects. The first is colored like this, where COLOR is some RGB color value:

```
<DiffuseMaterial Brush="COLOR" Color="White" />
```

The second has a *DiffuseMaterial* element like this:

```
<DiffuseMaterial Brush="White" Color="COLOR" />
```

In the first case, the *Brush* is the COLOR value and *Color* is the default value of *White*. This is how you customarily use *DiffuseMaterial*. In the second case, the two properties are swapped: *Brush* is *White* while *Color* is the COLOR value. Is there any difference between figures colored with these two *DiffuseMaterial* objects?

If you have only one *DirectionalLight* object, there is no difference. But with multiple *DirectionalLight* objects, the second object quite possibly will be lighter than the first. Obviously the first object can be no brighter than the COLOR value. But in the second case, the color calculated during vertex processing (which corresponds to the section of the preceding formula within square brackets) can have a value greater than COLOR. The primary values are clamped at 255, but then they're multiplied by the *Brush* values, which are 255 in this case. The color of the figure can be brighter than COLOR.

Let's look at an example. The following ColorKnobs.xaml file displayed two triangles with two *DirectionalLight* objects (one white and one gray) shining straight at them.

```
ColorKnobs.xaml
<!-- ===========================================
     ColorKnobs.xaml (c) 2007 by Charles Petzold
     =========================================== -->
<Page xmlns="http://schemas.microsoft.com/winfx/2006/xaml/presentation"
      xmlns:x="http://schemas.microsoft.com/winfx/2006/xaml"
      WindowTitle="Color Knobs"
      Title="Color Knobs">
    <Viewport3D>
        <ModelVisual3D>
            <ModelVisual3D.Content>
                <Model3DGroup>

                    <!-- Triangle on left. -->
                    <GeometryModel3D>
                        <GeometryModel3D.Geometry>
                            <MeshGeometry3D
                                Positions="-1 1 0, -2 0 0, 0 0 0"
                                TriangleIndices=" 0 1 2" />
                        </GeometryModel3D.Geometry>

                        <GeometryModel3D.Material>
                            <DiffuseMaterial Brush="#208080" Color="White" />
                        </GeometryModel3D.Material>
                    </GeometryModel3D>
```

```
                        <!-- Triangle on right. -->
                        <GeometryModel3D>
                            <GeometryModel3D.Geometry>
                                <MeshGeometry3D
                                        Positions="1 1 0, 0 0 0, 2 0 0"
                                        TriangleIndices=" 0 1 2" />
                            </GeometryModel3D.Geometry>

                            <GeometryModel3D.Material>
                                <DiffuseMaterial Brush="White" Color="#208080" />
                            </GeometryModel3D.Material>
                        </GeometryModel3D>

                        <!-- Light sources. -->
                        <DirectionalLight Color="White" Direction="0 0 -1" />
                        <DirectionalLight Color="Gray" Direction="0 0 -1" />
                    </Model3DGroup>
                </ModelVisual3D.Content>
            </ModelVisual3D>

            <Viewport3D.Camera>
                <PerspectiveCamera Position="0 0 10"
                                   LookDirection="0 0 -1"
                                   UpDirection="0 1 0"
                                   FieldOfView="30" />
            </Viewport3D.Camera>
        </Viewport3D>
    </Page>
```

The triangle on the left has its *Brush* property set to "#208080" and its *Color* property set to *White*, while the triangle on the right swaps those two values. Here's the result:

The one on the right is lighter. Using WhatColor, you can determine that the triangle on the left has an RGB color of 20-80-80, and the one on the right is 30-C0-C0. All three RGB values of the figure on the right are increased by 50 percent over the figure on the left as a result of the two *DirectionalLight* objects.

Let's verify these results. The two lights are shining straight on the triangle, so the *Normal-Factor* value is 1, but there are two *DirectionalLight* objects and no ambient light, so the formula for the red primary is:

Red = [*DirectionalLight1.Color.R* * *DiffuseMaterial.Color.R* +
       DirectionalLight2.Color.R * *DiffuseMaterial.Color.R*] *
       DiffuseMaterial.Brush.Color.R

Notice that the two *DirectionalLight* objects are labeled *DirectionalLight1* and *DirectionalLight2*. If we assume that color values range from 0 to 1 rather than 0 through 255, *Directional-Light1.Color.R* is 1 and *DirectionalLight2.Color.R* is 0.5.

For the triangle on the left, both *DirectionalLight1.Color.R* and *DirectionalLight2.Color.R* are multiplied by *DiffuseMaterial.Color.R* (which is 1) and the products are summed to 1.5, which is greater than the maximum possible color value. This value is clamped at 1.0, and that's the value multiplied by *DiffuseMaterial.Brush.Color.R*, which is 0.125. The result is 0.125, or the hexadecimal color value of 0x20.

For the triangle on the right, both *DirectionalLight1.Color.R* and *DirectionalLight2.Color.R* are multiplied by *DiffuseMaterial.Color.R*, which is 0.125 in this case. The products are summed to 0.1875. No clamping is required. This is then multiplied by *DiffuseMaterial.Brush.Color.R*, which is 1. The result is 0.1875, or the hexadecimal color value of 0x30.

If you copy and paste additional *DirectionalLight* objects in the markup, the figure on the right gets lighter and lighter until it becomes entirely white, which is vaguely what we might expect in real life. But notice that the figure would not become all white if any one of the three color primaries of *DiffuseMaterial.Color* were zero. A primary color value of zero remains zero regardless of what it's multiplied by.

This technique is only valid when you set the *Brush* property (either implicitly or explicitly) to an object of *SolidColorBrush*. In the next chapter I'll explore brushes of other types.

SpotLight and *PointLight*

As you've seen, *AmbientLight* mimics a light source similar to the diffusion of photons in our atmosphere, while *DirectionalLight* mimics a light source from a far distance, such as the sun. On any particular plane, *DirectionalLight* strikes all areas of that plane at a uniform angle:

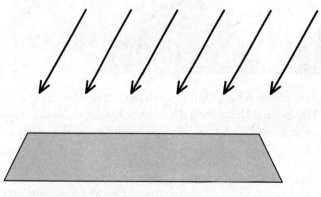

DirectionalLightRays.xaml

The *PointLight* and *SpotLight* classes bring the light source closer to home. A *PointLight* mimics a light bulb that emits light in all directions. A *PointLight* object has a particular position in 3D space so that the rays of light strike a planar surface at a variety of angles:

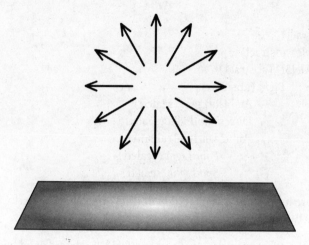

PointLightRays.xaml

In a room with a bare light bulb hanging from the ceiling, the center of the walls, ceiling, and floor are perpendicular to the light and are illuminated the most, while the corners of the room are darker.

SpotLight is more like a flashlight. The rays of light strike a planar surface at different angles, but the light is restricted to a cone:

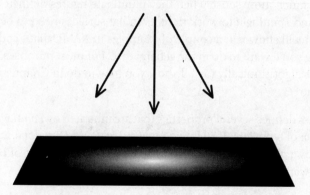

SpotLightRays.xaml

The following class hierarchy is complete beginning with the *Light* class:

Object
    DispatcherObject (abstract)
        DependencyObject
            Freezable (abstract)
                Animatable (abstract)
                    Model3D (abstract)
                        Light (abstract)
                            AmbientLight (sealed)
                            DirectionalLight (sealed)
                            PointLightBase (abstract)
                                PointLight (sealed)
                                SpotLight (sealed)

Both *PointLight* and *SpotLight* are lumped in with *DirectionalLight* when WPF 3D performs calculations with the *Color* property of the *Material* classes.

It is crucial to understand that the effects of *PointLight* and *SpotLight* are determined based on the vertices of the triangle mesh. If you define a rectangle plane based on two triangles, and if you position a *PointLight* close to that plane, the illumination of the entire plane will be based on the angles the light makes with the four vertex normals. Depending where that *PointLight* is positioned, you might not even see any difference in illumination over the plane. With *SpotLight*, where all the illumination is confined to a cone, you might not get any illumination at all if all the vertices fall outside that cone!

SpotLight and *PointLight* make much more sense when they illuminate figures defined with lots of vertices. For *SpotLight* and *PointLight* to work right, even flat surfaces need to be composed of lots of tiny triangles. I will show you a couple of examples in XAML that I coded by hand, but this is not something you'll want to do in the general case. For most purposes, you'll be generating mesh geometries algorithmically (as I'll show you how to do in Chapter 6) or obtaining them from other sources.

The abstract *PointLightBase* class defines several properties that are inherited by *PointLight* and *SpotLight*, most notably *Position* of type *Point3D*. Unlike *AmbientLight* and *DirectionalLight*, these other light sources occupy a particular location in 3D space. The default value of *Position* is (0, 0, 0), so you'll probably want to set it explicitly to something else.

The following program defines a square in the XY plane with its lower-left corner at the point (0, 0, 0) and its upper-right corner at (9, 9, 0). The square consists of 100 vertices and 162 triangles.

PointLightDemo.xaml

```
<!-- ================================================
      PointLightDemo.xaml (c) 2007 by Charles Petzold
     ================================================ -->
<Page xmlns="http://schemas.microsoft.com/winfx/2006/xaml/presentation"
      xmlns:x="http://schemas.microsoft.com/winfx/2006/xaml"
      WindowTitle="PointLight Demo"
      Title="PointLight Demo">
    <Viewport3D>
        <ModelVisual3D>
            <ModelVisual3D.Content>
                <GeometryModel3D>
                    <GeometryModel3D.Geometry>
                        <MeshGeometry3D

                Positions=
            "0 0 0, 1 0 0, 2 0 0, 3 0 0, 4 0 0, 5 0 0, 6 0 0, 7 0 0, 8 0 0, 9 0 0,
             0 1 0, 1 1 0, 2 1 0, 3 1 0, 4 1 0, 5 1 0, 6 1 0, 7 1 0, 8 1 0, 9 1 0,
             0 2 0, 1 2 0, 2 2 0, 3 2 0, 4 2 0, 5 2 0, 6 2 0, 7 2 0, 8 2 0, 9 2 0,
             0 3 0, 1 3 0, 2 3 0, 3 3 0, 4 3 0, 5 3 0, 6 3 0, 7 3 0, 8 3 0, 9 3 0,
             0 4 0, 1 4 0, 2 4 0, 3 4 0, 4 4 0, 5 4 0, 6 4 0, 7 4 0, 8 4 0, 9 4 0,
             0 5 0, 1 5 0, 2 5 0, 3 5 0, 4 5 0, 5 5 0, 6 5 0, 7 5 0, 8 5 0, 9 5 0,
             0 6 0, 1 6 0, 2 6 0, 3 6 0, 4 6 0, 5 6 0, 6 6 0, 7 6 0, 9 6 0, 9 6 0,
             0 7 0, 1 7 0, 2 7 0, 3 7 0, 4 7 0, 5 7 0, 6 7 0, 7 7 0, 8 7 0, 9 7 0,
             0 8 0, 1 8 0, 2 8 0, 3 8 0, 4 8 0, 5 8 0, 6 8 0, 7 8 0, 8 8 0, 9 8 0,
             0 9 0, 1 9 0, 2 9 0, 3 9 0, 4 9 0, 5 9 0, 6 9 0, 7 9 0, 8 9 0, 9 9 0"

                TriangleIndices="
   0  1 10,  1  2 11,  2  3 12,  3  4 13,  4  5 14,  5  6 15,  6  7 16,  7  8 17,  8  9 18,
   1 11 10,  2 12 11,  3 13 12,  4 14 13,  5 15 14,  6 16 15,  7 17 16,  8 18 17,  9 19 18,

  10 11 20, 11 12 21, 12 13 22, 13 14 23, 14 15 24, 15 16 25, 16 17 26, 17 18 27, 18 19 28,
  11 21 20, 12 22 21, 13 23 22, 14 24 23, 15 25 24, 16 26 25, 17 27 26, 18 28 27, 19 29 28,

  20 21 30, 21 22 31, 22 23 32, 23 24 33, 24 25 34, 25 26 35, 26 27 36, 27 28 37, 28 29 38,
  21 31 30, 22 32 31, 23 33 32, 24 34 33, 25 35 34, 26 36 35, 27 37 36, 28 38 37, 29 39 38,

  30 31 40, 31 32 41, 32 33 42, 33 34 43, 34 35 44, 35 36 45, 36 37 46, 37 38 47, 38 39 48,
  31 41 40, 32 42 41, 33 43 42, 34 44 43, 35 45 44, 36 46 45, 37 47 46, 38 48 47, 39 49 48,

  40 41 50, 41 42 51, 42 43 52, 43 44 53, 44 45 54, 45 46 55, 46 47 56, 47 48 57, 48 49 58,
  41 51 50, 42 52 51, 43 53 52, 44 54 53, 45 55 54, 46 56 55, 47 57 56, 48 58 57, 49 59 58,

  50 51 60, 51 52 61, 52 53 62, 53 54 63, 54 55 64, 55 56 65, 56 57 66, 57 58 67, 58 59 68,
  51 61 60, 52 62 61, 53 63 62, 54 64 63, 55 65 64, 56 66 65, 57 67 66, 58 68 67, 59 69 68,

  60 61 70, 61 62 71, 62 63 72, 63 64 73, 64 65 74, 65 66 75, 66 67 76, 67 68 77, 68 69 78,
  61 71 70, 62 72 71, 63 73 72, 64 74 73, 65 75 74, 66 76 75, 67 77 76, 68 78 77, 69 79 78,

  70 71 80, 71 72 81, 72 73 82, 73 74 83, 74 75 84, 75 76 85, 76 77 86, 77 78 87, 78 79 88,
  71 81 80, 72 82 81, 73 83 82, 74 84 83, 75 85 84, 76 86 85, 77 87 86, 78 88 87, 79 89 88,

  80 81 90, 81 82 91, 82 83 92, 83 84 93, 84 85 94, 85 86 95, 86 87 96, 87 88 97, 88 89 98,
  81 91 90, 82 92 91, 83 93 92, 84 94 93, 85 95 94, 86 96 95, 87 97 96, 88 98 97, 89 99 98"
                        />
```

```
                    </GeometryModel3D.Geometry>

                    <GeometryModel3D.Material>
                        <DiffuseMaterial Brush="Cyan" />
                    </GeometryModel3D.Material>
                </GeometryModel3D>
            </ModelVisual3D.Content>
        </ModelVisual3D>

        <!-- Light source. -->
        <ModelVisual3D>
            <ModelVisual3D.Content>
                <PointLight Position="4.5 4.5 4" />
            </ModelVisual3D.Content>
        </ModelVisual3D>

        <!-- Camera. -->
        <Viewport3D.Camera>
            <PerspectiveCamera Position="4.5 4.5 30"
                               LookDirection="0 0 -1"
                               UpDirection="0 1 0"
                               FieldOfView="22.5" />
        </Viewport3D.Camera>
    </Viewport3D>
</Page>
```

Notice that the camera is positioned to point at the center of the square at the point (4.5, 4.5, 0) and the *PointLight* is positioned at (4.5, 4.5, 4), which is even with the center of the square but four units away on the Z axis. And here's what it looks like:

You can clearly see that the illumination is greatest in the center where the rays of light from the *PointLight* strike the square perpendicularly. However, if you test the center color with

WhatColor, you'll discover that it's not 00-FF-FF as you might guess, but 00-FB-FB. The center square of the mesh has vertices at (4, 5, 0), (5, 5, 0), (4, 4, 0), and (5, 4, 0), and the *SpotLight* is positioned at (4.5, 4.5, 4). The light does not strike those vertices perpendicularly but is about 10 degrees off. The cosine of 10 degrees is about 0.985, which results in a color of 00-FB-FB rather than 00-FF-FF. At the corners of the large square, the light makes an angle of about 58 degrees, and the color is 00-88-88.

PointLight defines no properties of its own. The class inherits a *Color* property (with a default value of *White*) from the *Light* class, which works the same way as the *Color* property inherited by *DirectionalLight*.

PointLight also inherits several properties from *PointLightBase* besides the *Position* property. These include properties of type *double* named *ConstantAttenuation* (with a default value of 1) *LinearAttenuation* (with a default value of 0) and *QuadraticAttenuation* (default value of 0) that govern how the intensity of light decreases as it travels over a distance.

In real life, light decreases in intensity over a distance for two reasons: First, light is dispersed by the air. This effect is proportional to distance and would be reflected by a non-zero setting of *LinearAttenuation*. Second, light intensity is subject to an inverse square rule, and decreases proportionally to the square of the distance. This effect can be visualized by imagining a light bulb in the center of a sphere. The light bulb is emitting a fixed number of photons per second, so every square inch of the inside of that sphere gets hit with a certain number of photons per second. Now double the radius of the sphere. Because the surface of the sphere is proportional to the square of the radius, the inside surface of the sphere has increased by a factor of four. Each square inch is now getting one-quarter of the number of photons per second. Double the distance, quarter the light. The effect of the inverse-square rule is reflected in a non-zero setting of *QuadraticAttenuation*.

For any vertex at a distance equal to D from the *Position* property of the *PointLight*, an attenuation factor is calculated as:

ConstantAttenuation + *LinearAttenuation* * D + *QuadraticAttenuation* * D^2

The default attenuation factor is 1. If it's greater than 1, the light intensity is divided by the factor. For example, try inserting this attribute in the *PointLight* tag of PointLightDemo.xaml:

```
ConstantAttenuation="2"
```

All the RGB values across the square are halved. If you use *LinearAttenuation* and *QuadraticAttenuation*, you'll probably want to set them to very small values less than 1. Otherwise, the *PointLight* can easily be attenuated to nothing. The attenuation factor is ignored if it's less than 1, unless it's zero or negative, in which case the light disappears.

PointLightBase also defines a *Range* property of type *Double* with a default value of *Double.PositiveInfinity*. If the distance between the light and a vertex is greater than *Range*, the light is ignored.

The *SpotLight* object has a location but does not radiate in all directions. If *PointLight* mimics a naked light bulb, *SpotLight* is more like a flashlight or the headlights of a car. The *SpotLight* class inherits the *Color* property of *Light*, and the *Position*, *ConstantAttenuation*, *LinearAttenuation*, *QuadraticAttenuation*, and *Range* properties of *PointLightBase*.

SpotLight also defines three properties of its own. Like *DirectionalLight*, *SpotLight* defines a *Direction* property of type *Vector3D*. This is the direction in which the light is pointed, and the default value is (0, 0, −1).

Shining a flashlight straight at a wall results in a circular area of high illumination, but this circle is not clearly delimited and its border is rather fuzzy. *SpotLight* mimics a light source that emits light in a cone, which can be narrow or wide, and it simulates a falloff in intensity beyond this cone. *SpotLight* defines two properties of type *Double* named *InnerConeAngle* and *OuterConeAngle*. The defaults are rather oddly defined: In practice, you generally set *InnerConeAngle* less than the *OuterConeAngle*, but the defaults are 180 degrees and 90 degrees, respectively. Within *InnerConeAngle*, the light is affected by its angle to the vertex normals and any attenuation that might be defined. Outside of *OuterConeAngle*, the light has no effect. Between *InnerConeAngle* and *OuterConeAngle*, the light falls off in intensity. (But keep in mind that all illumination is always based on interpolations of the illumination at the triangle vertices!)

Here's a program similar to PointLightDemo.xaml with the same nine-unit square with 100 vertices, but with a *SpotLight* rather than a *PointLight*.

```
SpotLightDemo.xaml
<!-- =============================================
        SpotLightDemo.xaml (c) 2007 by Charles Petzold
     ============================================= -->

    • • •

        <!-- Light source. -->
        <ModelVisual3D>
            <ModelVisual3D.Content>
                <SpotLight Position="4.5 4.5 10" Direction="0 0 -1"
                        InnerConeAngle="30" OuterConeAngle="45" />
            </ModelVisual3D.Content>
        </ModelVisual3D>
    • • •
```

The *SpotLight* has a *Position* of (4.5, 4.5, 10), which is 10 units along the Z axis from the center of the square, and a *Direction* property of (0, 0, −1), which is the default. The *SpotLight* is given an *InnerConeAngle* of 30 degrees and an *OuterConeAngle* of 45 degrees.

At a distance of 10 units from the center of the square, an *InnerConeAngle* should result in an illuminated radius of about 2.7 units. (The calculation is 10 times the tangent of 30 degrees divided by 2.) The *OuterConeAngle* implies a radius of about 4.1 units. Here's what it looks like:

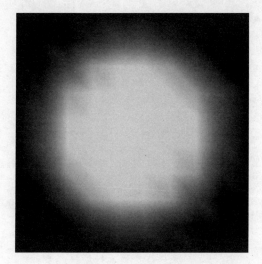

The image certainly seems to match the calculation, but get a load of those Mach bands! Even on the printed page, you can actually see some of the outlines of the smaller squares that comprise the large square. Around the edges of the illumination, you can also see instances where some vertices were within the *OuterConeAngle* but adjacent vertices were not, creating little spike-like effects.

If this were a real-life application, you'd almost definitely start making those little squares smaller and smaller until the Mach bands became less startling. And that's not something you want to be doing by hand. That's why the *for* loop was invented, and why mesh geometries are very often calculated algorithmically as I'll show you how to do in Chapter 6.

Chapter 5
Texture and Materials

Generally the worlds of two-dimensional graphics and three-dimensional graphics are kept far apart. Each world has its own paradigms, its own classes for defining visible objects, and its own transforms. But the two worlds meet where brushes are concerned: Three-dimensional figures are always covered with two-dimensional surfaces. It seems reasonable that these surfaces could be colored and patterned with the array of brushes WPF provides for two-dimensional graphics, and that's precisely the case.

So far I've been decorating 3D figures with solid colors. In this chapter I'll show you how to use gradient brushes and tile brushes, which encompass bitmap images, drawings, and even visuals derived from user-interface objects such as controls. You can even cover a 3D figure with a brush derived from another three-dimensional scene.

Gradient Brushes

I've been using two types of syntax for setting the *Brush* property of *DiffuseMaterial*. The first sets it to a named color:

```
<DiffuseMaterial Brush="Cyan" />
```

This syntax is a shortcut for

```
Brush="{x:Static Brushes.Cyan}"
```

Brushes is a class in the *System.Windows.Media* namespace that contains a collection of static read-only properties of type *Brush*. (The properties actually return objects of type *SolidColor-Brush*.) One of these properties is *Cyan*.

The other syntax I've been using is

```
<DiffuseMaterial Brush="#80FF00C0" />
```

This is also shortcut syntax. A more explicit rendition requires an element of type *SolidColor-Brush*:

```
<DiffuseMaterial>
    <DiffuseMaterial.Brush>
        <SolidColorBrush Color="#80FF00C0"
    </DiffuseMaterial.Brush>
</DiffuseMaterial>
```

And if you really want to get picky about it, that's also a shortcut for syntax that includes a *Color* element:

```
<DiffuseMaterial>
    <DiffuseMaterial.Brush>
        <SolidColorBrush>
            <SolidColorBrush.Color>
                <Color A="128" R="255" G="0" B="192" />
            </SolidColorBrush.Color>
        </SolidColorBrush>
    </DiffuseMaterial.Brush>
</DiffuseMaterial>
```

Such shortcut syntax is made possible by the *BrushConverter* and *ColorConverter* classes that come into play for XAML attributes of type *Brush* and *Color*.

I show you these extended sequences of markup so that you'll be prepared when you move from the simple comfort of *SolidColorBrush* into the more complex brush classes. The *Brush* property of *DiffuseMaterial* is of type *Brush*, and the abstract *Brush* class can be found in the following class hierarchy:

Object
    DispatcherObject (abstract)
        DependencyObject
            Freezable (abstract)
                Animatable (abstract)
                    Brush (abstract)
                        SolidColorBrush (sealed)
                        GradientBrush (abstract)
                            LinearGradientBrush (sealed)
                            RadialGradientBrush (sealed)
                        TileBrush (abstract)
                            DrawingBrush (sealed)
                            ImageBrush (sealed)
                            VisualBrush (sealed)

There are no special brushes for 3D graphics. Instead, you use these two-dimensional brushes to cover the surfaces of three-dimensional figures. As you'll probably recall from working with two-dimensional WPF graphics, brushes generally have no intrinsic size and conform to the size of the surface you're applying them to. This is doubly true when using these brushes with 3D: Brushes often resemble shrink wrap that conforms to the surface of the 3D figures.

In conventional two-dimensional WPF programming, you can define a *LinearGradientBrush* to cover the background of a *Page* element, for example. This is a complete XAML file:

```
<Page xmlns="http://schemas.microsoft.com/winfx/2006/xaml/presentation">
    <Page.Background>
        <LinearGradientBrush StartPoint="0 0" EndPoint="1 1">
            <GradientStop Offset="0" Color="Red" />
            <GradientStop Offset="0.5" Color="Yellow" />
            <GradientStop Offset="1" Color="Blue" />
        </LinearGradientBrush>
    </Page.Background>
</Page>
```

The *StartPoint* and *EndPoint* properties indicate the relative points where the gradient begins and ends; a *StartPoint* of (0, 0) indicates the upper-left corner and an *EndPoint* of (1, 1) indicates the lower-right corner. (These values are the defaults, by the way.) The *Offset* values of the *GradientStop* elements indicate a relative distance between those two points. The resultant gradient begins with red in the upper-left corner, goes to yellow in the center, and ends with blue in the lower-right corner. But the brush covers the entire *Page*, so the brush point of (1, 1) corresponds to the lower-right corner of the *Page* element.

Covering the background of a *Page* element with a *RadialGradientBrush* is similar:

```
<Page xmlns="http://schemas.microsoft.com/winfx/2006/xaml/presentation">
    <Page.Background>
        <RadialGradientBrush>
            <GradientStop Offset="0" Color="Red" />
            <GradientStop Offset="0.5" Color="Yellow" />
            <GradientStop Offset="1" Color="Blue" />
        </RadialGradientBrush>
    </Page.Background>
</Page>
```

Again, the brush conforms to the size and aspect ratio of the surface on which it appears. Whether you're working with brushes in two-dimensional graphics or three-dimensional graphics, you refer to coordinates within the brush using the following relative coordinate system:

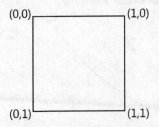

BrushCoordinates.xaml

In accordance with the conventions of two-dimensional WPF graphics, increasing values of Y go down. This is the opposite of the customary view of the Y axis in 3D, a difference that's likely to be confusing at first.

To cover a three-dimensional figure with a two-dimensional brush, you must establish a correspondence between the three-dimensional vertices of your figure and the two-dimensional relative coordinates of the brush. You do this using a property of *MeshGeometry3D* named *TextureCoordinates*. This property is of type *PointCollection*—not a *Point3DCollection*—and its collection of two-dimensional *Point* objects.

As you know, every triangle in your figure is defined by three consecutive indices in the *TriangleIndices* collection of *MeshGeometry3D*. Those indices index the *Positions* collection to obtain the 3D coordinates of the vertices of that triangle. These same indices also index the *TextureCoordinates* collection (if there is one) to obtain three two-dimensional coordinates of a brush. If you have duplicate vertices in the *Positions* collection, you can associate them with different points in the *TextureCoordinates* collection.

Suppose you've defined a *LinearGradientBrush* like this:

```
<LinearGradientBrush>
    <GradientStop Offset="0" Color="Yellow" />
    <GradientStop Offset="1" Color="Brown" />
</LinearGradientBrush>
```

The default *StartPoint* and *EndPoint* values are (0, 0) and (1, 1). The gradient begins in the upper-left corner with yellow and ends in the lower-right corner with brown. You can use any triangular subset of this brush to color a triangle in the 3D mesh. Suppose you want the following mapping:

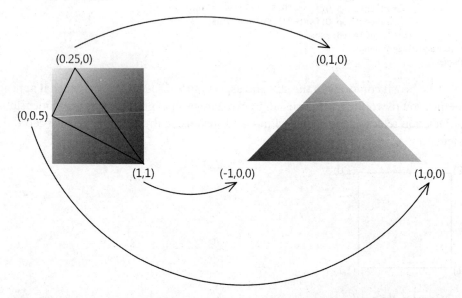

BrushMapping.xaml

The three-dimensional triangle shown on the right is covered with a triangular subset of the two-dimensional brush shown on the left. The selected subset of the brush is stretched to fit the entire 3D triangle. You define the *MeshGeometry3D* like so:

```
<MeshGeometry3D TriangleIndices="0 1 2"
                Positions="0 1 0, -1 0 0, 1 0 0"
                TextureCoordinates="0.25 0, 1 1, 0 0.5" />
```

The brush is a two-dimensional rectangle with four vertices, and the mesh consists of triangles with three vertices. It is simply not possible to specify *TextureCoordinates* values so that an entire rectangular brush fits in a single triangle. If you're working with objects in which pairs of triangles form rectangles, you can associate those rectangles with entire brushes. But in general, that's not the case.

With *TextureCoordinates* we've come to the last of the four properties defined by *MeshGeometry3D* that also include *Positions*, *TriangleIndices*, and *Normals*.

MeshGeometry3D also inherits a *Bounds* property from *Geometry3D*. This property is of type *Rect3D* and indicates the total size of the figure before any transforms are applied. Imagine the figure being entirely enclosed in a box whose sides are parallel to the XY, YZ, and XZ planes. The *Rect3D* structure defines a *Location* property of type *Point3D* (and also separate *X*, *Y*, and *Z* properties) that indicates the coordinate of the left bottom-rear corner of this bounding box. The *Size* property of type *Size3D* (or the separate *SizeX*, *SizeY*, and *SizeZ* properties) indicates the dimensions of the box. The *Bounds* property is sometimes useful for positioning a figure. For example, you might want to position a figure so that its bottom sits on the XZ plane. Set an *OffsetY* property of a *TranslateTransform3D* to the negative of the *Bounds.Y* property.

Keep in mind that each *GeometryModel3D* consists of one *MeshGeometry3D* and one object of type *Material*, so by necessity you use the same brush for all the triangles that comprise the figure. If you want to use different brushes for different triangles, you might want to split the figure into multiple *GeometryModel3D* objects or use a technique involving panels that I'll show you later in this chapter. In some cases you might cover a single *MeshGeometry3D* with two materials by defining the triangle indices in such a way that lets you use both *Material* and *BackMaterial*.

Here's a four-sided pyramid where opposite sides map to the same triangle of a gradient brush, but adjacent sides map to different triangles. To keep it simple, the pyramid has no bottom.

PyramidWithGradientBrush.xaml

```
<!-- =========================================================
        PyramidWithGradientBrush.xaml (c) 2007 by Charles Petzold
     ========================================================= -->
<Page xmlns="http://schemas.microsoft.com/winfx/2006/xaml/presentation"
      xmlns:x="http://schemas.microsoft.com/winfx/2006/xaml"
      WindowTitle="Pyramid with LinearGradientBrush"
      Title="Pyramid with LinearGradientBrush">
```

```
<DockPanel>
    <ScrollBar Name="horz" DockPanel.Dock="Bottom" Orientation="Horizontal"
            Minimum="-180" Maximum="180"
            LargeChange="10" SmallChange="1" />

    <Viewport3D>
        <ModelVisual3D>
            <ModelVisual3D.Content>
                <Model3DGroup>
                    <GeometryModel3D>
                        <GeometryModel3D.Geometry>

                            <!-- Pyramid: Front, back, left, right. -->
                            <MeshGeometry3D
                                Positions="0 1 0, -0.5 0  0.5,  0.5 0  0.5,
                                           0 1 0,  0.5 0 -0.5, -0.5 0 -0.5,
                                           0 1 0, -0.5 0 -0.5, -0.5 0  0.5,
                                           0 1 0,  0.5 0  0.5,  0.5 0 -0.5"

                                TriangleIndices="0 1 2, 3 4 5,
                                                 6 7 8, 9 10 11"

                                TextureCoordinates="1 0, 0 1, 1 1,
                                                    1 0, 0 1, 0 0,
                                                    1 0, 0 0, 0 1,
                                                    1 0, 1 1, 0 1" />
                        </GeometryModel3D.Geometry>

                        <GeometryModel3D.Material>
                            <DiffuseMaterial>
                                <DiffuseMaterial.Brush>
                                    <LinearGradientBrush StartPoint="0 0"
                                                         EndPoint="1 1">
                                        <GradientStop
                                            Color="#FF0000" Offset="0" />
                                        <GradientStop
                                            Color="#FFFF00" Offset="0.2" />
                                        <GradientStop
                                            Color="#00FF00" Offset="0.4" />
                                        <GradientStop
                                            Color="#00FFFF" Offset="0.6" />
                                        <GradientStop
                                            Color="#0000FF" Offset="0.8" />
                                        <GradientStop
                                            Color="#FF00FF" Offset="1" />
                                    </LinearGradientBrush>
                                </DiffuseMaterial.Brush>
                            </DiffuseMaterial>
                        </GeometryModel3D.Material>

                        <GeometryModel3D.Transform>
                            <RotateTransform3D>
                                <RotateTransform3D.Rotation>
                                    <AxisAngleRotation3D Axis="0 1 0"
```

```
                                         Angle="{Binding ElementName=horz,
                                                         Path=Value}" />
                        </RotateTransform3D.Rotation>
                    </RotateTransform3D>
                </GeometryModel3D.Transform>
            </GeometryModel3D>

            <!-- Light sources. -->
            <AmbientLight Color="Gray" />
            <DirectionalLight Color="Gray" Direction="2 -3 -1" />
        </Model3DGroup>
    </ModelVisual3D.Content>
</ModelVisual3D>

<!-- Camera. -->
<Viewport3D.Camera>
    <PerspectiveCamera Position="-2 2 4"
                       LookDirection="2 -2 -4"
                       UpDirection="0 1 0"
                       FieldOfView="22.5" />
</Viewport3D.Camera>
        </Viewport3D>
    </DockPanel>
</Page>
```

The upper-right corner of the brush—the point (1, 0)—is always mapped to the top of the pyramid—the point (0, 1, 0). The other three corners of the brush are mapped to various vertices at the base of the pyramid:

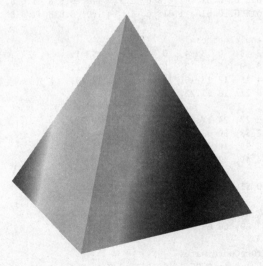

A horizontal scrollbar lets you confirm that the brush seems to continuously wrap around the pyramid.

To the rotating dodecahedron in Chapter 3, "Axis/Angle Rotation," I've added a *Texture-Coordinates* collection and a *RadialGradientBrush*.

DodecahedronWithRadialBrush.xaml

```
<!-- =========================================================
        DodecahedronWithRadialBrush.xaml (c) 2007 by Charles Petzold
     ========================================================= -->
<Page xmlns="http://schemas.microsoft.com/winfx/2006/xaml/presentation"
      xmlns:x="http://schemas.microsoft.com/winfx/2006/xaml"
      WindowTitle="Dodecahedron with RadialGradientBrush"
      Title="Dodecahedron with RadialGradientBrush">
    <Viewport3D>
        <ModelVisual3D>
            <ModelVisual3D.Content>
                <Model3DGroup>
                    <GeometryModel3D>
                        <GeometryModel3D.Geometry>
                            <MeshGeometry3D
                            Positions=
"1.171 -0.724 0, 1 -1 -1, 1.618 0 -0.618, 1.618 0  0.618, 1 -1  1, 0.618 -1.618 0,
-1.171 -0.724 0,-1 -1  1,-1.618 0  0.618,-1.618 0 -0.618,-1 -1 -1,-0.618 -1.618 0,
-1.171  0.724 0,-1  1 -1,-1.618 0 -0.618,-1.618 0  0.618,-1  1  1,-0.618  1.618 0,
 1.171  0.724 0, 1  1  1, 1.618 0  0.618, 1.618 0 -0.618, 1  1 -1, 0.618  1.618 0,
-0.724 0 -1.171,-1  1 -1,0  0.618 -1.618,0 -0.618 -1.618,-1 -1 -1,-1.618 0 -0.618,
-0.724 0  1.171,-1 -1  1,0 -0.618  1.618,0  0.618  1.618,-1  1  1,-1.618 0  0.618,
 0.724 0 -1.171, 1 -1 -1,0 -0.618 -1.618,0  0.618 -1.618, 1  1 -1, 1.618 0 -0.618,
 0.724 0  1.171, 1  1  1,0  0.618  1.618,0 -0.618  1.618, 1 -1  1, 1.618 0  0.618,
0 -1.171 -0.724, 1 -1 -1, 0.618 -1.618 0,-0.618 -1.618 0,-1 -1 -1,0 -0.618 -1.618,
0  1.171 -0.724,-1  1 -1,-0.618  1.618 0, 0.618  1.618 0, 1  1 -1,0  0.618 -1.618,
0 -1.171  0.724,-1 -1  1,-0.618 -1.618 0, 0.618 -1.618 0, 1 -1  1,0 -0.618  1.618,
0  1.171  0.724, 1  1  1, 0.618  1.618 0,-0.618  1.618 0,-1  1  1,0  0.618  1.618"

                            TriangleIndices=
"  0  1  2,   0  2  3,   0  3  4,   0  4  5,   0  5  1,
   6  7  8,   6  8  9,   6  9 10,   6 10 11,   6 11  7,
  12 13 14,  12 14 15,  12 15 16,  12 16 17,  12 17 13,
  18 19 20,  18 20 21,  18 21 22,  18 22 23,  18 23 19,

  24 25 26,  24 26 27,  24 27 28,  24 28 29,  24 29 25,
  30 31 32,  30 32 33,  30 33 34,  30 34 35,  30 35 31,
  36 37 38,  36 38 39,  36 39 40,  36 40 41,  36 41 37,
  42 43 44,  42 44 45,  42 45 46,  42 46 47,  42 47 43,

  48 49 50,  48 50 51,  48 51 52,  48 52 53,  48 53 49,
  54 55 56,  54 56 57,  54 57 58,  54 58 59,  54 59 55,
  60 61 62,  60 62 63,  60 63 64,  60 64 65,  60 65 61,
  66 67 68,  66 68 69,  66 69 70,  66 70 71,  66 71 67"

                            TextureCoordinates=
"0.5 0.5, 0.5 0, 1 0.4, 0.85 1, 0.15 1, 0 0.4
 0.5 0.5, 0.5 0, 1 0.4, 0.85 1, 0.15 1, 0 0.4
 0.5 0.5, 0.5 0, 1 0.4, 0.85 1, 0.15 1, 0 0.4
 0.5 0.5, 0.5 0, 1 0.4, 0.85 1, 0.15 1, 0 0.4
 0.5 0.5, 0.5 0, 1 0.4, 0.85 1, 0.15 1, 0 0.4
```

```
                    0.5 0.5, 0.5 0, 1 0.4, 0.85 1, 0.15 1, 0 0.4
                    0.5 0.5, 0.5 0, 1 0.4, 0.85 1, 0.15 1, 0 0.4
                    0.5 0.5, 0.5 0, 1 0.4, 0.85 1, 0.15 1, 0 0.4
                    0.5 0.5, 0.5 0, 1 0.4, 0.85 1, 0.15 1, 0 0.4
                    0.5 0.5, 0.5 0, 1 0.4, 0.85 1, 0.15 1, 0 0.4
                    0.5 0.5, 0.5 0, 1 0.4, 0.85 1, 0.15 1, 0 0.4
                    0.5 0.5, 0.5 0, 1 0.4, 0.85 1, 0.15 1, 0 0.4" />
                </GeometryModel3D.Geometry>

                <!-- RadialGradientBrush. -->
                <GeometryModel3D.Material>
                    <DiffuseMaterial>
                        <DiffuseMaterial.Brush>
                            <RadialGradientBrush>
                                <GradientStop Color="Cyan" Offset="0" />
                                <GradientStop Color="Red" Offset="1" />
                            </RadialGradientBrush>
                        </DiffuseMaterial.Brush>
                    </DiffuseMaterial>
                </GeometryModel3D.Material>

                <!-- Transform for animated rotation. -->
                <GeometryModel3D.Transform>
                    <RotateTransform3D>
                        <RotateTransform3D.Rotation>
                            <AxisAngleRotation3D x:Name="rotate"
                                            Axis="1 2 0"  />
                        </RotateTransform3D.Rotation>
                    </RotateTransform3D>
                </GeometryModel3D.Transform>
            </GeometryModel3D>

            <!-- Light sources. -->
            <AmbientLight Color="Gray" />
            <DirectionalLight Color="Gray" Direction="1, -3 -2" />

        </Model3DGroup>
      </ModelVisual3D.Content>
    </ModelVisual3D>

    <Viewport3D.Camera>
        <PerspectiveCamera Position="0 0 5"
                        LookDirection="0 0 -5"
                        UpDirection="0 1 0"
                        FieldOfView="45" />
    </Viewport3D.Camera>
</Viewport3D>

<!-- Animation -->
<Page.Triggers>
    <EventTrigger RoutedEvent="Page.Loaded">
        <BeginStoryboard>
            <Storyboard TargetName="rotate" TargetProperty="Angle">
                <DoubleAnimation To="360" Duration="0:0:30"
```

```
                                        RepeatBehavior="Forever" />
            </Storyboard>
          </BeginStoryboard>
        </EventTrigger>
    </Page.Triggers>
  </Page>
```

As you'll recall, each of the 12 lines in the *Positions* collection defines one pentagon of the figure. The first *Point3D* object is the center of the pentagon, and the other five points define the vertices of the pentagon in a clockwise direction. The 12 lines in the *TextureCoordinates* collection correspond to the *Positions* collection. The first *Point* object is the center of the brush, the point (0.5, 0.5), and the other five points roughly mark out a pentagon with points arranged clockwise around the circumference of the brush: (0.5, 0), (1, 0.4), (0.85, 1), (0.15, 1), and (0, 0.4).

Tile Brushes

The three remaining brush classes are *ImageBrush*, *DrawingBrush*, and *VisualBrush*. In theory, these brushes have quite a bit of overlapping functionality, but in most real-life applications you'll probably use them for these specific purposes:

- *ImageBrush* for brushes based on bitmaps
- *DrawingBrush* for brushes based on vector drawings
- *VisualBrush* for brushes based on visual objects, including user-interface elements and controls

ImageBrush defines only one property: The *ImageSource* property is of type *ImageSource*, which is the abstract class from which *BitmapSource* and *DrawingImage* descend. *BitmapSource* is the abstract class from which all the bitmap classes descend.

DrawingBrush also defines just one property: The *Drawing* property, which is of type *Drawing*, an abstract class from which five classes descend. Most often you'll probably use the *GeometryDrawing* class in connection with this brush, but you can also use objects of type *GlyphRunDrawing*, *ImageDrawing*, *VideoDrawing*, and *DrawingGroup*. In particular, *VideoDrawing* lets you play a video file on a 3D object.

VisualBrush defines two properties: The *Visual* property is of type *Visual*—the abstract class from which, most notably, *FrameworkElement* and *Control* derive. (The other property is named *AutoLayoutContent* and is *True* by default.) You use the *VisualBrush* to put elements, panels, and controls on 3D figures. These are not functional controls, but only the images of controls. (If you want actual functional controls on your 3D figures, you'll want to investigate the free software package "3D Tools for the Windows Presentation Foundation" available at *http://www.codeplex.com/3DTools*.) I find *VisualBrush* most useful in putting *TextBlock* elements on 3D figures, and also when using panels that can contain other elements.

ImageBrush, *DrawingBrush*, and *VisualBrush* all derive from *TileBrush*, so called because these styles of brushes are capable of repeating a rectangular image horizontally and vertically. The default behavior, however, is *not* to tile. *ImageBrush*, *DrawingBrush*, and *VisualBrush* all inherit eight properties from *TileBrush* that are essential for using the *TileBrush* classes in a flexible and powerful manner. Demonstrating these properties will be the main focus of this section.

Brushes Based on Bitmaps

Let's begin by using *ImageBrush* to put a picture of my face on a cube. (When you see where this exercise eventually goes, you'll understand why I use a picture of myself rather than someone else.) A bitmap can be applied to a cube in many different ways. This first stab is a fairly straightforward approach. The six faces of the cube are defined independently, with no shared vertices. In the *Positions* collection, the four sides perpendicular to the XZ plane have their vertices defined in this order: upper-left, upper-right, lower-left, and lower-right. The *TextureCoordinates* collection consists of the two-dimensional points $(0, 0)$, $(1, 0)$, $(0, 1)$, and $(1, 1)$ to correspond with that order. *TextureCoordinates* repeats those same four *Point* objects for each face of the cube.

```
FaceOnACube1.xaml
<!-- ===========================================
     FaceOnACube1.xaml (c) 2007 by Charles Petzold
     =========================================== -->
<Page xmlns="http://schemas.microsoft.com/winfx/2006/xaml/presentation"
      xmlns:x="http://schemas.microsoft.com/winfx/2006/xaml"
      WindowTitle="Face on a Cube #1"
      Title="Face on a Cube #1">
```

```
<DockPanel>
    <ScrollBar Name="horz" DockPanel.Dock="Bottom" Orientation="Horizontal"
            Minimum="-180" Maximum="180"
            LargeChange="10" SmallChange="1" />

    <ScrollBar Name="vert" DockPanel.Dock="Right" Orientation="Vertical"
            Minimum="-180" Maximum="180"
            LargeChange="10" SmallChange="1" />

    <Viewport3D>
        <ModelVisual3D>
            <ModelVisual3D.Content>
                <Model3DGroup>
                    <GeometryModel3D>
                        <GeometryModel3D.Geometry>

                            <!-- Unit cube: front, back, left,
                                            right, top, bottom. -->
                            <MeshGeometry3D
                                Positions="-0.5  0.5  0.5,   0.5  0.5  0.5,
                                           -0.5 -0.5  0.5,   0.5 -0.5  0.5,

                                            0.5  0.5 -0.5,  -0.5  0.5 -0.5,
                                            0.5 -0.5 -0.5,  -0.5 -0.5 -0.5,

                                           -0.5  0.5 -0.5,  -0.5  0.5  0.5,
                                           -0.5 -0.5 -0.5,  -0.5 -0.5  0.5,

                                            0.5  0.5  0.5,   0.5  0.5 -0.5,
                                            0.5 -0.5  0.5,   0.5 -0.5 -0.5,

                                           -0.5  0.5 -0.5,   0.5  0.5 -0.5,
                                           -0.5  0.5  0.5,   0.5  0.5  0.5,

                                            0.5 -0.5 -0.5,  -0.5 -0.5 -0.5,
                                            0.5 -0.5  0.5,  -0.5 -0.5  0.5"

                                TriangleIndices=" 0  2  1,   1  2  3,
                                                  4  6  5,   5  6  7,
                                                  8 10  9,   9 10 11,
                                                 12 14 13,  13 14 15,
                                                 16 18 17,  17 18 19
                                                 20 22 21,  21 22 23"

                                TextureCoordinates="0 0, 1 0, 0 1, 1 1,
                                                     0 0, 1 0, 0 1, 1 1,
                                                     0 0, 1 0, 0 1, 1 1,
                                                     0 0, 1 0, 0 1, 1 1,
                                                     0 0, 1 0, 0 1, 1 1,
                                                     0 0, 1 0, 0 1, 1 1" />
                        </GeometryModel3D.Geometry>
```

```
                            <GeometryModel3D.Material>
                                <DiffuseMaterial>
                                    <DiffuseMaterial.Brush>
                                        <ImageBrush
                    ImageSource="http://www.charlespetzold.com/PetzoldTattoo.jpg" />
                                    </DiffuseMaterial.Brush>
                                </DiffuseMaterial>
                            </GeometryModel3D.Material>

                            <GeometryModel3D.Transform>
                                <Transform3DGroup>
                                    <RotateTransform3D>
                                        <RotateTransform3D.Rotation>
                                            <AxisAngleRotation3D Axis="0 1 0"
                                                Angle="{Binding ElementName=horz,
                                                                Path=Value}" />
                                        </RotateTransform3D.Rotation>
                                    </RotateTransform3D>
                                    <RotateTransform3D>
                                        <RotateTransform3D.Rotation>
                                            <AxisAngleRotation3D Axis="1 0 0"
                                                Angle="{Binding ElementName=vert,
                                                                Path=Value}" />
                                        </RotateTransform3D.Rotation>
                                    </RotateTransform3D>
                                </Transform3DGroup>
                            </GeometryModel3D.Transform>
                        </GeometryModel3D>

                        <!-- Light source. -->
                        <AmbientLight Color="White" />
                    </Model3DGroup>
                </ModelVisual3D.Content>
            </ModelVisual3D>

            <!-- Camera. -->
            <Viewport3D.Camera>
                <PerspectiveCamera Position="-2 2 4"
                                   LookDirection="2 -2 -4"
                                   UpDirection="0 1 0"
                                   FieldOfView="22.5" />
            </Viewport3D.Camera>
        </Viewport3D>
    </DockPanel>
</Page>
```

Notice that only an *AmbientLight* is present, so the bitmap looks as bright as if it were viewed normally under Windows. Two *ScrollBar* controls on the right and bottom let you rotate the cube to view it from other directions.

The *DiffuseMaterial* object for the brush is defined like this:

```
<DiffuseMaterial>
    <DiffuseMaterial.Brush>
        <ImageBrush
            ImageSource="http://www.charlespetzold.com/PetzoldTattoo.jpg" />
    </DiffuseMaterial.Brush>
</DiffuseMaterial>
```

Very conveniently, the *ImageSource* attribute simply references a bitmap on my Web site via a URI. (You can thank the programmers of the *ImageSourceConverter* class for that convenience.) This is certainly the easiest way to reference a bitmap for an *ImageBrush*, but watch out: If the bitmap cannot be downloaded, the *ImageBrush* file will raise an exception. In a real-life program, you'll probably want to include images as resources in a Microsoft Visual Studio project, and create binary .exe or .xbap files rather than just XAML files. Here's the cube:

The original bitmap image is not square. It is 439 pixels wide by 521 pixels high. By default, WPF 3D stretches the image of the square face of the cube, in the process making my face look just a little squatter and pudgier than it actually is. This behavior is governed by the *Stretch* property, which *ImageBrush* inherits from *TileBrush* and which you set to a member of the *Stretch* enumeration. The default *Stretch* property is *Fill*, which stretches the image to fill the area without regard to its original aspect ratio. In general, the surfaces of a 3D figure are all different shapes and sizes, so stretching the image to fit is certainly the simplest generalized behavior. For some applications you'll want to try to preserve the correct aspect ratio of the bitmap.

You might want to experiment with the alternatives. Try this:

```
<ImageBrush Stretch="Uniform" ... />
```

Now the image assumes its correct aspect ratio on the faces of the cube. Although the brush covers the whole face of the cube, the image does not, and where there is no image, the brush is transparent. With this particular image, which is taller than it is wide, the uniformly stretched image sits in the horizontal center of the brush, creating gaps on both the left and right. You can set the *AlignmentX* property defined by *TileBrush* to *Left* or *Right* to move it to one side. (The default setting is *Center*.) Similarly, for an image that's wider than it is tall, you can set the *AlignmentY* property to *Top* or *Bottom* rather than the default *Center*.

Now try this:

```
<ImageBrush Stretch="UniformToFill" ... />
```

This lets the image have its correct aspect ratio *and* fill the area, but only at the cost of cropping part of the image. For this bitmap, part of the top and bottom are cropped. You can set *AlignmentY* to *Bottom* to crop the top of the image only, or to *Top* to crop the bottom of the image.

With the *Uniform* and *UniformToFill* options, the image appears in its correct aspect ratio only because it's displayed on a square surface. If this were not actually a cube, the image would be shrunk or cropped as if it were displayed on a square surface, but it wouldn't appear to have the correct aspect ratio. Setting the *Stretch* property to *None* is an option in the two-dimensional world because it lets the image assume its metrical size. For 3D figures, you need to specify *TextureCoordinates* in device-independent units.

You might be tempted to use the *TextureCoordinates* collection to crop the image. Let's try it. Replace the first line of *TextureCoordinates* with the following:

```
0.3 0.1, 0.8 0.1, 0.3 0.6, 0.8 0.6,
```

This means that I want the relative coordinate (0.3 0.1) of the brush to be aligned with the upper-left corner of the front face of the cube. The other relative coordinates of the brush are set to display only half the width and half the height of the bitmap. And sure enough, the front of the cube now displays a nicely cropped version of the image:

You can then go through *TextureCoordinates* and replace every line, but as you replace the last line, the image reverts to what it was initially! In effect, *TextureCoordinates* indicates a rendering size for the image, and if the coordinates do not range between 0 and 1, they are normalized to encompass the entire image.

If you need to crop the image, you can do so using the *Viewbox* property defined by *TileBrush*. Set *Viewbox* to an object of type *Rect* (a two-dimensional rectangle) indicating the desired portion of the image relative to the bounding box. The rectangle consists of four numbers: the left coordinate, the top coordinate, a width, and a height. To get the same cropping as shown in the preceding image, use:

```
<ImageBrush Viewbox="0.3 0.1 0.5 0.5" ...
```

And here it is:

You can use coordinates not in the range of 0 and 1, such as:

```
<ImageBrush Viewbox="-0.1 -0.1 1.2 1.2"
```

You can visualize this as setting a size of the brush as 1.2 units wide and high, with horizontal and vertical coordinates ranging from –0.1 to 1.1. The bitmap is displayed with a one-unit width and height between coordinates 0 and 1 within this brush. The result is that a margin of transparent brush surrounds the bitmap.

If you'd prefer, you can specify cropping or padding in terms of device-independent coordinates of the brush. As you'll recall, device-independent coordinates are 1/96th inch, so if your bitmap is 600 pixels wide and 900 pixels high, and the horizontal and vertical resolution of the bitmap is 300 dots per inch, the bitmap width is two inches, or 192 device-independent units, and the bitmap height is three inches, or 288 device-independent units.

Fortunately the image in FaceOnACube1.xaml has a resolution of 96 dots per inch, so device-independent units are the same as pixels. I said earlier that the bitmap is 439 pixels wide by 521 pixels high. To specify cropping in terms of device-independent units, set *ViewboxUnits* to the *Absolute* member of the *BrushMappingMode* enumeration (the default is *RelativeTo-BoundingBox*):

```
<ImageBrush ViewboxUnits="Absolute" Viewbox="132 52 220 260" ...
```

This markup performs the same cropping as shown earlier.

So far we haven't seen any tiling, and that's because the default *TileMode* property is the enumeration member *TileMode.None*. You can set this property to *Tile* to enable tiling, but that's not quite sufficient either, because by default the size of each tile is assumed to be the size of the brush. You also need to use the *Viewport* property to indicate the size of each tile relative to the bounding box. Like *Viewbox*, you set *Viewport* to a *Rect* object. Try this:

```
<ImageBrush TileMode="Tile" Viewport="0 0 0.20 0.25" ...
```

What this *Viewport* means is that horizontally you want each tile to occupy 20 percent of the width, and vertically you want each tile to be 25 percent of the height. Five tiles should appear horizontally and four vertically along each surface, and that's the case:

This tiling is about right to compensate for the non-square aspect ratio of the bitmap, so if you also set *Stretch* to *UniformToFill*, the change is only very slight.

There are five tiled images horizontally and four vertically because the width and height values of the *Rect* object set to *Viewport* are 0.20 and 0.25. If these numbers do not divide equally into one, partial tiles are displayed. For example, try this:

```
<ImageBrush TileMode="Tile" Viewport="0 0 0.40 0.67" ...
```

Now two-and-a-half images are tiled horizontally and one-and-a-half vertically:

The tile in the upper-left corner is aligned with the corner of the face of the cube. You can alter this behavior with the first two numbers in the *Rect* object that you set to the *Viewport* property. These indicate the coordinate of the upper-left tile. For example, the following markup causes the tiles in the first column to begin horizontally midway through the image:

```
<ImageBrush TileMode="Tile" Viewport="0.1 0 0.20 0.25" ...
```

The following causes tiles on the top and bottom to begin vertically midway through the image:

```
<ImageBrush TileMode="Tile" Viewport="0 0.125 0.20 0.25" ...
```

You can also set *TileMode* to the enumeration members *FlipX*, *FlipY*, or *FlipXY* to alter the orientation of alternate tiles. The *FlipX* option causes every other column of tiles to be flipped around its vertical axis. The *FlipY* option flips every other row of tiles around its horizontal axis. *FlipXY* combines the two effects:

```
<ImageBrush TileMode="FlipXY" Viewport="0 0 0.20 0.25" ...
```

That results in the following image:

Keep in mind that this has all been looking rather neat and pretty only because we've been tiling an image on six squares of the same size. If these were not squares, it wouldn't work quite as well. For example, in the *Positions* collection of the *MeshGeometry3D* in FaceOnA-Cube1.xaml, change all the Z values from 0.5 to 1.5 and from –0.5 to –1.5, and use the same tiling we've been experimenting with:

```
<ImageBrush TileMode="Tile" Viewport="0 0 0.20 0.25" ...
```

You'll have to pull back the camera a bit to get the entire figure in the frame. This figure is now a square cuboid, but each face of the figure still displays five images horizontally and four images vertically:

On the left and right sides, the image is stretched horizontally; on the top and bottom the image is stretched vertically. This might be what you want, or you might want the individual tiles to be the same size regardless of the size of the surface on which they appear. Is there a way to do that?

Yes there is. First, set the *TextureCoordinates* values to more closely reflect the relative distances between vertices. For example, if you have *TextureCoordinates* of (0, 0) and (1, 0) for two vertices of one face of the figure, and another face of the figure is three times wider, use *Texture-Coordinates* of (0, 0) and (3, 0) for that wider face. You might be a little hesitant that this will work because of the earlier experiment I described involving altering *TextureCoordinates* for cropping. That experiment didn't turn out to be very successful because WPF 3D normalized all the *TextureCoordinates*. But you can prevent that from happening. In the *ImageBrush* tag, set *ViewportUnits* to *Absolute*:

```
<ImageBrush TileMode="Tile" ViewportUnits="Absolute" Viewport="0 0 0.20 0.25" ...
```

The default value of *ViewportUnits* is *RelativeToBoundingBox*, which means that the *Viewport* rectangle is based on the bounding box of the *TextureCoordinates* collection—that is, the overall minimums and maximums normalized to the range 0 to 1. With a value of *Absolute*, the *Viewport* rectangle is based on the actual numbers in the *TextureCoordinates* collection. If two *TextureCoordinates* of a face of the figure have values of (0, 0) and (1, 0), the *Viewport* width of 0.20 indicates that five tiled images will appear horizontally. If two *TextureCoordinates* have values of (0, 0) and (3, 0), fifteen tiled images will appear instead.

Here's a program that demonstrates this technique. The XAML file defines a square cuboid with X and Y values ranging from −0.5 to 0.5, but Z values ranging from −3.5 to 0.5. For the left and right sides, the *TextureCoordinates* values are (0, 0), (4, 0), (0, 1), and (4, 1). For the top and bottom, the values are (0, 0), (1, 0), (0, 4), and (1, 4). Most of the file is identical to FaceOnACube1.xaml.

```
FaceOnACuboid.xaml
<!-- =================================================
      FaceOnACuboid.xaml (c) 2007 by Charles Petzold
     ================================================= -->

  • • •
                        <GeometryModel3D.Geometry>
                            <!-- Square cuboid: front, back, left,
                                              right, top, bottom. -->
                        <MeshGeometry3D
                            Positions="-0.5  0.5  0.5,   0.5  0.5  0.5,
                                       -0.5 -0.5  0.5,   0.5 -0.5  0.5,
                                        0.5  0.5 -3.5,  -0.5  0.5 -3.5,
                                        0.5 -0.5 -3.5,  -0.5 -0.5 -3.5,
                                       -0.5  0.5 -3.5,  -0.5  0.5  0.5,
                                       -0.5 -0.5 -3.5,  -0.5 -0.5  0.5,
                                        0.5  0.5  0.5,   0.5  0.5 -3.5,
                                        0.5 -0.5  0.5,   0.5 -0.5 -3.5,
                                       -0.5  0.5 -3.5,   0.5  0.5 -3.5,
                                       -0.5  0.5  0.5,   0.5  0.5  0.5,
```

```
                                         0.5 -0.5 -3.5, -0.5 -0.5 -3.5,
                                         0.5 -0.5  0.5, -0.5 -0.5  0.5"

                 TriangleIndices=" 0  2  1,  1  2  3,
                                   4  6  5,  5  6  7,
                                   8 10  9,  9 10 11,
                                  12 14 13, 13 14 15,
                                  16 18 17, 17 18 19,
                                  20 22 21, 21 22 23"

                 TextureCoordinates="0 0, 1 0, 0 1, 1 1,
                                     0 0, 1 0, 0 1, 1 1,
                                     0 0, 4 0, 0 1, 4 1,
                                     0 0, 4 0, 0 1, 4 1,
                                     0 0, 1 0, 0 4, 1 4,
                                     0 0, 1 0, 0 4, 1 4" />
    </GeometryModel3D.Geometry>

    <GeometryModel3D.Material>
        <DiffuseMaterial>
            <DiffuseMaterial.Brush>
                <ImageBrush TileMode="Tile"
                            ViewportUnits="Absolute"
                            Viewport="0 0 0.20 0.25"
    ImageSource="http://www.charlespetzold.com/PetzoldTattoo.jpg" />
            </DiffuseMaterial.Brush>
        </DiffuseMaterial>
    </GeometryModel3D.Material>
...
```

This does precisely what we desire: The long faces of the figure are now populated with sufficient tiles so that every tile is exactly the same size:

Of course, if you're attempting to tile a figure with non-rectangular faces, the tiles will be distorted anyway, but this is a good technique to keep the tiles at least reasonably consistent.

In summary, *TileBrush* defines two properties of type *Rect*: *Viewbox* and *Viewport*. These two properties are associated with two other properties named *ViewboxUnits* and *ViewportUnits*, both of type *BrushMappingMode*, an enumeration that has two members: *RelativeToBounding-Box* (the default) and *Absolute*.

You use *Viewbox* to indicate what portion of the image you want to use for tiling. You can crop or pad the image with *Viewbox*. Normally you indicate the portion of the image you want to use with relative coordinates ranging from 0 to 1, but if you set *ViewboxUnits* to *Absolute*, you can specify coordinates in device-independent units. If the bitmap has a resolution of 96 DPI, these units are pixels.

You use *Viewport* to indicate tiling. The width and height of the *Rect* indicate the fraction of the area to be occupied by a single tile. By default, these fractions are relative to the *Texture-Coordinates* collection normalized between 0 and 1, but if you set *ViewportUnits* to *Absolute*, these fractions are relative to the actual *TextureCoordinates* values.

In two-dimensional graphics programming, generally the *Viewport* rectangle is quite different depending on the setting of *ViewportUnits*. For example, if you wanted to have 10 tiles horizontally and 5 tiles vertically regardless of the size of the surface, you'd leave *ViewportUnits* at its default setting of *RelativeToBoundingBox* and set *Viewport* to the string "0 0 0.1 0.2". If instead you wanted each tile to occupy 100 device-independent units horizontally and 50 units vertically, you'd set *ViewportUnits* to *Absolute* and set *Viewport* to "0 0 100 50". But in this case you're probably tiling a surface that might be a thousand pixels in width or height. You usually don't see such large *Viewport* values in 3D programming because the *TextureCoordi-nates* values are not large. But you're not required to use small values in the *TextureCoordinates* collection. You could certainly set the *TextureCoordinates* values to three- or four-digit numbers and then use a *Viewport* value of "0 0 100 50" with a *ViewportUnits* setting of *Absolute*.

When I first began discussing *ImageBrush*, I showed a XAML file that put my face on the six sides of a cube. The FaceOnACube1.xaml file has obvious discontinuities at the edges where (for example) the left side the image meets the right side of the image. You might prefer some visual continuity at the edges, and you can partially do that by flipping images around the vertical axis. For example, the images on the front and back of the cube might be normal, but the images on the left and right sides would be flipped so the edges match up.

The big question then becomes: What are you going to do about the top and bottom? You can also preserve visual continuity on the top and bottom by essentially duplicating a single row of pixels across an entire surface. That's the premise behind the next program, which is mostly the same as FaceOnACube1.xaml.

FaceOnACube2.xaml

```xml
<!-- ============================================
     FaceOnACube2.xaml (c) 2007 by Charles Petzold
     ============================================ -->

. . .

                        <GeometryModel3D.Geometry>

                            <!-- Unit cube. -->
                            <MeshGeometry3D
                                Positions="-0.5  0.5  0.5,  0.5  0.5  0.5,
                                           -0.5 -0.5  0.5,  0.5 -0.5  0.5,
                                            0.5  0.5 -0.5, -0.5  0.5 -0.5,
                                            0.5 -0.5 -0.5, -0.5 -0.5 -0.5,
                                           -0.5  0.5 -0.5, -0.5  0.5  0.5,
                                           -0.5 -0.5 -0.5, -0.5 -0.5  0.5,
                                            0.5  0.5  0.5,  0.5  0.5 -0.5,
                                            0.5 -0.5  0.5,  0.5 -0.5 -0.5,
                                           -0.5  0.5 -0.5,  0.5  0.5 -0.5,
                                           -0.5  0.5  0.5,  0.5  0.5  0.5,
                                            0.5 -0.5 -0.5, -0.5 -0.5 -0.5,
                                            0.5 -0.5  0.5, -0.5 -0.5  0.5"

                                TriangleIndices=" 0  2  1,  1  2  3
                                                  4  6  5,  5  6  7,
                                                  8 10  9,  9 10 11,
                                                 12 14 13, 13 14 15,
                                                 16 18 17, 17 18 19,
                                                 20 22 23, 20 23 21"

                                TextureCoordinates="0 0, 1 0, 0 1, 1 1,
                                                    0 0, 1 0, 0 1, 1 1,
                                                    1 0, 0 0, 1 1, 0 1,
                                                    1 0, 0 0, 1 1, 0 1,
                                                    1 0, 0 0, 0 0, 1 0,
                                                    0 1, 1 1, 1 1, 0 1" />
                        </GeometryModel3D.Geometry>

                        <GeometryModel3D.Material>
                            <DiffuseMaterial>
                                <DiffuseMaterial.Brush>
                                    <ImageBrush
                    ImageSource="http://www.charlespetzold.com/PetzoldTattoo.jpg" />
                                </DiffuseMaterial.Brush>
                            </DiffuseMaterial>
                        </GeometryModel3D.Material>

. . .
```

In the *Positions* collection, the vertices for each face are defined in this order: upper-left, upper-right, lower-left, and lower-right. The first two lines in the *TextureCoordinates* collection are for the front and back, and the coordinates are (0, 0), (1, 0), (0, 1), and (1, 1). For the left and right faces, the order is (1, 0), (0, 0), (1, 1) and (0, 1), which swaps the left and right sides of the bitmap to make mirror images.

Take particular note of the treatment of the top and bottom, which are encoded in the last two lines of *TextureCoordinates*. The four points in the *TextureCoordinates* collection for the top of the cube are (1, 0), (0, 0), (0, 0), and (1, 0). These points reference only the top row of pixels of the bitmap, which means that the top of the cube is covered entirely by a single row of pixels swept out over two triangles:

It might seem odd that this works at all. But consider the triangle with indices 17, 18, and 19. This is the triangle on the top of the cube that abuts the front and right sides. The *Positions* values corresponding to these vertices are (0.5, 0.5 −0.5), (−0.5, 0.5, 0.5), and (0.5, 0.5, 0.5), and the *TextureCoordinates* are (0, 0), (0, 0), and (1, 0), so that any point within that triangle corresponds to a point on the image between (0, 0) and (1, 0).

If you're really detail oriented, you might even notice that I changed the last line of *Triangle-Indices* from these values used in previous incarnations of the unit cube:

```
20 22 21, 21 22 23
```

to these:

```
20 22 23, 20 23 21
```

The choice was purely aesthetic, and only affects the bottom of the cube, which you can scroll into view using the scrollbars. You might want to change the values back to see the effect. If you want to see something funny happen to the top of the cube, set the following attribute in the *ImageBrush*:

```
<ImageBrush Stretch="UniformToFill" ...
```

I draw the line at including an image like *that* in this book!

For complex 3D figures—faces or animals perhaps—often a custom bitmap is created that would look very odd if viewed normally because it contains exterior views of all sides of the figure. Similar to that concept is the following image, which consists of different views of my head rather crudely stitched together into one bitmap:

This image is stored on the home page of my Web site at *http://www.charlespetzold.com/ Petzold360.jpg*. It was originally created for wrapping around a sphere (and I'll demonstrate that in the next chapter) but there's no reason why it can't be wrapped around a cube.

Wrapping a single bitmap around a cube is fairly straightforward only if we ignore the top and bottom. But if you want part of the bitmap on the top and bottom of the cube—much like a real head—you must adjust the mesh geometry somewhat. The top and bottom of the image should fold over onto the top and bottom of the cube, like the following.

CubeHeadWithFlaps.xaml

The *Positions* collection needs to be redefined so that the top and bottom faces of the cube consist of six points rather than four. The point in the center of the top is shared among four triangles. That point maps to the point (0.5, 0) of the bitmap. Similarly, a point in the center of the bottom face of the cube maps to the bitmap point (0.5, 1). The right-rear vertex of the top and bottom face appears twice to accommodate the left and right sides of the bitmap. Most of the file is the same as FaceOnACube1.xaml.

FaceOnACube3.xaml

```
<!-- ===============================================
        FaceOnACube3.xaml (c) 2007 by Charles Petzold
     =============================================== -->

    ...

                    <GeometryModel3D.Geometry>

                        <!-- Unit cube. -->
                        <MeshGeometry3D
                            Positions="-0.5  0.5  0.5,   0.5  0.5  0.5,
                                       -0.5 -0.5  0.5,   0.5 -0.5  0.5,
                                        0.5  0.5 -0.5,  -0.5  0.5 -0.5,
                                        0.5 -0.5 -0.5,  -0.5 -0.5 -0.5,
                                       -0.5  0.5 -0.5,  -0.5  0.5  0.5,
                                       -0.5 -0.5 -0.5,  -0.5 -0.5  0.5,
                                        0.5  0.5  0.5,   0.5  0.5 -0.5,
                                        0.5 -0.5  0.5,   0.5 -0.5 -0.5,

                                        0    0.5  0,     0.5  0.5 -0.5,
                                       -0.5  0.5 -0.5,  -0.5  0.5  0.5,
                                        0.5  0.5  0.5,   0.5  0.5 -0.5,

                                        0   -0.5  0,     0.5 -0.5 -0.5,
                                       -0.5 -0.5 -0.5,  -0.5 -0.5  0.5,
                                        0.5 -0.5  0.5,   0.5 -0.5 -0.5"

                            TriangleIndices=" 0  2  1,   1  2  3
                                              4  6  5,   5  6  7,
                                              8 10  9,   9 10 11,
                                             12 14 13,  13 14 15,

                                             16 17 18,  16 18 19,
                                             16 19 20,  16 20 21,

                                             22 24 23,  22 25 24,
                                             22 26 25,  22 27 26"

                            TextureCoordinates=
                                "0.50 0.2, 0.75 0.2, 0.50 0.8, 0.75 0.8,
                                 0.00 0.2, 0.25 0.2, 0.00 0.8, 0.25 0.8,
                                 0.25 0.2, 0.50 0.2, 0.25 0.8, 0.50 0.8,
                                 0.75 0.2, 1.00 0.2, 0.75 0.8, 1.00 0.8,
```

```
                              0.50 0,   0     0.2, 0.25 0.2,
                              0.50 0.2, 0.75 0.2, 1.00 0.2,

                              0.50 1,   0     0.8, 0.25 0.8,
                              0.50 0.8, 0.75 0.8, 1.00 0.8" />
        </GeometryModel3D.Geometry>

        <GeometryModel3D.Material>
            <DiffuseMaterial>
                <DiffuseMaterial.Brush>
                    <ImageBrush
    ImageSource="http://www.charlespetzold.com/Petzold360.jpg" />
                </DiffuseMaterial.Brush>
            </DiffuseMaterial>
        </GeometryModel3D.Material>
```

. . .

The last part of both the *Positions* collection and the *TextureCoordinates* collections shows six vertices for the top of the cube and six for the bottom; the *TriangleIndices* collection shows four triangles for the top and four for the bottom. The center of the bitmap is aligned with the left-front edge of the cube. A seam—where the left of the bitmap meets the right—runs from the center of the top face, down the left-rear edge, and then to the center of the bottom face.

You might not think that looks very realistic, but it's probably better than the other image wrapped around the cube in the same way, as follows.

Efficiency Issues

An important blog entry on 3D performance (*http://blogs.msdn.com/wpfsdk/archive/2007/01/15/maximizing-wpf-3d-performance-on-tier-2-hardware.aspx*) ranked brushes from fastest to slowest:

- *SolidColorBrush*
- *LinearGradientBrush*
- *ImageBrush*
- *DrawingBrush* (cached)
- *VisualBrush* (cached)
- *RadialGradientBrush*
- *DrawingBrush* (uncached)
- *VisualBrush* (uncached)

The problem with *DrawingBrush* and *VisualBrush*—the two brushes I'm about to discuss—is that the brushes are re-rendered whenever the 3D scene needs to be updated. You can help speed things up in a couple of ways when you need to use these brushes.

If the content of the brush is entirely static and of a fixed size, you might want to create a bitmap from the image in code, and then use that bitmap in an *ImageBrush*. You do this by creating an object of type *RenderTargetBitmap*, specifying a particular pixel size and resolution in the constructor. You can then call the *Render* method to render objects of type *Visual* on the bitmap.

If the contents of the *DrawingBrush* or *VisualBrush* do not change, you can help the WPF 3D system by setting the attached property *Render.CachingHint* to the enumeration member

CachingHint.Cache. This property suggests to WPF 3D that the brush can be cached in memory and needn't be recreated. In code, if *brush* is an object of type *DrawingBrush* or *Visual-Brush*, you set the attached property like this:

```
RenderOptions.SetCachingHint(brush, CachingHint.Cache);
```

In XAML, you can supply the attached property along with other attributes in the *Drawing-Brush* or *VisualBrush* tag:

```
<DrawingBrush RenderOptions.CachingHint="Cache" ...
```

The *RenderOptions* class defines two other related properties that you can use in the same way: *CacheInvalidationThresholdMinimum* and *CacheInvalidationThresholdMaximum*. Both are of type *double.* You set these to values that indicate a change in size allowed before the brush is regenerated. For example, if you set *CacheInvalidationThresholdMinimum* to 0.25, the brush isn't regenerated until its size is one-quarter of its original size. Similarly, you set *CacheInvali-dationThresholdMaximum* to a value greater than one.

Brushes Based on Drawings

The *DrawingBrush* is very similar to the *ImageBrush* and inherits all the same properties from *TileBrush.* You generally use *DrawingBrush* to create a brush based on vector-graphics drawing objects, including straight lines, Bezier curves, rectangles, ellipses, and arcs.

DrawingBrush defines one property on its own named *Drawing* of type *Drawing. Drawing* is an abstract class from which descend *GeometryDrawing, ImageDrawing, GlyphRunDrawing, Video-Drawing,* and *DrawingGroup* (for combining *Drawing* objects).

Generally you'll use one or more *GeometryDrawing* objects in connection with a *DrawingBrush*; if you have more than one, you can combine them in a *DrawingGroup.* However, you can also combine drawings and bitmap images using the *ImageDrawing* class. This class defines a property named *ImageSource* that you set to a bitmap.

Here's the general syntax when you require only one *GeometryDrawing* object:

```
<DrawingBrush ...>
    <DrawingBrush.Drawing>
        <GeometryDrawing ...>
            ...
        </GeometryDrawing>
    </DrawingBrush.Drawing>
</DrawingBrush>
```

The *GeometryDrawing* class defines *Brush, Pen,* and *Geometry* properties. If the drawing includes some enclosed areas that you want filled with a brush, here's where you define that brush. If you only need a *SolidColorBrush*, you can specify the color in the *GeometryDrawing* tag:

```
<GeometryDrawing Brush="Magenta">
```

Otherwise, you'll have to break out the *Brush* property as a property element:

```
<GeometryDrawing>
    ...
    <GeometryDrawing.Brush>
        ...
    </GeometryDrawing.Brush>
    ...
</GeometryDrawing>
```

If you want lines in the drawing to be stroked with a pen, the pen must be specified as a property element:

```
<GeometryDrawing>
    ...
    <GeometryDrawing.Pen>
        <Pen Brush="Black" Thickness="2.5" />
    </GeometryDrawing.Pen>
    ...
</GeometryDrawing>
```

The *Pen* has other properties as well, including end caps and line joins. If you want to base the *Pen* on anything but a *SolidColorBrush*, you must again break out the *Brush* property of *Pen* as a property element.

If your drawing requires multiple pen colors or multiple fill colors, each different color combination must be a separate *GeometryDrawing* object. You can group multiple *GeometryDrawing* objects in a *DrawingGroup*.

The actual lines that define the drawing are specified as *Geometry* objects. *Geometry* is an abstract class that is parent to *LineGeometry*, *RectangleGeometry*, *EllipseGeometry*, *PathGeometry*, *StreamGeometry*, *CombinedGeometry*, and *GeometryGroup*. You can use *GeometryGroup* to combine multiple geometries in a single *GeometryDrawing*:

```
<GeometryDrawing>
    ...
    <GeometryDrawing.Geometry>
        <GeometryGroup>
            <EllipseGeometry ... />
            <LineGeometry ... />
            <LineGeometry ... />
        </GeometryGroup>
    </GeometryDrawing.Geometry>
    ...
</GeometryDrawing>
```

I've mentioned two types of groups. *DrawingGroup* generally combines multiple *Geometry-Drawing* objects, each of which has its own *Brush*, *Pen*, and *Geometry* properties. *Geometry-Group* combines multiple *Geometry* objects.

You can also set the *Geometry* property of *GeometryDrawing* to a string that encodes straight lines and curves:

```
<GeometryDrawing Geometry="M 0 0 L 100 50 ... ">
```

The syntax of this string is documented in a page entitled "Path Markup Syntax" found in the Geometry section of the Graphics section of the overviews of the Windows Presentation Foundation. This example shows codes for "move" and "line."

You construct a drawing using various coordinates. When you're all done, the whole drawing fits in a bounding box available as the get-only *Bounds* property (of type *Rect*) defined by the *Geometry* class. This rectangle is generally a bit larger than the coordinates you specified because it also includes pen widths. For example, an ellipse with a radius of 100 units drawn with a pen 6 units wide will have a total width and height of 206 units. This is the size of the rectangle that becomes a single tile of the brush.

It's important to make the coordinates of your drawing and the width of the pen consistent; otherwise, lines can look very thick or very thin. Watch out for drawings expanding into the space allowed for them: The default *Stretch* property is *Fill*, and if the drawing consists simply of a horizontal or vertical line, that line will fill the entire tile. If you want some margin around the drawing, you might want to begin with a rectangle filled with a background brush. That brush can be transparent if you want a margin of the drawing to be transparent.

The following program displays three cubes with three different *DrawingBrush* objects. To prevent excessive indentation, all three brushes (as well as the *MeshGeometry3D*) are defined as resources. Consequently, the three *GeometryModel3D* objects are very compact.

CubesWithDrawingBrushes.xaml

```xml
<!-- ==========================================================
     CubesWithDrawingBrushes.xaml (c) 2007 by Charles Petzold
     ========================================================== -->
<Page xmlns="http://schemas.microsoft.com/winfx/2006/xaml/presentation"
      xmlns:x="http://schemas.microsoft.com/winfx/2006/xaml"
      WindowTitle="Cubes with Drawing Brushes"
      Title="Cubes with Drawing Brushes">
    <Page.Resources>

        <!-- MeshGeometry3D of unit cube. -->
        <MeshGeometry3D x:Key="cube"
            Positions="-0.5  0.5  0.5,  0.5  0.5  0.5,
                       -0.5 -0.5  0.5,  0.5 -0.5  0.5,
                        0.5  0.5 -0.5, -0.5  0.5 -0.5,
                        0.5 -0.5 -0.5, -0.5 -0.5 -0.5,
                       -0.5  0.5 -0.5, -0.5  0.5  0.5,
                       -0.5 -0.5 -0.5, -0.5 -0.5  0.5,
                        0.5  0.5  0.5,  0.5  0.5 -0.5,
                        0.5 -0.5  0.5,  0.5  0.5 -0.5,
                       -0.5  0.5 -0.5,  0.5  0.5 -0.5,
                       -0.5  0.5  0.5,  0.5  0.5  0.5,
                        0.5 -0.5 -0.5, -0.5 -0.5 -0.5,
                        0.5 -0.5  0.5, -0.5 -0.5  0.5"
```

```
        TriangleIndices=" 0  2  1,  1  2  3
                          4  6  5,  5  6  7,
                          8 10  9,  9 10 11,
                         12 14 13, 13 14 15
                         16 18 17, 17 18 19
                         20 22 21, 21 22 23"

        TextureCoordinates="0 0, 1 0, 0 1, 1 1,
                            0 0, 1 0, 0 1, 1 1,
                            0 0, 1 0, 0 1, 1 1,
                            0 0, 1 0, 0 1, 1 1,
                            0 0, 1 0, 0 1, 1 1,
                            0 0, 1 0, 0 1, 1 1" />


    <!-- DrawingBrush with ellipse. -->
    <DiffuseMaterial x:Key="ellipse">
        <DiffuseMaterial.Brush>
            <DrawingBrush RenderOptions.CachingHint="Cache"
                    TileMode="Tile" Viewport="0 0 0.2 0.2">
                <DrawingBrush.Drawing>
                    <GeometryDrawing Brush="Cyan">
                        <GeometryDrawing.Pen>
                            <Pen Brush="Red" />
                        </GeometryDrawing.Pen>
                        <GeometryDrawing.Geometry>
                            <EllipseGeometry RadiusX="4"
                                             RadiusY="4" />
                        </GeometryDrawing.Geometry>
                    </GeometryDrawing>
                </DrawingBrush.Drawing>
            </DrawingBrush>
        </DiffuseMaterial.Brush>
    </DiffuseMaterial>


    <!-- DrawingBrush with bricks. -->
    <DiffuseMaterial x:Key="bricks">
        <DiffuseMaterial.Brush>
            <DrawingBrush RenderOptions.CachingHint="Cache"
                    TileMode="Tile" Viewport="0 0 0.1 0.1">
                <DrawingBrush.Drawing>
                    <DrawingGroup>

                        <GeometryDrawing Brush="LightGray">
                            <GeometryDrawing.Geometry>
                                <RectangleGeometry Rect="0 0 20 20" />
                            </GeometryDrawing.Geometry>
                        </GeometryDrawing>

                        <GeometryDrawing Brush="Brown">
                            <GeometryDrawing.Geometry>
                                <GeometryGroup>
                                    <RectangleGeometry Rect="0 1 9 8" />
                                    <RectangleGeometry Rect="11 1 9 8" />
                                    <RectangleGeometry Rect="1 11 18 8" />
                                </GeometryGroup>
```

```xml
                              </GeometryDrawing.Geometry>
                          </GeometryDrawing>

                      </DrawingGroup>
                  </DrawingBrush.Drawing>
              </DrawingBrush>
          </DiffuseMaterial.Brush>
      </DiffuseMaterial>

      <!-- DrawingBrush with diagonal hatch marks. -->
      <DiffuseMaterial x:Key="hatch">
          <DiffuseMaterial.Brush>
              <DrawingBrush RenderOptions.CachingHint="Cache"
                        TileMode="Tile" Viewport="0 0 0.2 0.2"
                        Viewbox="0 0 100 100" ViewboxUnits="Absolute">
                  <DrawingBrush.Drawing>
                      <DrawingGroup>

                          <GeometryDrawing Brush="White"
                              Geometry="M 0 0 L 100 0 L 100 100 L 0 100 Z" />

                          <GeometryDrawing Geometry="M  -10 77.5 L  22.5  110
                                                     M  -10 52.5 L  47.5  110
                                                     M  -10 27.5 L  72.5  110
                                                     M  -10  2.5 L  97.5  110
                                                     M  2.5  -10 L  110 97.5
                                                     M 27.5  -10 L  110 72.5
                                                     M 52.5  -10 L  110 47.5
                                                     M 77.5  -10 L  110 22.5">
                              <GeometryDrawing.Pen>
                                  <Pen Brush="Black" Thickness="4" />
                              </GeometryDrawing.Pen>
                          </GeometryDrawing>
                      </DrawingGroup>
                  </DrawingBrush.Drawing>
              </DrawingBrush>
          </DiffuseMaterial.Brush>
      </DiffuseMaterial>
  </Page.Resources>

  <DockPanel>
      <ScrollBar Name="horz" DockPanel.Dock="Bottom" Orientation="Horizontal"
              Minimum="-180" Maximum="180"
              LargeChange="10" SmallChange="1" />

      <ScrollBar Name="vert" DockPanel.Dock="Right" Orientation="Vertical"
              Minimum="-180" Maximum="180"
              LargeChange="10" SmallChange="1" />

      <Viewport3D>
          <ModelVisual3D>
              <ModelVisual3D.Content>
                  <Model3DGroup>
```

```xml
                    <!-- Cube with ellipse brush. -->
                    <GeometryModel3D Geometry="{StaticResource cube}"
                                Material="{StaticResource ellipse}"
                                BackMaterial="{StaticResource ellipse}">
                        <GeometryModel3D.Transform>
                            <TranslateTransform3D OffsetX="-1.5"
                                                OffsetY="1.5" />
                        </GeometryModel3D.Transform>
                    </GeometryModel3D>

                    <!-- Cube with bricks brush. -->
                    <GeometryModel3D Geometry="{StaticResource cube}"
                                Material="{StaticResource bricks}" />

                    <!-- Cube with hatch brush. -->
                    <GeometryModel3D Geometry="{StaticResource cube}"
                                Material="{StaticResource hatch}">
                        <GeometryModel3D.Transform>
                            <TranslateTransform3D OffsetX="1.5"
                                                OffsetY="-1.5" />
                        </GeometryModel3D.Transform>
                    </GeometryModel3D>
                </Model3DGroup>
            </ModelVisual3D.Content>

            <!-- Rotation transforms bound to scrollbars. -->
            <ModelVisual3D.Transform>
                <Transform3DGroup>
                    <RotateTransform3D>
                        <RotateTransform3D.Rotation>
                            <AxisAngleRotation3D Axis="0 1 0"
                                Angle="{Binding ElementName=horz,
                                                Path=Value}" />
                        </RotateTransform3D.Rotation>
                    </RotateTransform3D>
                    <RotateTransform3D>
                        <RotateTransform3D.Rotation>
                            <AxisAngleRotation3D Axis="1 0 0"
                                Angle="{Binding ElementName=vert,
                                                Path=Value}" />
                        </RotateTransform3D.Rotation>
                    </RotateTransform3D>
                </Transform3DGroup>
            </ModelVisual3D.Transform>
        </ModelVisual3D>

        <!-- Light source. -->
        <ModelVisual3D>
            <ModelVisual3D.Content>
                <AmbientLight Color="White" />
            </ModelVisual3D.Content>
        </ModelVisual3D>
```

```
            <!-- Camera. -->
            <Viewport3D.Camera>
                <PerspectiveCamera Position="0 0 10"
                                   LookDirection="0 0 -10"
                                   UpDirection="0 1 0"
                                   FieldOfView="30" />
            </Viewport3D.Camera>
        </Viewport3D>
    </DockPanel>
</Page>
```

The first *DrawingBrush* is the resource named "ellipse." The tiles consist of an ellipse with a red outline and a fill brush of cyan. The corners around the ellipse are transparent, so I used the same brush for the *BackMaterial* property of the *GeometryModel3D*. You can see through the corners of each tile to the same tiles on the inside of the cube:

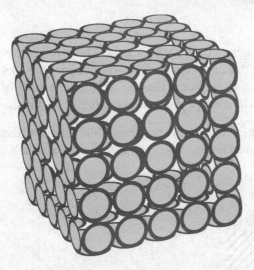

Notice how wide the outline of the ellipse is compared to its overall size. This is a result of having a radius of four units and a default pen width of one unit. Both the width and height of the brush measure nine units. (The pen renders the circumference of the ellipse as one unit wide and centered around the geometrical border of the ellipse so it extends beyond the radius one-half unit in all directions.)

The second *DrawingBrush* simulates bricks:

The tile is one-tenth of the width and height of the side of the cube. The brush consists of a light-gray background (the mortar) with three brown rectangles—the two partial bricks on the top of each tile and the full brick on the bottom. Notice that the rectangle for the light-gray background is given a size of 20 units, which effectively defines the size of the brush.

The third *DrawingBrush* was in theory the simplest and most basic, but it gave me the most trouble. It was intended to simulate diagonal hatch marks such as those available in Windows since its earliest versions:

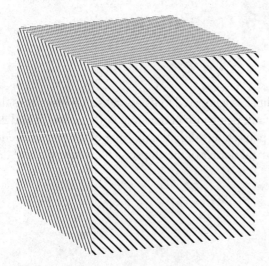

I defined a white background as a square with sides of 100 units. The hatch marks were originally defined like so:

```
<GeometryDrawing Geometry="M  0 75 L  25 100
                           M  0 50 L  50 100
                           M  0 25 L  75 100
                           M  0  0 L 100 100
                           M 25  0 L 100  75
                           M 50  0 L 100  50
                           M 75  0 L 100  25">
```

This geometry path draws lines from (0, 75) to (25, 100) and so forth. However, the image didn't look good at all. It was obvious where one tile ended and the other began because little gaps existed in the lines at the border of the square. The problem, I realized, was that the lines began and ended with a flat line cap. Rather than mess around with the line caps (which I feared wouldn't entirely solve the problem), I decided to decrease the coordinates of all the "move" points by 25 units and increase all the "line" points by 25 units so that the first one became a line from (−25, 50) to (50 125). That required me to add a *Viewbox* attribute to restrict the brush to just the area in the 100-unit square:

```
<DrawingBrush RenderOptions.CachingHint="Cache"
                     TileMode="Tile" Viewport="0 0 0.2 0.2"
                     Viewbox="0 0 100 100" ViewboxUnits="Absolute">
```

This fixed the problem except for the line now going from (−25, −25) to (125, 125). That line still had a little gap at the tile corners, and I realized it was the result of the *Viewbox* truncating the shape of the tile to a square. The corner of that square shaved off part of the line extending between the two corners. So I shifted all the lines over by 12.5 units, and that seemed to do the trick.

The *VisualBrush*

I began my discussion of tile brushes indicating that the *ImageBrush*, *DrawingBrush*, and *VisualBrush* all overlapped in functionality: You can set the *ImageSource* property of *Image-Brush* to an object of type *DrawingImage*, which is based on a *Drawing* object. Likewise, you can set the *Drawing* property of *DrawingBrush* to an object of type *ImageDrawing*, which itself has an *ImageSource* property that you can set to a bitmap.

The *VisualBrush* continues this virtuosity. *Visual* is the class from which *UIElement* and then *FrameworkElement* and then *Control* descend, so *VisualBrush* lets you base brushes on *Image* elements (to display bitmaps) or descendents of the *Shapes* class (to display vector drawings).

I find *VisualBrush* most useful for a couple of applications that can't be handled with *Image-Brush* or *DrawingBrush*. Basing a brush on a text string is easy if you set the *Visual* property of *VisualBrush* to an object of type *TextBlock*. If you need multiple lines of text in your brush with various fonts and colors, you can combine multiple *TextBlock* elements—or elements of any type—using one of the various *Panel* elements available, such as *StackPanel*, *Grid*, and *Canvas*. The *Panel* class derives from *FrameworkElement*, so it's also an object of type *Visual*.

This is a slightly updated version of one of the first animated 3D programs I ever wrote. A *DiffuseMaterial* based on a *VisualBrush* is defined as a resource and used for both the *Material* and *BackMaterial* properties of a *GeometryModel3D*.

Hello3D.xaml

```xml
<!-- =======================================
     Hello3D.xaml (c) 2007 by Charles Petzold
     ======================================= -->
<Page xmlns="http://schemas.microsoft.com/winfx/2006/xaml/presentation"
      xmlns:x="http://schemas.microsoft.com/winfx/2006/xaml"
      WindowTitle="Hello 3D"
      Title="Hello 3D">
    <Page.Resources>

        <!-- Define Material object as resource. -->
        <DiffuseMaterial x:Key="materialText">
            <DiffuseMaterial.Brush>
                <VisualBrush RenderOptions.CachingHint="Cache">
                    <VisualBrush.Visual>
                        <TextBlock FontFamily="Times New Roman"
                                   Text="Hello, 3D!" />
                    </VisualBrush.Visual>
                </VisualBrush>
            </DiffuseMaterial.Brush>
        </DiffuseMaterial>
    </Page.Resources>


    <Viewport3D>
        <ModelVisual3D>
            <ModelVisual3D.Content>
                <GeometryModel3D Material="{StaticResource materialText}"
                                 BackMaterial="{StaticResource materialText}">

                    <!-- Define a unit square. -->
                    <GeometryModel3D.Geometry>
                        <MeshGeometry3D
                            Positions="0 0 0, 0 1 0, 1 0 0, 1 1 0"
                            TriangleIndices="0 2 3, 0 3 1"
                            TextureCoordinates="0 1, 0 0, 1 1, 1 0" />
                    </GeometryModel3D.Geometry>

                    <!-- Transform applied to visual object. -->
                    <GeometryModel3D.Transform>
                        <RotateTransform3D>
                            <RotateTransform3D.Rotation>
                                <AxisAngleRotation3D x:Name="xform"
                                                     Axis="0,1,0" />
                            </RotateTransform3D.Rotation>
                        </RotateTransform3D>
                    </GeometryModel3D.Transform>
```

```
                        </GeometryModel3D>
                    </ModelVisual3D.Content>
                </ModelVisual3D>

                <!-- Ambient light. -->
                <ModelVisual3D>
                    <ModelVisual3D.Content>
                        <AmbientLight Color="White" />
                    </ModelVisual3D.Content>
                </ModelVisual3D>

                <!-- Camera. -->
                <Viewport3D.Camera>
                    <PerspectiveCamera Position="0 0.5 1.5" LookDirection="0 0 -1"
                                       UpDirection="0 1 0" FieldOfView="120" />
                </Viewport3D.Camera>
            </Viewport3D>

            <!-- Animate the transform. -->
            <Page.Triggers>
                <EventTrigger RoutedEvent="Page.Loaded">
                    <BeginStoryboard>
                        <Storyboard TargetName="xform" TargetProperty="Angle">
                            <DoubleAnimation From="360" To="0" Duration="0:0:10"
                                             RepeatBehavior="Forever" />
                        </Storyboard>
                    </BeginStoryboard>
                </EventTrigger>
            </Page.Triggers>
        </Page>
```

Suppose you wanted to display a cube with six different colors on its six sides. You can do this by splitting the cube up into six different *GeometryModel3D* objects, each with a separate *Material* object and a different color. Alternatively, you can use one *GeometryModel3D* and create a *DrawingBrush* with six different *Drawing* objects for the six different sides. You then reference different parts of that *Drawing* using the *TextureCoordinates* collection.

The following program is similar to that second approach except that it uses a *UniformGrid* panel containing six rows. Each of the rows contains a *Rectangle* object with a different fill brush. Most of the file is the same as FaceOnACube1.xaml.

PaneledCube.xaml

```
<!-- ===========================================
     PaneledCube.xaml (c) 2007 by Charles Petzold
     =========================================== -->

. . .

                        <GeometryModel3D.Geometry>

                            <!-- Unit cube. -->
```

```
                        <MeshGeometry3D
                            Positions="-0.5  0.5  0.5,   0.5  0.5  0.5,
                                       -0.5 -0.5  0.5,   0.5 -0.5  0.5,
                                        0.5  0.5 -0.5,  -0.5  0.5 -0.5,
                                        0.5 -0.5 -0.5,  -0.5 -0.5 -0.5,
                                       -0.5  0.5 -0.5,  -0.5  0.5  0.5,
                                       -0.5 -0.5 -0.5,  -0.5 -0.5  0.5,
                                        0.5  0.5  0.5,   0.5  0.5 -0.5,
                                        0.5 -0.5  0.5,   0.5 -0.5 -0.5,
                                       -0.5  0.5 -0.5,   0.5  0.5 -0.5,
                                       -0.5  0.5  0.5,   0.5  0.5  0.5,
                                        0.5 -0.5 -0.5,  -0.5 -0.5 -0.5,
                                        0.5 -0.5  0.5,  -0.5 -0.5  0.5"

                            TriangleIndices=" 0  2  1,   1  2  3
                                              4  6  5,   5  6  7,
                                              8 10  9,   9 10 11,
                                             12 14 13,  13 14 15
                                             16 18 17,  17 18 19
                                             20 22 21,  21 22 23"

                            TextureCoordinates=
                                "0.000 0, 0.167 0, 0.000 1, 0.167 1,
                                 0.167 0, 0.333 0, 0.167 1, 0.333 1,
                                 0.333 0, 0.500 0, 0.333 1, 0.500 1,
                                 0.500 0, 0.667 0, 0.500 1, 0.667 1,
                                 0.667 0, 0.833 0, 0.667 1, 0.833 1,
                                 0.833 0, 1.000 0, 0.833 1, 1.000 1" />
                    </GeometryModel3D.Geometry>

                    <GeometryModel3D.Material>
                        <DiffuseMaterial>
                            <DiffuseMaterial.Brush>
                                <VisualBrush
                                    RenderOptions.CachingHint="Cache">
                                    <VisualBrush.Visual>
<UniformGrid Rows="1" Columns="6">
    <Rectangle Width="10" Height="10" Fill="#FF0000" />
    <Rectangle Width="10" Height="10" Fill="#FFFF00" />
    <Rectangle Width="10" Height="10" Fill="#00FF00" />
    <Rectangle Width="10" Height="10" Fill="#00FFFF" />
    <Rectangle Width="10" Height="10" Fill="#0000FF" />
    <Rectangle Width="10" Height="10" Fill="#FF00FF" />
</UniformGrid>
                                    </VisualBrush.Visual>
                                </VisualBrush>
                            </DiffuseMaterial.Brush>
                        </DiffuseMaterial>
                    </GeometryModel3D.Material>
```

...

Another class that derives from *Visual* is *Viewport3D*, which means that you can cover a 3D figure with a brush based on... yes, another 3D figure! Not the *same* 3D figure, but perhaps another one very much like it.

That's the premise behind the following program. A *MeshGeometry3D* and a complete *Viewport3D* using that geometry are both defined as resources. (The only reason the *Viewport3D* is defined as a resource is to keep the indentation down to a minimum when the *VisualBrush* is defined.) The rest of the file looks rather normal: A *Viewport3D* references the *MeshGeometry3D* resource to display a cube.

```
3DCubeBrush.xaml
<!-- ==========================================
        3DCubeBrush.xaml (c) 2007 by Charles Petzold
     ========================================== -->
<Page xmlns="http://schemas.microsoft.com/winfx/2006/xaml/presentation"
      xmlns:x="http://schemas.microsoft.com/winfx/2006/xaml"
      WindowTitle="3D Cube Brush"
      Title="3D Cube Brush">
    <Page.Resources>
        <!-- Unit cube. -->
        <MeshGeometry3D x:Key="cube"
            Positions="-0.5  0.5  0.5,   0.5  0.5  0.5,
                       -0.5 -0.5  0.5,   0.5 -0.5  0.5,
                        0.5  0.5 -0.5,  -0.5  0.5 -0.5,
                        0.5 -0.5 -0.5,  -0.5 -0.5 -0.5,
                       -0.5  0.5 -0.5,  -0.5  0.5  0.5,
                       -0.5 -0.5 -0.5,  -0.5 -0.5  0.5,
                        0.5  0.5  0.5,   0.5  0.5 -0.5,
                        0.5 -0.5  0.5,   0.5 -0.5 -0.5,
                       -0.5  0.5 -0.5,   0.5  0.5 -0.5,
                       -0.5  0.5  0.5,   0.5  0.5  0.5,
                        0.5 -0.5 -0.5,  -0.5 -0.5 -0.5,
                        0.5 -0.5  0.5,  -0.5 -0.5  0.5"

            TriangleIndices=" 0  2  1,   1  2  3
                              4  6  5,   5  6  7,
                              8 10  9,   9 10 11,
                             12 14 13,  13 14 15
                             16 18 17,  17 18 19
                             20 22 21,  21 22 23"

            TextureCoordinates="0 0, 1 0, 0 1, 1 1,
                                0 0, 1 0, 0 1, 1 1,
                                0 0, 1 0, 0 1, 1 1,
                                0 0, 1 0, 0 1, 1 1,
                                0 0, 1 0, 0 1, 1 1,
                                0 0, 1 0, 0 1, 1 1" />

        <!-- Viewport3D to be used in VisualBrush. -->
        <Viewport3D x:Key="viewport3D" Width="100" Height="100">
            <ModelVisual3D>
                <ModelVisual3D.Content>
```

```
                <Model3DGroup>
                    <GeometryModel3D Geometry="{StaticResource cube}" >
                        <GeometryModel3D.Material>
                            <DiffuseMaterial Brush="Cyan" />
                        </GeometryModel3D.Material>
                    </GeometryModel3D>

                    <!-- Light sources. -->
                    <AmbientLight Color="#404040" />
                    <DirectionalLight Color="#C0C0C0" Direction="2 -3 -1" />
                </Model3DGroup>
            </ModelVisual3D.Content>
        </ModelVisual3D>

        <!-- Camera. -->
        <Viewport3D.Camera>
            <PerspectiveCamera Position="-2 2 4"
                               LookDirection="2 -2 -4"
                               UpDirection="0 1 0"
                               FieldOfView="22.5" />
        </Viewport3D.Camera>
    </Viewport3D>
</Page.Resources>

<DockPanel>
    <ScrollBar Name="horz" DockPanel.Dock="Bottom" Orientation="Horizontal"
               Minimum="-180" Maximum="180"
               LargeChange="10" SmallChange="1" />

    <ScrollBar Name="vert" DockPanel.Dock="Right" Orientation="Vertical"
               Minimum="-180" Maximum="180"
               LargeChange="10" SmallChange="1" />

    <Viewport3D>
        <ModelVisual3D>
            <ModelVisual3D.Content>
                <Model3DGroup>
                    <GeometryModel3D Geometry="{StaticResource cube}">

                        <GeometryModel3D.Material>
                            <DiffuseMaterial>
                                <DiffuseMaterial.Brush>
                                    <VisualBrush TileMode="Tile"
                                                 Viewport="0 0 0.2 0.2"
                                                 RenderOptions.CachingHint=
                                                     "Cache"
                                         Visual= "{StaticResource viewport3D}" />
                                </DiffuseMaterial.Brush>
                            </DiffuseMaterial>
                        </GeometryModel3D.Material>

                        <GeometryModel3D.Transform>
                            <Transform3DGroup>
                                <RotateTransform3D>
                                    <RotateTransform3D.Rotation>
                                        <AxisAngleRotation3D Axis="0 1 0"
```

```
                                          Angle="{Binding ElementName=horz,
                                                   Path=Value}" />
                           </RotateTransform3D.Rotation>
                       </RotateTransform3D>
                       <RotateTransform3D>
                           <RotateTransform3D.Rotation>
                               <AxisAngleRotation3D Axis="1 0 0"
                                     Angle="{Binding ElementName=vert,
                                              Path=Value}" />
                           </RotateTransform3D.Rotation>
                       </RotateTransform3D>
                   </Transform3DGroup>
               </GeometryModel3D.Transform>

           </GeometryModel3D>

           <!-- Light source. -->
           <AmbientLight Color="White" />
           <DirectionalLight Color="Gray" Direction="2 -3 -1" />
       </Model3DGroup>
     </ModelVisual3D.Content>
   </ModelVisual3D>

   <!-- Camera. -->
   <Viewport3D.Camera>
       <PerspectiveCamera Position="-2 2 4"
                          LookDirection="2 -2 -4"
                          UpDirection="0 1 0"
                          FieldOfView="22.5" />
   </Viewport3D.Camera>
  </Viewport3D>
 </DockPanel>
</Page>
```

The difference here is that the *Material* object is based on a *VisualBrush* that references the *Viewport3D* resource, so that the cube seems to be covered with miniature 3D cubes:

You might need to convince yourself that those brushes covering the sides of the cube are actually flat. Use the *ScrollBar* controls and the right and bottom to bring a side into a sharper viewing angle. Those little cubes are flat, although the cube certainly looks like it's built from 25 little cubes on each side.

You might also have a little fun by moving the two transforms (the block of markup beginning and ending with the *GeometryModel3D.Transform* tags) into the *GeometryModel3D* element in the resource section. Now the scrollbars rotate the little cubes used in the brush. You can actually *copy* that block of markup and have the scrollbars rotating both the large cube and the little brush cubes.

Some objects of type *Visual*—such as *TextBlock* when it contains some text or *Button* when it contains some content—have a specific metrical dimension that the *VisualBrush* uses for tiling. *Viewport3D*, however, does not, and you must explicitly assigned its *Width* and *Height* properties before you use it in a brush.

The *System.Windows.Media.Media3D* namespace defines a *Viewport3DVisual* class that inherits directly from *Visual*. This is a class used mostly internally in WPF to bridge the gap between WPF 3D and two-dimensional visuals. But you can also use it when defining a *VisualBrush*. In 3DCubeBrush.xaml, change the *Viewport3D* resource to a *Viewport3DVisual* resource by replacing the *Width* and *Height* attributes with a *Viewport* attribute:

```
<Viewport3DVisual x:Key="viewport3D" Viewport="0 0 100 100">
```

Specular and Emissive Materials

Like many classes in the *System.Windows.Media.Media3D* namespace, the abstract *Material* class derives from *Animatable*. It has four descendents, as shown in the following class hierarchy:

```
Object
    DispatcherObject (abstract)
        DependencyObject
            Freezable (abstract)
                Animatable (abstract)
                    Material (abstract)
                        DiffuseMaterial (sealed)
                        EmissiveMaterial (sealed)
                        MaterialGroup (sealed)
                        SpecularMaterial (sealed)
```

The *MaterialGroup* class lets you layer materials. It defines a content property named *Children* of type *MaterialCollection*, which is a collection of *Material* objects:

```
<GeometryModel3D.Material>
    <MaterialGroup>
        <DiffuseMaterial ... />
        <DiffuseMaterial ... />
    </MaterialGroup>
</GeometryModel3D.Material>
```

When stacking *DiffuseMaterial* objects, the second brush appears on top of the first one. Obviously this example wouldn't make much sense unless that second *DiffuseMaterial* brush were partially transparent. That second brush could be as simple as a partially transparent solid color providing a tint to the brush underneath, or a more complex brush in itself.

The following program is a variation of the FaceOnACube files presented earlier in this chapter. The *ImageBrush* is now in a *MaterialGroup* with a *DrawingBrush* on top that defines some quadratic splines that effectively draw a silly mustache on my face. Most of the file is the same as FaceOnACube1.xaml.

MustachedFaceOnACube.xaml

```
<!-- ========================================================
      MustachedFaceOnACube.xaml (c) 2007 by Charles Petzold
     ======================================================== -->

  • • •

                        <GeometryModel3D.Geometry>

                            <!-- Unit cube. -->
                            <MeshGeometry3D
                                Positions="-0.5  0.5  0.5,   0.5  0.5  0.5,
                                           -0.5 -0.5  0.5,   0.5 -0.5  0.5,
                                            0.5  0.5 -0.5,  -0.5  0.5 -0.5,
                                            0.5 -0.5 -0.5,  -0.5 -0.5 -0.5,
                                           -0.5  0.5 -0.5,  -0.5  0.5  0.5,
                                           -0.5 -0.5 -0.5,  -0.5 -0.5  0.5,
                                            0.5  0.5  0.5,   0.5  0.5 -0.5,
                                            0.5 -0.5  0.5,   0.5 -0.5 -0.5,
                                           -0.5  0.5 -0.5,   0.5  0.5 -0.5,
                                           -0.5  0.5  0.5,   0.5  0.5  0.5,
                                            0.5 -0.5 -0.5,  -0.5 -0.5 -0.5,
                                            0.5 -0.5  0.5,  -0.5 -0.5  0.5"

                                TriangleIndices=" 0  2  1,   1  2  3
                                                  4  6  5,   5  6  7,
                                                  8 10  9,   9 10 11,
                                                 12 14 13,  13 14 15
                                                 16 18 17,  17 18 19
                                                 20 22 21,  21 22 23"

                                TextureCoordinates="0 0,  1 0,  0 1,  1 1,
                                                    0 0,  1 0,  0 1,  1 1,
                                                    0 0,  1 0,  0 1,  1 1,
```

```
                                                0 0, 1 0, 0 1, 1 1,
                                                0 0, 1 0, 0 1, 1 1,
                                                0 0, 1 0, 0 1, 1 1" />
            </GeometryModel3D.Geometry>

            <GeometryModel3D.Material>
                <MaterialGroup>

                        <!-- ImageBrush overlayed with... -->
                        <DiffuseMaterial>
                            <DiffuseMaterial.Brush>
                                <ImageBrush
ImageSource="http://www.charlespetzold.com/PetzoldTattoo.jpg" />
                            </DiffuseMaterial.Brush>
                        </DiffuseMaterial>

                        <!-- DrawingBrush with drawing. -->
                        <DiffuseMaterial>
                            <DiffuseMaterial.Brush>

<DrawingBrush Viewbox="0 0 100 100" ViewboxUnits="Absolute">
    <DrawingBrush.Drawing>
        <GeometryDrawing Geometry="M 66 42 H 76
                                   Q 90 42 90 30 Q 90 25 85 25
                                   Q 80 25 80 30 Q 80 35 85 35
                                   M 61 42 H 51
                                   Q 37 42 37 30 Q 37 25 42 25
                                   Q 47 25 47 30 Q 47 35 42 35">
            <GeometryDrawing.Pen>
                <Pen Brush="Black" Thickness="3"
                     StartLineCap="Round" EndLineCap="Round" />
            </GeometryDrawing.Pen>
        </GeometryDrawing>
    </DrawingBrush.Drawing>
</DrawingBrush>
                            </DiffuseMaterial.Brush>
                        </DiffuseMaterial>
                    </MaterialGroup>
            </GeometryModel3D.Material>
```

Notice that the *Viewbox* of the *DrawingBrush* is set to a 100-unit square, and the coordinates of the geometry path are relative to that square. Here's the result:

The other two classes that derive from *Material* are intended to be in conjunction with *Diffuse-Material* objects within a *MaterialGroup*. Generally one or more *DiffuseMaterial* objects come first in the *MaterialGroup*, followed by an *EmissiveMaterial* or *SpecularMaterial* element, or maybe even both. You can use *EmissiveMaterial* and *SpecularMaterial* by themselves, but the results are not very satisfactory. If you come across an application in which you want just the effect of *EmissiveMaterial* or *SpecularMaterial* by itself, put the material on top of a *Diffuse-Material* element with *Brush* set to *Black*.

Both *EmissiveMaterial* and *SpecularMaterial* always tend to add brightness—if possible—to an existing texture. In other words, these materials increase the red, green, and blue components of a particular pixel color on a figure's surface. I added the caveat "if possible" because color values never go above 255. Once a surface becomes all white, it has no place left to go.

EmissiveMaterial is intended to mimic a surface that radiates light, such as a light bulb or glowing hot metal. This does *not* mean that the surface becomes a light source that illuminates other figures. However, a surface covered with *EmissiveMaterial* will have a visible color in the absence of all light sources. In the presence of light, *EmissiveMaterial* adds to the brightness of the figure provided by the underlying *DiffuseMaterial*.

EmissiveMaterial defines two properties named *Brush* and *Color*. By default *Brush* is *null* and *Color* is *White*. If *Brush* is actually a *SolidColorBrush*, *EmissiveMaterial* increases the red component of a particular pixel by *Brush.Color.R* times *Color.R*, and so forth for the other primaries. If *Brush* is not a *SolidColorBrush*, the calculation is based on the particular color of the brush at each point on the surface of the figure.

You'll recall the LandOfThePyramids program from Chapter 2, "Transforms and Animations." I originally made the sky another part of the 3D scene and discovered that it was not as illuminated as it should have been. I discussed one fix in Chapter 4, "Light and Shading," involving the *AmbientColor* property. Another solution would have been to give the sky an

EmissiveMaterial so the sky always shone *SkyBlue* regardless of the light sources. Here's a complete *ModelVisual3D* that you could add to that earlier program to create this visual:

```
<ModelVisual3D>
    <ModelVisual3D.Content>
        <GeometryModel3D>
            <GeometryModel3D.Geometry>
                <MeshGeometry3D
                    Positions="-1000     0 -1000, 1000     0 -1000,
                               -1000 1000 -1000, 1000 1000 -1000"
                    TriangleIndices="0 1 2, 1 3 2" />
            </GeometryModel3D.Geometry>

            <GeometryModel3D.Material>
                <MaterialGroup>
                    <DiffuseMaterial Brush="Black" />
                    <EmissiveMaterial Brush="SkyBlue" />
                </MaterialGroup>
            </GeometryModel3D.Material>
        </GeometryModel3D>
    </ModelVisual3D.Content>
</ModelVisual3D>
```

However, this is still not an entirely satisfactory solution. If you remove the light sources, the sky remains the same color, which isn't quite right.

The *SpecularMaterial* class also adds brightness to a figure, but in a more complex manner. It is intended to mimic light that bounces off glossy objects, such as flat metal or plastic or varnished wood. As you'll recall, a figure covered with *DiffuseMaterial* appears the same color regardless of the viewing angle. *SpecularMaterial* is different because the viewing angle affects the brightness. A glossy surface reflects light so that the angle of reflection equals the angle of incidence. A *SpecularMaterial* will appear the brightest when the angle between the light and the surface are opposite the angle from the surface to the camera.

The following XAML file covers both sides of the smooth quarter tube developed in Chapter 4 with a *SpecularMaterial* object on top of the *DiffuseMaterial*. Most of the file is the same as the ConvexSurfaceWithNormals.xaml file from Chapter 4.

ConvexSurfaceWithSpecularMaterial.xaml
```
<!-- =================================================================
     ConvexSurfaceWithSpecularMaterial.xaml (c) 2007 by Charles Petzold
     ================================================================= -->

    . . .

                        <GeometryModel3D.Material>
                            <MaterialGroup>
                                <DiffuseMaterial Brush="Cyan" />
                                <SpecularMaterial Brush="White" />
                            </MaterialGroup>
                        </GeometryModel3D.Material>

                        <GeometryModel3D.BackMaterial>
                            <MaterialGroup>
```

```
                    <DiffuseMaterial Brush="Pink" />
                    <SpecularMaterial Brush="Red" />
                </MaterialGroup>
            </GeometryModel3D.BackMaterial>
```

. . .

As you manipulate the vertical *ScrollBar* on the right, you can "catch the light" and see reflections from the surface. To examine the effect of the *SpecularMaterial* by itself, set the brush of the *DiffuseMaterial* objects to *Black*. Obviously *SpecularMaterial* works best with curved figures, which the next chapter is devoted to generating.

SpecularMaterial defines a *SpecularPower* property—40 by default—that indicates the focus of the reflection. A high number makes the reflective area very small, rather like a mirror (although *SpecularMaterial* only reflects light sources, not other images). When *SpecularPower* gets small, *SpecularMaterial* is more like *DiffuseMaterial*.

You can set the brush used with *SpecularMaterial* to *White*, or you can set it to a color the same as (or related to) the color of the underlying *DiffuseMaterial*. A *White* brush is sometimes used to simulate plastic surfaces, while you can simulate metal with *DiffuseMaterial* and *SpecularMaterial* brushes that are similar.

Or you can set the *Brush* to something other than a solid color. The following program defines half of a hollow cylinder and covers it with a *DiffuseMaterial* with a *Blue* brush and a *SpecularMaterial* with an *ImageBrush*. The *DirectionalLight* is animated to spin around the cylinder, and the *ImageBrush* appears only when the *DirectionalLight* shines on it.

TubeWithSpecularBrush.xaml

```xml
<!-- =========================================================
     TubeWithSpecularBrush.xaml (c) 2007 by Charles Petzold
     ========================================================= -->
<Page xmlns="http://schemas.microsoft.com/winfx/2006/xaml/presentation"
      xmlns:x="http://schemas.microsoft.com/winfx/2006/xaml"
      WindowTitle="Tube with Specular Brush"
      Title="Tube with Specular Brush">
    <Viewport3D>
        <ModelVisual3D>
            <ModelVisual3D.Content>
                <GeometryModel3D>
                    <GeometryModel3D.Geometry>
                        <!-- 1/2 of 40-sided polygonal tube:
                             Top points first, then bottom. -->
                        <MeshGeometry3D
                            Positions=
  "-1.00  1 0.00, -0.99  1 0.16, -0.95  1 0.31, -0.89  1 0.45,
   -0.81  1 0.59, -0.71  1 0.71,  0.59  1 0.81, -0.45  1 0.89,
   -0.31  1 0.95, -0.16  1 0.99,  0.00  1 1.00,  0.16  1 0.99,
    0.31  1 0.95,  0.45  1 0.89,  0.59  1 0.81,  0.71  1 0.71,
    0.81  1 0.59,  0.89  1 0.45,  0.95  1 0.31,  0.99  1 0.16, 1.00  1 0.00,
```

```
          -1.00 -1 0.00, -0.99 -1 0.16, -0.95 -1 0.31, -0.89 -1 0.45,
          -0.81 -1 0.59, -0.71 -1 0.71, -0.59 -1 0.81, -0.45 -1 0.89,
          -0.31 -1 0.95, -0.16 -1 0.99,  0.00 -1 1.00,  0.16 -1 0.99,
           0.31 -1 0.95,  0.45 -1 0.89,  0.59 -1 0.81,  0.71 -1 0.71,
           0.81 -1 0.59,  0.89 -1 0.45,  0.95 -1 0.31,  0.99 -1 0.16, 1.00 -1 0.00"

                         Normals=
          "-1.00 0 0.00, -0.99 0 0.16, -0.95 0 0.31, -0.89 0 0.45,
          -0.81 0 0.59, -0.71 0 0.71, -0.59 0 0.81, -0.45 0 0.89,
          -0.31 0 0.95, -0.16 0 0.99,  0.00 0 1.00,  0.16 0 0.99,
           0.31 0 0.95,  0.45 0 0.89,  0.59 0 0.81,  0.71 0 0.71,
           0.81 0 0.59,  0.89 0 0.45,  0.95 0 0.31,  0.99 0 0.16, 1.00  0 0.00,

          -1.00 0 0.00, -0.99 0 0.16, -0.95 0 0.31, -0.89 0 0.45,
          -0.81 0 0.59, -0.71 0 0.71, -0.59 0 0.81, -0.45 0 0.89,
          -0.31 0 0.95, -0.16 0 0.99,  0.00 0 1.00,  0.16 0 0.99,
           0.31 0 0.95,  0.45 0 0.89,  0.59 0 0.81,  0.71 0 0.71,
           0.81 0 0.59,  0.89 0 0.45,  0.95 0 0.31,  0.99 0 0.16, 1.00  0 0.00"

                      TextureCoordinates=
          "0.00 0, 0.05 0, 0.10 0, 0.15 0, 0.20 0, 0.25 0, 0.30 0,
          0.35 0, 0.40 0, 0.45 0, 0.50 0, 0.55 0, 0.60 0, 0.65 0,
          0.70 0, 0.75 0, 0.80 0, 0.85 0, 0.90 0, 0.95 0, 1.00 0,

          0.00 1, 0.05 1, 0.10 1, 0.15 1, 0.20 1, 0.25 1, 0.30 1,
          0.35 1, 0.40 1, 0.45 1, 0.50 1, 0.55 1, 0.60 1, 0.65 1,
          0.70 1, 0.75 1, 0.80 1, 0.85 1, 0.90 1, 0.95 1, 1.00 1"

                      TriangleIndices=
          " 0 21  1,  1 21 22,  1 22  2,  2 22 23,  2 23  3,  3 23 24,
           3 24  4,  4 24 25,  4 25  5,  5 25 26,  5 26  6,  6 26 27,
           6 27  7,  7 27 28,  7 28  8,  8 28 29,  8 29  9,  9 29 30,
           9 30 10, 10 30 31, 10 31 11, 11 31 32, 11 32 12, 12 32 33,
          12 33 13, 13 33 34, 13 34 14, 14 34 35, 14 35 15, 15 35 36,
          15 36 16, 16 36 37, 16 37 17, 17 37 38, 17 38 18, 18 38 39,
          18 39 19, 19 39 40, 19 30 20, 20 40 41" />

             </GeometryModel3D.Geometry>

             <!-- Diffuse material and specular material. -->
             <GeometryModel3D.Material>
                 <MaterialGroup>
                     <DiffuseMaterial Brush="Blue" Color="Black" />
                     <SpecularMaterial SpecularPower="20">
                         <SpecularMaterial.Brush>
                             <ImageBrush
             ImageSource="http://www.charlespetzold.com/PetzoldTattoo.jpg" />
                         </SpecularMaterial.Brush>
                     </SpecularMaterial>
                 </MaterialGroup>
             </GeometryModel3D.Material>
         </GeometryModel3D>
     </ModelVisual3D.Content>
 </ModelVisual3D>
```

```
            <!-- Ambient light. -->
            <ModelVisual3D>
                <ModelVisual3D.Content>
                    <AmbientLight Color="Gray" />
                </ModelVisual3D.Content>
            </ModelVisual3D>

            <!-- Directional light with transform. -->
            <ModelVisual3D>
                <ModelVisual3D.Content>
                    <DirectionalLight Color="#C0C0C0" Direction="0 0 -1" />
                </ModelVisual3D.Content>

                <ModelVisual3D.Transform>
                    <RotateTransform3D>
                        <RotateTransform3D.Rotation>
                            <AxisAngleRotation3D x:Name="rotate" Axis="0 1 0" />
                        </RotateTransform3D.Rotation>
                    </RotateTransform3D>
                </ModelVisual3D.Transform>
            </ModelVisual3D>

            <!-- Camera. -->
            <Viewport3D.Camera>
                <PerspectiveCamera Position="0 0 4"
                                   LookDirection="0 0 -1"
                                   UpDirection="0 1 0"
                                   FieldOfView="45" />
            </Viewport3D.Camera>
        </Viewport3D>

        <!-- Animation to rotate directional light. -->
        <Page.Triggers>
            <EventTrigger RoutedEvent="Page.Loaded">
                <BeginStoryboard>
                    <Storyboard TargetName="rotate" TargetProperty="Angle">
                        <DoubleAnimation From="0" To="360" Duration="0:0:3"
                                         RepeatBehavior="Forever" />
                    </Storyboard>
                </BeginStoryboard>
            </EventTrigger>
        </Page.Triggers>
    </Page>
```

Many of the more esoteric 3D features—such as the *PointLight* and *SpotLight* classes covered in the last chapter, and the *SpecularMaterial* class demonstrated here—really cry out for curved surfaces and lots of triangles. These triangles are often generated algorithmically, as the next chapter will demonstrate.

Chapter 6
Algorithmic Mesh Geometries

Every figure in a 3D scene is composed of triangles, but some figures have more triangles than others, and some figures might have hundreds or even thousands of triangles. The simulation of curved surfaces often requires many triangles, but as you saw toward the end of Chapter 4, "Light and Shading," even flat surfaces require a subdivision into many triangles if you illuminate them with *PointLight* or *SpotLight*.

It's sometimes fun to calculate a curved surface using just a calculator, as I did with the convex surfaces in Chapter 4 and Chapter 5, "Texture and Materials." But as the number of vertices increases, the fun quickly dissipates, and you realize you really should be generating these *MeshGeometry3D* objects algorithmically in code. That's what this chapter is all about. The process of generating polygons that cover a surface is known as *tessellation*. If only triangles are involved—as they are in WPF 3D—the word *triangulation* is appropriate.

This transition to code can actually be rather sad because it seems to imply that you can no longer define an entire 3D scene in a XAML file. But fear not: I will show you how to generate *MeshGeometry3D* objects in code and then convert these objects to text and insert them into your XAML files.

Everybody's needs are different. In the course of this chapter, I'll show you the techniques of writing both custom code and reusable code to generate the triangle meshes you require. To a certain extent, people's needs overlap, and that is why certain primitives such as spheres and cylinders are often required. For your ease, I have developed classes that generate triangle meshes for these common figures, and which are part of a dynamic-link library named Petzold.Media3D.dll that you can use in your own programs.

Triangulation Basics

Although the classes in the Petzold.Media3D library will probably suffice for simple figures, you will likely encounter a need that the library does not satisfy. For that reason, it's important that you learn not only how to use the classes in this library, but also the principles under which they were developed.

Parametric Equations

Let's begin with a sphere. The equation of a unit sphere–a sphere with a radius of 1 with its center at the origin–is:

$$x^2 + y^2 + z^2 = 1$$

Every point (x, y, z) that satisfies this equation is a point on the surface of the sphere. The equation for points inside the sphere is the same except that the equal sign changes to a less-than sign.

The equation can be generalized for a sphere of radius r:

$$x^2 + y^2 + z^2 = r^2$$

And now it's clear that this equation is really just a restatement of the Pythagorean Theorem in three dimensions. Any point on the surface of the sphere is an equal distance r from the center. If the center is not the origin, but instead the point (x_0, y_0, z_0), the equation is further generalized as:

$$(x - x_0)^2 + (y - y_0)^2 + (z - z_0)^2 = r^2$$

Regardless of how simplified or generalized this equation is, for the purpose of generating a MeshGeometry3D, it's just about worthless. These are *analytic* equations common in analytic geometry: They let you easily *test* whether a particular point is on the surface of the sphere, but there's no obvious way to generate points on the sphere.

What we need instead are *parametric equations*. Parametric equations express a series of points representing a line or surface in terms of one or more independent variables called *parameters*.

In two-dimensional graphics, parametric equations generally represent x and y as functions of the variable t, which you can imagine as vaguely representing "time." For example, pages 806 through 809 of *Applications = Code + Markup* show the derivation of the parametric equations for a two-dimensional Bézier spline with end-points (x_0, y_0) and (x_3, y_3) and control points (x_1, y_1) and (x_2, y_2):

$$x(t) = (1-t)^3 x_0 + 3t(1-t)^2 x_1 + 3t^2(1-t)x_2 + t^3 x_3$$
$$y(t) = (1-t)^3 y_0 + 3t(1-t)^2 y_1 + 3t^2(1-t)y_2 + t^3 y_3$$

As t goes from 0 to 1, the equations generate points (x, y) on the curve. As you can easily verify, when t equals 0, the equations yield the point (x_0, y_0), and when t equals 1, the equations yield (x_3, y_3). Once you have the parametric equations, it's generally easy to convert them to code. You generate the points inside a *for* loop that varies the independent variable t from 0 to 1. You can achieve as much resolution as you want by adjusting the increment of t.

Parametric and analytic equations are often quite different. The analytic equation for a two-dimensional circle centered on the point (x_0, y_0) with radius r is:

$$(x - x_0)^2 + (y - y_0)^2 = r^2$$

The parametric equations for a circle use an independent variable often called θ (theta) that represents an angle:

$$x(\theta) = x_0 + r \cdot \cos(\theta)$$
$$y(\theta) = y_0 + r \cdot \sin(\theta)$$

The angle θ ranges from 0 to 360 degrees, or 0 to 2π if you're using radians.

Three-dimensional figures are covered with two-dimensional surfaces, so generally the parametric equations you'll use for 3D figures involve *two* independent variables. A useful source for obtaining parametric equations is Wikipedia (*http://www.wikipedia.org*); Wolfram's MathWorld (*http://mathworld.wolfram.com*) has heavier math content and is also useful. Or you can derive parametric equations on your own from general principles. Be prepared to use some trigonometry!

Analyzing the Sphere

The sphere is a particularly troublesome figure for newcomers because the immediate impulse is to triangulate the surface with uniform triangles—that is, triangles with the same shape and size. Doing this seems reasonable at first, yet it is mathematically impossible. In fact, covering a sphere with triangles that are only *approximately* uniform is a higher-level mathematical challenge. (For an example, see this paper from Microsoft Research: *http://research.microsoft.com/ research/pubs/view.aspx?type=Technical%20Report&id=977.*)

To actually get a sphere up and running, it's probably best to begin with familiar concepts, such as longitude and latitude. Following is a sphere marked with lines of longitude and latitude every 15 degrees.

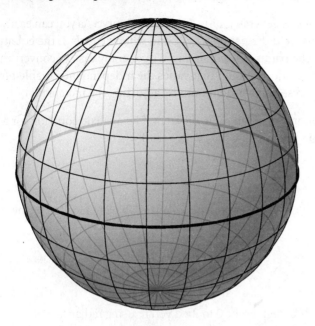

LongitudeAndLatitude.xaml

The lines of longitude and latitude are very different from each other. All the lines of longitude are great circles (which are circles that are centered at the center of the sphere) and share common points at the North Pole and South Pole. All the lines of latitude are parallel to the plane of the equator (shown with a thicker line); only the equator itself is a great circle.

Since I've chosen the same 15-degree increment of longitude and latitude, the areas near the equator are very nearly square. The triangulation algorithm will further divide each of these areas into two triangles. As you approach the poles, the lines of longitude get closer together and the areas where the lines of longitude and latitude intersect get skinnier. The only real problem is that more triangles are involved than are required to maintain the same resolution as around the equator. At each pole are 24 very skinny triangles. But we'll live with that asymmetry in the interest of getting the algorithm working.

For purposes of simplicity, let's first assume that the sphere is centered on the origin and has a unit radius. The North Pole is the point (0, 1, 0) and the South Pole is (0, −1, 0). The equator is on the XZ plane. Let θ (theta) represent an angle of longitude ranging from 0 to 360 degrees. For reasons that will become apparent shortly, I want zero degrees of longitude to be the rear of the sphere where Z equals −1. Assume that increasing angles of longitude circle the sphere in an eastward direction. The parametric equations for the equator are similar to those for a circle in two dimensions:

$$x(\theta) = -\sin(\theta)$$
$$z(\theta) = -\cos(\theta)$$

where θ ranges from 0 to 360 degrees. The negative signs are required for starting the equator at the point (0, 0, −1) and going eastward. For example, when θ equals 90 degrees, the point on the equator is (−1, 0, 0).

Let φ (phi) be an angle of latitude. Positive angles are north of the equator and negative angles are south. The possible values of φ range from 90 degrees (the North Pole) to −90 degrees (the South Pole). As you'll recall, all the circles of latitude are parallel to the equator. These circles are offset from the equator, which means that if the equator is on the XZ plane, the lines of latitude have non-zero y values. Also, the circles of latitude have smaller radii than the equator. Fortunately, both of these differences are easily quantifiable.

For any angle of latitude φ, the distance from the equator y is obviously the sine of that angle:

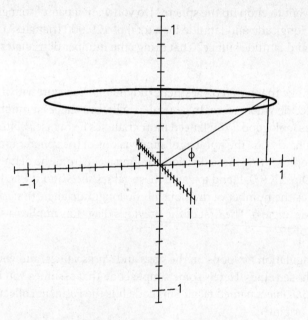

LatitudeCalculation.xaml

In addition, the radius of the circle of latitude is the cosine of φ, which means that you can calculate an equation for any circle of latitude by scaling the x and z values in the parametric equations by that cosine. Therefore, the composite parametric equations for the unit sphere centered on the origin are:

$$x(\theta,\phi) = -\cos(\phi)\sin(\theta)$$
$$y(\theta,\phi) = \sin(\phi)$$
$$z(\theta,\phi) = -\cos(\phi)\cos(\theta)$$

where angle θ ranges from 0 to 360 degrees and ϕ ranges from 90 degrees to −90 degrees. For a sphere with a radius of r centered on the point (x_0, y_0, z_0) the equations are only slightly more complex:

$$x(\theta,\phi) = x_0 - r \cdot \cos(\phi)\sin(\theta)$$
$$y(\theta,\phi) = y_0 + r \cdot \sin(\phi)$$
$$z(\theta,\phi) = z_0 - r \cdot \cos(\phi)\cos(\theta)$$

Triangulating the Sphere

Code that triangulates the sphere will contain two *for* loops that essentially vary the angles θ and ϕ. But how finely do you want to chop up the sphere? Do you want a pair of triangles corresponding to every degree of longitude and latitude for a total of 129,600 triangles? Or will every 10 degrees of longitude and latitude suffice? That brings the number of triangles down to 1,296.

In truth, you'll make decisions like that based on aesthetic judgments. You start with a guess, look at the results, and then decide where to go. In general, you'll want the least number of triangles that make your figures look good. (You'll need more triangles if you use *PointLight* or *SpotLight*, of course.) You can't hard-code the number of subdivisions of the sphere, and you'll have to come up with names representing these divisions. Taking a cue from the definition of methods in the *Mesh* class in DirectX 9.0, I tend to name these values *slices* and *stacks*. For the sphere, the *slices* value indicates the number of divisions of the longitude angle θ; *stacks* indicates the division of the latitude angle ϕ. The first of the previous diagrams implies a *slices* value of 24 and a *stacks* value of 12.

So in reality, you base the triangulation *for* loops on the *slices* and *stacks* values, and you calculate the angles θ and ϕ from those values. Here's some simple code that assumes you have a freshly created *MeshGeometry3D* object named *mesh*. This code fills the *Positions* collection for a unit sphere centered on the origin.

```
for (int stack = 0; stack <= stacks; stack++)
{
    double phi = Math.PI / 2 - stack * Math.PI / stacks;
    double y = Math.Sin(phi);
    double scale = -Math.Cos(phi);

    for (int slice = 0; slice <= slices; slice++)
    {
        double theta = slice * 2 * Math.PI / slices;
        double x = scale * Math.Sin(theta);
        double z = scale * Math.Cos(theta);
        mesh.Positions.Add(new Point3D(x, y, z));
    }
}
```

Notice the use of singular *stack* and plural *stacks*, and similarly *slice* and *slices*. The value of *stack* ranges from 0 (which corresponds to a latitude of 90 degrees at the North Pole) to *stacks* (a latitude of −90 degrees at the South Pole), while *slice* goes from 0 (a longitude of 0 degrees) to *slices* (a longitude of 360 degrees, back where it started). Each intersection of one of these lines of latitude and lines of longitude is a new *Point3D* for the *Positions* collection. The *scale* value is the negative cosine of ϕ, so that θ essentially begins at the rear of the sphere and increases eastward.

Calculating the *Normals* collection at the same time as *Positions* is quite simple for the sphere. The normal is the vector from the center of the sphere to the vertex, and if the center of the sphere is the origin, that normal is the same as the vertex. Just add the following code:

```
mesh.Normals.Add(new Vector3D(x, y, z));
```

Accommodating a *radius* value and a *center* value (of type *Point3D*) in this code would also be fairly easy. The *radius* value is just a multiplicative value applied to *x*, *y*, and *z*. To accommodate a *center* value, replace the preceding code that adds the *Point3D* object to the *vertices* collection with this:

```
Vector3D normal = new Vector3D(x, y, z);
mesh.Normals.Add(normal);
mesh.Positions.Add(normal + center);
```

The *normal* value is calculated first, assuming that the sphere is centered on the origin, and then the *center* value is added to the normal vector to calculate the vertex. (Another way to think about it is to remember that the normal vector equals the vertex point minus the center point.)

These *for* loops seem to calculate a few more points than are actually needed. It's clear that *stack* needs to range from 0 up to (and including) the *stacks* value to encompass both the North Pole and South Pole. But the second loop generates values of *theta* that are the same at the beginning and end. Vertices on the line of zero degrees longitude are duplicated. That second loop also generates (*slices* + 1) vertices for both the North Pole and the South Pole, which seem to be *slices* more than are needed.

These little flukes are for the benefit of the *TextureCoordinates* property. In general, triangulation is often *much* easier if you forget about calculating the *TextureCoordinates* property entirely, but that's a luxury you have only if you're covering the surface of the figure with a solid color brush. Programming 3D graphics is much more fun with gradient brushes and tiled brushes, so you should give serious thought beforehand to how the vertices of the figure will correspond to the two-dimensional vertices of the brush.

It's often helpful to draw a rectangle representing the brush and indicate how parts of the brush correspond to the figure you're generating:

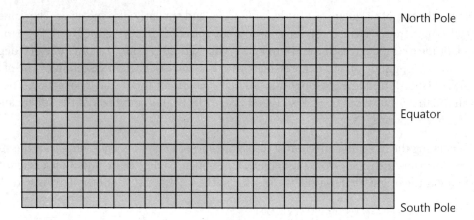

North Pole

Equator

South Pole

RectangularBrush.xaml

This brush will wrap around the sphere. Obviously some distortion will occur! But there must be an angle of longitude on the sphere where the left edge of the brush meets up with the right edge of the brush in a *seam*. Operating under the philosophy that seams should be out of sight, I've defined zero degrees of longitude to be the rear of the sphere, and that's why vertices are duplicated on that line. The first set of vertices corresponds to the left side of the brush, and the second set corresponds to the right side of the brush.

Moreover, I've defined the two loops in the mesh-generation logic so that the *stack* value starts at the top and goes down, while the *slice* value goes eastward around the sphere, which is left to right across the brush. Everything seemingly peculiar that I've done in the previous code has been leading up to the ability to write this simple and elegant statement:

```
mesh.TextureCoordinates.Add(new Point((double)slice / slices,
                                       (double)stack / stacks));
```

You can insert this statement at the end of the inner loop shown previously.

In writing triangulation code, don't wait until the very end to figure out the *TextureCoordinates* property. Begin by considering how the surface of the figure will be covered with a rectangular brush, and base your logic around that. The whole process will be a lot more confusing if you try to add some *TextureCoordinates* logic later on.

If you think that something is not quite right with the North and South Poles, you're absolutely correct. The problem becomes more evident when you tackle the final job, which is filling the *TriangleIndices* collection. Generally you'll want to use a different set of loops for this job because *stack* and *slice* only need to range up to (but not including) *stacks* and *slices*. For each rectangle, you need to calculate two sets of three indices:

```
for (int stack = 0; stack < stacks; stack++)
    for (int slice = 0; slice < slices; slice++)
    {
        TriangleIndices.Add((stack + 0) * (slices + 1) + slice);
```

```
        TriangleIndices.Add((stack + 1) * (slices + 1) + slice);
        TriangleIndices.Add((stack + 0) * (slices + 1) + slice + 1);

        TriangleIndices.Add((stack + 0) * (slices + 1) + slice + 1);
        TriangleIndices.Add((stack + 1) * (slices + 1) + slice);
        TriangleIndices.Add((stack + 1) * (slices + 1) + slice + 1);
    }
```

I know this looks messy, but if you add triangles to the earlier diagram of the rectangular brush and label a few representative vertices, you'll see that the code is basically correct:

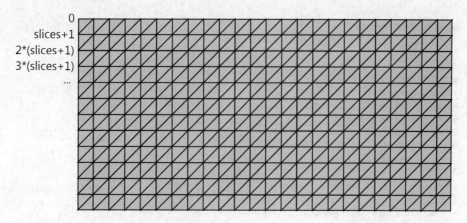

RectangularTriangulatedBrush1.xaml

But look at those top and bottom rows. All those points along the top and bottom of the brush correspond to the North Pole and South Pole, respectively, and half the triangles actually collapse into lines and aren't visible. Here's a better representation of how the brush is mapped to the surface of the sphere:

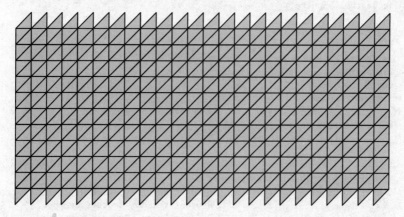

RectangularTriangulatedBrush2.xaml

Yes, it's sad but true: Part of the brush won't be making the journey to the surface of the sphere. That is unavoidable, and the best you can do is increase the *stacks* value to minimize the damage. In the loops to fill the *TriangleIndices* collection, you can add a couple *if* statements to avoid executing the first block of assignment statements when *stack* equals zero, and the second block when *stack* equals *stacks* minus one.

The following C# file incorporates all the code I've shown so far in a method named *Generate-Sphere*. The four parameters are *center*, *radius*, *slices*, and *stacks*.

BeachBallSphere.cs

```
//-------------------------------------------------
// BeachBallSphere.cs (c) 2007 by Charles Petzold
//-------------------------------------------------
using System;
using System.Windows;
using System.Windows.Controls;
using System.Windows.Media;
using System.Windows.Media.Animation;
using System.Windows.Media.Media3D;
using System.Windows.Shapes;

namespace Petzold.BeachBallSphere
{
    public class BeachBallSphere : Window
    {
        [STAThread]
        public static void Main()
        {
            Application app = new Application();
            app.Run(new BeachBallSphere());
        }

        public BeachBallSphere()
        {
            Title = "Beachball Sphere";

            // Create Viewport3D as content of window.
            Viewport3D viewport = new Viewport3D();
            Content = viewport;

            // Get the MeshGeometry3D from the GenerateSphere method.
            MeshGeometry3D mesh =
                GenerateSphere(new Point3D(0, 0, 0), 1, 36, 18);
            mesh.Freeze();

            // Define a brush for the sphere.
            Brush[] brushes = new Brush[6] { Brushes.Red, Brushes.Blue,
                                             Brushes.Yellow, Brushes.Orange,
                                             Brushes.Green, Brushes.White };
            DrawingGroup drawgrp = new DrawingGroup();

            for (int i = 0; i < brushes.Length ; i++)
```

```
        {
            RectangleGeometry rectgeo =
                new RectangleGeometry(new Rect(10 * i, 0, 10, 60));

            GeometryDrawing geodraw =
                new GeometryDrawing(brushes[i], null, rectgeo);

            drawgrp.Children.Add(geodraw);
        }
        DrawingBrush drawbrsh = new DrawingBrush(drawgrp);
        drawbrsh.Freeze();

        // Define the GeometryModel3D.
        GeometryModel3D geomod = new GeometryModel3D();
        geomod.Geometry = mesh;
        geomod.Material = new DiffuseMaterial(drawbrsh);

        // Create a ModelVisual3D for the GeometryModel3D.
        ModelVisual3D modvis = new ModelVisual3D();
        modvis.Content = geomod;
        viewport.Children.Add(modvis);

        // Create another ModelVisual3D for light.
        Model3DGroup modgrp = new Model3DGroup();
        modgrp.Children.Add(new AmbientLight(Color.FromRgb(128, 128, 128)));
        modgrp.Children.Add(
            new DirectionalLight(Color.FromRgb(128, 128, 128),
                                 new Vector3D(2, -3, -1)));

        modvis = new ModelVisual3D();
        modvis.Content = modgrp;
        viewport.Children.Add(modvis);

        // Create the camera.
        PerspectiveCamera cam = new PerspectiveCamera(new Point3D(0, 0, 8),
                       new Vector3D(0, 0, -1), new Vector3D(0, 1, 0), 45);
        viewport.Camera = cam;

        // Create a transform for the GeometryModel3D.
        AxisAngleRotation3D axisangle =
            new AxisAngleRotation3D(new Vector3D(1, 1, 0), 0);
        RotateTransform3D rotate = new RotateTransform3D(axisangle);
        geomod.Transform = rotate;

        // Animate the RotateTransform3D.
        DoubleAnimation anima =
            new DoubleAnimation(360, new Duration(TimeSpan.FromSeconds(5)));
        anima.RepeatBehavior = RepeatBehavior.Forever;
        axisangle.BeginAnimation(AxisAngleRotation3D.AngleProperty, anima);
    }
    MeshGeometry3D GenerateSphere(Point3D center, double radius,
                                  int slices, int stacks)
    {
        // Create the MeshGeometry3D.
```

```
            MeshGeometry3D mesh = new MeshGeometry3D();

            // Fill the Position, Normals, and TextureCoordinates collections.
            for (int stack = 0; stack <= stacks; stack++)
            {
                double phi = Math.PI / 2 - stack * Math.PI / stacks;
                double y = radius * Math.Sin(phi);
                double scale = -radius * Math.Cos(phi);

                for (int slice = 0; slice <= slices; slice++)
                {
                    double theta = slice * 2 * Math.PI / slices;
                    double x = scale * Math.Sin(theta);
                    double z = scale * Math.Cos(theta);

                    Vector3D normal = new Vector3D(x, y, z);
                    mesh.Normals.Add(normal);
                    mesh.Positions.Add(normal + center);
                    mesh.TextureCoordinates.Add(
                            new Point((double)slice / slices,
                                      (double)stack / stacks));
                }
            }

            // Fill the TriangleIndices collection.
            for (int stack = 0; stack < stacks; stack++)
                for (int slice = 0; slice < slices; slice++)
                {
                    int n = slices + 1; // Keep the line length down.

                    if (stack != 0)
                    {
                        mesh.TriangleIndices.Add((stack + 0) * n + slice);
                        mesh.TriangleIndices.Add((stack + 1) * n + slice);
                        mesh.TriangleIndices.Add((stack + 0) * n + slice + 1);
                    }
                    if (stack != stacks - 1)
                    {
                        mesh.TriangleIndices.Add((stack + 0) * n + slice + 1);
                        mesh.TriangleIndices.Add((stack + 1) * n + slice);
                        mesh.TriangleIndices.Add((stack + 1) * n + slice + 1);
                    }
                }
            return mesh;
        }
    }
}
```

The *GenerateSphere* method is in C#, so I wrote the whole rest of the program in C#. The brush used to cover the sphere consists of six rectangles arranged horizontally across the brush with the colors red, blue, yellow, orange, green, and white. These rectangles meet at points at the North and South Poles:

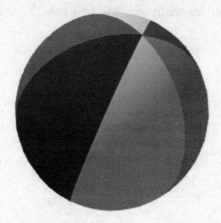

This particular mapping of brush to sphere works best when the *slices* parameter is a multiple of six—the number of rectangles in the brush. Try setting *slices* to nine, for example, and you'll see some waviness in the borders between colors because that division between colors doesn't match a line of longitude.

The program animates the beach ball through a *RotateTransform3D* with an *AxisAngle-Rotation3D* applied to the *GeometryModel3D*. Notice the code that animates the *Angle* property of the *AxisAngleRotation3D* object named *axisangle*:

```
DoubleAnimation anima =
    new DoubleAnimation(360, new Duration(TimeSpan.FromSeconds(5)));
anima.RepeatBehavior = RepeatBehavior.Forever;
axisangle.BeginAnimation(AxisAngleRotation3D.AngleProperty, anima);
```

This is called a non-storyboard animation and it can only be done in code. In XAML, animations require *Storyboard* elements. The *BeginAnimation* method is defined by the *Animatable* class, from which *AxisAngleRotation3D* (and many other classes in the *System.Windows.Media.Media3D* namespace) derive. The two arguments are a dependency property of the object being animated, and an instance of one of the many classes that derive from *AnimationTimeline*—in this case, *DoubleAnimation*.

The convenience of non-storyboard animation is a compelling reason to derive a class from *Animatable* (when appropriate), as I shall do later in this chapter.

The Problem of Inheritance

Although the approach shown in the BeachBallSphere program is adequate for a one-time "quickie" triangulation method, in general you'll want the option of writing the triangulation code in C# but referencing it in XAML files. The best approach is to devote a whole class to the sphere-generation code with properties named *Center*, *Radius*, *Slices*, and *Stacks*. This class can be the beginning of a whole library to generate mesh geometries algorithmically for use in XAML files.

As you first conceive this *Sphere* class, you'll undoubtedly want to derive the class from *MeshGeometry3D*:

```
namespace MyMeshGeometryLibrary
{
    public class Sphere : MeshGeometry3D
    {
        ...
    }
}
```

In your XAML file, you can include an XML namespace declaration to associate an XML namespace with the .NET namespace you've used:

```
xmlns:src="clr-namespace:MyMeshGeometryLibrary"
```

If the *Sphere* class is in a DLL rather than part of the project, the namespace declaration also needs to indicate the DLL assembly name:

```
xmlns:src="clr-namespace:MyMeshGeometryLibrary;assembly=MyMeshGeometryLibrary"
```

You could then refer to the *Sphere* class where you'd normally refer to a *MeshGeometry3D* element:

```
<ModelVisual3D>
    <ModelVisual3D.Content>
        <GeometryModel3D>
            <GeometryModel3D.Geometry>
                <src:Sphere Center="0 -1 2" Radius="1.5" />
            </GeometryModel3D.Geometry>
            ...
        </GeometryModel3D>
    </ModelVisual3D.Content>
</ModelVisual3D>
```

This all seems quite wonderful and straightforward. There's only one problem: *You can't do it.* The big, big obstacle is that the *MeshGeometry3D* class is sealed—you cannot inherit from it. Moreover, if you try to inherit from the abstract *Geometry3D* class instead, you'll discover that you'll need to override methods that are internal to the PresentationCore dynamic-link library, and that is not possible.

In fact, every class in the *System.Windows.Media.Media3D* namespace is either abstract or sealed, with the exception of *ModelVisual3D*. That's certainly an important exception, and I'll be making use of that special characteristic of *ModelVisual3D* shortly. But deriving from *ModelVisual3D* involves complications of its own, so let's pursue a somewhat different approach first.

Triangulation Resources

You can't derive a class from *MeshGeometry3D*, but all is not lost. Instead, you can define a mesh-generation class to be used as a resource in XAML files, and then refer to that resource in your markup with a data binding.

Resource Mechanics

Here's a mesh-generation class that doesn't explicitly inherit from anything:

```
namespace MyMeshGeometryLibrary
{
    public class SphereMeshGenerator
    {
        ...
        public MeshGeometry3D Geometry
        {
            get { ... }
        }
        ...
    }
}
```

This *SphereMeshGenerator* class probably has several properties named *Slices*, *Stacks*, *Radius*, and *Center*, but it also has a get-only property of type *MeshGeometry3D* that I've named *Geometry*. The *get*-accessor of this *Geometry* property creates a new *MeshGeometry3D*, fills all four collections, and then returns that object.

In a XAML file you can't just insert a *SphereMeshGenerator* element within a *ModelVisual3D* element. You instead must define a *SphereMeshGenerator* object in the *Resources* section of an XAML file:

```
<Page.Resources>
    <src:SphereMeshGenerator x:Key="sphere" Center="0 -1 2" Radius="1.5" />
    ...
</Page.Resources>
```

Within a *GeometryModel3D* element you can then reference that resource with a binding:

```
<GeometryModel3D Geometry="{Binding Source={StaticResource sphere},
                           Path=Geometry}">
```

Notice that the binding references the static resource named *sphere* and the *Geometry* property, which is of type *MeshGeometry3D*. This *MeshGeometry3D* object is assigned to the *Geometry* property of the *GeometryModel3D* element.

This might seem like a rather undesirable approach, but it's really better than it looks. Remember that resources are meant to be shared, so you can use a single resource to provide a *MeshGeometry3D* for several different figures. Each of these figures can apply transforms to the *GeometryModel3D* (or the *ModelVisual3D*) to change the size, location, or orientation of the figure. If you want to use *SphereMeshGenerator* in code, you can simply create an instance of the class and assign the *Geometry* property of a *GeometryModel3D* object from the *Geometry* property of the *SphereMeshGenerator* instance.

Here is a class named *SphereMeshGenerator1* that implements basically the same mesh-generation logic I described earlier but in the context of a class with properties for *Radius*, *Center*, *Slices*, and *Stacks*, and a get-only *Geometry* property.

```
SphereMeshGenerator1.cs
//------------------------------------------------------
// SphereMeshGenerator1.cs (c) 2007 by Charles Petzold
//------------------------------------------------------
using System;
using System.Windows;
using System.Windows.Media;
using System.Windows.Media.Media3D;

namespace Petzold.SphereResourceDemo
{
    public class SphereMeshGenerator1
    {
        // Four private initialized fields.
        int slices = 32;
        int stacks = 16;
        Point3D center = new Point3D();
        double radius = 1;

        // Four public properties allow access to private fields.
        public int Slices
        {
            set { slices = value; }
            get { return slices; }
        }

        public int Stacks
        {
            set { stacks = value; }
            get { return stacks; }
        }

        public Point3D Center
        {
            set { center = value; }
            get { return center; }
        }

        public double Radius
        {
            set { radius = value; }
            get { return radius; }
        }

        // Get-only property generates MeshGeometry3D.
        public MeshGeometry3D Geometry
        {
```

```
        get
        {
            // Create a MeshGeometry3D.
            MeshGeometry3D mesh = new MeshGeometry3D();

            // Fill the vertices, normals, and textures collections.
            for (int stack = 0; stack <= Stacks; stack++)
            {
                double phi = Math.PI / 2 - stack * Math.PI / Stacks;
                double y = Radius * Math.Sin(phi);
                double scale = -Radius * Math.Cos(phi);

                for (int slice = 0; slice <= Slices; slice++)
                {
                    double theta = slice * 2 * Math.PI / Slices;
                    double x = scale * Math.Sin(theta);
                    double z = scale * Math.Cos(theta);

                    Vector3D normal = new Vector3D(x, y, z);
                    mesh.Normals.Add(normal);
                    mesh.Positions.Add(normal + Center);
                    mesh.TextureCoordinates.Add(
                                new Point((double)slice / Slices,
                                          (double)stack / Stacks));
                }
            }

            // Fill the indices collection.
            for (int stack = 0; stack < Stacks; stack++)
            {
                int top = (stack + 0) * (Slices + 1);
                int bot = (stack + 1) * (Slices + 1);

                for (int slice = 0; slice < Slices; slice++)
                {
                    if (stack != 0)
                    {
                        mesh.TriangleIndices.Add(top + slice);
                        mesh.TriangleIndices.Add(bot + slice);
                        mesh.TriangleIndices.Add(top + slice + 1);
                    }

                    if (stack != Stacks - 1)
                    {
                        mesh.TriangleIndices.Add(top + slice + 1);
                        mesh.TriangleIndices.Add(bot + slice);
                        mesh.TriangleIndices.Add(bot + slice + 1);
                    }
                }
            }
            return mesh;
        }
    }
  }
}
```

Every time the *Geometry* property is accessed it calculates a fresh *MeshGeometry3D* object based on the current settings of the four properties.

The SphereMeshGenerator1.cs file and the following XAML file are part of the Sphere-ResourceDemo project. The *SphereMeshGenerator1* class shows up as a resource with the *Center* and *Radius* properties set.

```
SphereResourceDemo.xaml
<!-- =====================================================
        SphereResourceDemo.xaml (c) 2007 by Charles Petzold
     ===================================================== -->
<Window xmlns="http://schemas.microsoft.com/winfx/2006/xaml/presentation"
        xmlns:x="http://schemas.microsoft.com/winfx/2006/xaml"
        xmlns:src="clr-namespace:Petzold.SphereResourceDemo"
        x:Class="Petzold.SphereResourceDemo.SphereResourceDemo"
        Title="Sphere Resource Demo">
    <Window.Resources>
        <src:SphereMeshGenerator1 x:Key="sphere" Center="1 0 0 " Radius="0.5" />
    </Window.Resources>

        <Viewport3D>
            <ModelVisual3D>
                <ModelVisual3D.Content>
                    <Model3DGroup>
                        <GeometryModel3D
                            Geometry="{Binding Source={StaticResource sphere},
                                               Path=Geometry}">

                            <GeometryModel3D.Material>
                                <DiffuseMaterial>
                                    <DiffuseMaterial.Brush>
                                        <ImageBrush
                                            ImageSource="Petzold360.jpg" />
                                    </DiffuseMaterial.Brush>
                                </DiffuseMaterial>
                            </GeometryModel3D.Material>

                            <GeometryModel3D.Transform>
                                <RotateTransform3D>
                                    <RotateTransform3D.Rotation>
                                        <AxisAngleRotation3D x:Name="rotate"
                                                             Axis="0 1 0" />
                                    </RotateTransform3D.Rotation>
                                </RotateTransform3D>
                            </GeometryModel3D.Transform>
                        </GeometryModel3D>

                        <!-- Light source. -->
                        <AmbientLight Color="White" />

                    </Model3DGroup>
                </ModelVisual3D.Content>
            </ModelVisual3D>
```

```
            <!-- Camera. -->
            <Viewport3D.Camera>
                <PerspectiveCamera Position="0 0 4"
                                   LookDirection="0 0 -1"
                                   UpDirection="0 1 0"
                                   FieldOfView="45" />
            </Viewport3D.Camera>
        </Viewport3D>

    <Window.Triggers>
        <EventTrigger RoutedEvent="Window.Loaded">
            <BeginStoryboard>
                <Storyboard TargetName="rotate" TargetProperty="Angle">
                    <DoubleAnimation From="0" To="360" Duration="0:0:5"
                                     RepeatBehavior="Forever" />
                </Storyboard>
            </BeginStoryboard>
        </EventTrigger>
    </Window.Triggers>
</Window>
```

The SphereResourceDemo project also includes the Petzold360.jpg file that contains a crudely panoramic picture of my head, and the following C# file.

SphereResourceDemo.cs
```
//----------------------------------------------------
// SphereResourceDemo.cs (c) 2007 by Charles Petzold
//----------------------------------------------------
using System;
using System.Windows;

namespace Petzold.SphereResourceDemo
{
    public partial class SphereResourceDemo : Window
    {
        [STAThread]
        public static void Main()
        {
            Application app = new Application();
            app.Run(new SphereResourceDemo());
        }

        public SphereResourceDemo()
        {
            InitializeComponent();
        }
    }
}
```

The XAML file applies an animated rotation transform to the sphere, which spins it around the point (0, 0, 0):

You might try experimenting with different *Stacks* and *Slices* values. You'll notice that you can set *Stacks* as low as 2 and *Slices* as low as 3 before the mesh-generation logic breaks down.

There is nothing really wrong with the *SphereMeshGenerator1* class. The structure of the class illustrates yet another "quickie" way to define a *MeshGeometry3D*, but one that is suitable for use as a shareable resource in a XAML file. As the program illustrates, you can certainly animate the *GeometryModel3D* or the *ModelVisual3D* that makes use of this figure.

However, you might want to animate properties of the *SphereMeshGenerator1* object itself such as *Radius* and *Center*, and that you cannot do. The animation facilities in the Windows Presentation Foundation allow animation only of properties backed by dependency properties. And even if you set up a *DispatcherTimer* or *CompositionTarget* to generate timer or vertical-retrace events, changing the *Radius* or *Center* properties in a *SphereMeshGenerator1* object really doesn't do much of anything. Only when the *Geometry* property is accessed do the new property settings have an effect.

Another limitation is that you can't make the properties of *SphereMeshGenerator1* the targets of data bindings. For example, you can't control the *Radius* property using a scrollbar.

These problems are all solved by a total restructuring of the mesh-generator class to accommodate dependency properties.

Dependency Properties and Animation

In the earlier .NET client programming interface known as Windows Forms, the *SphereMesh-Generator1* class might have been enhanced with notification logic through an event named (for example) *GeometryChanged*. Whenever the *Radius*, *Center*, *Slices*, or *Stacks* property changed, the class would fire the *GeometryChanged* event. Any class using a *SphereMesh-Generator1* object would then be informed that a new *Geometry* property was available based on updated properties. The other class would then access that new *Geometry* property and perform its own updates.

In the Windows Presentation Foundation, a different notification system has been implemented involving dependency properties. Rather than a "pull" architecture that might be used in Windows Forms programs, dependency properties involve a "push" architecture. Whenever the *Radius*, *Center*, *Slices*, or *Stacks* property changes, the mesh-generator class responds by immediately changing its *Geometry* property. Because this property is probably bound to the *Geometry* property of a *GeometryModel3D* element, the *GeometryModel3D* element receives its own notification of the change, and the change notifications ripple up through the system and eventually cause the visuals to change.

The *SphereMeshGenerator2* class (coming up soon) will include dependency properties for *Center*, *Radius*, *Slices*, *Stacks*, and *Geometry*. The inclusion of these dependency properties requires *SphereMeshGenerator2* to derive from *DependencyObject*.

The class's *Center* property, for example, must be backed by a dependency property named *CenterProperty* defined as a static field like this:

```
public static readonly DependencyProperty CenterProperty =
    DependencyProperty.Register("Center",
        typeof(Point3D),
        typeof(SphereMeshGenerator2),
        new PropertyMetadata(new Point3D(), PropertyChanged));
```

It is normal to define this field as *public* and *readonly* as well as *static*. The static *Dependency-Property.Register* method registers the dependency property. The first argument is the text name of the property, the second argument is the type of the property, the third argument is the class registering the property, and the fourth argument is an object of type *PropertyMeta-data*. This object includes the default value of the property and a reference to a static *Property-Changed* method (it can actually have any name) defined in the class.

The *Center* property itself is defined solely in terms of the dependency property:

```
public Point3D Center
{
    set { SetValue(CenterProperty, value); }
    get { return (Point3D)GetValue(CenterProperty); }
}
```

This definition is sometimes called the CLR (Common Language Runtime) property to distinguish it from the dependency property. The *SetValue* and *GetValue* methods are defined by the *DependencyObject* class from which *SphereMeshGenerator2* derives. Logic implemented in the *DependencyObject* class is responsible for storing current values of the property and returning them. The CLR property shouldn't do anything *except* call *SetValue* and *GetValue*. Notice that *GetValue* returns an object of type *object* so that it must be cast to the proper type.

You can define dependency properties and CLR properties for *Radius*, *Slices*, and *Stacks* similarly. These properties can have their own property-changed handlers, or they can all reference the same *PropertyChanged* handler. (I prefer the latter approach.) You define the *PropertyChanged* handler in the class like this:

```
static void PropertyChanged(DependencyObject obj,
                            DependencyPropertyChangedEventArgs args)
{
    ...
}
```

This *PropertyChanged* handler is called whenever the *SetValue* method is called with an argument of *CenterProperty* (or *RadiusProperty* or *SlicesProperty* or *StackProperty*) and the value of the new property is different from its previous value.

Notice that the *PropertyChanged* method is static! Of course it has to be static because it's referenced by a static field. Fortunately the first argument is the particular instance of *SphereMeshGenerator2* whose property is changing. The second argument identifies the particular dependency property being changed—that's why you can share property-changed handlers among multiple properties—and its old and new values. I usually like to implement the static *PropertyChanged* handler like this:

```
static void PropertyChanged(DependencyObject obj,
                            DependencyPropertyChangedEventArgs args)
{
    (obj as SphereMeshGenerator2).PropertyChanged(args);
}
```

That single statement references a non-static overload of *PropertyChanged* defined like so:

```
void PropertyChanged(DependencyPropertyChangedEventArgs args)
{
    ...
}
```

This method can now reference the properties of the class with ease. In this example, the *PropertyChanged* method is responsible for filling the four collections of a *MeshGeometry3D* object based on the new property settings. This *MeshGeometry3D* object is publicly accessible through the class's *Geometry* property.

The *SphereMeshGenerator2* class must define a dependency property for *Geometry*, but the *Geometry* property is a little different because the *SphereMeshGenerator2* class is responsible for generating the value of this property, and to external classes the property must be read-only. The standard way to do this with dependency properties is to first define a static object of type *DependencyPropertyKey*

```
static readonly DependencyPropertyKey GeometryKey =
    DependencyProperty.RegisterReadOnly("Geometry",
        typeof(MeshGeometry3D),
        typeof(SphereMeshGenerator2),
        new PropertyMetadata(new MeshGeometry3D()));
```

Notice that the *GeometryKey* object is the return value of the static *DependencyProperty.RegisterReadOnly* method, and that this object is private to the class. The type of the *Geometry* property is *MeshGeometry3D* and the *PropertyMetadata* includes a default *MeshGeometry3D* property. But no property-changed handler is associated with this property. The *SphereMesh-Generator2* class changes this property internally, and that's the only way the property is changed.

The class also defines a public *DependencyProperty* object but it's derived from the *DependencyPropertyKey* object:

```
public static readonly DependencyProperty GeometryProperty =
    GeometryKey.DependencyProperty;
```

The *SetValue* method won't work with this *DependencyProperty* object but will work with the *DependencyPropertyKey* object. The definition of the *Geometry* CLR property indicates another little difference between this property and the others:

```
public MeshGeometry3D Geometry
{
    protected set { SetValue(GeometryKey, value); }
    get { return (MeshGeometry3D)GetValue(GeometryProperty); }
}
```

Notice that the *set* accessor is defined as *protected* so that it can't be called from outside the class (although it's still available to a derived class), and that the argument to *SetValue* is the *DependencyPropertyKey* object that is also invisible from outside the class. When defining a read-only property, it's important to make both the *DependencyPropertyKey* and the *set* accessor of the CLR property either private or protected.

All the real activity in *SphereMeshGenerator2* occurs in the *PropertyChanged* method. This property is responsible for filling the *MeshGeometry3D* collections with new values based on the new settings of the *Center*, *Radius*, *Stacks*, and *Slices* values.

Does *PropertyChanged* create a new instance of *MeshGeometry3D* every time it is called? No it definitely does *not*! The big reason we're rewriting this second mesh-generation class is to allow animation and data binding. This means that the *PropertyChanged* method might be called many times per second for very long periods of time. The method shouldn't make *any* memory allocations because all these memory allocations will pile up and require garbage collection, and the last thing you want is for the .NET garbage truck to come through and disrupt your animations.

Any *new* expression involving structures, such as *new Point3D* or *new Vector3D*, is fine because structures don't involve allocations from the application heap. However, expressions resulting in heap allocations such as *new MeshGeometry3D* or *new Point3DCollection* should be strictly avoided.

The *PropertyChanged* method must not create a new *MeshGeometry3D* or new collections. Instead, it modifies the existing collections of the existing *MeshGeometry3D* object stored as the *Geometry* property. The *PropertyChanged* method might begin by getting a reference to its *Geometry* property and storing it in a local variable for convenience:

```
void PropertyChanged(DependencyPropertyChangedEventArgs args)
{
    MeshGeometry3D mesh = Geometry;
    ...
}
```

Now you have another problem: The four collections in *MeshGeometry3D*—the collections that *PropertyChanged* will be modifying—are themselves backed by dependency properties. In fact, the collections themselves are derived from *Freezable*, which means that these collections are firing change notifications whenever any item in the collections change, and these changes are rippling up through the *GeometryModel3D* and *ModelVisual3D*.

To avoid a lot of needless activity behind the scenes, it's a very good idea for the *Property-Changed* method to detach the four collections from the *MeshGeometry3D* object. Here's the code:

```
void PropertyChanged(DependencyPropertyChangedEventArgs args)
{
    // Get reference to Geometry property for local ease.
    MeshGeometry3D mesh = Geometry;

    // Get references to all four collections.
    Point3DCollection vertices = mesh.Positions;
    Vector3DCollection normals = mesh.Normals;
    Int32Collection indices = mesh.TriangleIndices;
    PointCollection textures = mesh.TextureCoordinates;

    // Set the MeshGeometry3D properties to null to inhibit notifications.
    mesh.Positions = null;
    mesh.Normals = null;
    mesh.TriangleIndices = null;
    mesh.TextureCoordinates = null;

    // Clear the four collections.
    vertices.Clear();
    normals.Clear();
    indices.Clear();
    textures.Clear();
```

```
    // Fill the collections with new values.
    ...

    // Set the collections back to the properties.
    mesh.TextureCoordinates = textures;
    mesh.TriangleIndices = indices;
    mesh.Normals = normals;
    mesh.Positions = vertices;
}
```

I know this looks crazy, but it really speeds up the code. The method first stores a local reference to the *MeshGeometry3D* obtained from the *Geometry* property. It then gets references to all four collections in local variables. These statements don't involve any memory allocations, of course; the references to the collections are just copied.

The next step is to set the four properties of the *MeshGeometry3D* object to *null*. Now the method can change these collections without generating a bunch of notifications to the *MeshGeometry3D* object. Notice that the first property to be set to *null* is *Positions*. With a *null* *Positions* property, the *MeshGeometry3D* can't do much of anything.

Now the method can clear the existing collections and generate new items for the collections, which will involve similar code to that in the *SphereMeshGenerator1* class, except that it can refer to the collections using the local variables *vertices*, *normals*, and so forth rather than the *MeshGeometry3D* properties.

The *PropertyChanged* method concludes by setting these updated collections back to the *MeshGeometry3D* properties. Notice that the *Positions* property is last in this list. Once you set *Positions*, WPF 3D can use all the changes that you have made to generate new visuals.

Preventing memory allocations in the *PropertyChanged* method and disabling change notifications in the *MeshGeometry3D* object are the two most important lessons of this whole exercise. Everything else is just detail.

One detail I've glossed over is that the *PropertyChanged* method won't actually be able to alter the default *MeshGeometry3D* originally specified in the *Geometry* dependency property. The *MeshGeometry3D* class derives from *Freezable*, and when a *Freezable* object is set as the default value of a dependency property, it is frozen, which means that it cannot be altered. If you think about it, it makes perfect sense: The *GeometryProperty* dependency property is static, and so is the *MeshGeometry3D* object assigned as the default value, which means that it's shared among all instances of the *SphereMeshGenerator2* class in the application. If each instance of *SphereMeshGenerator2* modified the same *MeshGeometry3D* object, crazy things would happen.

The fix: Define a constructor for *SphereMeshGenerator2* and assign the *Geometry* property a new instance of *MeshGeometry3D*:

```
Geometry = new MeshGeometry3D();
```

This will also work:

```
Geometry = Geometry.Clone();
```

You can leave the default value of the *Geometry* dependency property as I've shown it (and you must leave it if you use the second method) so that programs examining the dependency properties know that the class initializes this property to a non-*null* value.

Incidentally, the code in the class's constructor to initialize the *Geometry* property is the only time the *set* accessor of the *Geometry* property needs to be called.

Another little fix: If you create a new object of type *SphereMeshGenerator2* (either as a XAML resource or in code) and leave all the properties set to their default values, the *Property-Changed* method won't ever be called, and the *MeshGeometry3D* collections will never be filled. You'll also want to initialize the *MeshGeometry3D* by adding this statement to the constructor:

```
PropertyChanged(new DependencyPropertyChangedEventArgs());
```

Suppose you define *SphereMeshGenerator2* object as a XAML resource similar to the way you defined a *SphereMeshGenerator1* object:

```
<src:SphereMeshGenerator2 x:Key="sphere" />
```

Then suppose that you've referenced this resource in a *GeometryModel3D* and all is well. Now you want to animate the *Radius* property in XAML. You define a *DoubleAnimation* element for this purpose. You set the *Storyboard.TargetProperty* attached property to "Angle" and the *Storyboard.TargetName* attached property to...what? You can't use the name you've assigned to the *x:Key* attribute for this purpose, so you add an *x:Name* attribute to the resource:

```
<src:SphereMeshGenerator2 x:Key="sphere" x:Name="sphere" />
```

Whether you assign *x:Name* to the same string as *x:Key* or not, the name won't be recognized. In fact, the documentation of *x:Name* clearly states: "*x:Name* cannot be applied in certain scopes. For instance, items in a *ResourceDictionary* cannot have names, because they already have the *x:Key* attribute as their unique identifier."

The solution? Define a *Name* property in *SphereMeshGenerator2*—and yes, you should back the *Name* property with a dependency property (for reasons I'll discuss shortly). You can actually give this property any name you want, but you have to indicate that name in an attribute for the class:

```
[RuntimeNameProperty("Name")]
```

You'll also need a *using* directive for *System.Windows.Markup*, or you can precede *Runtime-NameProperty* with that namespace. The *Name* dependency property does not need a property-changed handler.

Now you can define the resource like this:

```
<src:SphereMeshGenerator2 x:Key="sphere" Name="sphere" />
```

Well, actually not. You'll get this very mysterious error message: "Because *SphereMesh-Geometry2* is implemented in the same assembly, you must set the *x:Name* attribute rather than the *Name* attribute." Just change it to *x:Name* and it'll work. You can use *Name* if the class is implemented in a DLL.

So far, I've shown you the code you need to have in *SphereMeshGenerator2* if the class inherits from *DependencyObject*, which is the minimum requirement to implement dependency properties used for animations and targets of data bindings. But if you also want to use *Begin-Animation* with properties of the class, you'll need to inherit from *Animatable*, the class shown in this hierarchy:

Object
    DispatcherObject (abstract)
        DependencyObject
            Freezable (abstract)
                Animatable (abstract)

By inheriting from *Animatable*, you're also deriving from *Freezable*, and that little fact has some serious consequences. The tutorial on the *Freezable* class in the WPF documentation lists several methods you need to implement. However, if all the properties in the class are backed by dependency properties (which I certainly recommend), you need to override only one method, *CreateInstanceCore*, and you can simply return a new instance of the class:

```
protected override Freezable CreateInstanceCore()
{
    return new SphereMeshGenerator2();
}
```

Here at long last is the *SphereMeshGenerator2* class. At this point everything should look familiar:

SphereMeshGenerator2.cs
```
//----------------------------------------------------
// SphereMeshGenerator2.cs (c) 2007 by Charles Petzold
//----------------------------------------------------
using System;
using System.Windows;
using System.Windows.Markup;
using System.Windows.Media;
using System.Windows.Media.Animation;
using System.Windows.Media.Media3D;
```

```
namespace Petzold.AnimatableResourceDemo
{
    [RuntimeNameProperty("Name")]
    public class SphereMeshGenerator2 : Animatable
    {
        // Constructor performs initialization.
        public SphereMeshGenerator2()
        {
            Geometry = Geometry.Clone();
            PropertyChanged(new DependencyPropertyChangedEventArgs());
        }

        // Name dependency property and CLR property.
        public static readonly DependencyProperty NameProperty =
            DependencyProperty.Register("Name",
                typeof(string),
                typeof(SphereMeshGenerator2));

        public string Name
        {
            set { SetValue(NameProperty, value); }
            get { return (string)GetValue(NameProperty); }
        }

        // Center dependency property and CLR property.
        public static readonly DependencyProperty CenterProperty =
            DependencyProperty.Register("Center",
                typeof(Point3D),
                typeof(SphereMeshGenerator2),
                new PropertyMetadata(new Point3D(), PropertyChanged));

        public Point3D Center
        {
            set { SetValue(CenterProperty, value); }
            get { return (Point3D)GetValue(CenterProperty); }
        }

        // Radius dependency property and CLR property.
        public static readonly DependencyProperty RadiusProperty =
            DependencyProperty.Register("Radius",
                typeof(double),
                typeof(SphereMeshGenerator2),
                new PropertyMetadata(1.0, PropertyChanged));

        public double Radius
        {
            set { SetValue(RadiusProperty, value); }
            get { return (double)GetValue(RadiusProperty); }
        }

        // Slices dependency property and CLR property.
        public static readonly DependencyProperty SlicesProperty =
            DependencyProperty.Register("Slices",
                typeof(int),
```

```
                typeof(SphereMeshGenerator2),
                new PropertyMetadata(32, PropertyChanged));

    public int Slices
    {
        set { SetValue(SlicesProperty, value); }
        get { return (int)GetValue(SlicesProperty); }
    }

    // Stacks dependency property and CLR property.
    public static readonly DependencyProperty StacksProperty =
        DependencyProperty.Register("Stacks",
            typeof(int),
            typeof(SphereMeshGenerator2),
            new PropertyMetadata(16, PropertyChanged));

    public int Stacks
    {
        set { SetValue(StacksProperty, value); }
        get { return (int)GetValue(StacksProperty); }
    }

    // Geometry dependency property and CLR property.
    static readonly DependencyPropertyKey GeometryKey =
        DependencyProperty.RegisterReadOnly("Geometry",
            typeof(MeshGeometry3D),
            typeof(SphereMeshGenerator2),
            new PropertyMetadata(new MeshGeometry3D()));

    public static readonly DependencyProperty GeometryProperty =
        GeometryKey.DependencyProperty;

    public MeshGeometry3D Geometry
    {
        protected set { SetValue(GeometryKey, value); }
        get { return (MeshGeometry3D)GetValue(GeometryProperty); }
    }

    // PropertyChanged methods.
    static void PropertyChanged(DependencyObject obj,
                                DependencyPropertyChangedEventArgs args)
    {
        (obj as SphereMeshGenerator2).PropertyChanged(args);
    }

    void PropertyChanged(DependencyPropertyChangedEventArgs args)
    {
        // Get reference to Geometry property for local ease.
        MeshGeometry3D mesh = Geometry;

        // Get references to all four collections.
        Point3DCollection vertices = mesh.Positions;
        Vector3DCollection normals = mesh.Normals;
        Int32Collection indices = mesh.TriangleIndices;
        PointCollection textures = mesh.TextureCoordinates;
```

```
            // Set the MeshGeometry3D properties to null to inhibit notifications.
            mesh.Positions = null;
            mesh.Normals = null;
            mesh.TriangleIndices = null;
            mesh.TextureCoordinates = null;

            // Clear the four collections.
            vertices.Clear();
            normals.Clear();
            indices.Clear();
            textures.Clear();

            // Fill the vertices, normals, and textures collections.
            for (int stack = 0; stack <= Stacks; stack++)
            {
                double phi = Math.PI / 2 - stack * Math.PI / Stacks;
                double y = Radius * Math.Sin(phi);
                double scale = -Radius * Math.Cos(phi);

                for (int slice = 0; slice <= Slices; slice++)
                {
                    double theta = slice * 2 * Math.PI / Slices;
                    double x = scale * Math.Sin(theta);
                    double z = scale * Math.Cos(theta);

                    Vector3D normal = new Vector3D(x, y, z);
                    normals.Add(normal);
                    vertices.Add(normal + Center);
                    textures.Add(new Point((double)slice / Slices,
                                           (double)stack / Stacks));
                }
            }

            // Fill the indices collection.
            for (int stack = 0; stack < Stacks; stack++)
            {
                int top = (stack + 0) * (Slices + 1);
                int bot = (stack + 1) * (Slices + 1);

                for (int slice = 0; slice < Slices; slice++)
                {
                    if (stack != 0)
                    {
                        indices.Add(top + slice);
                        indices.Add(bot + slice);
                        indices.Add(top + slice + 1);
                    }

                    if (stack != Stacks - 1)
                    {
                        indices.Add(top + slice + 1);
                        indices.Add(bot + slice);
                        indices.Add(bot + slice + 1);
                    }
                }
            }
```

```
            // Set the collections back to the properties.
            mesh.TextureCoordinates = textures;
            mesh.TriangleIndices = indices;
            mesh.Normals = normals;
            mesh.Positions = vertices;
        }

        // Required override of CreateInstanceCore.
        protected override Freezable CreateInstanceCore()
        {
            return new SphereMeshGenerator2();
        }
    }
}
```

Notice that the default value of the *Radius* property is set to 1.0. When I set default values of dependency properties of type *double*, I almost never use a decimal point and just put in 1 (for example) in the *PropertyMetadata* constructor. However, this argument is of type *object*, and a 1 by itself is considered an integer. The problem doesn't reveal itself until run time.

The SphereMeshGenerator2.cs file is part of the AnimatableResourceDemo project, which also includes the following XAML file. The file creates two instances of *SphereMeshGenerator2* as resources and animates the *Radius* properties. One gets larger while the other gets smaller, and then the process reverses.

AnimatableResourceDemo.xaml
```
<!-- =======================================================
        AnimatableResourceDemo.xaml (c) 2007 by Charles Petzold
     ======================================================= -->
<Window xmlns="http://schemas.microsoft.com/winfx/2006/xaml/presentation"
        xmlns:x="http://schemas.microsoft.com/winfx/2006/xaml"
        xmlns:src="clr-namespace:Petzold.AnimatableResourceDemo"
        x:Class="Petzold.AnimatableResourceDemo.AnimatableResourceDemo"
        Title="Animatable Resource Demo">
    <Window.Resources>
        <src:SphereMeshGenerator2 x:Key="sphere1" x:Name="sphere1"
                            Center="-0.5 0 0" />
        <src:SphereMeshGenerator2 x:Key="sphere2" x:Name="sphere2"
                            Center="0.5 0 0" />
    </Window.Resources>

    <Viewport3D>
        <ModelVisual3D>
            <ModelVisual3D.Content>
                <Model3DGroup>
```

```xml
                    <!-- First sphere. -->
                    <GeometryModel3D
                        Geometry="{Binding Source={StaticResource sphere1},
                                           Path=Geometry}">
                        <GeometryModel3D.Material>
                            <DiffuseMaterial Brush="Cyan" />
                        </GeometryModel3D.Material>
                    </GeometryModel3D>

                    <!-- Second sphere. -->
                    <GeometryModel3D
                        Geometry="{Binding Source={StaticResource sphere2},
                                           Path=Geometry}">
                        <GeometryModel3D.Material>
                            <DiffuseMaterial Brush="Pink" />
                        </GeometryModel3D.Material>
                    </GeometryModel3D>

                    <!-- Light sources. -->
                    <AmbientLight Color="#404040" />
                    <DirectionalLight Color="#C0C0C0" Direction="2 -3 -1" />
                </Model3DGroup>
            </ModelVisual3D.Content>
        </ModelVisual3D>

        <!-- Camera. -->
        <Viewport3D.Camera>
            <PerspectiveCamera Position="0 0 4"
                               LookDirection="0 0 -1"
                               UpDirection="0 1 0"
                               FieldOfView="45" />
        </Viewport3D.Camera>
    </Viewport3D>

    <Window.Triggers>
        <EventTrigger RoutedEvent="Window.Loaded">
            <BeginStoryboard>
                <Storyboard>
                    <DoubleAnimation Storyboard.TargetName="sphere1"
                                     Storyboard.TargetProperty="Radius"
                                     From="0" To="1" Duration="0:0:3"
                                     AutoReverse="True"
                                     RepeatBehavior="Forever" />

                    <DoubleAnimation Storyboard.TargetName="sphere2"
                                     Storyboard.TargetProperty="Radius"
                                     From="1" To="0" Duration="0:0:3"
                                     AutoReverse="True"
                                     RepeatBehavior="Forever" />
                </Storyboard>
            </BeginStoryboard>
        </EventTrigger>
    </Window.Triggers>
</Window>
```

The AnimatableResourceDemo project is completed with the code half of the *Window* class defined by the following file:

```
AnimatableResourceDemo.cs
//----------------------------------------------------------
// AnimatableResourceDemo.cs (c) 2007 by Charles Petzold
//----------------------------------------------------------
using System;
using System.Windows;

namespace Petzold.AnimatableResourceDemo
{
    public partial class AnimatableResourceDemo : Window
    {
        [STAThread]
        public static void Main()
        {
            Application app = new Application();
            app.Run(new AnimatableResourceDemo());
        }

        public AnimatableResourceDemo()
        {
            InitializeComponent();
        }
    }
}
```

I warned you about memory allocations during the *PropertyChanged* method, which basically means no *new* expressions involving classes (but *new* expressions with structures are allowed). However, memory allocations haven't been entirely eliminated from *Property-Changed*. In particular, the collections that comprise the four properties of *MeshGeometry3D* are dynamically allocated if more space is required. Certainly the first time that *Property-Changed* is called, memory allocations will occur as the collections achieve the required capacity. Also, if you animate *Slices* or *Stacks* (which is entirely possible) the collection objects might have to reallocate themselves. These memory allocations are generally not dangerous because they don't occur very often. If this idea bothers you, you can use the constructor to initialize the properties of the *MeshGeometry3D* objects to collections of an adequate size. For example:

```
Geometry.Positions = new Point3DCollection((Stacks + 1) * (Slices + 1));
```

Initializing these collections is more crucial when you know they're going to be very large.

As written, the *PropertyChanged* method recalculates all four collections whenever the *Center*, *Radius*, *Slices*, or *Stacks* property changes. However, if the *Center* or *Radius* property is being changed, only the *Positions* collection needs to be recalculated; the *TriangleIndices*, *Normals*, and *TextureCoordinates* collections will remain the same. This means that you can avoid some work in the *PropertyChanged* method by checking the *Property* property of the *Dependency-PropertyChangedEventArgs* argument. This type of enhancement tends to muddy up the

PropertyChanged method; you should probably attempt it only when you're otherwise very happy with the method and it's raining outside.

The *SphereMeshGenerator2* class doesn't have checks against invalid settings of the *Radius*, *Slices*, and *Stacks* properties. Interestingly enough, if you set *Radius* to negative values, the figure is unchanged. However, *Slices* should have values of 3 and higher, and *Stacks* should be set to 2 and higher.

Dependency properties have a built-in mechanism for validity checking. It's another argument to the *DependencyProperties.Register* method following the property metadata:

```
public static readonly DependencyProperty SlicesProperty =
    DependencyProperty.Register("Slices",
        typeof(int),
        typeof(SphereMeshGenerator2),
        new PropertyMetadata(32, PropertyChanged),
        ValidateSlices);
```

The validation callback has a very simple signature and is generally very simply implemented:

```
static bool ValidateSlices(object obj)
{
    return (int)obj > 2;
}
```

If the property is set to an invalid value, an *ArgumentException* is raised.

Converting Objects to XAML

You might want to use the *MeshGeometry3D* object generated by the *SphereMeshGenerator2* class in an all-XAML program. Fortunately, WPF provides ways to convert from objects to XAML—a process called *serialization*.

Here's a little console program from a project named SerializeGeometry that also contains a link to the SphereMeshGenerator2.cs file.

```
SerializeGeometry.cs
//-------------------------------------------------
// SerializeGeometry.cs (c) 2007 by Charles Petzold
//-------------------------------------------------
using System;
using System.Text;
using System.Windows;
using System.Windows.Markup;
using System.Windows.Media.Media3D;
using System.Xml;
using Petzold.AnimatableResourceDemo;

namespace Petzold.SerializeGeometry
{
```

```
public class SerializeGeometry
{
    [STAThread]
    public static void Main()
    {
        // Create mesh-generator object and set properties.
        SphereMeshGenerator2 meshgen = new SphereMeshGenerator2();
        meshgen.Slices = 10;
        meshgen.Stacks = 5;

        // Make the XML look nice.
        XmlWriterSettings settings = new XmlWriterSettings();
        settings.Indent = true;
        settings.IndentChars = new string(' ', 4);
        settings.NewLineOnAttributes = true;
        settings.OmitXmlDeclaration = true;

        // Dump the MeshGeometry3D.
        MeshGeometry3D mesh = meshgen.Geometry;
        StringBuilder strbuild = new StringBuilder();
        XmlWriter xmlwrite = XmlWriter.Create(strbuild, settings);
        XamlWriter.Save(mesh, xmlwrite);

        // Copy it to the clipboard.
        Clipboard.SetText(strbuild.ToString());
    }
}
```

The key call here is *XamlWriter.Save*, which converts a WPF object to XAML. The program then copies the result to the clipboard. You can then paste the XAML Document wherever you want it.

Deriving from *ModelVisual3D*

In the entire *System.Windows.Media.Media3D* namespace, only one class is neither abstract nor sealed. That class is *ModelVisual3D*, and you might be wondering: What happened? Did they just forget to add the *sealed* modifier?

No, *ModelVisual3D* was deliberately made available for inheritance. The problem is that it's not that easy to do so, and has a certain built-in hassle factor.

As you'll recall, *ModelVisual3D* defines three properties: *Children*, *Content*, and *Transform*. When you use *ModelVisual3D* for three-dimensional figures, you set the *Content* property to an object of type *GeometryModel3D*, which defines the *Geometry*, *Material*, and *BackMaterial* properties that define the figure.

The implication here is simple: If you derive from *ModelVisual3D* to generate a *MeshGeometry3D* object, your class must also define *Material* and *BackMaterial* properties. The class's constructor must create a *GeometryModel3D* object to set to its *Content* property, and a *MeshGeometry3D* object to set to the *Geometry* property of the *GeometryModel3D*. Any objects set to your class's *Material* and *BackMaterial* properties should then be transferred to the *Material* and *BackMaterial* properties of the *GeometryModel3D*.

The big advantage of this approach is that you can use the class right in your markup as a child of the *Viewport3D*. For example:

```
<Viewport3D>
    <src:Sphere ...>
        ...
    </src:Sphere>
    ...
</Viewport3D>
```

I've left room between the *Sphere* start and end tags for the definition of (at least) the *Material* property.

Here is yet another sphere class, but this one derives from *ModelVisual3D* and defines *Material* and *BackMaterial* properties along with *Center*, *Radius*, *Slices*, and *Stacks* properties. This class has no public *Geometry* property.

```
SphereVisual.cs
//---------------------------------------------
// SphereVisual.cs (c) 2007 by Charles Petzold
//---------------------------------------------
using System;
using System.Windows;
using System.Windows.Media;
using System.Windows.Media.Media3D;

namespace Petzold.SphereVisualDemo
{
    public class SphereVisual : ModelVisual3D
    {
        // Private fields store necessary content.
        GeometryModel3D model;
        MeshGeometry3D mesh;

        // Constructor.
        public SphereVisual()
        {
            // Create objects and set the Content property.
            model = new GeometryModel3D();
            mesh = new MeshGeometry3D();
            model.Geometry = mesh;
            Content = model;

            // Initialize the MeshGeometry3D.
            PropertyChanged(new DependencyPropertyChangedEventArgs());
        }
```

```csharp
// Material dependency property and CLR property.
public static readonly DependencyProperty MaterialProperty =
    GeometryModel3D.MaterialProperty.AddOwner(
        typeof(SphereVisual),
        new PropertyMetadata(MaterialPropertyChanged));

public Material Material
{
    set { SetValue(MaterialProperty, value); }
    get { return (Material)GetValue(MaterialProperty); }
}


// BackMaterial dependency property and CLR property.
public static readonly DependencyProperty BackMaterialProperty =
    GeometryModel3D.BackMaterialProperty.AddOwner(
        typeof(SphereVisual),
        new PropertyMetadata(MaterialPropertyChanged));

public Material BackMaterial
{
    set { SetValue(BackMaterialProperty, value); }
    get { return (Material)GetValue(BackMaterialProperty); }
}


// Center dependency property and CLR property.
public static readonly DependencyProperty CenterProperty =
    DependencyProperty.Register("Center",
        typeof(Point3D),
        typeof(SphereVisual),
        new PropertyMetadata(new Point3D(), PropertyChanged));

public Point3D Center
{
    set { SetValue(CenterProperty, value); }
    get { return (Point3D)GetValue(CenterProperty); }
}


// Radius dependency property and CLR property.
public static readonly DependencyProperty RadiusProperty =
    DependencyProperty.Register("Radius",
        typeof(double),
        typeof(SphereVisual),
        new PropertyMetadata(1.0, PropertyChanged));

public double Radius
{
    set { SetValue(RadiusProperty, value); }
    get { return (double)GetValue(RadiusProperty); }
}


// Slices dependency property and CLR property.
public static readonly DependencyProperty SlicesProperty =
    DependencyProperty.Register("Slices",
        typeof(int),
```

```
                        typeof(SphereVisual),
                        new PropertyMetadata(32, PropertyChanged));

    public int Slices
    {
        set { SetValue(SlicesProperty, value); }
        get { return (int)GetValue(SlicesProperty); }
    }

    // Stacks dependency property and CLR property.
    public static readonly DependencyProperty StacksProperty =
        DependencyProperty.Register("Stacks",
            typeof(int),
            typeof(SphereVisual),
            new PropertyMetadata(16, PropertyChanged));

    public int Stacks
    {
        set { SetValue(StacksProperty, value); }
        get { return (int)GetValue(StacksProperty); }
    }

    // MaterialPropertyChanged methods.
    static void MaterialPropertyChanged(DependencyObject obj,
                            DependencyPropertyChangedEventArgs args)
    {
        (obj as SphereVisual).MaterialPropertyChanged(args);
    }

    void MaterialPropertyChanged(DependencyPropertyChangedEventArgs args)
    {
        if (args.Property == MaterialProperty)
            model.Material = args.NewValue as Material;

        else if (args.Property == BackMaterialProperty)
            model.BackMaterial = args.NewValue as Material;
    }

    // PropertyChanged methods.
    static void PropertyChanged(DependencyObject obj,
                            DependencyPropertyChangedEventArgs args)
    {
        (obj as SphereVisual).PropertyChanged(args);
    }

    void PropertyChanged(DependencyPropertyChangedEventArgs args)
    {
        // Get references to all four collections.
        Point3DCollection vertices = mesh.Positions;
        Vector3DCollection normals = mesh.Normals;
        Int32Collection indices = mesh.TriangleIndices;
        PointCollection textures = mesh.TextureCoordinates;

        // Set the MeshGeometry3D properties to null to inhibit notifications.
```

```
mesh.Positions = null;
mesh.Normals = null;
mesh.TriangleIndices = null;
mesh.TextureCoordinates = null;

// Clear the four collections.
vertices.Clear();
normals.Clear();
indices.Clear();
textures.Clear();

// Fill the vertices, normals, and textures collections.
for (int stack = 0; stack <= Stacks; stack++)
{
    double phi = Math.PI / 2 - stack * Math.PI / Stacks;
    double y = Radius * Math.Sin(phi);
    double scale = -Radius * Math.Cos(phi);

    for (int slice = 0; slice <= Slices; slice++)
    {
        double theta = slice * 2 * Math.PI / Slices;
        double x = scale * Math.Sin(theta);
        double z = scale * Math.Cos(theta);

        Vector3D normal = new Vector3D(x, y, z);
        normals.Add(normal);
        vertices.Add(normal + Center);
        textures.Add(new Point((double)slice / Slices,
                               (double)stack / Stacks));
    }
}


// Fill the indices collection.
for (int stack = 0; stack < Stacks; stack++)
{
    int top = (stack + 0) * (Slices + 1);
    int bot = (stack + 1) * (Slices + 1);

    for (int slice = 0; slice < Slices; slice++)
    {
        if (stack != 0)
        {
            indices.Add(top + slice);
            indices.Add(bot + slice);
            indices.Add(top + slice + 1);
        }

        if (stack != Stacks - 1)
        {
            indices.Add(top + slice + 1);
            indices.Add(bot + slice);
            indices.Add(bot + slice + 1);
        }
    }
```

```
        }

        // Set the collections back to the properties.
        mesh.TextureCoordinates = textures;
        mesh.TriangleIndices = indices;
        mesh.Normals = normals;
        mesh.Positions = vertices;
    }
  }
}
```

Notice that the *GeometryModel3D* and *MeshGeometry3D* associated with this *ModelVisual3D* are stored as fields. The constructor sets the *MeshGeometry3D* object to the *Geometry* property of the *GeometryModel3D* and the *GeometryModel3D* object to the base class's *Content* property.

The class creates the dependency properties for *Material* and *BackMaterial* by registering a new owner for the existing properties in *GeometryModel3D*. These two properties are associated with a property-changed handler named *MaterialPropertyChanged*, which transfers any new values of these properties to the same property in the *GeometryModel3D* object saved as a field.

The rest of the program should look very familiar by now. But note that the *PropertyChanged* method that performs the triangulation logic needs merely to access the *MeshGeometry3D* object stored as a field.

The *SphereVisual* class is part of the SphereVisualDemo project. The following XAML file creates a *SphereVisual* object in its markup, and then independently animates the three components of a *ScaleTransform3D* object to make the sphere assume nonspherical shapes.

SphereVisualDemo.xaml

```
<!-- ================================================
       SphereVisualDemo.xaml (c) 2007 by Charles Petzold
     ================================================ -->
<Page xmlns="http://schemas.microsoft.com/winfx/2006/xaml/presentation"
      xmlns:x="http://schemas.microsoft.com/winfx/2006/xaml"
      xmlns:src="clr-namespace:Petzold.SphereVisualDemo"
      Title="SphereVisual Demo"
      WindowTitle="SphereVisual Demo">
    <Viewport3D>
        <!-- Sphere. -->
        <src:SphereVisual Slices="72" Stacks="36">
            <src:SphereVisual.Material>
                <DiffuseMaterial Brush="Cyan" />
            </src:SphereVisual.Material>

            <src:SphereVisual.Transform>
                <ScaleTransform3D x:Name="scale" />
            </src:SphereVisual.Transform>
        </src:SphereVisual>
```

```
                <!-- Light sources. -->
                <ModelVisual3D>
                    <ModelVisual3D.Content>
                        <Model3DGroup>
                            <AmbientLight Color="#404040" />
                            <DirectionalLight Color="#C0C0C0" Direction="2 -3 -1" />
                        </Model3DGroup>
                    </ModelVisual3D.Content>
                </ModelVisual3D>

                <!-- Camera. -->
                <Viewport3D.Camera>
                    <PerspectiveCamera Position="4 4 4"
                                       LookDirection="-1 -1 -1"
                                       UpDirection="0 1 0"
                                       FieldOfView="45" />
                </Viewport3D.Camera>
            </Viewport3D>

            <!-- Animations. -->
            <Page.Triggers>
                <EventTrigger RoutedEvent="Page.Loaded">
                    <BeginStoryboard>
                        <Storyboard TargetName="scale">
                            <DoubleAnimation Storyboard.TargetProperty="ScaleX"
                                             From="0.5" To="2" Duration="0:0:3"
                                             AutoReverse="True"
                                             RepeatBehavior="Forever" />

                            <DoubleAnimation Storyboard.TargetProperty="ScaleY"
                                             From="0.5" To="2" Duration="0:0:5"
                                             AutoReverse="True"
                                             RepeatBehavior="Forever" />

                            <DoubleAnimation Storyboard.TargetProperty="ScaleZ"
                                             From="0.5" To="2" Duration="0:0:7"
                                             AutoReverse="True"
                                             RepeatBehavior="Forever" />
                        </Storyboard>
                    </BeginStoryboard>
                </EventTrigger>
            </Page.Triggers>
        </Page>
```

An application definition file completes the project.

```
SphereVisualDemoApp.xaml
<!-- =====================================================
        SphereVisualDemoApp.xaml (c) 2007 by Charles Petzold
     ===================================================== -->
<Application xmlns="http://schemas.microsoft.com/winfx/2006/xaml/presentation"
             StartupUri="SphereVisualDemo.xaml" />
```

The Petzold.Media3D Library

To make WPF 3D programming easier for me and for you, I have assembled several helpful classes in a dynamic-link library with the file name Petzold.Media3D.dll. This DLL (and source code) is available with the downloadable code associated with this book. The code for each chapter is stored in directories named *Chapter 1*, *Chapter 2*, and so forth; the *Petzold.Media3D* directory stores the Petzold.Media3D library.

Later versions of the DLL will be found on my Web site at *http://www.charlespetzold.com/3D*. That page of my Web site also includes a program that displays documentation of the classes in the library.

Purchasing this book gives you a royalty-free license to use and distribute the Petzold.Media3D library with your own code, including commercial software products. You can't sell or publish the library by itself, however, or modify it. If you want to provide enhancements, do so by inheriting from the existing classes in the library.

Most of the classes in the Petzold.Media3D library have a namespace of *Petzold.Media3D*. However, a very small number of classes have the namespace *Petzold.Media2D* and are for use with two-dimensional graphics. These few classes draw lines with arrows on the ends, and were used to construct some diagrams in this book involving vectors.

For organizational convenience, the source code that contributes to the Petzold.Media3D library has been divided into various directories in the Visual Studio project. (The classes that draw two-dimensional lines with arrows are in the *Media2D* directory.) Each source code file is either a single class or structure, or occasionally an enumeration.

The Mesh Geometry Classes

Several classes in the Petzold.Media3D library are intended for use as resources. These classes generate a *MeshGeometry3D* object very much like *SphereMeshGenerator2*. You can find the source code for these classes in the *Meshes* directory of the Visual Studio project.

The abstract *MeshGeneratorBase* class derives from *Animatable* and provides base services for the other classes in the *Meshes* directory by defining *Name* and *Geometry* properties. The *Geometry* property is of type *MeshGeometry3D* and has a public *get* accessor and a protected *set* accessor.

MeshGeneratorBase also defines a static and protected method named *PropertyChanged*. This static *PropertyChanged* method calls a private non-static *PropertyChanged* method, which is structured much like the corresponding *PropertyChanged* method in *SphereMeshGenerator2*: It obtains the *MeshGeometry3D* object from the *Geometry* property, stores references to the collections in local variables, and then sets the four properties of the *MeshGeometry3D* to *null*. *PropertyChanged* then calls an abstract method named *Triangulate*, passing to it the *DependencyPropertyChangedEventArgs* object and the four collections.

Non-abstract classes that derive from *MeshGeneratorBase* must provide a *Triangulate* method. Generally this method begins by clearing the four collections of the *MeshGeometry3D*, but it's not required to.

Any class that derives from *MeshGeneratorBase* probably defines several properties such as *Center*, *Radius*, *Slices*, and *Stacks*. These dependency properties should reference the static *PropertyChanged* method in *MeshGeneratorBase*. Doing so causes a call to *Triangulate* whenever any property changes. If the class generates something valid with default properties, it should also call this static *PropertyChanged* method in its constructor:

```
PropertyChanged(this, new DependencyPropertyChangedEventArgs());
```

The class must also override the *CreateInstanceCore* method defined by *Freezable*.

The Petzold.Media3D library provides several classes that derive from *MeshGeneratorBase*, including *SphereMesh*, *BoxMesh*, *CylinderMesh*, *TorusMesh*, and *TeapotMesh*. The *TeapotMesh* class generates a *MeshGeometry3D* for the famous Utah Teapot created in 1975 at the University of Utah and commonly used in 3D computer graphics. I obtained the mesh information in this class from the static *Mesh.Teapot* method in DirectX 9.0.

The Petzold.Media3D library also includes an abstract class named *FlatSurfaceMeshBase* that derives from *MeshGeneratorBase* and provides services for classes that generate objects with flat surfaces. Although a polygon with N sides is easily triangulated with N triangles, if you're using the figure with *PointLight* or *SpotLight*, you'll want each triangle divided into many more triangles. *FlatSurfaceMeshBase* implements a *TriangleSubdivide* method for performing this calculation. *FlatSurfaceMeshBase* is parent to *PolygonMesh* and the abstract *PolyhedronMeshBase* class from which classes such as *DodecahedronMesh* and *IcosahedronMesh* derive.

Using the Library with Visual Studio

If you want to use the Petzold.Media3D library in a Visual Studio project, you should store the Petzold.Media3D.dll file somewhere locally. Create a WPF project as normal. In Solution Explorer, right-click the References items and select Add Reference from the drop-down menu. (Or, select Add Reference from the Project menu.) The Add Reference dialog box appears. Select the Browse tab. You can then locate the Petzold.Media.dll file and select it.

In your C# source code files, you only need to add a *using* directive for the namespace for the classes in the library:

```
using Petzold.Media3D;
```

You can alternatively (or additionally) supply a *using* directive for the *Petzold.Media2D* namespace. Visual Studio IntelliSense should now work with all the classes, properties, and methods in the library.

To reference Petzold.Media3D classes in XAML files, you must include an XML namespace declaration that associates a particular prefix with the *Petzold.Media3D* namespace and dynamic link library. I like to use the initials of my name ("cp") for the XML namespace prefix:

```
xmlns:cp="clr-namespace:Petzold.Media3D;assembly=Petzold.Media3D"
```

You can use something similar for the *Petzold.Media2D* namespace.

Alternatively you can use the following URI in the XML namespace declaration:

```
xmlns:cp="http://schemas.charlespetzold.com/2007/xaml"
```

This, of course, is very similar to the URIs referenced normally in XAML files. I associated that URI with the *Petzold.Media3D* and *Petzold.Media2D* namespaces in the AssemblyInfo.cs file that's part of the Visual Studio project for the library:

```
[assembly: XmlnsDefinition("http://schemas.charlespetzold.com/2007/xaml",
                           "Petzold.Media3D")]
[assembly: XmlnsDefinition("http://schemas.charlespetzold.com/2007/xaml",
                           "Petzold.Media2D")]
```

Don't bother looking at that location on the Web. There's nothing there! This is simply a URI that I have jurisdiction over because I own the domain name *charlespetzold.com*.

The SpinningWheel project shown next uses the Petzold.Media3D library. This project doesn't make a spinning wheel, but it does make a wheel out of a sphere (the hub), cylinders (the spokes), and a torus (the tire), and then sets it spinning with an animation.

SpinningWheel.xaml

```
<!-- ===============================================
     SpinningWheel.xaml (c) 2007 by Charles Petzold
     =============================================== -->
<Page xmlns="http://schemas.microsoft.com/winfx/2006/xaml/presentation"
      xmlns:x="http://schemas.microsoft.com/winfx/2006/xaml"
      xmlns:cp="http://schemas.charlespetzold.com/2007/xaml"
      WindowTitle="Spinning Wheel"
      Title="Spinning Wheel">
    <Page.Resources>

        <!-- Primitive shapes. -->
        <cp:SphereMesh x:Key="hub" Radius="0.2" />
        <cp:HollowCylinderMesh x:Key="spoke" Radius="0.03" Length="1" />
        <cp:TorusMesh x:Key="tire" Radius="1" TubeRadius="0.2" />

        <!-- Two materials. -->
        <DiffuseMaterial x:Key="matSteel" Brush="SteelBlue" />
        <DiffuseMaterial x:Key="matTire" Brush="DarkGray" />

        <!-- Assemble three spokes in a group. -->
        <Model3DGroup x:Key="spokeGroup">
            <GeometryModel3D Geometry="{Binding Source={StaticResource spoke},
```

```
                                            Path=Geometry}"
                        Material="{StaticResource matSteel}" />


    <GeometryModel3D Geometry="{Binding Source={StaticResource spoke},
                                        Path=Geometry}"
                     Material="{StaticResource matSteel}">
        <GeometryModel3D.Transform>
            <RotateTransform3D>
                <RotateTransform3D.Rotation>
                    <AxisAngleRotation3D Axis="0 0 -1" Angle="30" />
                </RotateTransform3D.Rotation>
            </RotateTransform3D>
        </GeometryModel3D.Transform>
    </GeometryModel3D>


    <GeometryModel3D Geometry="{Binding Source={StaticResource spoke},
                                        Path=Geometry}"
                     Material="{StaticResource matSteel}">
        <GeometryModel3D.Transform>
            <RotateTransform3D>
                <RotateTransform3D.Rotation>
                    <AxisAngleRotation3D Axis="0 0 -1" Angle="60" />
                </RotateTransform3D.Rotation>
            </RotateTransform3D>
        </GeometryModel3D.Transform>
    </GeometryModel3D>
</Model3DGroup>

<!-- Assemble the complete wheel. -->
<Model3DGroup x:Key="wheel">
    <GeometryModel3D Geometry="{Binding Source={StaticResource hub},
                                        Path=Geometry}"
                     Material="{StaticResource matSteel}" />

    <StaticResource ResourceKey="spokeGroup" />

    <Model3DGroup>
        <StaticResource ResourceKey="spokeGroup" />
        <Model3DGroup.Transform>
            <RotateTransform3D>
                <RotateTransform3D.Rotation>
                    <AxisAngleRotation3D Axis="0 0 -1" Angle="90" />
                </RotateTransform3D.Rotation>
            </RotateTransform3D>
        </Model3DGroup.Transform>
    </Model3DGroup>

    <Model3DGroup>
        <StaticResource ResourceKey="spokeGroup" />
        <Model3DGroup.Transform>
            <RotateTransform3D>
                <RotateTransform3D.Rotation>
                    <AxisAngleRotation3D Axis="0 0 -1" Angle="100" />
                </RotateTransform3D.Rotation>
```

```
                    </RotateTransform3D>
                </Model3DGroup.Transform>
        </Model3DGroup>

        <Model3DGroup>
            <StaticResource ResourceKey="spokeGroup" />
            <Model3DGroup.Transform>
                <RotateTransform3D>
                    <RotateTransform3D.Rotation>
                        <AxisAngleRotation3D Axis="0 0 -1" Angle="270" />
                    </RotateTransform3D.Rotation>
                </RotateTransform3D>
            </Model3DGroup.Transform>
        </Model3DGroup>

        <GeometryModel3D Geometry="{Binding Source={StaticResource tire},
                                            Path=Geometry}"
                         Material="{StaticResource matTire}" />
    </Model3DGroup>
</Page.Resources>

<Viewport3D>

    <!-- Show the wheel. -->
    <ModelVisual3D Content="{StaticResource wheel}">
        <ModelVisual3D.Transform>
            <RotateTransform3D>
                <RotateTransform3D.Rotation>
                    <AxisAngleRotation3D x:Name="rotate" Axis="0 0 -1" />
                </RotateTransform3D.Rotation>
            </RotateTransform3D>
        </ModelVisual3D.Transform>
    </ModelVisual3D>

    <!-- Light sources. -->
    <ModelVisual3D>
        <ModelVisual3D.Content>
            <Model3DGroup>
                <AmbientLight Color="#404040" />
                <DirectionalLight Color="#C0C0C0" Direction="2 -3 -1" />
            </Model3DGroup>
        </ModelVisual3D.Content>
    </ModelVisual3D>

    <!-- Camera. -->
    <Viewport3D.Camera>
        <PerspectiveCamera Position="-4 0 4"
                           LookDirection="4 0 -4"
                           UpDirection="0 1 0"
                           FieldOfView="45" />
    </Viewport3D.Camera>
</Viewport3D>

<Page.Triggers>
```

```
        <EventTrigger RoutedEvent="Page.Loaded">
            <BeginStoryboard>
                <Storyboard>
                    <DoubleAnimation Storyboard.TargetName="rotate"
                                     Storyboard.TargetProperty="Angle"
                                     From="0" To="360" Duration="0:0:5"
                                     RepeatBehavior="Forever" />
                </Storyboard>
            </BeginStoryboard>
        </EventTrigger>
    </Page.Triggers>
</Page>
```

Everything except the mesh-generator classes is in the XAML file, and its root element is a *Page*, so the only other file the project needs is an application definition.

SpinningWheelApp.xaml
```
<!-- ==================================================
        SpinningWheelApp.xaml (c) 2007 by Charles Petzold
     ================================================== -->
<Application xmlns="http://schemas.microsoft.com/winfx/2006/xaml/presentation"
             StartupUri="SpinningWheel.xaml" />
```

When Visual Studio compiles a program that references the Petzold.Media3D library, it copies the DLL to the same directory as the executable so that the executable can get access to this DLL at run time. If you publish the program to a Web site using Visual Studio, the DLL is copied along with the executable.

And here's the wheel:

If you'd rather not bother with the DLL but you still want to use classes in the Petzold.Media3D library in your own programs, you can copy individual source code files into your project and compile those along with your own source code. In this case, you can treat the library source code just like any source code in this book, and modify it as you like. In the XAML files, you'll want to change the XML namespace declaration to this:

```
xmlns:cp="clr-namespace:Petzold.Media3D"
```

Using the Library with XamlCruncher 2.0

If you enjoy experimenting with XAML files in my XamlCruncher program, you might be disappointed that you can't play with XAML files that reference the Petzold.Media3D library. XamlCruncher 2.0 (available from the *http://www.charlespetzold.com/wpf* page of my Web site) has a feature that lets you overcome that limitation. You can specify additional assemblies to load into the execution space of XamlCruncher, which are then available to XAML files you create in XamlCruncher.

To use this feature, select Load Assembly from the Xaml menu. The Load Assembly dialog box appears. Click the Add button. You get a File Open dialog box, which you can use to select the DLL file you want to load into the execution space. Navigate to the Petzold.Media3D.dll file and select it. XamlCruncher 2.0 calls the static *Assembly.LoadFrom* method to load the DLL for use by the application, which then makes it available to the *XamlReader.Load* method that the program calls to convert XAML to WPF objects. XamlCruncher 2.0 also saves the names of the DLLs you select and automatically loads them the next time you run the program.

XamlCruncher only attempts to load an assembly when you select a new one with the Add button from the Load Assembly dialog box and when XamlCruncher starts up. You can check the Load Assembly dialog box at any time to see what's been loaded, and you can delete DLLs from the list. However, you can't "unload" an assembly. If you're referencing a DLL that you're also developing, and you want to recompile the DLL, you need to exit XamlCruncher.

This new facility in XamlCruncher 2.0 is strictly for experimentation. It makes no sense to distribute the files as standalone XAML; they won't run in Microsoft Internet Explorer.

XamlCruncher 2.0 has a couple of other new features. You can display horizontal and vertical rulers and grid lines, which are helpful if you're using the program to design some visuals. You can print the rendered XAML or save it to a bitmap. (That's how many of the diagrams in this book were made.)

In the downloadable code for this book, some Visual Studio projects consist solely of two XAML files: a XAML file with a root element of *Page* that references the Petzold.Media3D library, and an application definition file. You can load those *Page* files into XamlCruncher 2.0 if you've also loaded the Petzold.Media3D library from the Load Assembly dialog box.

Using the Library with Standalone XAML

At times you might want to create a standalone XAML file that displays a sphere, cylinder, torus, teapot, or other object generated from classes in the Petzold.Media3D library. You realize that the resultant XAML file might be a bit long and contain mostly long strings of numbers, but you don't care.

In that case, you'll want to use the MeshGeometry3DExtractor program, which is included with the source code with the other Chapter 6 programs, but which I won't show you in the pages of this book because it has much more to do with regular WPF programming than with 3D programming, and you've already seen how it's done with the SerializeGeometry program.

MeshGeometry3DExtractor lists all the classes in the Petzold.Media3D library that contain a *Geometry* property of type *MeshGeometry3D*. Select one, and you'll be presented with the class's public properties that you can alter. The resultant *MeshGeometry3D* markup is displayed in the *TextBox* control, courtesy of the static *XamlWriter.Save* method. Just copy and paste into your own XAML files. You'll probably want to delete the namespace declaration and possibly add an *x:Key* attribute if you're using it as a resource. But it doesn't have to be a resource: You can insert this markup right into a *GeometryModel3D.Geometry* property element.

ModelVisual3D Derivations

The Petzold.Media3D library also includes several classes that derive from *ModelVisual3D*. These classes are located in the *Visuals* directory of the Petzold.Media3D project. The classes generally have simple names such as *Sphere*, *Cylinder*, and *Billboard*, and they derive from the abstract *ModelVisualBase*, which provides the definition of the *Material* and *BackMaterial* properties, and also provides the structural overhead for the derivative classes.

I took a somewhat different design philosophy with the classes that derive from *ModelVisual3D* than I did with the classes that generate mesh geometries. The mesh-generation classes are often used as resources and are shared among multiple visuals; in practice, you alter these figures with transforms.

When deriving from *ModelVisual3D*, however, you're probably not sharing the figure, so you might appreciate having greater control over the appearance of the figure by setting properties rather than using transforms. For example, the *CylinderMesh* class lets you set *Radius* and *Length* properties but the cylinder always begins at the origin and extends along the Z axis. The *Cylinder* class lets you specify the points where the cylinder begins and ends, and the two radii at either end.

The *Sphere* class lets you specify a range of longitude and latitude so that you can display a partial sphere. This feature is put to use in the following file, which you can also load into XamlCruncher 2.0.

OpenAndClose.xaml

```xml
<!-- =============================================
        OpenAndClose.xaml (c) 2007 by Charles Petzold
     ============================================= -->
<Page xmlns="http://schemas.microsoft.com/winfx/2006/xaml/presentation"
      xmlns:x="http://schemas.microsoft.com/winfx/2006/xaml"
      xmlns:cp="http://schemas.charlespetzold.com/2007/xaml"
      WindowTitle="Open and Close"
      Title="Open and Close">
    <Viewport3D>
        <cp:Sphere x:Name="sphere">
            <cp:Sphere.Material>
                <DiffuseMaterial Brush="Cyan" />
            </cp:Sphere.Material>

            <cp:Sphere.BackMaterial>
                <DiffuseMaterial>
                    <DiffuseMaterial.Brush>
                        <SolidColorBrush x:Name="inside" />
                    </DiffuseMaterial.Brush>
                </DiffuseMaterial>
            </cp:Sphere.BackMaterial>

            <cp:Sphere.Transform>
                <RotateTransform3D>
                    <RotateTransform3D.Rotation>
                        <AxisAngleRotation3D x:Name="rotate" Axis="0 0 1" />
                    </RotateTransform3D.Rotation>
                </RotateTransform3D>
            </cp:Sphere.Transform>
        </cp:Sphere>

        <!-- Light sources. -->
        <ModelVisual3D>
            <ModelVisual3D.Content>
                <Model3DGroup>
                    <AmbientLight Color="#404040" />
                    <DirectionalLight Color="#C0C0C0" Direction="2, -3 -1" />
                </Model3DGroup>
            </ModelVisual3D.Content>
        </ModelVisual3D>

        <!-- Camera. -->
        <Viewport3D.Camera>
            <PerspectiveCamera Position="0 0 5"
                               LookDirection="0 0 -1"
                               UpDirection="0 1 0"
                               FieldOfView="45" />
        </Viewport3D.Camera>
    </Viewport3D>

    <Page.Triggers>
        <EventTrigger RoutedEvent="Page.Loaded">
            <BeginStoryboard>
```

```
            <Storyboard RepeatBehavior="Forever">
                <DoubleAnimation Storyboard.TargetName="sphere"
                                Storyboard.TargetProperty="LongitudeFrom"
                                From="0.001" To="60" Duration="0:0:3"
                                AutoReverse="True"
                                RepeatBehavior="2x" />

                <DoubleAnimation Storyboard.TargetName="sphere"
                                Storyboard.TargetProperty="LongitudeTo"
                                From="-0.001" To="-60" Duration="0:0:3"
                                AutoReverse="True"
                                RepeatBehavior="2x" />

                <DoubleAnimationUsingKeyFrames
                                Storyboard.TargetName="rotate"
                                Storyboard.TargetProperty="Angle">
                    <DiscreteDoubleKeyFrame
                                KeyTime="0:0:0" Value="0" />

                    <DiscreteDoubleKeyFrame
                                KeyTime="0:0:6" Value="90" />
                </DoubleAnimationUsingKeyFrames>

                <ColorAnimationUsingKeyFrames
                                Storyboard.TargetName="inside"
                                Storyboard.TargetProperty="Color">
                    <DiscreteColorKeyFrame
                                KeyTime="0:0:0" Value="Red" />

                    <DiscreteColorKeyFrame
                                KeyTime="0:0:6" Value="Blue" />
                </ColorAnimationUsingKeyFrames>


            </Storyboard>
          </BeginStoryboard>
        </EventTrigger>
    </Page.Triggers>
</Page>
```

The XAML file animates the *LongitudeFrom* and *LongitudeTo* properties of *Sphere* so that it appears to open and close. If you'd rather compile this XAML file than run it in Xaml-Cruncher 2.0, the OpenAndClose project includes the following application definition file.

OpenAndCloseApp.xaml

```
<!-- =================================================
       OpenAndCloseApp.xaml (c) 2007 by Charles Petzold
     ================================================= -->
<Application xmlns="http://schemas.microsoft.com/winfx/2006/xaml/presentation"
             StartupUri="OpenAndClose.xaml" />
```

I've given the classes in Petzold.Media3D that derive from *ModelVisual3D* a public get-only *Geometry* property, so you can use the MeshGeometry3DExtractor program with these classes as well.

I have not yet finished discussing the contents of the Petzold.Media3D library. More is to come in the next chapter.

Chapter 7
Matrix Transforms

My coverage of transforms in Chapter 2, "Transforms and Animation," and Chapter 3, "Axis/ Angle Rotation," omitted one of the classes that derive from *Transform3D*. That mystery class is *MatrixTransform3D*, which has the flexibility to encompass all the standard translate, scale, and rotation transforms—and much more. Naturally, it's not nearly as easy to use: The single read/write *Matrix* property is of type *Matrix3D*, a structure with 16 of its own read/write properties. In XAML, you can either set these properties of the *Matrix3D* object individually or indicate a complete *Matrix3D* with a string of 16 numbers.

If you find the standard translate, scale, and rotation transforms entirely sufficient for your needs, you might be able to avoid the *Matrix3D* structure entirely. But understanding its role in 3D graphics programming is the key to several advanced techniques.

The *Matrix3D* structure encapsulates a mathematical entity that was given the name *matrix* around the mid-nineteenth century by English mathematician James Joseph Sylvester (1814– 1897). Graphical transforms are often represented as matrices because matrix algebra makes the transforms easy to manipulate. For example, compound transforms are equivalent to matrix multiplications, and inverse transforms are equivalent to matrix inversions. I suspect you've encountered matrices in your education but if you're a little rusty, I've provided a brief review.

Transforms are categorized in various ways, and I'll define these categories as we encounter them. My presentation of matrices in this chapter focuses on linear transforms first, then affine transforms, and then non-affine transforms. If at first you think I'm omitting something from this discussion, rest assured that it will appear at the proper time.

Linear Transforms

In mathematics, a function f is said to be *linear* if the following relationships are true for variables x and y and constant k:

$$f(x+y) = f(x) + f(y)$$
$$f(kx) = kf(x)$$

In 3D graphics, that function f could very well be a transform, and rather than being numbers, x and y could be three-dimensional points and vectors. It's actually easier to think in terms of vectors rather than points because vectors can be added, and vectors can be multiplied by a constant, but those concepts make no sense with points.

The scale transform is linear. The rotation transform is linear. Other types of transforms (such as the shear, also known as skew) are also linear. But translation—in one sense the simplest of all transforms—is *not* linear. Fortunately, this little problem involves a solution that also offers other benefits.

A Review of Matrix Algebra

A matrix is a rectangular array of numbers with a fixed number of rows and columns. A 3×4 matrix has three rows and four columns:

$$\begin{vmatrix} 27 & 0.5 & -2 & 0 \\ 1.2 & 0 & 0 & 1 \\ 8 & 18 & -3 & -0.5 \end{vmatrix}$$

The matrix is written with vertical lines enclosing the array. Often bold-faced capital letters (such as $\mathbf{A}$) indicate an entire matrix. Each number is referred to as an *element* or an *entry* of the matrix. Sometimes the matrix is said to contain *cells*. A particular element is notated with two subscripts—for example, $a_{i,j}$ where i is the row and j is the column. These subscripts are one-based rather than zero-based. In the above array, $a_{1,1}$ is the element in the upper-left corner and $a_{3,4}$ is the element in the lower-right corner.

You can add or subtract two matrices of the same size by simply adding or subtracting the corresponding elements. You can multiply a matrix by a scalar (a single number) by multiplying all the elements by that scalar.

The more interesting operation is the multiplication of two matrices. Suppose $\mathbf{A}$ and $\mathbf{B}$ are two matrices with entries $a_{i,j}$ and $b_{i,j}$ and $\mathbf{C}$ is their product with entries $c_{i,j}$:

$$\mathbf{A} \times \mathbf{B} = \mathbf{C}$$

The product is defined only if the number of columns in $\mathbf{A}$ equals the number of rows in $\mathbf{B}$. The product $\mathbf{C}$ has the same number of rows as $\mathbf{A}$ and the same number of columns as $\mathbf{B}$. You can calculate each entry in $\mathbf{C}$ with the following formula, where N is the number of columns in $\mathbf{A}$ and rows in $\mathbf{B}$:

$$c_{i,j} = \sum_{n=1}^{N} a_{i,n} \times b_{n,j}$$

The large Greek sigma indicates a summation of n ranging from 1 to N. Matrix multiplication is actually much easier in practice than in the abstract. Consider the following three matrices:

$$\begin{vmatrix} 2 & 3 & 4 \\ 7 & 5 & 3 \end{vmatrix} \times \begin{vmatrix} 1 & 2 & 3 & 4 \\ 4 & 3 & 2 & 1 \\ 2 & 4 & 1 & 3 \end{vmatrix} = \begin{vmatrix} 22 & 29 & 16 & 23 \\ 33 & 41 & 34 & 42 \end{vmatrix}$$

I've already filled in the elements of the product. As you can see, the number of columns in the first matrix (three) is the same as the number of rows in the second matrix. The product has the same number of rows as the first matrix (two), and the same number of columns as the second matrix (four).

Begin with the first row of the first matrix, which consists of the numbers 2, 3, and 4. In your mind, twist it sideways so that it's vertical. Line it up with the first column of the second matrix (the numbers 1, 4, and 2). Multiply corresponding numbers and add them up: 2 times 1, plus 3 times 4, plus 4 times 2 equals 22. That's the number that goes in the first row and first column of the result. Continue with the first row of the first matrix and the second, third, and fourth columns of the second matrix to complete the first row of the result. Now consider the second row of the first matrix—the numbers 7, 5, and 3. Again, twist it sideways and multiply by the first column of the second matrix: 7 times 1, plus 5 times 4, plus 3 times 2 equals 33. That's the result for the first column of the second row. Now continue multiplying the second row from the first matrix by the second, third, and fourth columns in the second matrix to fill in the subsequent columns of the second row of the result.

In general, matrix multiplication is not commutative. In other words, the product $\mathbf{A} \times \mathbf{B}$ does not necessarily equal $\mathbf{B} \times \mathbf{A}$. This is obvious in my example because the number of columns in the first matrix must equal the number of rows in the second matrix, and that's no longer true if you switch them around. But even if the matrices are square (that is, if they have the same number of rows and columns), matrix multiplication is generally not commutative. However, matrix multiplication is associative: In the multiplication $\mathbf{A} \times \mathbf{B} \times \mathbf{C}$ it doesn't matter which multiplication you do first. Matrix multiplication is also distributive over addition:

$$\mathbf{A} \times (\mathbf{B} + \mathbf{C}) = \mathbf{A} \times \mathbf{B} + \mathbf{A} \times \mathbf{C}$$

Matrices and Transforms

A point in 3D space (x, y, z) can be represented by a 1×3 matrix:

$$\begin{vmatrix} x & y & z \end{vmatrix}$$

A linear transform can be represented as a 3×3 matrix:

$$\begin{vmatrix} M11 & M12 & M13 \\ M21 & M22 & M23 \\ M31 & M32 & M33 \end{vmatrix}$$

I've shown the elements in this matrix using the property names defined by the *Matrix3D* structure that conveniently indicate the row and column. The transform is a multiplication of the 3D point and the 3×3 matrix:

$$|x \quad y \quad z| \times \begin{vmatrix} M11 & M12 & M13 \\ M21 & M22 & M23 \\ M31 & M32 & M33 \end{vmatrix} = |x' \quad y' \quad z'|$$

The original point (x, y, z) is transformed to a new point (x', y', z') with the following formulas implied by the matrix multiplication:

$$x' = M11 \cdot x + M21 \cdot y + M31 \cdot z$$
$$y' = M12 \cdot x + M22 \cdot y + M32 \cdot z$$
$$z' = M13 \cdot x + M23 \cdot y + M33 \cdot z$$

A transform could be said to *map* a point (x, y, z) to the point (x', y', z').

(I am obliged to note here that some graphics books show this matrix multiplication a little differently: The matrix has its rows and columns switched, which requires that the three-dimensional point be represented as a 3×1 matrix that appears to the right of the transform matrix in the multiplication. Although that syntax has some advantages, I will stick to the convention implied by the names of the *Matrix3D* properties.)

The transform represented by this 3×3 matrix is called a *linear* transform because each formula involves only constants multiplied by the x, y, and z components of the point, and that satisfies the requirements for mathematical linearity. I want you to get a good feel for the formulas for x', y', and z' so that when you see a 3×3 matrix, you know that the first column provides the factors for x', the second column provides the factors for y', and the third column provides the factors for z'.

Here's another way of looking at it: Suppose that (x, y, z) isn't a point but a vector: $(\mathbf{x}, \mathbf{y}, \mathbf{z})$. The three columns of the matrix can also be represented as vectors: $(\mathbf{M11}, \mathbf{M21}, \mathbf{M31})$, $(\mathbf{M12}, \mathbf{M22}, \mathbf{M32})$, and $(\mathbf{M13}, \mathbf{M23}, \mathbf{M33})$. The transformed x', y', and z' are the three dot products of $(\mathbf{x}, \mathbf{y}, \mathbf{z})$ with the three column vectors that make up the matrix:

$$x' = (\mathbf{x}, \mathbf{y}, \mathbf{z}) \bullet (\mathbf{M11}, \mathbf{M21}, \mathbf{M31})$$
$$y' = (\mathbf{x}, \mathbf{y}, \mathbf{z}) \bullet (\mathbf{M12}, \mathbf{M22}, \mathbf{M32})$$
$$z' = (\mathbf{x}, \mathbf{y}, \mathbf{z}) \bullet (\mathbf{M13}, \mathbf{M23}, \mathbf{M33})$$

This approach to interpreting transforms proves to be quite useful.

Using *MatrixTransform3D*

When you create a new *MatrixTransform3D* object, the *Matrix* property stores a default *Matrix3D* object that has values of 1 only in the diagonal:

$$\begin{vmatrix} 1 & 0 & 0 \\ 0 & 1 & 0 \\ 0 & 0 & 1 \end{vmatrix}$$

This is known as the *identity matrix*, and it's the object created by the *Matrix3D* parameterless constructor. The identity matrix is the matrix equivalent to the number 1: Multiplying any matrix by the identity matrix has no effect. The transform formulas associated with the identity matrix are simply:

$$x' = x$$
$$y' = y$$
$$z' = z$$

You probably know that the default parameterless constructor of a structure always sets all fields of the structure to zero, so it may seem a little odd that the parameterless constructor of the *Matrix3D* structure results in the identity matrix, where some properties are set to 1. Internally, all fields of the *Matrix3D* structure are zero, but the *M11*, *M22*, and *M33* properties obviously add 1 to the values stored in their associated fields.

You can use a *MatrixTransform3D* element wherever you use a *TranslateTransform3D*, *ScaleTransform3D*, or *RotateTransform3D*. The following approach encloses a *Matrix3D* element in a *MatrixTransform3D.Matrix* property element:

```
<MatrixTransform3D>
    <MatrixTransform3D.Matrix>
        <Matrix3D M11="1" M12="0" M13="0"
                   M21="0" M22="1" M23="0"
                   M31="0" M32="0" M33="1" />
    </MatrixTransform3D.Matrix>
</MatrixTransform3D>
```

This markup shows the properties of *Matrix3D* arranged in a convenient array form with their default values set. The following LinearTransformExperimenter.xaml file contains a similar *Matrix3D* element that you can experiment with.

LinearTransformExperimenter.xaml

```xml
<!-- ===========================================================
        LinearTransformExperimenter.xaml (c) 2007 by Charles Petzold
     =========================================================== -->
<Page xmlns="http://schemas.microsoft.com/winfx/2006/xaml/presentation"
      xmlns:x="http://schemas.microsoft.com/winfx/2006/xaml"
      WindowTitle="Linear Transform Experimenter"
      Title="Linear Transform Experimenter">
    <DockPanel>

        <!-- Scrollbars to view object from different sides. -->
        <ScrollBar Name="horz" DockPanel.Dock="Bottom" Orientation="Horizontal"
                   Minimum="-180" Maximum="180"
                   LargeChange="10" SmallChange="1" />

        <ScrollBar Name="vert" DockPanel.Dock="Right" Orientation="Vertical"
                   Minimum="-180" Maximum="180"
                   LargeChange="10" SmallChange="1" />

        <Viewport3D>
            <ModelVisual3D>
                <ModelVisual3D.Content>
                    <Model3DGroup>
                        <GeometryModel3D>
                            <GeometryModel3D.Geometry>
                                <!-- House: front, back, left roof, left,
                                            right roof, right, bottom. -->
                                <MeshGeometry3D
                                    Positions=
                                        " 0 1  1, -0.5 0.6 1,  0.5  0.6 1,
                                                 -0.5 0 1,  0.5  0    1,

                                          0 1 -1,  0.5 0.6 -1, -0.5 0.6 -1,
                                                   0.5 0   -1, -0.5 0   -1,

                                          0   1  -1, 0   1   1,
                                         -0.5 0.6 -1, -0.5 0.6 1,

                                         -0.5 0.6 -1, -0.5 0.6 1,
                                         -0.5 0   -1, -0.5 0    1,

                                          0   1   1, 0   1   -1,
                                          0.5 0.6 1,  0.5 0.6 -1,

                                          0.5 0.6 1,  0.5 0.6 -1,
                                          0.5 0   1   0.5 0   -1,

                                          0.5 0   1,  0.5 0   -1,
                                         -0.5 0   1, -0.5 0   -1"

                                    TriangleIndices=
                                        " 0  1  2,  1  3  2,  2  3  4,
                                          5  6  7,  6  8  7,  7  8  9,
                                         10 12 11, 11 12 13,
```

```xml
                             14 16 15, 15 16 17,
                             18 20 19, 19 20 21,
                             22 24 23, 23 24 25,
                             26 28 27, 27 28 29" />
            </GeometryModel3D.Geometry>

            <GeometryModel3D.Material>
                <DiffuseMaterial Brush="Cyan" />
            </GeometryModel3D.Material>

            <GeometryModel3D.BackMaterial>
                <DiffuseMaterial Brush="Red" />
            </GeometryModel3D.BackMaterial>

            <!-- Matrix transform. -->
            <GeometryModel3D.Transform>
                <MatrixTransform3D>
                    <MatrixTransform3D.Matrix>
                        <Matrix3D
                            M11="1" M12="0" M13="0"
                            M21="0" M22="1" M23="0"
                            M31="0" M32="0" M33="1" />
                    </MatrixTransform3D.Matrix>
                </MatrixTransform3D>
            </GeometryModel3D.Transform>
        </GeometryModel3D>

        <!-- Light sources. -->
        <AmbientLight Color="#404040" />
        <DirectionalLight Color="#C0C0C0" Direction="2, -3 -1" />
    </Model3DGroup>
  </ModelVisual3D.Content>
</ModelVisual3D>

<!-- Camera. -->
<Viewport3D.Camera>

    <OrthographicCamera Position="0 0 4"
                    LookDirection="0 0 -1"
                    UpDirection="0 1 0"
                    Width="4">

        <OrthographicCamera.Transform>
            <Transform3DGroup>
                <RotateTransform3D>
                    <RotateTransform3D.Rotation>
                        <AxisAngleRotation3D Axis="0 1 0"
                            Angle="{Binding ElementName=horz,
                                        Path=Value}" />
                    </RotateTransform3D.Rotation>
                </RotateTransform3D>
                <RotateTransform3D>
                    <RotateTransform3D.Rotation>
                        <AxisAngleRotation3D Axis="1 0 0"
```

```
                                    Angle="{Binding ElementName=vert,
                                                    Path=Value}" />
                        </RotateTransform3D.Rotation>
                    </RotateTransform3D>
                </Transform3DGroup>
            </OrthographicCamera.Transform>
        </OrthographicCamera>
    </Viewport3D.Camera>
</Viewport3D>
</DockPanel>
</Page>
```

The file displays a simple 3D house sitting on the XZ plane. The house is one unit wide, one unit high, and two units deep, and the X and Z axes both pass under the center of the house. An *OrthographicCamera* looks at the house head on, so you'll initially only see the front, but you can use the two scrollbars to get a better view.

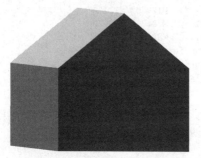

It is most educational to load LinearTransformExperimenter.xaml into XamlCruncher or a similar program, and experiment with the properties of the *Matrix3D* element. The three diagonal entries *M11*, *M22*, and *M33* govern scaling in the X, Y, and Z directions. Setting these three properties is the same as setting the *ScaleX*, *ScaleY*, and *ScaleZ* properties of *ScaleTransform3D*. If you set all three properties to 5, the house will actually encompass the camera and you'll see the bright red interior.

You can also rotate the figure around the X, Y, and Z axes. Rotation around the Z axis involves the following transform matrix:

$$\begin{vmatrix} \cos(\theta) & \sin(\theta) & 0 \\ -\sin(\theta) & \cos(\theta) & 0 \\ 0 & 0 & 1 \end{vmatrix}$$

The transform formulas are:

$$x' = x \cdot \cos(\theta) - y \cdot \sin(\theta)$$
$$y' = x \cdot \sin(\theta) + y \cdot \cos(\theta)$$
$$z' = z$$

These formulas are similar to the formulas for generating a circle that you encountered in the last chapter. Rotation of 30 degrees around the Z axis requires the following values:

$$\begin{vmatrix} 0.87 & 0.50 & 0 \\ -0.50 & 0.87 & 0 \\ 0 & 0 & 1 \end{vmatrix}$$

And here it is, viewed slightly off center:

Rotation around the X axis is the matrix:

$$\begin{vmatrix} 1 & 0 & 0 \\ 0 & \cos(\theta) & \sin(\theta) \\ 0 & -\sin(\theta) & \cos(\theta) \end{vmatrix}$$

And rotation around the Y axis is:

$$\begin{vmatrix} \cos(\theta) & 0 & -\sin(\theta) \\ 0 & 1 & 0 \\ \sin(\theta) & 0 & \cos(\theta) \end{vmatrix}$$

Notice that each of these basic rotation matrices leaves the coordinate corresponding to the rotation axis untouched. For example, the matrix that rotates around the Y axis leaves all y values unchanged.

Rotation about an arbitrary axis $(\mathbf{x}, \mathbf{y}, \mathbf{z})$ is rather messy, but since you asked, here it is. I've simplified the trigonometry syntax by removing parentheses to make it a bit easier to read:

$$\begin{vmatrix} (1-\cos\theta)x^2+\cos\theta & (1-\cos\theta)xy+(\sin\theta)z & (1-\cos\theta)xz-(\sin\theta)y \\ (1-\cos\theta)yx-(\sin\theta)z & (1-\cos\theta)y^2+\cos\theta & (1-\cos\theta)yz+(\sin\theta)x \\ (1-\cos\theta)zx+(\sin\theta)y & (1-\cos\theta)zy-(\sin\theta)x & (1-\cos\theta)z^2+\cos\theta \end{vmatrix}$$

Keep in mind that the values of x, y, and z in this matrix are the elements of the axis of rotation and not the point being transformed. If you set x and y to zero and z to 1 for rotation around the z axis, the matrix reduces to the one shown earlier, and similarly for the other fundamental unit vectors.

So far you haven't seen anything you can't do with *ScaleTransform3D* or *RotateTransform3D*, but only *MatrixTransform3D* lets you define shear transforms (also known as skew). In a shear transform, right angles become acute or oblique. For example, try this matrix:

$$\begin{vmatrix} 1 & 0 & 0 \\ 1 & 1 & 0 \\ 0 & 0 & 1 \end{vmatrix}$$

It's just the identity matrix with one extra element set to 1 so that the formula for x' is:

$$x' = x + y$$

For points above the XZ plane, values of x become increasingly more positive, while for points below the plane, x values become increasingly more negative. The house tilts over:

You can shear the house in many different directions by setting those zero elements of the matrix to non-zero values. Here's one little variation:

$$\begin{vmatrix} 1 & 0 & 0 \\ 0 & 1 & 0 \\ 1.25 & 0.5 & 1 \end{vmatrix}$$

Values of z are left unchanged, but values of x and y are shifted based on the value of z:

$$x' = x + 1.25z$$
$$y' = y + 0.5z$$

For example, when *z* equals 1, which is the plane corresponding to the front of the house, the transform formulas are:

$$x' = x + 1.25$$
$$y' = y + 0.5$$

And here's what it looks like:

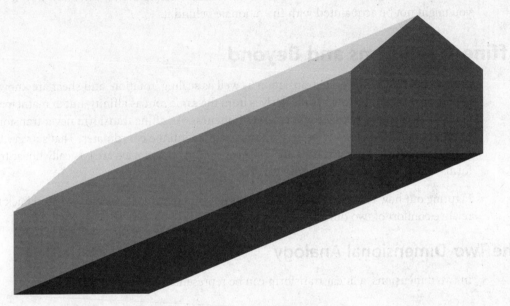

I want you to keep that image in your head for a little while. It might be useful soon.

Something is missing from the linear transform matrix, and you might find it truly disturbing that we've developed a mathematical technique to represent scale transforms, rotate transforms, and shear transforms, and any combination of scaling, rotation, and shear—and yet we cannot represent simple translation.

The problem is that the 3×3 matrix represents a *linear* transform in three-dimensional space, and translation is simply not a linear function. For example, consider the points (1, 2, 3) and (3, 2, 1), which can also be represented by the vectors (**1, 2, 3**) and (**3, 2, 1**) positioned with their tails at the origin. (I'm switching to vectors so that the arithmetical operations make sense.) Add those two vectors to get (**4, 4, 4**) and translate by 1 unit in the X direction: (**5, 4, 4**). Now do the translation first to get the vectors (**2, 2, 3**) and (**4, 2, 1**) and then add them. The result is (**6, 4, 4**), which is not the same as the first result, demonstrating that translation is not a linear function or a linear transform.

The scale, rotation, and shear transforms always operate proportionally on a figure. It doesn't matter how large or small the figure is—if it's scaled by a factor of 2 it's always doubled in size.

But translation is different: It's an additive factor rather than a multiplicative factor. Translation is based on actual units and requires that we actually assign numbers to the tick marks of the coordinate axes.

How can we incorporate translation into the convenient matrix we've developed for the other types of transforms?

The problem is solvable, but the solution is not intuitive, and even if you know how it's done, you might not be acquainted with the rationale behind it.

Affine Transforms and Beyond

Transforms that incorporate translation as well as scaling, rotation, and shear are known as *affine* transforms. The word affine derives from the same root as affinity, but in mathematics it usually refers to something that preserves finiteness. An affine transform never transforms a point in finite 3D space to a point with one or more infinite coordinates. That's a very broad definition, but where transforms are concerned, affine transforms are basically linear transforms with an additional translation factor.

Figuring out how to represent affine transforms with matrices is easier if we drop back to the relative comfort of two dimensions.

The Two-Dimensional Analogy

In two dimensions, a linear transform can be represented by a 2×2 matrix:

$$\begin{vmatrix} x & y \end{vmatrix} \times \begin{vmatrix} M11 & M12 \\ M21 & M22 \end{vmatrix} = \begin{vmatrix} x' & y' \end{vmatrix}$$

The transform formulas are:

$$x' = M11 \cdot x + M21 \cdot y$$
$$y' = M12 \cdot x + M22 \cdot y$$

These transform formulas allow scaling, rotation, and shear, but like the linear transform formulas in 3D, they do not allow translation. Here are three views of a little 2D house sitting on the origin:

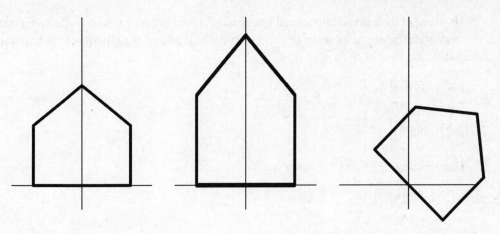

TwoDimensionalHouse.xaml

In the second view, the house has been scaled 50% in the Y direction; the third view shows it rotated 45 degrees clockwise around the origin. But translation isn't possible with the 2×2 matrix.

This 2D house is actually identical to the front of the 3D house used in the LinearTransformExperimenter.xaml file, except that all coordinates are 100 times as large so that they are better suited to the WPF two-dimensional coordinate system of 96 units to the inch.

Curiously enough, you've already seen an example where a two-dimensional house has been translated. The three-dimensional house shown earlier in this chapter contains a two-dimensional house on its front plane. The last shear example I showed you translates the front of the house away from the origin but otherwise leaves that plane undistorted:

The front of that three-dimensional house has Z coordinates of 1, so it is effectively translated away from the origin by shear factors set to the *M31* and *M32* elements of the transform matrix:

$$\begin{vmatrix} 1 & 0 & 0 \\ 0 & 1 & 0 \\ 1.25 & 0.5 & 1 \end{vmatrix}$$

That matrix implies the following transform formulas:

$$x' = x + 1.25z$$
$$y' = y + 0.5z$$
$$z' = z$$

But if we're only interested in the plane where z equals 1, these transform formulas reduce to translation formulas on x and y:

$$x' = x + 1.25$$
$$y' = y + 0.5$$

This is a powerful revelation: Three-dimensional shear using the *M31* and *M32* elements of the transform matrix effectively translates two-dimensional objects on the plane where z equals 1. That's the key to incorporating translation into two-dimensional graphics. Whenever we want to draw in two dimensions, we can pretend that we're actually drawing in three dimensions. We can conceptually draw all of our two-dimensional figures on the plane in three-dimensional space where z equals 1, shown here as a translucent gray surface:

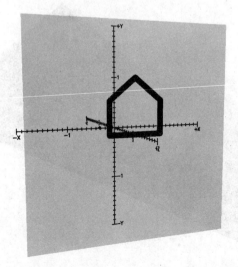

2Don3D.xaml

Because we're now drawing in 3D, instead of specifying two-dimensional points (x, y), we're actually specifying three-dimensional points $(x, y, 1)$. Make no mistake: We're still drawing flat figures on a flat surface. The 3D points have the same amount of information as the 2D points. But now we can apply a three-dimensional skew transform to translate figures on this plane:

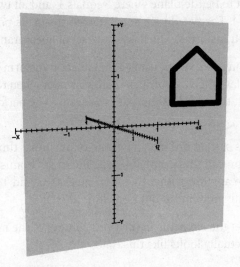

Of course, in practice we don't actually have to draw 2D figures in 3D space. This process is solely conceptual. All we really need is a bigger transform. I trust that nobody will be surprised to learn that the regular *Matrix* structure defined in the *System.Windows.Media* namespace for two-dimensional WPF graphics actually encapsulates a 3×3 matrix with these properties:

$$\begin{vmatrix} M11 & M12 & 0 \\ M21 & M22 & 0 \\ OffsetX & OffsetY & 1 \end{vmatrix}$$

Conceptually, all points (x, y) are represented as $(x, y, 1)$ for the matrix multiplication:

$$\begin{vmatrix} x & y & 1 \end{vmatrix} \times \begin{vmatrix} M11 & M12 & 0 \\ M21 & M22 & 0 \\ OffsetX & OffsetY & 1 \end{vmatrix} = \begin{vmatrix} x' & y' & 1 \end{vmatrix}$$

The transform formulas are:

$$x' = M11 \cdot x + M21 \cdot y + OffsetX$$
$$y' = M12 \cdot x + M22 \; y + OffsetY$$

In summary, to incorporate translation into two-dimensional graphics, it is necessary to use a three-dimensional linear transform matrix. This technique makes itself evident when we realize that three-dimensional shear in the X and Y directions is equivalent to two-dimensional translation on a plane parallel to (but not equal to) the XY plane. To make the math work out nicely, that plane is generally assumed to be the plane where z equals 1, and all two-dimensional points are of the form $(x, y, 1)$. The two-dimensional transforms made possible with this larger matrix are known as affine transforms, which is a superset of linear transforms.

What about the third column in that 3×3 matrix? When using a 3×3 linear transform matrix in the 3D world, that column comes into play when Z coordinates are scaled, or when rotation occurs around anything but the Z axis. But that third column doesn't seem to be performing any useful function for 2D graphics.

In fact, the two-dimensional WPF graphics system doesn't allow you to touch that third column of the *Matrix* object. But in theory, you can think of that third column as "bonus squares." If you *could* set those elements to anything other than the values 0, 0, and 1, you'd be able to define a transform that is not only non-linear, but non-affine as well.

Let's pretend for a moment that you *can* set the elements in the third column of the matrix, and that the two-dimensional transform actually looks like this:

$$\begin{vmatrix} x & y & 1 \end{vmatrix} \times \begin{vmatrix} M11 & M12 & M13 \\ M21 & M22 & M23 \\ OffsetX & OffsetY & M33 \end{vmatrix} = \begin{vmatrix} x' & y' & z' \end{vmatrix}$$

Now the translation formulas are:

$$x' = M11 \cdot x + M21 \cdot y + OffsetX$$
$$y' = M12 \cdot x + M22 \cdot y + OffsetY$$
$$z' = M13 \cdot x + M23 \cdot y + M33$$

If the values in that third column are anything but 0, 0, and 1, the transformed point has actually moved off the plane where z equals 1. Because we're still working with 2D graphics in this exercise, we have to get that transformed point back on the plane somehow. We must somehow alter the x', y', and z' values in such a way that the Z coordinate becomes 1 again and the figure is on the plane.

The simplest solution is to divide all three coordinates by z':

$$(x', y', z') \rightarrow \left(\frac{x'}{z'}, \frac{y'}{z'}, \frac{z'}{z'} \right) \rightarrow \left(\frac{x'}{z'}, \frac{y'}{z'}, 1 \right)$$

Now we're back to a point on the plane where z equals 1. But we've potentially introduced something very dangerous here: The division involved in this calculation is potentially a division by zero, which means that the transformed coordinate could be infinite. The prospect of infinity is what makes this a non-affine transform. By definition, affine transforms are those that do *not* result in infinite coordinates.

The particular type of non-affine transform I'm describing here is sometimes known as a *taper* transform because it does not preserve parallel lines and instead causes figures to get narrower on one side and wider on another. For example, consider the following two-dimensional non-affine transform matrix:

$$\begin{vmatrix} 1 & 0 & -0.01 \\ 0 & 1 & 0 \\ 0 & 0 & 1 \end{vmatrix}$$

That value of −0.01 for $M13$ seems small but it has a big impact for 2D graphics with a coordinate system of 96 units to the inch. The transform formulas are:

$$x' = x$$
$$y' = y$$
$$z' = 1 - 0.01x$$

The point (x, y) is transformed to the point:

$$\left(\frac{x}{1-0.01x}, \frac{y}{1-0.01x} \right)$$

When x equals 100, the denominator is zero and the coordinates are infinite. Fortunately, the little two-dimensional house is restricted to x coordinates between −50 and 50, so the denominator ranges from 1.5 to 0.5. Here's what the transformed version looks like:

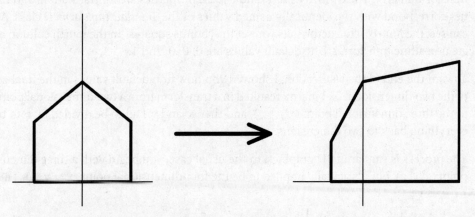

TaperTransformedHouse.xaml

Points to the right of the origin get bigger while points to the left of the origin get smaller. If this looks like something akin to a perspective effect, you're certainly anticipating where this two-dimensional analogy is headed.

When you represent a two-dimensional point (x, y) with an extra coordinate, you are using *homogeneous coordinates*, a concept developed by German mathematician August Ferdinand Möbius (1790–1868), who is best known today for the topological oddity known as the Möbius strip. In 3D, homogeneous coordinates are not only useful for representing translation, but also play a major role in perspective.

Three-Dimensional Homogeneous Coordinates

If translation in two dimensions is equivalent to three-dimensional shear, it seems reasonable that translation in 3D is equivalent to a shear transform in 4D. We need a bigger matrix for that job. Analogously to the two-dimensional case, the bottom row of the expanded matrix indicates the three translation factors in the X, Y, and Z directions.

Can you visualize a shear transform in four dimensions? Of course you can't! And don't even try: Attempting to visualize four-dimensional space is one of the leading causes of exploding heads. (And if you actually *can* visualize a four-dimensional shear transform, you probably shouldn't be wasting your time reading this book.) Fortunately we are dealing with math, and if the math works, we don't need to visualize it. The *Matrix3D* structure in the *System.Windows.Media.Media3D* namespace is actually defined with 16 properties:

$$\begin{vmatrix} M11 & M12 & M13 & M14 \\ M21 & M22 & M23 & M24 \\ M31 & M32 & M33 & M34 \\ OffsetX & OffsetY & OffsetZ & M44 \end{vmatrix}$$

The upper three rows and leftmost three columns constitute the three-dimensional linear transform matrix. The *OffsetX*, *OffsetY*, and *OffsetZ* properties are for translation, and their values correspond with the identically named values of the *TranslateTransform3D* class. As you can see, the *Matrix3D* structure lets you set the "bonus squares" in the fourth column and create non-affine transforms. The default values are 0, 0, 0, and 1.

Toward the end of the last section, I showed you how non-default values in the final column of the two-dimensional 3×3 matrix resulted in a transform from a two-dimensional point (x, y) to the three-dimensional point (x', y', z'), and then x' and y' had to be divided by z' to bring everything back to two dimensions.

The process is similar in 3D graphics. In the usual case, you begin with a three-dimensional point (x, y, z), but it's actually implied to be the four-dimensional point $(x, y, z, 1)$. The

Matrix3D structure transforms that point to the four-dimensional point (*x'*, *y'*, *z'*, and we're at the end of the alphabet, so the fourth dimension is represented by *w'*):

$$|x \quad y \quad z \quad 1| \times \begin{vmatrix} M11 & M12 & M13 & M14 \\ M21 & M22 & M23 & M24 \\ M31 & M32 & M33 & M34 \\ OffsetX & OffsetY & OffsetZ & M44 \end{vmatrix} = |x' \quad y' \quad z' \quad w'|$$

The transform formulas are:

$$x' = M11 \cdot x + M21 \cdot y + M31 \cdot z + OffsetX$$
$$y' = M12 \cdot x + M22 \cdot y + M32 \cdot z + OffsetY$$
$$z' = M13 \cdot x + M23 \cdot y + M33 \cdot z + OffsetZ$$
$$w' = M14 \cdot x + M24 \cdot y + M34 \cdot z + M44$$

For an affine transform, *M14*, *M24*, and *M34* are all zero, and *M44* is 1, so *w'* is just 1. Regardless, the transformed three-dimensional point that results from this process is:

$$\left(\frac{x'}{w'}, \frac{y'}{w'}, \frac{z'}{w'} \right)$$

Notice that you can use *M44* as an overall scaling factor: If *M14*, *M24*, and *M34* are all zero but *M44* is 0.25, for example, everything is scaled by a factor of four. Otherwise *M14*, *M24*, and *M34* are attenuation factors based on the *x*, *y*, and *z* coordinates of the original point.

For advanced purposes, the *System.Windows.Media.Media3D* namespace defines a structure named *Point4D* with properties *X*, *Y*, *Z*, and *W*. In the *Point4D* constructor, and when specifying a *Point4D* object in XAML (which is highly unlikely), and when calling *ToString* on a *Point4D* object, the *W* property is always the *last* of the four coordinates. It's the fourth dimension.

The *Point3D* structure defines an explicit cast from a *Point3D* object to a *Point4D* object; the *X*, *Y*, and *Z* properties are just copied directly into the *Point4D* object, and the *W* property is set to 1. The *Matrix3D* structure and the *Transform3D* class define methods to transform *Point4D* objects, and the matrix multiplication looks like this:

$$|x \quad y \quad z \quad w| \times \begin{vmatrix} M11 & M12 & M13 & M14 \\ M21 & M22 & M23 & M24 \\ M31 & M32 & M33 & M34 \\ OffsetX & OffsetY & OffsetZ & M44 \end{vmatrix} = |x' \quad y' \quad z' \quad w'|$$

Because you're starting out with a *w* coordinate that's not necessarily equal to 1, the transform formulas are a little different from those I showed earlier:

$$x' = M11 \cdot x + M21 \cdot y + M31 \cdot z + OffsetX \cdot w$$
$$y' = M12 \cdot x + M22 \cdot y + M32 \cdot z + OffsetY \cdot w$$
$$z' = M13 \cdot x + M23 \cdot y + M33 \cdot z + OffsetZ \cdot w$$
$$w' = M14 \cdot x + M24 \cdot y + M34 \cdot z + M44 \cdot w$$

Sometimes it's convenient to work with *Point4D* objects, but those occasions fortunately don't arise very often.

The default parameterless constructor of *Matrix3D* creates a matrix with *M11*, *M22*, *M33*, and *M44* set to one and everything else set to zero, which is the 4×4 identity matrix. The static *Matrix3D.Identity* property returns the same object, and the *SetIdentity* method sets an existing *Matrix3D* object to the identity matrix. The *IsIdentity* property returns *true* if the matrix is the identity matrix. The *IsAffine* property returns true if *M14*, *M24*, and *M34* are all zero, and *M44* is one, which is the case for an affine transform.

The *Matrix3D* structure defines a 16-argument constructor that lets you specify all the elements of the matrix starting with the first row. The *Matrix3D* structure also defines many methods that let you apply various types of transforms to the matrix, and to transform points and vectors using the resultant matrix.

In XAML, the *Matrix3DConverter* class works behind the scenes so that you can set the *Matrix* property of a *MatrixTransform3D* element using a string that consists of the word "identity" or all 16 values beginning with the top row. For example, the following string scales by 2 in the X direction, and by 3 in the Z direction:

```
<MatrixTransform3D Matrix="2 0 0 0, 0 1 0 0, 0 0 3 0, 0 0 0 1" />
```

I've included the commas between the rows to make it bit easier to read. But you can't do this:

```
<!-- Not allowed. -->
<GeometryModel3D ... Transform="2 0 0 0, 0 1 0 0, 0 0 3 0, 0 0 0 1" ... >
```

Although it seems reasonable that you can set a property of type *Transform3D* with such a string, no *Transform3DConverter* class exists that lets you do it.

The *Transform3D* class defines a get-only *Value* property of type *Matrix3D* that provides the matrix corresponding to the transform encapsulated by the object. I'll show you how to profitably use this property in the next section.

One of the classes in the Petzold.Media3D library is called *Matrix3DPanel*, which is an element that lets you use 16 scrollbars to set the 16 properties of a *Matrix3D* object. You can then use a binding to set that resultant transform on a 3D figure. The following XAML file includes a *Matrix3DPanel* that lets you interactively experiment with affine transforms and non-affine transforms.

3DTransformExperimenter.xaml

```xml
<!-- =========================================================
        3DTransformExperimenter.xaml (c) 2007 by Charles Petzold
     ========================================================= -->
<Page xmlns="http://schemas.microsoft.com/winfx/2006/xaml/presentation"
      xmlns:x="http://schemas.microsoft.com/winfx/2006/xaml"
      xmlns:cp="http://schemas.charlespetzold.com/2007/xaml"
      WindowTitle="3D Transform Experimenter"
      Title="3D Transform Experimenter">
    <DockPanel>
        <!-- Scrollbars to view object from different sides. -->
        <ScrollBar Name="horz" DockPanel.Dock="Bottom" Orientation="Horizontal"
                   Minimum="-180" Maximum="180"
                   LargeChange="10" SmallChange="1" />

        <ScrollBar Name="vert" DockPanel.Dock="Right" Orientation="Vertical"
                   Minimum="-180" Maximum="180"
                   LargeChange="10" SmallChange="1" />

        <!-- Matrix3DPanel to change transform. -->
        <cp:Matrix3DPanel Name="matxpnl" DockPanel.Dock="Bottom" />

        <Viewport3D>
            <ModelVisual3D>
                <ModelVisual3D.Content>
                    <Model3DGroup>
                        <GeometryModel3D>
                            <GeometryModel3D.Geometry>
                                <!-- House. -->
                                <MeshGeometry3D
                                    Positions=
                                        " 0 1  1, -0.5  0.6  1,  0.5  0.6  1,
                                                 -0.5 0 1,  0.5  0    1,
                                          0 1 -1,  0.5  0.6 -1, -0.5  0.6 -1,
                                                  0.5  0   -1, -0.5  0   -1,
                                          0   1   -1,  0   1    1,
                                         -0.5 0.6 -1, -0.5 0.6  1,
                                         -0.5 0.6 -1, -0.5 0.6  1,
                                         -0.5 0   -1, -0.5 0    1,
                                          0   1    1,  0   1   -1,
                                          0.5 0.6  1,  0.5 0.6 -1,
                                          0.5 0.6  1,  0.5 0.6 -1,
                                          0.5 0    1   0.5 0   -1,
                                          0.5 0    1,  0.5 0   -1,
                                         -0.5 0    1, -0.5 0   -1"

                                    TriangleIndices=
                                        " 0  1  2,  1  3  2,  2  3  4,
                                          5  6  7,  6  8  7,  7  8  9,
                                         10 12 11, 11 12 13,
                                         14 16 15, 15 16 17,
                                         18 20 19, 19 20 21,
                                         22 24 23, 23 24 25,
                                         26 28 27, 27 28 29" />
                            </GeometryModel3D.Geometry>
```

```xml
                        <GeometryModel3D.Material>
                            <DiffuseMaterial Brush="Cyan" />
                        </GeometryModel3D.Material>

                        <GeometryModel3D.BackMaterial>
                            <DiffuseMaterial Brush="Red" />
                        </GeometryModel3D.BackMaterial>

                        <!-- Matrix transform. -->
                        <GeometryModel3D.Transform>
                            <MatrixTransform3D
                                Matrix="{Binding ElementName=matxpnl,
                                                 Path=Matrix, Mode=OneWay}" />
                        </GeometryModel3D.Transform>
                    </GeometryModel3D>

                    <!-- Light sources. -->
                    <AmbientLight Color="#404040" />
                    <DirectionalLight Color="#C0C0C0" Direction="2, -3 -1" />
                </Model3DGroup>
            </ModelVisual3D.Content>
        </ModelVisual3D>

        <!-- Camera. -->
        <Viewport3D.Camera>
            <OrthographicCamera Position="0 0 4"
                                LookDirection="0 0 -1"
                                UpDirection="0 1 0"
                                Width="4">
                <OrthographicCamera.Transform>
                    <Transform3DGroup>
                        <RotateTransform3D>
                            <RotateTransform3D.Rotation>
                                <AxisAngleRotation3D Axis="0 1 0"
                                    Angle="{Binding ElementName=horz,
                                                    Path=Value}" />
                            </RotateTransform3D.Rotation>
                        </RotateTransform3D>
                        <RotateTransform3D>
                            <RotateTransform3D.Rotation>
                                <AxisAngleRotation3D Axis="1 0 0"
                                    Angle="{Binding ElementName=vert,
                                                    Path=Value}" />
                            </RotateTransform3D.Rotation>
                        </RotateTransform3D>
                    </Transform3DGroup>
                </OrthographicCamera.Transform>
            </OrthographicCamera>
        </Viewport3D.Camera>
    </Viewport3D>
</DockPanel>
</Page>
```

Although you can run that XAML file in XamlCruncher 2.0 with the Petzold.Media3D library loaded, I've also supplied an application definition file so that you can compile and run the program as a standalone window:

```
3DTransformExperimenterApp.xaml
<!-- =============================================================
        3DTransformExperimenterApp.xaml (c) 2007 by Charles Petzold
     ============================================================= -->
<Application xmlns="http://schemas.microsoft.com/winfx/2006/xaml/presentation"
             StartupUri="3DTransformExperimenter.xaml" />
```

Again, I encourage you to play with this program to get a good feel for matrix transforms. Clicking the arrows on the scrollbars changes the values by 0.01, and clicking either side of the thumb changes the values by 0.1, so it's easy to select values to two decimal places without dragging the scrollbar thumb.

In particular, try setting non-default values in that last column. You'll find that non-zero values of $M14$ cause the house to get larger or smaller on either side of the YZ plane, similar to the two-dimensional tapered house I showed you earlier. Non-zero values of $M24$ makes the top of the house larger or smaller than the bottom. Negative values of $M34$ cause a familiar perspective effect: The front of the house gets larger while the rear of the house gets smaller. For example, when $M34$ is −0.5, the transform formulas are:

$$x' = \frac{x}{1 - 0.5z}$$

$$y' = \frac{y}{1 - 0.5z}$$

$$z' = \frac{z}{1 - 0.5z}$$

Everything in front of the XY plane gets larger and everything to the rear gets smaller. These are not exactly the same transform formulas that implement perspective, but they're close. Positive values of $M34$ reverse the effect.

Compound Transforms

When I first introduced transforms in Chapter 2, I showed you how multiple transforms can be grouped in a *Transform3DGroup*, but that the order of the transforms makes a difference in the result. Compound transforms are equivalent to matrix multiplication, so the fact that matrix multiplication is not commutative pretty much clinches the whole question.

Let's look at an example from the perspective of matrix multiplication. Suppose you have a scale transform that scales in the X direction by 1.5, in the Y direction by 2, and in the Z direction by 2.5. A translate transform translates along the X axis by 10, the Y axis by 20, and the

Z axis by 30. Here's how you might represent such a composite transform in XAML with the scale transform first:

```
<Transform3DGroup>
    <ScaleTransform3D ScaleX="1.5" ScaleY="2" ScaleZ="2.5" />
    <TranslateTransform3D OffsetX="10" OffsetY="20" OffsetZ="30" />
</Transform3DGroup>
```

The composite transform applied to the point (x, y, z) looks like this:

$$|x \quad y \quad z \quad 1| \times \begin{vmatrix} 1.5 & 0 & 0 & 0 \\ 0 & 2 & 0 & 0 \\ 0 & 0 & 2.5 & 0 \\ 0 & 0 & 0 & 1 \end{vmatrix} \times \begin{vmatrix} 1 & 0 & 0 & 0 \\ 0 & 1 & 0 & 0 \\ 0 & 0 & 1 & 0 \\ 10 & 20 & 30 & 1 \end{vmatrix} = |x' \quad y' \quad z' \quad 1|$$

Matrix multiplication isn't commutative but it is associative. You might begin by multiplying the point by the first matrix and then multiplying the result by the second matrix, or you might begin by multiplying both matrices together. Here's what you get in that case:

$$|x \quad y \quad z \quad 1| \times \begin{vmatrix} 1.5 & 0 & 0 & 0 \\ 0 & 2 & 0 & 0 \\ 0 & 0 & 2.5 & 0 \\ 10 & 20 & 30 & 1 \end{vmatrix} = |x' \quad y' \quad z' \quad 1|$$

If the matrices were in the opposite order (translation first and then scaling), the result would be:

$$|x \quad y \quad z \quad 1| \times \begin{vmatrix} 1.5 & 0 & 0 & 0 \\ 0 & 2 & 0 & 0 \\ 0 & 0 & 2.5 & 0 \\ 15 & 40 & 75 & 1 \end{vmatrix} = |x' \quad y' \quad z' \quad 1|$$

When the translate transform comes first, essentially the translation factors end up getting multiplied by the scaling factors.

As you'll recall, the *ScaleTransform3D* class lets you specify a center point that remains unchanged by the transform. Here's a scale transform with symbolic values:

```
<ScaleTransform3D ScaleX="SX" ScaleY="SY" ScaleZ="SZ"
                  CenterX="CX" CenterY="CY" CenterZ="CZ" />
```

I indicated in Chapter 2 that this was equivalent to a translation involving the negative center values, followed by scaling around the origin, and concluding with another translation. Here's the explicit matrix multiplication:

$$
\begin{vmatrix} 1 & 0 & 0 & 0 \\ 0 & 1 & 0 & 0 \\ 0 & 0 & 1 & 0 \\ -CX & -CY & -CZ & 1 \end{vmatrix}
\times
\begin{vmatrix} SX & 0 & 0 & 0 \\ 0 & SY & 0 & 0 \\ 0 & 0 & SZ & 0 \\ 0 & 0 & 0 & 1 \end{vmatrix}
\times
\begin{vmatrix} 1 & 0 & 0 & 0 \\ 0 & 1 & 0 & 0 \\ 0 & 0 & 1 & 0 \\ CX & CY & CZ & 1 \end{vmatrix}
$$

I suspect that the *ScaleTransform3D* method doesn't actually perform this matrix multiplication, and instead just creates the equivalent matrix:

$$
\begin{vmatrix} SX & 0 & 0 & 0 \\ 0 & SY & 0 & 0 \\ 0 & 0 & SZ & 0 \\ CX(1-SX) & CY(1-SY) & CZ(1-SZ) & 1 \end{vmatrix}
$$

This matrix leaves the point (*CX*, *CY*, *CZ*) unchanged.

If you define a *Transform3DGroup* containing multiple transforms, you might want to keep the transforms distinct for animation or data binding purposes. But it's also possible that you assembled the individual transforms in a *Transform3DGroup* in a way that made sense to you, but these individual transforms will be static the entire time that the program is running. You might get some improved efficiency by replacing the *Transform3DGroup* with a single *MatrixTransform3D*.

Do you need to perform the matrix multiplications yourself to determine the matrix for the *MatrixTransform3D*? No, you do not. The abstract *Transform3D* class defines a get-only *Value* property of type *Matrix3D*, and this property is inherited by all derivatives of *Transform3D*, including *Transform3DGroup*. You can get access to this property directly in XAML by giving the *Transform3DGroup* a name:

```
<Transform3DGroup x:Name="xform">
```

Then, somewhere else in the XAML file, you can reference the *Value* property of that object with a data binding:

```
<Label Name="lbl" Content="{Binding ElementName=xform, Path=Value}" />
```

The *Content* property of *Label* is of type *object*, and if the object set to *Content* doesn't derive from *UIElement* (as *Transform3D* does not), *Label* just uses the *ToString* method to get a string rendition of the object. The *ToString* method of *Transform3D* converts the *Value* property to a string so that *Label* displays the 16 numbers of the composite matrix:

```
1.5,0,0,0,0,2,0,0,0,0,2.5,0,10,20,30,1
```

Unfortunately, you can't select this text and copy it to the clipboard. But that's why I also gave the *Label* control a *Name* property. You can define another binding from the *Label* to a *TextBox*:

```
<TextBox Text="{Binding ElementName=lbl, Path=Content}" />
```

You can't bind the *TextBox* directly to the *Transform3DGroup* because the *Text* property wants a real string rather than an object with a *ToString* method. But with the *Label* intermediary you can now select the text in the *TextBox* and press Ctrl+C to copy it to the clipboard. You can then replace the entire *Transform3DGroup* with a single *MatrixTransform3D* and paste the text into the markup:

```
<MatrixTransform3D Matrix="1.5,0,0,0,0,2,0,0,0,0,2.5,0,10,20,30,1" />
```

In code, you could also use a *Transform3DGroup* if you wanted to keep the individual transforms distinct for animation or data-binding purposes. If you just want to generate a composite transform, you can use methods in the *Matrix3D* structure:

```
Matrix3D matx = new Matrix3D();
matx.Scale(new Vector3D(1.5, 2, 2.5));
matx.Translate(new Vector3D(10, 20, 30));
```

With each successive call to one of the methods in *Matrix3D*, the existing transform (which starts out as the identity matrix) is multiplied by the new transform, with the existing transform conceptually on the left of the times sign and the specified transform on the right. After these three statements of code, the *ToString* method of the *matx* object returns the string:

```
1.5,0,0,0,0,2,0,0,0,0,2.5,0,10,20,30,1
```

After you're done accumulating a transform in the *Matrix3D* object you can set the object to the *Matrix* property of *MatrixTransform3D*.

For every method such as *Scale* and *Translate*, the *Matrix3D* structure also defines methods named *ScalePrepend* and *TranslatePrepend*. These methods cause the multiplication to occur as if the specified transform is on the left and the existing transform is on the right. For example, the following code is equivalent to the preceding code:

```
Matrix3D matx = new Matrix3D();
matx.Translate(new Vector3D(10, 20, 30));
matx.ScalePrepend(new Vector3D(1.5, 2, 2.5));
```

Although the *Translate* transform is indicated first, the composite transform is calculated with the scale transform on the left of the times sign.

You can use the following code to reverse the order of the two transforms:

```
Matrix3D matx = new Matrix3D();
matx.Translate(new Vector3D(10, 20, 30));
matx.Scale(new Vector3D(1.5, 2, 2.5));
```

This code is equivalent:

```
Matrix3D matx = new Matrix3D();
matx.Scale(new Vector3D(1.5, 2, 2.5));
matx.TranslatePrepend(new Vector3D(10, 20, 30));
```

In either of these cases, the *ToString* method of *matx* returns:

```
1.5,0,0,0,0,2,0,0,0,0,2.5,0,15,40,75,1
```

Notice that it doesn't matter whether you use the regular form of the method or the *Prepend* form for the first call after creating a default *Matrix3D*–multiplication with the identity matrix is always commutative.

Inverse Transforms

Let's suppose we're dealing with 4×4 matrices. I'll use the capital boldface **I** to refer to the identity matrix:

$$\begin{vmatrix} 1 & 0 & 0 & 0 \\ 0 & 1 & 0 & 0 \\ 0 & 0 & 1 & 0 \\ 0 & 0 & 0 & 1 \end{vmatrix}$$

Suppose **A** and **B** are matrices such that the following is true:

$$\mathbf{A} \times \mathbf{B} = \mathbf{I}$$

Then **B** is known as the *inverse* of **A** and is commonly denoted $\mathbf{A}^{-1}$. Also, **A** is the inverse of **B**, which means that the multiplication of a matrix and its inverse is commutative:

$$\mathbf{A} \times \mathbf{A}^{-1} = \mathbf{A}^{-1} \times \mathbf{A} = \mathbf{I}$$

Inverse matrices do not always exist! For example, consider a 4×4 matrix filled with zeroes. You won't find any matrix that will equal the identity matrix when multiplied by that zero matrix.

That is why the *Matrix3D* structure defines a Boolean property named *HasInverse*. If that property is *false*, the matrix encapsulated by the *Matrix3D* object has no inverse. However, if *HasInverse* is *true*, you can safely call the *Invert* method. The *Invert* method has no arguments and returns *void*; it inverts the matrix stored by the *Matrix3D* object and stores the result back in the object.

In 3D graphics, inverse matrices are often very handy. If matrix **A** transforms the point (x, y, z) to (x', y', z'), the inverse matrix $\mathbf{A}^{-1}$ transforms the point (x', y', z') to (x, y, z).

Obviously WPF 3D performs all the transforms necessary to render 3D figures on the video display. But what if you want to begin with screen coordinates (for example, a mouse click) and obtain the 3D coordinates corresponding to that point? You need an inverse transform, as I'll demonstrate in a program in Chapter 9, "Applications and Curiosa," that lets the user interact with 3D figures using the mouse.

Coordinate Transforms

You sometimes encounter situations in which you need to find a transform that moves a particular figure to a particular location. This task becomes very, very easy when you can answer the following questions:

- Where do I want the point (0, 0, 0) transformed to?
- Where do I want the point (1, 0, 0) transformed to?
- Where do I want the point (0, 1, 0) transformed to?
- Where do I want the point (0, 0, 1) transformed to?

If you can answer those four questions you can easily define an affine transform that does exactly what you want. Suppose you want the four points transformed like so:

$$(0,0,0) \rightarrow (x_0, y_0, z_0)$$
$$(1,0,0) \rightarrow (x_1, y_1, z_1)$$
$$(0,1,0) \rightarrow (x_2, y_2, z_2)$$
$$(0,0,1) \rightarrow (x_3, y_3, z_3)$$

Let's examine a generalized affine transform applied to the first of those four points:

$$\begin{vmatrix} 0 & 0 & 0 & 1 \end{vmatrix} \times \begin{vmatrix} M11 & M12 & M13 & 0 \\ M21 & M22 & M23 & 0 \\ M31 & M32 & M33 & 0 \\ OffsetX & OffsetY & OffsetZ & 1 \end{vmatrix} = \begin{vmatrix} x_0 & y_0 & z_0 & 1 \end{vmatrix}$$

It's clear that *OffsetX*, *OffsetY*, and *OffsetZ* must be set to x_0, y_0, and z_0. Let's put those in the matrix and try the second point:

$$\begin{vmatrix} 1 & 0 & 0 & 1 \end{vmatrix} \times \begin{vmatrix} M11 & M12 & M13 & 0 \\ M21 & M22 & M23 & 0 \\ M31 & M32 & M33 & 0 \\ x_0 & y_0 & z_0 & 1 \end{vmatrix} = \begin{vmatrix} x_1 & y_1 & z_1 & 1 \end{vmatrix}$$

Now you know that $M11$ must be (x_1-x_0) and so forth. The complete matrix is:

$$\begin{vmatrix} x_1-x_0 & y_1-y_0 & z_1-z_0 & 0 \\ x_2-x_0 & y_2-y_0 & z_2-z_0 & 0 \\ x_3-x_0 & y_3-y_0 & z_3-z_0 & 0 \\ x_0 & y_0 & z_0 & 1 \end{vmatrix}$$

Of course, depending on the four points you've chosen, the figure might be somewhat distorted with a combination of different scaling factors and shear. That's fine if that's what you want.

In many cases, however, what you really want is to reorient a figure in space without otherwise changing it. In other words, you just want to perform a *rigid-body rotation*: rotating a figure in a way that does not alter its size and shape. In addition, you might also want to offset the figure from its current location with a translation.

For the moment, let's forget about translation. Once you determine a matrix that performs the proper rotation in space you can always tack on a translation. Forgetting about translation for a moment allows us to go back to using 3×3 matrices because we're only interested in a linear transform.

The figure you want to reorient in space is defined by coordinate points relative to the three basis vectors $(1, 0, 0)$, $(0, 1, 0)$, and $(0, 0, 1)$, commonly called **i**, **j**, and **k**. What we're going to do here is define a new coordinate system based on three new unit vectors that we can call **u**, **v**, and **w**. (The **w** here has no relation to the w used in four-dimensional coordinate points.)

The transformed figure will have the same relationship to these new axes that it had to the original three unit vectors **i**, **j**, and **k**:

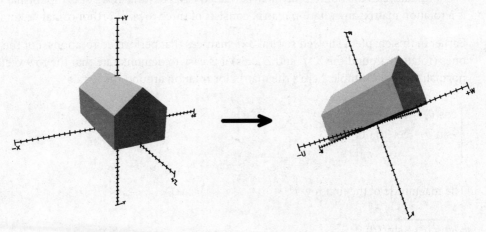

TransformingCoordinates.xaml

The new X axis is the unit vector **u**, which you can also write as (u_x, u_y, u_z) to show the x, y, and z components of the vector **u**. We want a matrix that performs the following transform:

$$(1,0,0) \rightarrow (u_x, u_y, u_z)$$
$$(0,1,0) \rightarrow (v_x, v_y, v_z)$$
$$(0,0,1) \rightarrow (w_x, w_y, w_z)$$

Because we're working with linear transforms here, the point (0, 0, 0) will remain the same under this transform. I've shown how the transform affects three points, but those are really vectors, and rather special vectors at that. The three vectors (u_x, u_y, u_z), (v_x, v_y, v_z), and (w_x, w_y, w_z) are all normalized—that is, their magnitudes equal 1—and they are mutually orthogonal, which means that they form right angles to each other. As a collection, these three vectors are thus called *orthonormal* vectors.

I contend that the transform matrix we want simply consists of these three orthonormal vectors as rows:

$$\begin{vmatrix} u_x & u_y & u_z \\ v_x & v_y & v_z \\ w_x & w_y & w_z \end{vmatrix}$$

It is easy to demonstrate that this matrix performs the desired transform on the points (1, 0, 0), (0, 1, 0), and (0, 0, 1).

This particular matrix is called a *rotation* matrix. All it does is perform a rotation from one set of coordinate axes to another. Any matrix that consists of three rows of orthonormal vectors is a rotation matrix; any rotation matrix consists of three rows of orthonormal vectors.

Earlier in this chapter I showed several 3×3 matrices that performed rotations. For the simple ones (rotation around the X, Y, and Z axes) it is easy to demonstrate that the row vectors are normalized. For example, here's the matrix for rotation around the Z axis:

$$\begin{vmatrix} \cos(\theta) & \sin(\theta) & 0 \\ -\sin(\theta) & \cos(\theta) & 0 \\ 0 & 0 & 1 \end{vmatrix}$$

The magnitude of the first row is:

$$\sqrt{\cos^2(\theta) + \sin^2(\theta)}$$

The sum of the squares of the sine and cosine of the same angle is always 1, so the magnitude is 1. The point (cosθ, sinθ, 0) is at right angles (relative to the origin) to the point (−sinθ, cosθ, 0), and both of those are at right angles to (0, 0, 1), which is the Z axis. So the rows are orthogonal as well. You can think of this matrix as performing a coordinate transform to the coordinates indicated by the three rows.

What is the inverse of the matrix that rotates around the Z axis? Rather than going through an elaborate calculation of matrix inversions, we can simply define a matrix that rotates the same number of degrees but in the opposite direction:

$$\begin{vmatrix} \cos(-\theta) & \sin(-\theta) & 0 \\ -\sin(-\theta) & \cos(-\theta) & 0 \\ 0 & 0 & 1 \end{vmatrix}$$

The cosine of an angle is always equal to the cosine of the negative of that angle. The sine of an angle is equal to the negative sine of the negative of that angle. The inverse matrix is equal to:

$$\begin{vmatrix} \cos(\theta) & -\sin(\theta) & 0 \\ \sin(\theta) & \cos(\theta) & 0 \\ 0 & 0 & 1 \end{vmatrix}$$

As you can see, it's just the original matrix with the rows and columns swapped. (A matrix with the rows and columns swapped is called a *transpose*.) The first row has become the first column; the second row has become the second column, and so forth.

In fact, that little trick is a characteristic of rotation matrices: The inverse of a rotation matrix is the same as its transpose. Here's the rotation matrix for rotating θ degrees around the axis (**x, y, z**):

$$\begin{vmatrix} (1-\cos\theta)x^2+\cos\theta & (1-\cos\theta)xy+(\sin\theta)z & (1-\cos\theta)xz-(\sin\theta)y \\ (1-\cos\theta)yx-(\sin\theta)z & (1-\cos\theta)y^2+\cos\theta & (1-\cos\theta)yz+(\sin\theta)x \\ (1-\cos\theta)zx+(\sin\theta)y & (1-\cos\theta)zy-(\sin\theta)x & (1-\cos\theta)z^2+\cos\theta \end{vmatrix}$$

It's easy to see that making all the sine factors negative is equivalent to swapping the rows and columns.

Here's the rotation matrix I just developed with the three orthonormal vectors as rows as it's applied to the point $(1, 0, 0)$:

$$\begin{vmatrix} 1 & 0 & 0 \end{vmatrix} \times \begin{vmatrix} u_x & u_y & u_z \\ v_x & v_y & v_z \\ w_x & w_y & w_z \end{vmatrix} = \begin{vmatrix} u_x & u_y & u_z \end{vmatrix}$$

Here's the inverse matrix showing how it reverses the transform:

$$\begin{vmatrix} u_x & u_y & u_z \end{vmatrix} \times \begin{vmatrix} u_x & v_x & w_x \\ u_y & v_y & w_y \\ u_z & v_z & w_z \end{vmatrix} = \begin{vmatrix} 1 & 0 & 0 \end{vmatrix}$$

Just offhand, this looks like an exceedingly difficult calculation to prove, but it's actually quite easy: Think of (u_x, u_y, u_z) and the columns of the matrix as vectors. Under the rules of matrix multiplication, the first step is to multiply the three components of the point by the corresponding entries in the first column of the matrix:

$$u_x \cdot u_x + u_y \cdot u_y + u_z \cdot u_z$$

But that's a vector dot product, and we already know that the dot product of a vector times itself equals 1. Let's move onto the second column:

$$u_x \cdot v_x + u_y \cdot v_y + u_z \cdot v_z$$

That's a dot product of two vectors, but the two vectors are orthogonal to each other, which means that the result is zero, and similarly for the third column of the matrix.

Sometimes it's easier to derive a coordinate transform by going in the opposite direction: You pick points in the figure that you want transformed to the normal X, Y, and Z axes. For example, consider the little house displayed by the two transform experimentation programs shown earlier in this chapter. Suppose you want to determine a transform that orients the house so that the lower-left corner of the house, which is the point $(-0.5, 0, 1)$, is aligned at the origin, and the Y axis extends from that point through the rear peak of the roof, which is the point $(0, 1, -1)$. That's not enough information to derive the complete rotation matrix because we've only anchored two points of the house in space, and the house is free to spin around that axis. But it's a start, and perhaps you visualize something like this:

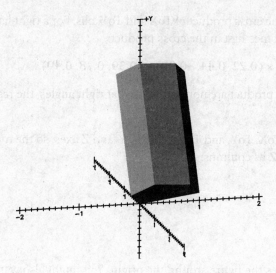

UprootedHouse.xaml

Let's first calculate a vector from the lower-left front corner of the house to the rear peak of the roof. This is the vector that the transform must map to the Y axis. Let me call this vector the **ToY** vector because it will map *to* the Y axis:

Unnormalized **ToY** = (0, 1, −1) − (−0.5, 0, 1) = **(0.5, 1, −2)**

Normalize that vector by dividing each of the components by the magnitude (which is approximately 2.29):

ToY = (0.22, 0.44, −0.87)

Now calculate a **ToX** vector, which must be orthogonal to the **ToY** axis. What's usually easiest is to first find an approximate Z axis, which is the vector that's approximately on the YZ plane and orthogonal to **ToY**. I'll call that **TrialZ**. Then calculate the cross product of that vector and the **ToY** axis. The **ToX** result will be orthogonal to both vectors. Approximately on the XZ plane in the preceding image is the vector from the lower-left front corner of the house to the front peak of the roof:

TrialZ = (0, 1, 1) − (−0.5, 0, 1) = **(0.5, 1, 0)**

Now calculate the cross product of that vector and the **ToY** vector. The order of the cross product determines the direction of the result based on the right-hand rule. The following order makes the positive **ToX** axis extend from the left side of the house to the right:

Unnormalized **ToX** = **ToY** × **TrialZ** = (0.22, 0.44, −0.87) × (0.5, 1, 0) = **(0.87, −0.44, 0)**

The magnitude is 0.97, so you can normalize the vector by dividing the components by 0.97:

ToX = (0.89, −0.45, 0)

Now calculate the **ToZ** vector from the cross product of **ToX** and **ToY** axis. For a right-handed coordinate system, the **ToX** vector comes first in the cross product:

ToZ = **ToX** × **ToY** = (0.89, −0.45, 0) × (0.22, 0.44, −0.87) = (0.39, 0.78, 0.49)

Because the two vectors in the cross product are normalized and at right angles, the result is normalized as well.

The rotation matrix we want maps **ToX**, **ToY**, and **ToZ** to the X, Y, and Z axes, so the rotation matrix consists of **ToX**, **ToY**, and **ToZ** as columns:

$$\begin{vmatrix} 0.89 & 0.22 & 0.39 \\ -0.45 & 0.44 & 0.78 \\ 0 & -0.87 & 0.49 \end{vmatrix}$$

This is a rotation matrix and it rotates the figure around the origin. You might also want to translate the origin as well to define a whole coordinate-transform matrix. The preceding illustration of the uprooted house shows the lower-left front corner of the house—the point $(-0.5, 0, 1)$—at the origin. When you apply the transform to that point, the result should be the point $(0, 0, 0)$:

$$\begin{vmatrix} -0.5 & 0 & 1 & 1 \end{vmatrix} \times \begin{vmatrix} 0.89 & 0.22 & 0.39 & 0 \\ -0.45 & 0.44 & 0.78 & 0 \\ 0 & -0.87 & 0.49 & 0 \\ OffsetX & OffsetY & OffsetZ & 1 \end{vmatrix} = \begin{vmatrix} 0 & 0 & 0 & 1 \end{vmatrix}$$

It's easy to see here that *OffsetX* must be the negative of the dot product of the vector $(-0.5, 0, 1)$, which is the point being transformed, and the first column of the rotation matrix, which is the **ToX** vector, and similarly for *OffsetY* and *OffsetZ*:

OffsetX = − $(-0.5, 0, 1)$ • **ToX** = 0.45
OffsetY = − $(-0.5, 0, 1)$ • **ToY** = 0.98
OffsetZ = − $(-0.5, 0, 1)$ • **ToZ** = −0.29

And here's the complete transform matrix:

$$\begin{vmatrix} 0.89 & 0.22 & 0.39 & 0 \\ -0.45 & 0.44 & 0.78 & 0 \\ 0 & -0.87 & 0.49 & 0 \\ 0.45 & 0.98 & -0.29 & 1 \end{vmatrix}$$

If you "dial up" these numbers in 3DTransformExperimenter you'll see precisely the transform that we set out to create.

Composite Rotations

In the eighteenth century, the Swiss mathematician Leonhard Euler (1707–1783) demonstrated that any rotation in three-dimensional space can be represented as a composite of three unique simple rotations around the X, Y, and Z axes. These three simple rotations are commonly known as *Euler angles*. One application of Euler angles is flight dynamics, where the rotations are called *roll* (around the X axis), *pitch* (around the Y axis) and *yaw* (around the Z axis). The coordinate system implied here has the X axis through the front and back of the aircraft, the Y axis from left to right, and a vertical Z axis.

Different applications use Euler angles in different ways. The order of multiplication of the Euler angles is not standard, and the order definitely matters. One simple approach in 3D graphics is to rotate first around the X axis by the angle ψ (psi), then the Y axis by the angle θ (theta), and then the Z axis by the angle ϕ (phi), which is a composite rotation that looks like this:

$$\begin{vmatrix} 1 & 0 & 0 \\ 0 & \cos(\psi) & \sin(\psi) \\ 0 & -\sin(\psi) & \cos(\psi) \end{vmatrix} \times \begin{vmatrix} \cos(\theta) & 0 & -\sin(\theta) \\ 0 & 1 & 0 \\ \sin(\theta) & 0 & \cos(\theta) \end{vmatrix} \times \begin{vmatrix} \cos(\phi) & \sin(\phi) & 0 \\ -\sin(\phi) & \cos(\phi) & 0 \\ 0 & 0 & 1 \end{vmatrix}$$

Each of these simple rotations is associated with a different angle. You can perform the matrix multiplications yourself, but be forewarned that the result does not simplify into anything pleasant, although it is definitely a rotation matrix.

Euler's rotation theorem implies that every rotation can be represented by just three numbers, such as the three angles of simple rotation that contribute to a composite rotation in three-dimensional space. In Chapter 3, you learned how to specify a rotation using an axis vector and an angle. The vector has three numbers and the angle is another number for a total of four. Why the discrepancy?

Simple: The magnitude of the axis vector is irrelevant. Only its direction is important, so the vector could be normalized and the rotation would be the same. A normalized vector seems like three numbers but it's not because the third number can be calculated from the other two.

A rotation matrix has nine numbers, but obviously those nine numbers are not independent because they define three orthonormal vectors. The first normalized vector is just two numbers because the third component can be calculated from the other two, and the second vector is really just one number because it's constrained by being orthogonal to the first vector. The third vector is entirely constrained because it's a cross product of the first two vectors.

Earlier in this chapter I showed you the transform matrix corresponding to a rotation of θ degrees around the axis $(\mathbf{x}, \mathbf{y}, \mathbf{z})$:

$$\begin{vmatrix} (1-\cos\theta)x^2 + \cos\theta & (1-\cos\theta)xy + (\sin\theta)z & (1-\cos\theta)xz - (\sin\theta)y \\ (1-\cos\theta)yx - (\sin\theta)z & (1-\cos\theta)y^2 + \cos\theta & (1-\cos\theta)yz + (\sin\theta)x \\ (1-\cos\theta)zx + (\sin\theta)y & (1-\cos\theta)zy - (\sin\theta)x & (1-\cos\theta)z^2 + \cos\theta \end{vmatrix}$$

If the rotation axis $(\mathbf{x}, \mathbf{y}, \mathbf{z})$ is normalized, this matrix qualifies as a rotation matrix. This matrix provides the key for converting any rotation matrix into a rotation axis and angle for use in an *AxisAngleRotation3D* object. Suppose you had the following rotation matrix:

$$\begin{vmatrix} M11 & M12 & M13 \\ M21 & M22 & M23 \\ M31 & M32 & M33 \end{vmatrix}$$

This could be the result of a manual calculation using the technique I described earlier, or the result of multiplying three matrices representing Euler angle rotation or any other rotation matrix. You can equate the elements of this matrix with those of the axis/angle rotation matrix and derive the following equalities:

$$\cos(\theta) = \frac{M11 + M22 + M33 - 1}{2}$$

$$x = \frac{M23 - M32}{2 \cdot \sin(\theta)}$$

$$y = \frac{M31 - M13}{2 \cdot \sin(\theta)}$$

$$z = \frac{M12 - M21}{2 \cdot \sin(\theta)}$$

Therefore, you can duplicate the rotation matrix by rotating θ degrees around the axis $(\mathbf{x}, \mathbf{y}, \mathbf{z})$. For the uprooted house I calculated this rotation matrix:

$$\begin{vmatrix} 0.89 & 0.22 & 0.39 \\ -0.45 & 0.44 & 0.78 \\ 0 & -0.87 & 0.49 \end{vmatrix}$$

When we apply the formulas, we find that this matrix is equivalent to a rotation of 66 degrees around the axis $(\mathbf{0.90}, \mathbf{-0.21}, \mathbf{0.37})$. The coordinate transform of the house also included a translation from the point $(0, 0, 0)$ to the point $(0.45, 0.98, -0.29)$, so the complete translation can be represented in XAML as:

```
<Transform3DGroup>
    <RotateTransform3D>
        <RotateTransform3D.Rotation>
            <AxisAngleRotation3D Angle="66" Axis="0.90 -0.21 0.37" />
        </RotateTransform3D.Rotation>
    </RotateTransform3D>
    <TranslateTransform3D OffsetX="0.45" OffsetY="0.98" OffsetZ="-0.29" />
</Transform3DGroup>
```

Camera Transforms

Although I introduced the *PerspectiveCamera* and *OrthographicCamera* classes in Chapter 1, "Lights! Camera! Mesh Geometries!" I neglected the *MatrixCamera* class. *MatrixCamera* is much harder to use, but just figuring out how to use it provides many insights into the mathematics behind 3D graphics. Having a good grasp of camera transforms is also important whenever you need to let the user manipulate 3D objects with the mouse.

When WPF 3D is composing a 3D scene, many transforms might be involved in determining where the coordinates of a figure are located. The application of transforms begins with the *GeometryModel3D*, then any *Model3DGroup* that the *GeometryModel3D* might be a part of, then the *ModelVisual3D*, and then any parent *ModelVisual3D* objects that might be present.

When all those transforms have been applied, the resultant coordinates are said to be in *3D space*. The next transform that WPF 3D applies is the *Transform* property of the camera, but this transform can't be used directly: Instead, the *inverse* of this transform moves the scene relative to the camera.

Next are two transforms associated with the camera. These are called the *view transform* and the *projection transform*, which are both defined by 4×4 matrices called the *view matrix* and the *projection matrix*. Internally, the *PerspectiveCamera* and the *OrthographicCamera* objects calculate a view matrix and a projection matrix based on the camera properties—*Position, LookDirection, UpDirection, NearPlaneDistance, FarPlaneDistance,* and either *FieldOfView* or *Width*. The view transform and projection transform result in normalized coordinates that then assist in clipping and which finally are mapped to the two-dimensional viewport that's part of the screen.

When you use the *MatrixCamera* you specify the two camera matrices yourself by setting two properties of type *Matrix3D* named *ViewMatrix* and *ProjectionMatrix*. To understand how to use the *ViewMatrix* and *ProjectionMatrix* properties of *MatrixCamera*—and to unlock some additional capabilities of 3D programming—it's very helpful to derive the view and projection matrices associated with the two standard cameras.

The View Matrix

The view matrix takes into account the location of the camera, the direction it's pointed, and the up direction, corresponding to the *Position*, *LookDirection*, and *UpDirection* properties defined by *ProjectionCamera* and inherited by *PerspectiveCamera* and *OrthographicCamera*.

A newly created *PerspectiveCamera* or *OrthographicCamera* has a default *Position* property of $(0, 0, 0)$, a *LookDirection* of $(0, 0, -1)$, and an *UpDirection* of $(0, 1, 0)$. With these default settings, the view matrix is the identity matrix. For other settings, the view matrix is a coordinate transform, which is a rotation transform with translation. This transform reorients everything in the 3D scene so that it seems as though the camera has default settings.

Because the view matrix is a coordinate transform, let's begin by determining the rotation transform component. You can think of the properties of the camera as defining the camera's coordinate system. We want to transform that camera coordinate system into the X, Y, and Z coordinates.

The camera's Z axis is the negative of the normalized *LookDirection* vector. The camera's Y axis is not exactly the normalized *UpDirection* vector because WPF 3D doesn't require the *UpDirection* vector to be orthogonal to *LookDirection*. What we do know, however, is that the camera's X axis is orthogonal to the plane of the *LookDirection* and *UpDirection*, so once we get the camera's X axis from a cross product, it's easy to get the camera's Y axis from another cross product.

In the following code, assume that *cam* is an object of type *ProjectionCamera*. The objective is to derive the view matrix from the camera properties. First, get the camera's Z axis:

```
Vector3D zAxis = -cam.LookDirection;
zAxis.Normalize();
```

You can calculate the camera's X axis with a cross product:

```
Vector3D xAxis = Vector3D.CrossProduct(cam.UpDirection, zAxis);
xAxis.Normalize();
```

The camera's Y axis is then another cross product:

```
Vector3D yAxis = Vector3D.CrossProduct(zAxis, xAxis);
```

Because the two vectors entering the calculation are normalized, the cross product will also be normalized. The three columns of the rotation matrix are *xAxis*, *yAxis*, and *zAxis*. The translation factors are the negative dot products of the three axes with the *Position* property of the camera:

```
Vector3D pos = (Vector3D)cam.Position;
double offsetX = -Vector3D.DotProduct(xAxis, pos);
double offsetY = -Vector3D.DotProduct(yAxis, pos);
double offsetZ = -Vector3D.DotProduct(zAxis, pos);
```

Here's the complete view matrix:

$$\begin{vmatrix} xAxis.X & yAxis.X & zAxis.X & 0 \\ xAxis.Y & yAxis.Y & zAxis.Y & 0 \\ xAxis.Z & yAxis.Z & zAxis.Z & 0 \\ offsetX & offsetY & offsetZ & 1 \end{vmatrix}$$

And here it is in code:

```
Matrix3D matxView =
    new Matrix3D(xAxis.X, yAxis.X, zAxis.X, 0,
                 xAxis.Y, yAxis.Y, zAxis.Y, 0,
                 xAxis.Z, yAxis.Z, zAxis.Z, 0,
                 offsetX, offsetY, offsetZ, 1);
```

The Projection Matrix

The projection transform is responsible for determining what is potentially visible within the *Viewport3D*. This transform takes the following into account:

- The *NearPlaneDistance* and *FarPlaneDistance* properties defined by *ProjectionCamera* and inherited by *PerspectiveCamera* and *OrthographicCamera*
- The *Width* property of *OrthographicCamera* or the *FieldOfView* property of *Perspective-Camera*
- The aspect ratio of the *Viewport3D*

The projection transform is applied after the view transform. The view transform has shifted everything in the scene so that it seems as though the camera is positioned at the origin and pointed in the direction of the negative Z axis.

Let's look at *OrthographicCamera* first. The *Width* property determines what part of the scene is visible in the *Viewport3D*. Any part of a 3D space that has an X coordinate greater than half the *Width* or less than half the negative *Width* should be eliminated. But this elimination is performed systematically. The projection transform essentially reduces the 3D scene to normalized coordinates. Only the parts of the scene with the following coordinates are rendered on the screen:

- X coordinates between −1 and 1
- Y coordinates between −1 and 1
- Z coordinates between 0 and 1

The projection transform is mostly just scaling with a little translation along the Z axis. Suppose the width and height of the *Viewport3D* are stored in the variables *width* and *height*. All we really need for this exercise is an aspect ratio:

```
double aspectRatio = width / height;
```

If *width* is 800 device-independent units and height is 400 device-independent units, *aspect-Ratio* equals 2.

As before, the camera object is *cam*, and the *cam.Width* property indicates the width of the viewable image along the X axis centered at the origin (because that's where the view matrix has positioned the camera).

The projection transform must be such that an X coordinate of −*cam.Width* / 2 is transformed to −1, and an X coordinate of *cam.Width* / 2 is transformed to 1. The scaling factor is:

```
double xScale = 2 / cam.Width;
```

The scaling of the 3D scene on the screen is governed by the width of the *Viewport3D*; the height of the *Viewport3D* just tags along. For example, with an aspect ratio of 2 (a viewport half as high as it is wide), a Y coordinate of −*cam.Width* / 4 must be transformed to −1, and a Y coordinate of *cam.Width* / 4 is transformed to 1. The scaling factor is:

```
double yScale = aspectRatio * 2 / cam.Width;
```

or:

```
double yScale = aspectRatio * xScale;
```

The scaling and translation of the Z coordinate is actually the trickiest. The *NearPlaneDistance* and *FarPlaneDistance* properties of the camera indicate a range of viewable objects. These are positive values representing distances from the camera. Because the view matrix has positioned the camera at the origin and pointed it in the direction of the negative Z axis, the projection transform must map a Z coordinate of −*cam.NearPlaneDistance* to 0 and a Z coordinate of −*cam.FarPlaneDistance* to 1. Let's suppose we've defined a couple of variables to reduce the typing:

```
double zNear = cam.NearPlaneDistance;
double zFar = cam.FarPlaneDistance;
```

The transform of Z coordinates is defined by:

```
double zScale = 1 / (zNear - zFar);
double zOffset = zNear / (zNear - zFar);
```

or:

```
double zOffset = zNear * zScale;
```

The resultant transform formula is:

$$z' = \frac{1}{zNear - zFar} \cdot z + \frac{zNear}{zNear - zFar}$$

or perhaps more clearly expressed as:

$$z' = \frac{z + zNear}{zNear - zFar}$$

This formula maps a Z coordinate of $-zNear$ to 0 and a Z coordinate of $-zFar$ to 1.

The complete projection transform matrix for *OrthographicCamera* is thus:

$$\begin{vmatrix} xScale & 0 & 0 & 0 \\ 0 & yScale & 0 & 0 \\ 0 & 0 & zScale & 0 \\ 0 & 0 & zOffset & 1 \end{vmatrix}$$

Unfortunately, the default *FarPlaneDistance* property is set to *Double.PositiveInfinity*, which causes these formulas to break down. I'm not sure how that problem is handled internally, but when simulating an *OrthographicCamera* with a *MatrixCamera*, you can use a very large value for *zFar* (such as the value 1E10), but not *Double.PositiveInfinity*.

I know you've been waiting for the projection matrix for *PerspectiveCamera* because that's where a non-affine transform simulates perspective. The view matrix has already positioned the camera at the origin pointing in the negative Z direction, so here's an overhead view of the camera showing the *FieldOfView* property, as well as *NearPlaneDistance* and *FarPlaneDistance* measured on the Z axis. Keep in mind that these two values are positive but they represent negative values on the Z axis.

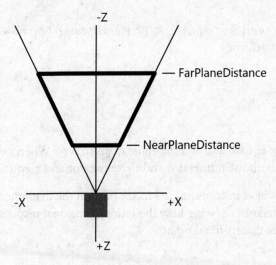

PerspectiveFrustum.xaml

The three-dimensional space of viewable objects is a four-sided frustum: basically a four-sided pyramid with the top cut off. The projection transform must map that frustum into a box so that everything with X and Y coordinates between –1 and 1, and Z coordinates between 0 and 1, is potentially visible on the screen.

We have an *aspectRatio* variable that equals the width of the *Viewport3D* divided by its height, and we have a *PerspectiveCamera* stored as *cam*. It's easiest to develop the transform formulas first and then go back to derive the actual matrix.

The transform formula for X coordinates is:

$$x' = \frac{x}{-z \cdot \tan(cam.FieldOfView \,/\, 2)}$$

If *FieldOfView* is 90 degrees, the tangent of half that angle is 1, and the calculation simplifies considerably. For example, at the plane where *z* equals –4, the field of view encompasses a width of 8 units along the X axis, or everything from –4 to 4. The formula maps –4 to –1 and 4 to 1. If *FieldOfView* is 45 degrees (the default), the tangent of 22.5 degrees is approximately 0.414, so at the plane where *z* equals –4, the field of view encompasses a width of 3.3 units, or everything from –1.65 to 1.65.

The transform formula for Y coordinates is identical except that it takes into account the aspect ratio:

$$y' = \frac{y \cdot aspectRatio}{-z \cdot \tan(cam.FieldOfView \,/\, 2)}$$

If *zNear* equals *cam.NearPlaneDistance* and *zFar* equals *cam.FarPlaneDistance*, I propose that this is the transform formula for Z coordinates:

$$z' = \frac{\dfrac{zFar}{zNear - zFar} \cdot z + \dfrac{zNear \cdot zFar}{zNear - zFar}}{-z}$$

When *z* equals –*zNear*, the numerator equals zero and the value maps to zero. When *z* equals –*zFar*, a factor of *zFar* cancels out in both the numerator and denominator and *z'* equals one.

What these three transform formulas have in common is a factor of –*z* in the denominator. Here's the generalized non-affine transform showing how the four-dimensional result of the matrix multiplication becomes a three-dimensional point:

$$\begin{vmatrix} x & y & z & 1 \end{vmatrix} \times \begin{vmatrix} M11 & M12 & M13 & M14 \\ M21 & M22 & M23 & M24 \\ M31 & M32 & M33 & M34 \\ OffsetX & OffsetY & OffsetZ & M44 \end{vmatrix} = \begin{vmatrix} x' & y' & z' & w' \end{vmatrix} \rightarrow \left(\frac{x'}{w'}, \frac{y'}{w'}, \frac{z'}{w'} \right)$$

That means that w' should equal $-z$, which means that $M34$ equals -1. Now that we know what the transform formulas are, we can write code to calculate the other elements of the matrix:

```
double xScale = 1 / Math.Tan(Math.PI * cam.FieldOfView / 360);
```

The static *Math.Tan* method requires an angle in radians; the conversion formula for degrees to radians normally divides by 180, but only half the angle is required.

```
double yScale = aspectRatio * xScale;
```

The formula for *zScale* takes the possibility of *zFar* equaling *Double.PositiveInfinity* into account:

```
zScale = zFar == Double.PositiveInfinity ? -1 : zFar / (zNear - zFar);
zOffset = zNear * zScale;
```

The final projection matrix for a *PerspectiveCamera* object is:

$$\begin{vmatrix} xScale & 0 & 0 & 0 \\ 0 & yScale & 0 & 0 \\ 0 & 0 & zScale & -1 \\ 0 & 0 & zOffset & 0 \end{vmatrix}$$

Notice the -1 in the $M34$ cell and a zero in the $M44$ cell. It's a non-affine transform.

What happens when the Z coordinate is zero? The transform formulas divide by zero, strongly suggesting that coordinates where Z equals zero are invalid. In fact, the point $(0, 0, 0)$ is the perspective point. In theory, any figure at that point has an infinite dimension.

In the final stages of processing, WPF 3D uses the transformed Z values of objects to determine what is visible, what is hidden from view, and what is blocked by partially transparent objects. When all that is finished, the coordinates are collapsed to two dimensions. Both the X and Y coordinates range from -1 to 1 for visible parts of the scene. These coordinates are scaled to the device-independent coordinates of the actual size of the *Viewport3D* for rendering on the screen.

MatrixCamera in Use

The PerspectiveSquareCuboid.xaml file from Chapter 1 contained a camera object defined like this:

```
<PerspectiveCamera Position="-2 2 4"
                   LookDirection="2 -1 -4"
                   UpDirection="0 1 0"
                   FieldOfView="45" />
```

Is it possible to mimic this camera in XAML with a *MatrixCamera* object? Well, not exactly. It's fairly straightforward to calculate the view matrix from the properties of the *Perspective-Camera*:

$$\begin{vmatrix} 0.89 & 0.098 & -0.44 & 0 \\ 0 & 0.98 & 0.22 & 0 \\ 0.45 & -0.20 & 0.87 & 0 \\ 0 & -0.98 & -4.8 & 1 \end{vmatrix}$$

However, calculating a projection matrix requires knowledge of the aspect ratio of the *Viewport3D*, and in the XAML files I've been showing you, that aspect ratio is ultimately controlled by the user, who can size the *Viewport3D* in a variety of different ways. If you assume that the aspect ratio is 1, the view matrix corresponding to that *PerspectiveCamera* is:

$$\begin{vmatrix} 2.414 & 0 & 0 & 0 \\ 0 & 2.414 & 0 & 0 \\ 0 & 0 & -1 & -1 \\ 0 & 0 & -0.125 & 0 \end{vmatrix}$$

You can enforce an aspect ratio of 1 on a *Viewport3D* with a little binding:

```
<Viewport3D Height="{Binding RelativeSource={RelativeSource self},
                     Path=ActualWidth}">
```

This binding sets the *Height* property of the *Viewport3D* from its *ActualWidth* property. The following XAML file uses that technique to reproduce the image from the original Perspective-SquareCuboid.xaml file but using a *MatrixCamera*:

MatrixCameraSquareCuboid.xaml

```xml
<!-- ===========================================================
        MatrixCameraSquareCuboid.xaml (c) 2007 by Charles Petzold
     =========================================================== -->
<Page xmlns="http://schemas.microsoft.com/winfx/2006/xaml/presentation"
      xmlns:x="http://schemas.microsoft.com/winfx/2006/xaml"
      WindowTitle="MatrixCamera Square Cuboid"
      Title="MatrixCamera Square Cuboid">
    <Viewport3D Height="{Binding RelativeSource={RelativeSource self},
                         Path=ActualWidth}"
                VerticalAlignment="Center" >
        <ModelVisual3D>
            <ModelVisual3D.Content>
                <Model3DGroup>
                    <GeometryModel3D>
                        <GeometryModel3D.Geometry>

                            <!-- Square cuboid. -->
                            <MeshGeometry3D
                                Positions="0 1 0, 0 0 0, 1 1 0, 1 0 0,
                                           0 1 -4, 0 0 -4, 0 1 0, 0 0 0,
                                           1 1 -4, 0 1 -4, 1 1 0, 0 1 0,
                                           1 1 0, 1 0 0, 1 1 -4, 1 0 -4,
                                           1 0 0, 0 0 0, 1 0 -4, 0 0 -4,
                                           1 1 -4, 1 0 -4, 0 1 -4, 0 0 -4"

                                TriangleIndices=" 0  1  2,  1  3  2,
                                                  4  5  6,  5  7  6,
                                                  8  9 10,  9 11 10,
                                                 12 13 14, 13 15 14,
                                                 16 17 18, 17 19 18,
                                                 20 21 22, 21 23 22" />
                        </GeometryModel3D.Geometry>

                        <GeometryModel3D.Material>
                            <DiffuseMaterial Brush="Cyan" />
                        </GeometryModel3D.Material>
                    </GeometryModel3D>

                    <!-- Light sources. -->
                    <AmbientLight Color="#404040" />
                    <DirectionalLight Color="#C0C0C0" Direction="2 -3 -1" />
                </Model3DGroup>
            </ModelVisual3D.Content>
        </ModelVisual3D>
```

```
<!-- Camera. -->
<Viewport3D.Camera>
    <MatrixCamera>
        <MatrixCamera.ViewMatrix>
            <Matrix3D
                M11="0.89"  M12="0.098"  M13="-0.44"  M14="0"
                M21="0"     M22="0.98"   M23="0.22"   M24="0"
                M31="0.45"  M32="-0.20"  M33="0.87"   M34="0"
                OffsetX="0" OffsetY="-0.98" OffsetZ="-4.8" M44="1" />
        </MatrixCamera.ViewMatrix>

        <MatrixCamera.ProjectionMatrix>
            <Matrix3D
                M11="2.414" M12="0"      M13="0"      M14="0"
                M21="0"     M22="2.414"  M23="0"      M24="0"
                M31="0"     M32="0"      M33="-1"     M34="-1"
                OffsetX="0" OffsetY="0" OffsetZ="-0.125" M44="0" />
        </MatrixCamera.ProjectionMatrix>
    </MatrixCamera>
</Viewport3D.Camera>
    </Viewport3D>
</Page>
```

3D Figures in 2D Units

The Petzold.Media3D library contains a class named *CameraInfo* that calculates the view matrix and project matrix for camera objects using the logic I showed you earlier. The class contains static public methods that calculate the matrices for a particular camera and aspect ratio, but you can also create an instance of *CameraInfo* as a XAML resource. You can then define bindings that let you look at the view and projection matrices for a camera that might be controlled by other bindings or an animation.

The *CameraInfo* class also includes properties that obtain the total transform for the camera—which includes the inverted *Transform* property—and the inverse of the total camera transform. Another class in the Petzold.Media3D library named *ViewportInfo* obtains the total transform corresponding to a particular *GeometryModel3D* and *ModelVisual3D*, and the inverse of that transform as well.

This information is useful for programs that need to let the user interact with 3D figures using the mouse. It's fairly easy to use the WPF hit-testing logic to determine whether a particular figure has been clicked with the mouse. I showed you how to do this toward the end of Chapter 3. However, if you also want to allow the user to grab a 3D figure with the mouse and move it—or to draw 3D figures with the mouse—you need transforms that go back and forth between the 3D and the 2D worlds. A program in Chapter 9 demonstrates how to do this.

I originally began exploring the camera transforms after using the *ScreenSpaceLines3D* class that's part of the WPF 3D team's collection of handy classes called 3DTools, available for downloading at *http://www.codeplex.com/3DTools*. The *ScreenSpaceLines3D* class lets you draw lines in 3D space that have a constant width, usually corresponding to one device-independent unit (1/96th inch) in the two-dimensional world. Normally if you tried to draw lines in 3D using very thin cylinders, the lines would have different widths depending on their distance from the camera. A single line could actually become thinner as it receded from the camera! *ScreenSpaceLines3D* solves this problem by accessing the camera transforms to make the 3D lines the proper thickness so that they appear to be of uniform width and always have a flat side toward the camera.

I loved this technique so much that I shamelessly used it myself in a bunch of classes in the Petzold.Media3D library. These classes begin with the word *Wire*, such as *WireLine*, *WireLines*, *WirePolyline*, and *WirePath*. This last class is further supported by classes that parallel the *Path-Geometry*, *PathFigure*, and *PathSegment* classes in the WPF 2D graphics world. You can use *WirePath* to draw Bézier curves in 3D space, for example. The *WireText* class lets you display text based on the old polyline stroke fonts dating from the original version of Microsoft Windows. Finally, the *Axes* class uses both lines and text to draw coordinate axes that you've seen in some of the diagrams in this book.

Chapter 8
Quaternions

Rotation is one of the most common tasks of 3D graphics programming, and yet also the task fraught with the scariest mathematics. Fortunately, the programmer working with WPF 3D is insulated from much of the difficult mathematics with the convenience of the *Rotate-Transform3D* and *AxisAngleRotation3D* classes, which I first discussed in Chapter 3, "Axis/Angle Rotation." When used in conjunction, these two classes let you define a rotation by specifying the axis of rotation, an angle of rotation around that axis, and an optional center of rotation. Using a rotation axis and angle requires very little information, and seems natural and straightforward—so much so that you might regard alternative approaches to rotation as completely unnecessary and even cruel.

Usually when you define an animation involving *AxisAngleRotation3D*, you're only interested in changing the *Angle* property while keeping the *Axis* constant. However, if you need to animate the *Axis* property (either by itself or in synchronization with the angle), problems begin to reveal themselves. These problems stem from the interpolation of the *Vector3D* object defining the rotation axis. For example, consider the AnimatingTheAxis.xaml program from the end of Chapter 3. As the name suggests, that file animates the *Axis* property of an *AxisAngleRotation3D* object but the effect just doesn't seem right. I discussed why the animation seems to slow down and speed up, but I offered no hints for fixing the problem.

The solution involves quaternions. Quaternions are an alternative way to define rotations in 3D space with the big advantage that they can be interpolated to preserve uniform angular velocity—an effect that can't easily be mimicked with an animated rotation axis. Quaternions provide a slight performance improvement over axis/angle rotations as well.

The word *quaternion* derives from the Latin "four at a time." (The word shows up in *Acts* 12:4 in the King James Version of the *Bible* to refer to a band of four soldiers.) Notice that the first two syllables are *not* the word *quarter*. You pronounce the first syllable "kwə" and accent the second syllable.

The Convenience of Complex Numbers

Quaternions are apt to seem a bit odd on first encounter, so it's helpful to explore some of the historical background that led to their development. The impetus for quaternions arose from the relatively simple task of rotation in two dimensions. Let's begin with the standard Cartesian coordinate system:

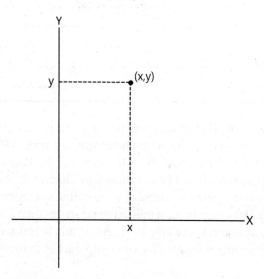

TwoDimensionalCoordinates1.xaml

Any point in this plane can be represented as the number pair (x, y). If you draw a line from the origin to the point, that line has a length r and makes an angle θ (theta) with the positive X axis:

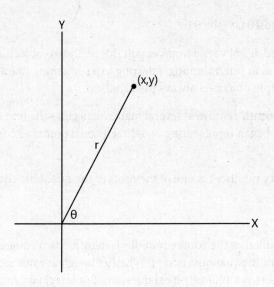

TwoDimensionalCoordinates2.xaml

This is an alternative representation of the point in polar coordinates. You can calculate *r* and θ like so:

$$r = \sqrt{x^2 + y^2}$$

$$\tan(\theta) = \frac{y}{x}$$

Alternatively, you can express *x* and *y* in terms of *r* and θ. Simply project the line on the X and Y axes:

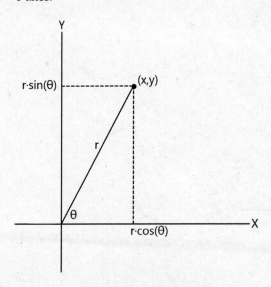

TwoDimensionalCoordinates3.xaml

The point (x, y) is also the point $(r \cdot \cos(\theta), r \cdot \sin(\theta))$.

Regardless of how the point is denoted, it's always a number *pair*. It's really two objects rather than just one object. In mathematics as in programming, referring to a something like a point with a single object rather than multiple objects is always preferred.

In the late eighteenth and early nineteenth centuries, several mathematicians—the first seems to have been Caspar Wessel in 1797—began representing two-dimensional points as complex numbers.

As you'll recall, the so-called imaginary number i is one of the roots of the quadratic equation:

$$x^2 + 1 = 0$$

Although i is sometimes loosely identified as the square root of −1, there are two square roots of −1, and two solutions to that quadratic equation: i and $-i$. Whether imaginary numbers are less real than the so-called real numbers is a philosophical question. But imaginary numbers have so many applications in the "real world" that they probably deserve a more dignified name.

A complex number c is the sum of a real number a and a real number b multiplied by i:

$$c = a + bi$$

These two real numbers are called the *real part* and the *imaginary part* of the complex number.

If you define a plane so that the horizontal axis represents real numbers and the vertical axis represents imaginary numbers, you can plot any complex number on this complex plane:

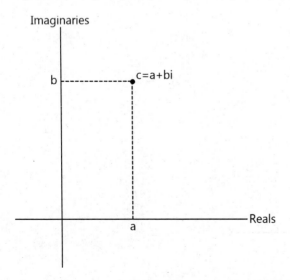

TwoDimensionalCoordinates4.xaml

Just as in the standard Cartesian coordinate system, you can draw a line from the origin to the point, and you can project that line on the axes:

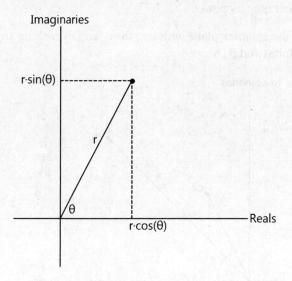

TwoDimensionalCoordinates5.xaml

Now it is obvious that you can represent any point on the plane by a complex number:

$$r \cdot \cos(\theta) + ir \cdot \sin(\theta)$$

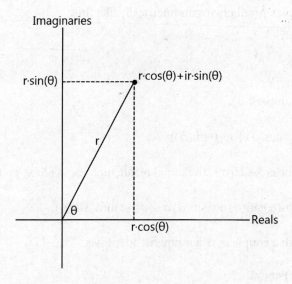

TwoDimensionalCoordinates6.xaml

You can add and subtract complex numbers simply by adding and subtracting their corresponding real and imaginary parts. You can also multiply two complex numbers, and this is where the complex plane starts revealing its power.

Suppose you have two points on the complex plane with lengths r_1 and r_2, making angles with the positive real axis of α (alpha) and β (beta):

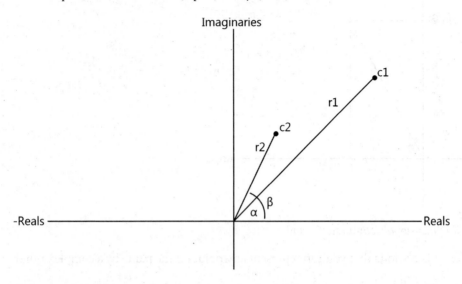

TwoDimensionalCoordinates7.xaml

You can represent these two complex numbers trigonometrically like this:

$$c_1 = r_1 \cos(\alpha) + ir_1 \sin(\alpha)$$
$$c_2 = r_2 \cos(\beta) + ir_2 \sin(\beta)$$

Let's multiply the two complex numbers:

$$c_1 c_2 = \left(r_1 \cdot \cos(\alpha) + r_1 \cdot i \cdot \sin(\alpha)\right) \cdot \left(r_2 \cdot \cos(\beta) + r_2 \cdot i \cdot \sin(\beta)\right)$$

When you begin multiplying all the cross terms, the initial result sure doesn't look pretty:

$$c_1 c_2 = (r_1 \cdot r_2) \cdot \left(\cos(\alpha)\cos(\beta) + i \cdot \cos(\alpha)\sin(\beta) + i \cdot \sin(\alpha)\cos(\beta) - \sin(\alpha)\sin(\beta)\right)$$

However, it helps to be armed with a couple of trigonometric identities:

$$\sin(x + y) = \sin(x)\cos(y) + \cos(x)\sin(y)$$
$$\cos(x + y) = \cos(x)\cos(y) - \sin(x)\sin(y)$$

Now you can reduce that monstrosity to something a little more civilized and revealing:

$$c_1 c_2 = (r_1 \cdot r_2)\big(\cos(\alpha + \beta) + i \cdot \sin(\alpha + \beta)\big)$$

The result is pictured here:

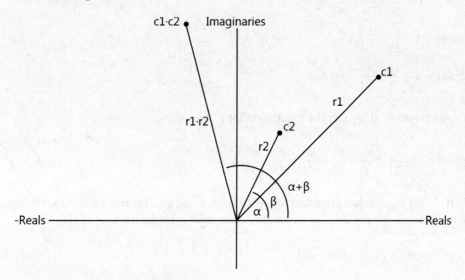

TwoDimensionalCoordinates8.xaml

The magnitude of the result is the product of the two magnitudes, but the angle is the *sum* of the two angles. It's a rotation: The product represents the first point rotated around the origin by an angle of β or the second point rotated by an angle of α.

Rather than dealing with sines and cosines and resurrecting long-forgotten trigonometric identities, you might prefer to represent the two points with their real and complex parts:

$$c_1 = a_1 + b_1 i$$
$$c_2 = a_2 + b_2 i$$

Now multiply these points:

$$c_1 c_2 = a_1 a_2 - b_1 b_2 + (a_1 b_2 + b_1 a_2)i$$

You have now performed a rotation in two dimensions without the use of trigonometry. On the complex plane, rotation is equivalent to multiplication.

You can represent points on the complex plane even more concisely by making use of Euler's formula:

$$e^{i\theta} = \cos(\theta) + i \cdot \sin(\theta)$$

Although this formula looks quite bizarre when first encountered, it can be proven in several ways. Perhaps the most straightforward approach uses infinite series (also called Taylor series) for exponents, cosines, and sines:

$$e^x = 1 + x + \frac{x^2}{2!} + \frac{x^3}{3!} + \frac{x^4}{4!} + \cdots$$

$$\cos(x) = 1 - \frac{x^2}{2!} + \frac{x^4}{4!} - \frac{x^6}{6!} + \cdots$$

$$\sin(x) = x - \frac{x^3}{3!} + \frac{x^5}{5!} - \frac{x^7}{7!} + \cdots$$

If you substitute $i\theta$ for x in the expansion for e^x, you get:

$$e^{i\theta} = 1 + i\theta - \frac{\theta^2}{2!} - \frac{i\theta^3}{3!} + \frac{\theta^4}{4!} + \frac{i\theta^5}{5!} - \frac{\theta^6}{6!} - \frac{i\theta^7}{7!} + \cdots$$

That clearly equals the expansion for $\cos(\theta)$ plus $i \cdot \sin(\theta)$. This means that the multiplication of the preceding two complex numbers can be represented as simply as this:

$$\left(r_1 e^{i\alpha} \right) \cdot \left(r_2 e^{i\beta} \right) = r_1 r_2 \cdot e^{i(\alpha + \beta)}$$

Again, notice how the sum of the angles indicates rotation around the origin.

The use of complex numbers to represent two-dimensional points provided so many interesting and elegant conveniences that mathematicians began to wonder: Could this concept be extended to three dimensions? How? A three-dimensional coordinate system requires three axes. If the first axis is real numbers and the second is imaginary numbers, what's the third axis?

And is that even the right question?

Hamilton and Quaternions

One of the people intrigued by the concept of extending complex numbers into three dimensions was Irish mathematician Sir William Rowan Hamilton (1805–1865). In one of the most famous stories in the history of mathematics, Hamilton and his wife were walking along the Royal Canal in Dublin on October 16, 1843, when he was struck with the solution. To help him remember, he used a pocket knife to carve a simple equation in a stone on Brougham Bridge (also called Broome Bridge):

$$i^2 = j^2 = k^2 = ijk = -1$$

Hamilton's graffito is no longer present, but a plaque on the bridge commemorates the event.

These i, j, and k values form the basis of quaternions. But what are they? They do not equal each other, but they have the common characteristic of squares that equal -1. In a sense, they are three different imaginary numbers, and because they extend the concept of complex numbers, they are sometimes known as hypercomplex numbers. Mathematically, conceiving three different imaginary numbers is a perfectly legitimate exercise as long as we don't run into any contradictions along the way. Let's see what we can deduce from Hamilton's equation.

If k^2 equals -1 and the product ijk also equals -1, the product ij must equal k. Similarly, jk equals i. That means that jki equals i^2 or -1, which means that ki equals j. Here's a summary so far:

$$ij = k$$
$$jk = i$$
$$ki = j$$

What does ji equal? The immediate instinct is to say that ji equals k because ij equals k. But that can't be true because if ji equaled k, jji would equal both i (substituting k for ji) and $-i$ (substituting -1 for jj).

These three imaginary numbers apparently do not obey the commutative law for multiplication. What works instead is that each pair of multiplied values becomes negative when the terms are switched:

$$ji = -k$$
$$kj = -i$$
$$ik = -j$$

These days, algebras that don't have commutative multiplication are common. We've already encountered two of these algebras in this book: The vector cross product is not commutative and matrix multiplication is not commutative. But non-commutative algebras were not considered quite orthodox in 1843, and the non-commutativity of quaternions made them controversial in their early years.

Historically, quaternions preceded vectors.[1] Or rather, vector algebra emerged as a part of quaternion algebra that proved useful on its own, and then quaternions were largely abandoned, only to be resurrected for aerospace applications and computer graphics. These days, we have no qualms about studying vectors entirely on their own and then merging vector algebra and quaternion algebra if it proves convenient.

---

1 A good history of quaternions and vectors—unfortunately not covering the resurgence of quaternions in recent decades—is *A History of Vector Analysis: The Evolution of the Idea of the Vectorial System* by Michael J. Crowe (Notre Dame Press, 1967; Dover Press, 1985, 1994).

Is it just a coincidence that the three letters i, j, and k are the same letters used for the three fundamental unit vectors $(1, 0, 0)$, $(0, 1, 0)$, and $(0, 0, 1)$ that form the basis of the three-dimensional coordinate system? No, it is not a coincidence. They are the same, and to commemorate that revelation, I will now switch to boldface for these three letters to indicate that they are truly vectors:

$$\mathbf{i} = (1,0,0)$$
$$\mathbf{j} = (0,1,0)$$
$$\mathbf{k} = (0,0,1)$$

However, it's essential to keep in mind that the multiplicative relationships that Hamilton inscribed on the bridge in 1843 are the definitions of *quaternion* multiplication and *not* vector multiplication. It is indeed true that the vector cross product of any two of these unit vectors equals the third unit vector or its negative:

$$\mathbf{i} \times \mathbf{j} = \mathbf{k} = -\mathbf{j} \times \mathbf{i}$$
$$\mathbf{j} \times \mathbf{k} = \mathbf{i} = -\mathbf{k} \times \mathbf{j}$$
$$\mathbf{k} \times \mathbf{i} = \mathbf{j} = -\mathbf{i} \times \mathbf{k}$$

Quaternion multiplication has these same rules. However, in quaternion multiplication, a basis vector multiplied by itself equals −1. The cross product of a vector times itself is a vector of zero magnitude.

The vector dot product is a real oddity in the mathematics world: The dot product of two vectors isn't even a vector! It's a scalar, and you can't represent a scalar as a vector. Quaternion multiplication has no such peculiarities: When you multiply two quaternions, the result is always another quaternion. Not only are $\mathbf{i}$, $\mathbf{j}$, and $\mathbf{k}$ quaternions, but so is −1, which is the product of $\mathbf{i}$, $\mathbf{j}$, and $\mathbf{k}$.

In fact, all real numbers are quaternions, just as all real numbers are also complex numbers. Recall that a complex number c is a real number plus an imaginary number:

$$c = a + bi$$

A quaternion q is the sum of a real number and three imaginary numbers:

$$q = a + b\mathbf{i} + c\mathbf{j} + d\mathbf{k}$$

The a, b, c, and d factors are all real numbers. I will not be using boldface for the quaternion itself. Boldface is reserved for vectors, and the quaternion is not a vector, although it certainly encompasses vectors.

Why Are Quaternions So Weird?

When we move from two dimensions to three dimensions, our use of Cartesian coordinates requires only one additional number. In two dimensions we represent points as (x, y) and in three dimensions we use (x, y, z).

It seems reasonable that extending complex numbers from two dimensions to three dimensions should be equally straightforward. If it's possible to represent a two-dimensional point as the complex number $a + bi$, we should be able to represent a three-dimensional point as $a + bi + cj$. One additional axis implies one more imaginary number, right?

Not quite. If the extension of complex numbers to three dimensions were this simple, somebody surely would have come up with a solution long before William Rowan Hamilton. Hamilton recognized that a fourth factor was required, so that the three axes **i**, **j**, and **k** are associated with the basis quaternions i, j, and k. This was Hamilton's breakthrough and it wasn't trivial.

In two dimensions, we can use the complex numbers to represent both points *and* rotations. That's what makes the complex plane so convenient and powerful. Multiplying two complex points together is the same as multiplying a point by a rotation, which is equivalent to rotating that point. This equivalence between points and rotations is a characteristic of two-dimensional space *only*. The concept breaks down in higher dimensionalities.

Rotation always occurs in a plane. In two-dimensional space, the X and Y axes form only one plane, so there is only one plane of rotation. In three-dimensional space, however, the additional Z axis extends the number of orthogonal rotation planes to three: the XY plane, the XZ plane, and the YZ plane. There's no longer an equivalence between points and rotations. A three-dimensional version of the complex number plane needs to represent *rotations* as well as points, and that's what makes quaternions stranger than we might originally anticipate.

In general, for an N-dimensional coordinate space, the number of orthogonal planes is:

$$\frac{N!}{(N-2)!2} = \frac{N(N-1)}{2}$$

In four-dimensional space, the number of orthogonal rotation planes is six, and entities called *octonians* get involved.[2]

---

2 John H. Conway and Derek A. Smith, *On Quaternions and Octonians: Their Geometry, Arithmetic, and Symmetry* (A.K. Peters, 2003) has an overview of both algebras from a mathematical perspective.

The *Quaternion* Structure

Different authors use different letters for the four real numbers of the quaternion. I earlier represented the quaternion as:

$$q = a + b\mathbf{i} + c\mathbf{j} + d\mathbf{k}$$

Here's one variation:

$$q = q_0 + q_1\mathbf{i} + q_2\mathbf{j} + q_3\mathbf{k}$$

The *Quaternion* structure defined in the *System.Windows.Media.Media3D* namespace defines properties named W, X, Y, and Z for the four components, so to avoid confusion I will tend to use those same letters in lower case:

$$q = w + x\mathbf{i} + y\mathbf{j} + z\mathbf{k}$$

Although this is the standard order for notating these components, unfortunately the *Quaternion* structure uses a different order in its four-argument constructor:

```
Quaternion q = new Quaternion(x, y, z, w);
```

The *ToString* method displays these components in that order as well. The *Parse* method of *Quaternion* can convert a string of four numbers into a *Quaternion* object, but expects the four components in the same order as the constructor. In XAML, you can specify a quaternion as a string containing four values, but these four values are also in the order x, y, z, w. In other words, the *Quaternion* structure is internally consistent, but it's inconsistent with standard mathematical notation that shows the scalar part first. In the mathematical analysis that follows, I will use the standard notation because it often parallels the notation of complex numbers.

The *Quaternion* structure provides methods that perform several basic quaternion operations, but it's still useful to see how these operations are derived, even if my exposition delays demonstrating the application of quaternions. Just hold on for a little while: What seems at first like an excessive amount of preparation eventually does lead to the point where you can use quaternions to express three-dimensional rotations.

Just as you can notate a vector by putting the three numbers in parentheses, you can indicate a quaternion as a four-tuple:

$$q = (w, x, y, z)$$

Just as complex numbers have a real part and an imaginary part, a quaternion has a real part (the w component) and a vector part (the rest). A quaternion can alternatively be written as:

$$q = w + \mathbf{q}$$

where $\mathbf{q}$ is the vector $(\mathbf{x}, \mathbf{y}, \mathbf{z})$ that equals the quaternion $x\mathbf{i} + y\mathbf{j} + z\mathbf{k}$. The quaternion can also be written with the real part and vector part in parentheses:

$$q = (w, \mathbf{q})$$

A "pure" quaternion is a quaternion whose scalar part (the w component) is equal to zero. A pure quaternion is a vector, and I will give a pure quaternion a bold-face identifier to remind you of that fact:

$$\mathbf{q} = x\mathbf{i} + y\mathbf{j} + z\mathbf{k}$$

Addition and subtraction of quaternions is trivial: Simply add and subtract the corresponding components. The *Quaternion* structure defines addition and subtraction operators for your convenience. Similarly, multiplication of a quaternion by a scalar involves only multiplying each component by the scalar. This operation is not explicitly provided by the *Quaternion* structure, but it's a subset of regular quaternion multiplication.

The multiplication of two quaternions is bit messy, but it helps to begin by examining the multiplication of two pure quaternions, such as these two:

$$\mathbf{q}_1 = x_1\mathbf{i} + y_1\mathbf{j} + z_1\mathbf{k}$$
$$\mathbf{q}_2 = x_2\mathbf{i} + y_2\mathbf{j} + z_2\mathbf{k}$$

When multiplying the two pure quaternions, multiply each of the three components of the first by the three components of the second. Take special care to preserve the order of the $\mathbf{i}, \mathbf{j}$, and $\mathbf{k}$ factors because multiplication of these basis vectors is not commutative:

$$\mathbf{q}_1\mathbf{q}_2 = x_1x_2\mathbf{ii} + x_1y_2\mathbf{ij} + x_1z_2\mathbf{ik} + y_1x_2\mathbf{ji} + y_1y_2\mathbf{jj} + y_1z_2\mathbf{jk} + z_1x_2\mathbf{ki} + z_1y_2\mathbf{kj} + z_1z_2\mathbf{kk}$$

The next step involves reducing those products of $\mathbf{i}, \mathbf{j}$, and $\mathbf{k}$. Remember: This is not a vector dot product or a cross product. The rules that you must apply are the basic assumptions for quaternions:

$$\mathbf{q}_1\mathbf{q}_2 = -x_1x_2 + x_1y_2\mathbf{k} - x_1z_2\mathbf{j} - y_1x_2\mathbf{k} - y_1y_2 + y_1z_2\mathbf{i} + z_1x_2\mathbf{j} - z_1y_2\mathbf{i} - z_1z_2$$

You can rearrange and regroup these terms like so:

$$\mathbf{q}_1\mathbf{q}_2 = (y_1z_2 - z_1y_2)\mathbf{i} + (z_1x_2 - x_1z_2)\mathbf{j} + (x_1y_2 - y_1x_2)\mathbf{k} - (x_1x_2 + y_1y_2 + z_1z_2)$$

Now this might start looking a little familiar. The last parenthetical expression is the dot product of vectors $\mathbf{q}_1$ and $\mathbf{q}_2$. The rest of the expression on the right side of the equal sign is the cross product of the vectors $\mathbf{q}_1$ and $\mathbf{q}_2$:

$$\mathbf{q}_1\mathbf{q}_2 = \mathbf{q}_1 \times \mathbf{q}_2 - \mathbf{q}_1 \bullet \mathbf{q}_2$$

The multiplication of two pure quaternions is equivalent to the vector cross product minus the vector dot product. Remember that the result of a vector dot product is not a vector. It is a scalar, so that the multiplication of two pure quaternions does not, in general, produce another pure quaternion. But the product of two pure quaternions is a quaternion, and that's more than you can say about the dot product of two vectors.

Because a pure quaternion *is* a vector, we can also say that the quaternion multiplication of two vectors is equal to the vector cross product minus the vector dot product. In fact, the vector cross product and the dot product originally came from quaternion mathematics.

Now that we've derived the multiplication of two pure quaternions, the multiplication of two full quaternions will be a snap. Here are the two quaternions:

$$q_1 = w_1 + \mathbf{q}_1$$
$$q_2 = w_2 + \mathbf{q}_2$$

Finding the product is trivial:

$$q_1 q_2 = w_1 w_2 + w_1 \mathbf{q}_2 + w_2 \mathbf{q}_1 + \mathbf{q}_1 \times \mathbf{q}_2 - \mathbf{q}_1 \bullet \mathbf{q}_2$$

It's the product of the scalar parts, plus each scalar part times the other vector part, plus the cross product of the vector parts, minus the dot product of the vector parts. It's long, but it's symmetrical and easy to memorize. Of course, the *Quaternion* structure will multiply two quaternions for you.

The *Quaternion* structure defines a static *Identity* property that creates a *Quaternion* object with the *X*, *Y*, and *Z* properties set to 0 and the *W* property set to 1. The identity quaternion has no effect when multiplied by any quaternion. The parameterless *Quaternion* constructor also creates an identity quaternion. The *IsIdentity* property returns *true* if *X*, *Y*, and *Z* are 0 and *W* equals 1.

A few more operations involving quaternions will be necessary before we really start to make progress here. But let's return to complex numbers for a moment. Here's a complex number:

$$c = a + bi$$

The norm of the complex number (also called the magnitude or absolute value) is just the two-dimensional form of the Pythagorean Theorem:

$$|c| = \sqrt{a^2 + b^2}$$

You can normalize a complex number by dividing the two components by the norm. The norm of a normalized complex number is 1.

The *complex conjugate* is often denoted with an asterisk following the symbol used for the complex number. The complex conjugate consists of the real part of the complex number minus the imaginary part:

$$c* = a - bi$$

It's easy to determine that the product of a complex number and its conjugate is the sum of the squares of the components a and b:

$$c \cdot c* = a^2 + b^2$$

This is the same as the square of the norm:

$$c \cdot c* = |c|^2$$

The multiplicative *inverse* of a complex number is denoted by c^{-1} and is calculated like this:

$$c^{-1} = \frac{c*}{|c|^2}$$

It's easy to see that this inverse is equivalent to our customary concept of a multiplicative inverse:

$$c^{-1} = \frac{c*}{|c|^2} = \frac{c*}{c \cdot c*} = \frac{1}{c}$$

The product of a complex number and its multiplicative inverse equals one. This is obvious because a complex number times its conjugate is equal to the square of the magnitude:

$$c \cdot c^{-1} = c \cdot \frac{c*}{|c|^2} = \frac{|c|^2}{|c|^2} = 1$$

A complex number has no inverse if its norm equals zero. For a normalized complex number, the inverse is the same as the conjugate.

Now let's find the analogous items for quaternions. Quaternions have a norm, which is loosely the "length" of the quaternion as calculated by the four-dimensional form of the Pythagorean Theorem:

$$|q| = \sqrt{w^2 + x^2 + y^2 + z^2}$$

You can normalize a quaternion by dividing each of its components by its norm. A normalized quaternion is also called a *unit* quaternion. The *Quaternion* structure includes a *Normalize* method and an *IsNormalized* property that returns *true* if the sum of the squares of the quaternion's components add to one.

A quaternion also has a conjugate that is the real part of the quaternion minus the vector part:

$$q^* = w - x\mathbf{i} - y\mathbf{j} - z\mathbf{k}$$

The quaternion conjugate looks much more like the complex conjugate when written like this:

$$q^* = w - \mathbf{q}$$

Just as with complex numbers, the product of a quaternion and its conjugate is the square of the norm:

$$q \cdot q^* = w^2 + x^2 + y^2 + z^2$$

Again, just as with complex numbers, the inverse of a quaternion is the quaternion conjugate divided by the square of its norm:

$$q^{-1} = \frac{q^*}{|q|^2}$$

Or:

$$q^{-1} = \frac{q^*}{q \cdot q^*} = \frac{1}{q}$$

The inverse is not defined if all the components of the quaternion are zero. For a unit quaternion, the inverse equals the conjugate.

The *Quaternion* structure defines a *Conjugate* method, which conjugates an existing quaternion, and an *Invert* method, which inverts an existing quaternion.

Quaternions and Rotation

So far, quaternions have been fairly abstract, except that a pure quaternion is a vector, so it's just as useful as vectors are. Now let's define a quaternion that represents a rotation in three-dimensional space.

Again, it's helpful to look at complex numbers to get a general pattern, and then apply that pattern to quaternions. The following complex number represents a rotation in two-dimensional space:

$$c_{rotate} = \cos(\theta_{rotation}) + i \cdot \sin(\theta_{rotation})$$

Multiply this complex number by any point (also represented by a complex number) and the point is rotated around the origin by $\theta_{rotation}$ degrees. This complex number we've called c_{rotate} is normalized because for any angle θ,

$$\sin^2(\theta) + \cos^2(\theta) = 1$$

For a rotation in three-dimensional space, not only must you specify an angle but an axis of rotation as well. The following quaternion represents a rotation of $\theta_{rotation}$ degrees around a normalized axis of $\mathbf{q_{axis}}$:

$$q_{rotate} = \cos\left(\frac{\theta_{rotation}}{2}\right) + \mathbf{q_{axis}} \cdot \sin\left(\frac{\theta_{rotation}}{2}\right)$$

This is called a "rotation quaternion." The real part—the w component—equals the cosine of half the rotation angle. The x, y, and z components of the quaternion are all equal to the sine of half the rotation angle multiplied by the x, y, and z components of the axis of rotation.

$$w = \cos\left(\frac{\theta_{rotation}}{2}\right)$$

$$x = x_{axis} \cdot \sin\left(\frac{\theta_{rotation}}{2}\right)$$

$$y = y_{axis} \cdot \sin\left(\frac{\theta_{rotation}}{2}\right)$$

$$z = z_{axis} \cdot \sin\left(\frac{\theta_{rotation}}{2}\right)$$

Aside from the peculiar use of half the angle, it's analogous to the complex number: The real part is a cosine and the imaginary part is a sine.

If the axis vector is normalized, is the rotation quaternion also normalized? Yes, it is, as this calculation shows:

$$\left|q_{rotate}\right|^2 = \cos^2\left(\frac{\theta_{rotation}}{2}\right) + (x^2 + y^2 + z^2) \cdot \sin^2\left(\frac{\theta_{rotation}}{2}\right)$$

The sum $(x^2 + y^2 + z^2)$ equals 1, so we're left with just the sum of the squares of the cosine and sine of the same angle, which always equals one. Whenever I refer to a "rotation quaternion," you should assume that the quaternion is normalized. Normalized pure quaternions (including the basis quaternions **i**, **j**, and **k**) are also rotation quaternions associated with a rotation of 180 degrees. Half that angle is 90 degrees so the sine is 1 and the cosine is 0.

The *Quaternion* structure includes a constructor that creates a rotation quaternion from an axis of rotation and an angle:

```
Quaternion qRotate = new Quaternion(vectAxis, angle);
```

The axis of rotation is normalized before the quaternion is calculated, so the rotation quaternion is normalized as well.

Once you have this rotation quaternion, can you just multiply it by a three-dimensional point to rotate that point?

Not quite. The first problem is that multiplication between a quaternion and a point is not defined. You must convert the point to a quaternion, which you can simply accomplish by expressing the point as a vector, which is a pure quaternion. However, this is not quite satisfactory either, because in general the product of a rotation quaternion times a pure quaternion is not another pure quaternion. If you performed the calculation, you'd be left with a scalar term that you wouldn't know what to do with.

Instead, you also need the conjugate of the rotation quaternion, which you can obtain like so:

$$q^*_{rotate} = \cos\left(\frac{\theta_{rotation}}{2}\right) - \mathbf{q_{axis}} \cdot \sin\left(\frac{\theta_{rotation}}{2}\right)$$

Because rotation quaternions are normalized, this conjugate is also the inverse of the quaternion.

To rotate a vector **v**, you multiply the vector by the rotation quaternion on the left and the conjugate of the rotation quaternion on the right:

$$\mathbf{v_{rotated}} = q_{rotate} \cdot \mathbf{v} \cdot q^*_{rotate}$$

Although this formula is certainly simple, it is not, of course, intuitively obvious, except in that it succeeds in eliminating any scalar part and also doubling the half angles.[3]

To assure ourselves that this rotation formula works (at least for simple cases) examine the case in which the axis of rotation $\mathbf{q_{axis}}$ is the Z axis or **(0, 0, 1)** or simply **k**:

---

3 If you'd like to understand quaternions and their applications in more depth, I can recommend two books: Jack B. Kuipers, *Quaternions and Rotation Sequences: A Primer with Applications to Orbits, Aerospace, and Virtual Reality* (Princeton University Press, 1999) and Andrew J. Hanson, *Visualizing Quaternions* (Elsevier, 2006).

$$q_{rotate} = \cos\left(\frac{\theta_{rotation}}{2}\right) + \mathbf{k} \cdot \sin\left(\frac{\theta_{rotation}}{2}\right)$$

Let's generalize the vector $\mathbf{v}$ being rotated as (x, y, z) or the pure quaternion $x\mathbf{i} + y\mathbf{j} + z\mathbf{k}$:

$$\mathbf{v_{rotated}} = q_{rotate} \cdot (x\mathbf{i} + y\mathbf{j} + z\mathbf{k}) \cdot q^*_{\ rotate}$$

Carrying out these two multiplications might be a good exercise. You'll make use of the following common trigonometric identities:

$$\sin(\theta)\cos(\theta) = \frac{\sin(2\theta)}{2}$$
$$\sin^2(\theta) = \frac{1 - \cos(2\theta)}{2}$$
$$\cos^2(\theta) = \frac{1 + \cos(2\theta)}{2}$$
$$\sin^2(\theta) + \cos^2(\theta) = 1$$

What you get is this:

$$\mathbf{v_{rotated}} = \left(x\cos(\theta) - y\sin(\theta)\right)\mathbf{i} + \left(x\sin(\theta) + y\cos(\theta)\right)\mathbf{j}$$

Or:

$$x_{rotated} = x\cos(\theta) - y\sin(\theta)$$
$$y_{rotated} = x\sin(\theta) + y\cos(\theta)$$

And that should look very comforting. You can reverse the rotation by multiplying by the conjugate first:

$$\mathbf{v} = q^*_{\ rotate} \cdot \mathbf{v_{rotated}} \cdot q_{rotate}$$

You can think about the inverse rotation in two ways: First, because the conjugate involves the negative of the vector part of the quaternion, it's making the axis vector point in the opposite direction, which reverses the rotation. Also, you can think of an inverse rotation as based on a negative angle. For a negative angle, the cosine remains the same but the sine is negative, and that's also a characteristic of the quaternion conjugate.

I've shown you how to construct a rotation quaternion from an axis vector and an angle, and the *Quaternion* structure provides a constructor that does the job for you. You can also get back the axis and angle (in radians) from a rotation quaternion. Here's some simple code for a *Quaternion* object named *q*:

```
double angle = 2 * Math.ACos(q.W);
double sine = Math.Sin(angle / 2);
Vector3D axis = new Vector3D(q.X / sine, q.Y / sine, q.Z / sine);
```

Again, you don't have to perform these calculations yourself. The *Quaternion* structure defines get-only *Angle* and *Axis* properties. The *Angle* property returns the angle in degrees, whereas the code I just showed uses radians.

Low-Level Quaternion Rotation

If you want to write code yourself that performs rotations, you can use the *Quaternion* structure with the rotation formulas I've shown you. For example, suppose you want to rotate the variable *point* of type *Point3D* by *angle* degrees around the *axis* vector. You first need to get a rotation quaternion and its conjugate:

```
Quaternion qRotate = new Quaternion(axis, angle);
Quaternion qConjugate = qRotate;
qConjugate.Conjugate();
```

Now convert the *Point3D* object to a pure quaternion:

```
Quaternion qPoint = new Quaternion(point.X, point.Y, point.Z, 0);
```

Multiply that point by the rotation quaternion on the left and its conjugate on the right:

```
Quaternion qRotatedPoint = qRotate * qPoint * qConjugate;
```

And convert back to a *Point3D*:

```
pointRotated = new Point3D(qRotatedPoint.X, qRotatedPoint.Y, qRotatedPoint.Z);
```

The *Quaternion* structure does not provide the logic to perform this calculation directly, but as you can see, it's simple enough to do it in code. Here's a C# program that uses this logic to perform a rotation of a square cuboid without using any WPF matrix transforms or animation facilities.

```
LowLevelQuaternionRotation.cs
//-----------------------------------------------------------
// LowLevelQuaternionRotation.cs (c) 2007 by Charles Petzold
//-----------------------------------------------------------
using System;
using System.Diagnostics;
using System.Windows;
using System.Windows.Controls;
using System.Windows.Media;
using System.Windows.Media.Media3D;
```

```
namespace Petzold.LowLevelQuaternionRotation
{
    public class LowLevelQuaternionRotation : Window
    {
        const double secondsPerCycle = 3;
        static readonly Vector3D axis = new Vector3D(1, 1, 0);
        static readonly Quaternion qCenter = new Quaternion(0.5, 0.5, -2, 0);

        Stopwatch stopwatch;
        MeshGeometry3D mesh;
        Point3D[] pointsCuboid =
            {
                new Point3D(0, 1,  0), new Point3D(0, 0,  0),
                new Point3D(1, 1,  0), new Point3D(1, 0,  0),
                new Point3D(0, 1, -4), new Point3D(0, 0, -4),
                new Point3D(0, 1,  0), new Point3D(0, 0,  0),
                new Point3D(1, 1, -4), new Point3D(0, 1, -4),
                new Point3D(1, 1,  0), new Point3D(0, 1,  0),
                new Point3D(1, 1,  0), new Point3D(1, 0,  0),
                new Point3D(1, 1, -4), new Point3D(1, 0, -4),
                new Point3D(1, 0,  0), new Point3D(0, 0,  0),
                new Point3D(1, 0, -4), new Point3D(0, 0, -4),
                new Point3D(1, 1, -4), new Point3D(1, 0, -4),
                new Point3D(0, 1, -4), new Point3D(0, 0, -4)
            };

        [STAThread]
        public static void Main()
        {
            Application app = new Application();
            app.Run(new LowLevelQuaternionRotation());
        }
        public LowLevelQuaternionRotation()
        {
            Title = "Low-Level Quaternion Rotation";

            // Create Viewport3D as content of window.
            Viewport3D viewport = new Viewport3D();
            Content = viewport;

            // Create MeshGeometry3D.
            mesh = new MeshGeometry3D();
            mesh.Positions = new Point3DCollection(pointsCuboid);
            mesh.TriangleIndices = new Int32Collection(new Int32[]
                {
                    0, 1, 2, 1, 3, 2, 4, 5, 6, 5, 7, 6,
                    8, 9, 10, 9, 11, 10, 12, 13, 14, 13, 15, 14,
                    16, 17, 18, 17, 19, 18, 20, 21, 22, 21, 23, 22
                });

            // Assemble all the models together.
            Model3DGroup grp = new Model3DGroup();
            grp.Children.Add(new GeometryModel3D(mesh,
                                new DiffuseMaterial(Brushes.Cyan)));
```

```
            grp.Children.Add(new AmbientLight(Color.FromRgb(64, 64, 64)));
            grp.Children.Add(new DirectionalLight(Color.FromRgb(192, 192, 192),
                                            new Vector3D(2, -3, -1)));

            // Create ModelVisual3D and camera.
            ModelVisual3D vis = new ModelVisual3D();
            vis.Content = grp;
            viewport.Children.Add(vis);
            viewport.Camera =
                new PerspectiveCamera(new Point3D(-2, 2, 4),
                        new Vector3D(2, -1, -4), new Vector3D(0, 1, 0), 45);

            stopwatch = new Stopwatch();
            stopwatch.Start();
            CompositionTarget.Rendering += OnRendering;
        }

        void OnRendering(object sender, EventArgs args)
        {
            // Detach collection from MeshGeometry3D.
            Point3DCollection points = mesh.Positions;
            mesh.Positions = null;
            points.Clear();

            // Calculation rotation quaternion.
            double angle = 360.0 * (stopwatch.Elapsed.TotalSeconds %
                                        secondsPerCycle) / secondsPerCycle;
            Quaternion qRotate = new Quaternion(axis, angle);
            Quaternion qConjugate = qRotate;
            qConjugate.Conjugate();

            // Apply rotation to each point.
            foreach (Point3D point in pointsCuboid)
            {
                Quaternion qPoint = new Quaternion(point.X, point.Y, point.Z, 0);
                qPoint -= qCenter;
                Quaternion qRotatedPoint = qRotate * qPoint * qConjugate;
                qRotatedPoint += qCenter;
                points.Add(new Point3D(qRotatedPoint.X, qRotatedPoint.Y,
                                            qRotatedPoint.Z));
            }

            // Re-attach collections to MeshGeometry3D.
            mesh.Positions = points;
        }
    }
}
```

At each vertical refresh of the screen, the *OnRendering* method calculates a new rotation angle, creates a *Quaternion* and its conjugate, and rotates the array of points that define the square cuboid. Notice that the program also stores a center point as a *Quaternion* object so that each point can essentially be translated based on that point before and after the rotation.

If you wanted to perform this same "manual" rotation without the use of quaternions, you'd need to create a transform matrix based on the axis and angle. You could consult the generalized rotation matrix for axis/angle rotations I showed you in the last chapter and construct a *Matrix3D* object from that. Or you could use an *AxisAngleRotation3D* object combined with a *RotateTransform3D* object. You could then apply the resultant transform to the array of points using the *Transform* method defined by either *Matrix3D* or *Transform3D* (from which *RotateTransform3D* derives). Just offhand, the quaternion approach appears to involve fewer numbers and fewer calculations, and that is one reason why quaternions have achieved such popularity in 3D graphics.

Quaternions and Rotation Matrices

The *Matrix3D* structure defines *Rotate*, *RotateAt*, *RotatePrepend*, and *RotateAtPrepend* methods to apply a rotation transform to the current transform stored by the *Matrix3D* object. However, the argument to these methods is not an angle and rotation axis, but a quaternion. If you want to create a *Matrix3D* object from an angle and rotation axis using these methods, you first need to create a *Quaternion* object from the constructor that accepts an angle and rotation axis.

Or, you could define the *Matrix3D* object itself directly from the four properties of the *Quaternion* object. Converting a rotation quaternion to a rotation matrix is fairly straightforward, but it's written in a couple different ways. (All of them are equivalent, of course.) For a quaternion (w, x, y, z), the rotation matrix is:

$$\begin{vmatrix} w^2 + x^2 - y^2 - z^2 & 2xy + 2wz & 2xz - 2wy \\ 2xy - 2wz & w^2 - x^2 + y^2 - z^2 & 2yz + 2wx \\ 2xz + 2wy & 2yz - 2wx & w^2 - x^2 - y^2 + z^2 \end{vmatrix}$$

The other two ways the rotation matrix is written are different only in the diagonals. Here's one:

$$\begin{vmatrix} 2w^2 + 2x^2 - 1 & 2xy + 2wz & 2xz - 2wy \\ 2xy - 2wz & 2w^2 + 2y^2 - 1 & 2yz + 2wx \\ 2xz + 2wy & 2yz - 2wx & 2w^2 + 2z^2 - 1 \end{vmatrix}$$

And here's the other:

$$\begin{vmatrix} 1 - 2y^2 - 2z^2 & 2xy + 2wz & 2xz - 2wy \\ 2xy - 2wz & 1 - 2x^2 - 2z^2 & 2yz + 2wx \\ 2xz + 2wy & 2yz - 2wx & 1 - 2x^2 - 2y^2 \end{vmatrix}$$

These are all equivalent because the rotation quaternion is normalized, which means:

$$w^2 + x^2 + y^2 + z^2 = 1$$

Let's examine a simple case where the axis of rotation is $(0, 0, 1)$, which means that w is the cosine of half the rotation angle, z is the sine of half the rotation angle, and x and y are zero. The rotation matrix based on the last of the three equivalent matrices is:

$$\begin{vmatrix} 1-2\sin^2\left(\dfrac{\theta}{2}\right) & 2\cos\left(\dfrac{\theta}{2}\right)\sin\left(\dfrac{\theta}{2}\right) & 0 \\ -2\cos\left(\dfrac{\theta}{2}\right)\sin\left(\dfrac{\theta}{2}\right) & 1-2\sin^2\left(\dfrac{\theta}{2}\right) & 0 \\ 0 & 0 & 1 \end{vmatrix}$$

Using trigonometric identities shown earlier in this chapter, you can easily simplify this matrix to our old friend:

$$\begin{vmatrix} \cos(\theta) & \sin(\theta) & 0 \\ -\sin(\theta) & \cos(\theta) & 0 \\ 0 & 0 & 1 \end{vmatrix}$$

Suppose you have a rotation matrix that you either calculated manually or obtained from some other source, and you want to convert it to a quaternion. Here's your rotation matrix labeled with the *Matrix3D* properties:

$$\begin{vmatrix} M11 & M12 & M13 \\ M21 & M22 & M23 \\ M31 & M32 & M33 \end{vmatrix}$$

You can often obtain the quaternion corresponding to this matrix using the following formulas:

$$w = \frac{1}{2}\sqrt{1 + M11 + M22 + M33}$$

$$x = \frac{M32 - M23}{4w}$$

$$y = \frac{M13 - M31}{4w}$$

$$z = \frac{M21 - M12}{4w}$$

However, it could be that the sum of *M11*, *M22*, and *M33* equals −1, in which case *w* equals zero (which means the angle is 180 degrees), and the formulas for *x*, *y*, and *z* aren't valid. In that case, you can use the following formulas for *x*, *y*, and *z*:

$$x = \frac{M12 \cdot M13}{\sqrt{(M12 \cdot M13)^2 + (M12 \cdot M23)^2 + (M13 \cdot M23)^2}}$$

$$y = \frac{M12 \cdot M23}{\sqrt{(M12 \cdot M13)^2 + (M12 \cdot M23)^2 + (M13 \cdot M23)^2}}$$

$$z = \frac{M13 \cdot M23}{\sqrt{(M12 \cdot M13)^2 + (M12 \cdot M23)^2 + (M13 \cdot M23)^2}}$$

Notice that the denominators are all the same. The numerator is always one of the products in the denominator, and $x^2 + y^2 + z^2$ equals 1. If the denominator is zero, the rotation is around the X, Y, or Z axis. If *M12* and *M13* are zero, the rotation is around the X axis; if *M12* and *M23* are zero, rotation is around the Y axis; if *M23* and *M13* are zero, rotation is around the Z axis. These cases must all be handled individually.

SLERP and Animation

The *RotateTransform3D* class defines a property named *Rotation* that you set to an object of type *Rotation3D*, which is an abstract class from which both *AxisAngleRotation3D* and *QuaternionRotation3D* descend. In previous chapters, I've shown only *AxisAngleRotation3D*. *QuaternionRotation3D* has a single property named *Quaternion* of type *Quaternion*. In XAML, it looks like this:

```
<RotateTransform3D>
    <RotateTransform3D.Rotation>
        <QuaternionRotation3D Quaternion="0 0 0.5 0.866" />
    </RotateTransform3D.Rotation>
</RotateTransform3D>
```

That's a rotation of 60 degrees around the Z axis or **(0, 0, 1)**. The number 0.5 is the sine of half the angle (or 30 degrees), and 0.866 is the cosine of 30 degrees. Remember: In XAML, the *w* term comes last. You can optionally specify a center for the rotation in the *Rotate-Transform3D* tag.

But for a case like this—where you're probably manually calculating the quaternion from an axis and angle—it really makes little sense not to use the *AxisAngleRotation3D* object itself. Quaternions are most valuable where animations are involved for two reasons. First, quaternions are marginally faster. I've tested the code, and setting the property of a *Quaternion-Rotation3D* is a little faster than setting the properties of an *AxisAngleRotation3D*. Perhaps more important, however, an interpolation formula for quaternions exists that preserves angular velocity. As you saw in the AnimatingTheAxis.xaml file at the conclusion of Chapter 3, animating the axis of an *AxisAngleRotation3D* object results in an animation of varying speed.

Although quaternions had already been used for several decades in the aerospace industry for spacecraft dynamics, quaternions entered computer graphics in a big way in 1985 with the publication of Ken Shoemake's article "Animating Rotation with Quaternion Curves" in SIGGRAPH '85 (also known as *Computer Graphics*, Volume 19, Number 3), pages 245–254. In this article, Shoemake introduced SLERP (which stands for spherical *linear interpolation*) to interpolate quaternions. Because a quaternion itself has four numbers, it really describes a point in four-dimensional space. A rotation quaternion, however, is normalized, so it represents a point on the surface of a four-dimensional sphere. SLERP is an interpolation on the surface of that sphere along the four-dimensional equivalent of a great circle.

The *Quaternion* structure defines a static *Slerp* method that performs this interpolation between two *Quaternion* objects. This is the method that the animation classes use when you animate a property of type *Quaternion*, which is most likely the *Quaternion* property of a *QuaternionRotation3D* object.

Here is a quaternion version of the AnimatingTheAxis.xaml file shown at the end of Chapter 3. As you might recall, that program kept the angle of rotation constant at 60 degrees but animated the axis between the positive and negative X and Y axes.

```
AnimatingTheQuaternion.xaml
<!-- =========================================================
         AnimatingTheQuaternion.xaml (c) 2007 by Charles Petzold
     ========================================================= -->
<Page xmlns="http://schemas.microsoft.com/winfx/2006/xaml/presentation"
      xmlns:x="http://schemas.microsoft.com/winfx/2006/xaml"
      WindowTitle="Animating the Quaternion"
      Title="Animating the Quaternion">
    <Viewport3D>
        <ModelVisual3D>
            <ModelVisual3D.Content>
                <Model3DGroup>
                    <GeometryModel3D>
                        <GeometryModel3D.Geometry>
                            <MeshGeometry3D
                                Positions="-0.5  0.5  0,  0.5  0.5  0,
                                           -0.5 -0.5  0,  0.5 -0.5  0"

                                TriangleIndices="0 2 1, 1 2 3" />
                        </GeometryModel3D.Geometry>

                        <GeometryModel3D.Material>
                            <DiffuseMaterial Brush="Cyan" />
                        </GeometryModel3D.Material>

                        <GeometryModel3D.Transform>
                            <RotateTransform3D>
                                <RotateTransform3D.Rotation>
                                    <QuaternionRotation3D x:Name="rotate" />
                                </RotateTransform3D.Rotation>
                            </RotateTransform3D>
```

```
                </GeometryModel3D.Transform>
            </GeometryModel3D>

            <!-- Light sources. -->
            <AmbientLight Color="#404040" />
            <DirectionalLight Color="#C0C0C0" Direction="2, -3 -1" />

        </Model3DGroup>
    </ModelVisual3D.Content>
</ModelVisual3D>

<Viewport3D.Camera>
    <PerspectiveCamera Position="0 0 3"
                        LookDirection="0 0 -1"
                        UpDirection="0 1 0"
                        FieldOfView="45" />
</Viewport3D.Camera>
</Viewport3D>

<Page.Triggers>
    <EventTrigger RoutedEvent="Page.Loaded">
        <BeginStoryboard>
            <Storyboard TargetName="rotate" TargetProperty="Quaternion">
                <QuaternionAnimationUsingKeyFrames RepeatBehavior="Forever">
                    <LinearQuaternionKeyFrame KeyTime="0:0:0"
                                            Value="-0.5 0 0 0.866" />
                    <LinearQuaternionKeyFrame KeyTime="0:0:1"
                                            Value="0 -0.5 0 0.866" />
                    <LinearQuaternionKeyFrame KeyTime="0:0:2"
                                            Value="0.5 0 0 0.866" />
                    <LinearQuaternionKeyFrame KeyTime="0:0:3"
                                            Value="0 0.5 0 0.866" />
                    <LinearQuaternionKeyFrame KeyTime="0:0:4"
                                            Value="-0.5 0 0 0.866" />
                </QuaternionAnimationUsingKeyFrames>
            </Storyboard>
        </BeginStoryboard>
    </EventTrigger>
</Page.Triggers>
</Page>
```

It will be instructional for you to run AnimatingTheAxis.xaml and this new program and then compare the results. It's easy to see that the quaternion animation keeps the angular velocity constant. With each step of the key-frame animation, the figure makes a sudden change in direction but maintains the same speed. The previous program seemed to slow down and speed up as the axis of rotation changed. You might actually prefer the appearance of the earlier program, and there's nothing wrong with that! But you can certainly see that the quaternion interpolation provides consistent results while the vector interpolation does not.

You can actually make use of quaternion SLERP without having any explicit quaternions in your program. This feat is possible through two additional animation classes designed specifically for 3D: *Rotation3DAnimation* and *Rotation3DAnimationUsingKeyFrames*. These classes animate objects of type *Rotation3D*, which is the abstract base class to *AxisAngleRotation3D* and *QuaternionRotation3D*. However, even if you define the *Rotation3D* animation entirely in terms of a rotation axis and angle, the animation uses quaternion SLERP for the interpolation.

In your markup, you'll probably define a rotation transform something like this:

```
<RotateTransform3D x:Name="rotate" />
```

By itself, this would make no sense because the *RotateTransform3D* is useless without setting the *Rotation* property to an object of type *AxisAngleRotation3D* or *QuaternionRotation3D*. But that's the property that's going to be animated. In a *Rotation3DAnimation* element, you set the target of the animation to the "rotate" element and the target property to *Rotation*—that is, the *Rotation* property of the *RotateTransform3D*. Normally in an animation element you simply set the *From* and *To* properties to strings indicating their values. But for *Rotation3DAnimation*, the *From* and *To* properties appear as property elements because the values are objects of type *AxisAngleRotation3D* or *QuaternionRotation3D*:

```
<Rotation3DAnimation Storyboard.TargetName="rotate"
                     Storyboard.TargetProperty="Rotation" ...>
    <Rotation3DAnimation.From>
        <AxisAngleRotation3D ... />
    </Rotation3DAnimation.From>
    <Rotation3DAnimation.To>
        <QuaternionRotation3D ... />
    </Rotation3DAnimation.To>
</Rotation3DAnimation>
```

Notice that the *From* value is indicated as an *AxisAngleRotation3D* while the *To* value is a *QuaternionRotation3D*. You can use either class for either property, and mix and match as you like. The actual interpolation always uses SLERP.

The following program uses *Rotation3DAnimationUsingKeyFrames* with objects of type *AxisAngleRotation3D* to specify the same constant angle and animated axes used in both AnimatingTheAxis.xaml and AnimatingTheQuaternion.xaml.

AnimatingTheRotation3D.xaml
```
<!-- ======================================================
     AnimatingTheRotation3D.xaml (c) 2007 by Charles Petzold
     ====================================================== -->
<Page xmlns="http://schemas.microsoft.com/winfx/2006/xaml/presentation"
      xmlns:x="http://schemas.microsoft.com/winfx/2006/xaml"
      WindowTitle="Animating the Rotation3D"
      Title="Animating the Rotation3D">
    <Viewport3D>
        <ModelVisual3D>
            <ModelVisual3D.Content>
```

```
            <Model3DGroup>
                <GeometryModel3D>
                    <GeometryModel3D.Geometry>
                        <MeshGeometry3D
                            Positions="-0.5  0.5  0,   0.5  0.5   0,
                                       -0.5 -0.5  0,   0.5 -0.5   0"

                            TriangleIndices="0 2 1, 1 2 3" />
                    </GeometryModel3D.Geometry>

                    <GeometryModel3D.Material>
                        <DiffuseMaterial Brush="Cyan" />
                    </GeometryModel3D.Material>

                    <GeometryModel3D.Transform>
                        <RotateTransform3D x:Name="rotate" />
                    </GeometryModel3D.Transform>
                </GeometryModel3D>

                <!-- Light sources. -->
                <AmbientLight Color="#404040" />
                <DirectionalLight Color="#C0C0C0" Direction="2, -3 -1" />

            </Model3DGroup>
        </ModelVisual3D.Content>
    </ModelVisual3D>

    <Viewport3D.Camera>
        <PerspectiveCamera Position="0 0 3"
                           LookDirection="0 0 -1"
                           UpDirection="0 1 0"
                           FieldOfView="45" />
    </Viewport3D.Camera>
</Viewport3D>

<Page.Triggers>
    <EventTrigger RoutedEvent="Page.Loaded">
        <BeginStoryboard>
            <Storyboard TargetName="rotate" TargetProperty="Rotation">
                <Rotation3DAnimationUsingKeyFrames RepeatBehavior="Forever">
                    <LinearRotation3DKeyFrame KeyTime="0:0:0">
                        <LinearRotation3DKeyFrame.Value>
                            <AxisAngleRotation3D Angle="60" Axis="-1 0 0" />
                        </LinearRotation3DKeyFrame.Value>
                    </LinearRotation3DKeyFrame>

                    <LinearRotation3DKeyFrame KeyTime="0:0:1">
                        <LinearRotation3DKeyFrame.Value>
                            <AxisAngleRotation3D Angle="60" Axis="0 -1 0" />
                        </LinearRotation3DKeyFrame.Value>
                    </LinearRotation3DKeyFrame>

                    <LinearRotation3DKeyFrame KeyTime="0:0:2">
                        <LinearRotation3DKeyFrame.Value>
```

```
                        <AxisAngleRotation3D Angle="60" Axis="1 0 0" />
                    </LinearRotation3DKeyFrame.Value>
                </LinearRotation3DKeyFrame>

                <LinearRotation3DKeyFrame KeyTime="0:0:3">
                    <LinearRotation3DKeyFrame.Value>
                        <AxisAngleRotation3D Angle="60" Axis="0 1 0" />
                    </LinearRotation3DKeyFrame.Value>
                </LinearRotation3DKeyFrame>

                <LinearRotation3DKeyFrame KeyTime="0:0:4">
                    <LinearRotation3DKeyFrame.Value>
                        <AxisAngleRotation3D Angle="60" Axis="-1 0 0" />
                    </LinearRotation3DKeyFrame.Value>
                </LinearRotation3DKeyFrame>
            </Rotation3DAnimationUsingKeyFrames>
        </Storyboard>
    </BeginStoryboard>
  </EventTrigger>
 </Page.Triggers>
</Page>
```

Despite the use of *AxisAngleRotation3D* to specify the values of the animation key frames, it's very clear when you run the program that the interpolation is the same as if quaternions had been specified.

If you dare, you can animate both the rotation axis *and* the angle in synchronization. The downloadable code for this chapter contains a file named AnimatingTheAxisAndAngle.xaml that does precisely that.

Chapter 9
Applications and Curiosa

I said in the Introduction to this book that the 3D facilities of the Windows Presentation Foundation were not designed for graphics-intensive games or the next animated blockbuster movie. Instead, they are intended to let you easily integrate 3D into your WPF applications to provide a richer experience for your users.

I created the programs in this chapter to demonstrate some interesting techniques in 3D graphics, but also to give you some ideas—and perhaps stimulate your imagination—about how 3D can play a role in your own applications.

Control Templates

Sometimes programmers need to write their own controls, and sometimes they need to enhance existing controls by deriving from a control class and adding properties or methods. But very often the *functionality* of a control is quite suitable, and the only real problem is its *appearance*.

In traditional graphical programming environments, very often the code that governed the appearance of a control was very intertwined with the code for the control functionality, and all of this code was buried deep inside the control. Changing the appearance of a control without access to the source code often required that the control be completely rewritten.

In the Windows Presentation Foundation, however, control functionality and appearance have been separated. The *Control* class defines a property named *Template* that is set to an object of type *ControlTemplate*. This is the object that defines the appearance of the control. Every control has a default *ControlTemplate* object set to its *Template* property, but application programmers can replace that template with a template of their own creation. These *Control-Template* objects are usually defined in XAML and can contain a combination of two-dimensional and three-dimensional graphics.

You've probably seen plenty of *CheckBox* controls in your life. The standard *CheckBox* control consists of a little box and some text. If the *CheckBox* is checked, a little X or checkmark appears in the box. In the abstract, however, a *CheckBox* is basically a way for a user to specify the value of a Boolean variable. (Let's ignore tri-state *CheckBox* controls for this discussion.) A control can graphically display a Boolean in many ways. Here, for example, are two *CheckBox* controls with a new template that makes use of 3D graphics:

These have the appearance of old-fashioned knife switches. When you click anywhere on the control, the "knife" swivels to its new position in a one-second animation.

The *ControlTemplate* for this switch is defined in the Resources section of the following XAML file. The file concludes by creating the two *CheckBox* controls that use this template.

```
KnifeSwitchCheckBox.xaml
<!-- =================================================
     KnifeSwitchCheckBox.xaml (c) 2007 by Charles Petzold
     ================================================= -->
<Page xmlns="http://schemas.microsoft.com/winfx/2006/xaml/presentation"
      xmlns:x="http://schemas.microsoft.com/winfx/2006/xaml"
      Title="Knife Switch CheckBox"
      WindowTitle="Knife Switch CheckBox">
    <Page.Resources>
        <ControlTemplate x:Key="templateKnifeSwitchCheckBox"
                         TargetType="CheckBox">
            <ControlTemplate.Resources>

                • • •

            </ControlTemplate.Resources>

            <!-- The control begins with a border. -->
            <Border BorderBrush="{TemplateBinding BorderBrush}"
                    BorderThickness="{TemplateBinding BorderThickness}"
                    Background="{TemplateBinding Background}"
                    MinWidth="100"
                    MinHeight="210">
```

```xml
<!-- Viewport3D contains 3D parts. -->
<Viewport3D>
    <ModelVisual3D Content="{StaticResource base}" />

    <ModelVisual3D Content="{StaticResource switcher}">
        <ModelVisual3D.Transform>
            <RotateTransform3D CenterY="0.25" CenterZ="0.25" >
                <RotateTransform3D.Rotation>
                    <AxisAngleRotation3D x:Name="rotate"
                                         Axis="1 0 0" Angle="-90" />
                </RotateTransform3D.Rotation>
            </RotateTransform3D>
        </ModelVisual3D.Transform>
    </ModelVisual3D>

    <!-- This visual displays the control content. -->
    <ModelVisual3D>
        <ModelVisual3D.Content>
            <GeometryModel3D>
                <GeometryModel3D.Geometry>
                    <MeshGeometry3D
                        Positions=
                            "-0.2  0.1 0.01, 0.2  0.1 0.01,
                             -0.2 -0.1 0.01, 0.2 -0.1 0.01"
                        TextureCoordinates="0 0, 1 0, 0 1, 1 1"
                        TriangleIndices="1 0 2, 1 2 3" />
                </GeometryModel3D.Geometry>
                <GeometryModel3D.Material>
                    <DiffuseMaterial>
                        <DiffuseMaterial.Brush>
<!-- VisualBrush displays control content. -->
<VisualBrush>
    <VisualBrush.Visual>
        <ContentPresenter
            Content="{TemplateBinding Content}"
            ContentTemplate="{TemplateBinding ContentTemplate}"
            Margin="{TemplateBinding Padding}"
            HorizontalAlignment="{TemplateBinding
                                  HorizontalContentAlignment}"
            VerticalAlignment="{TemplateBinding
                                VerticalContentAlignment}" />
    </VisualBrush.Visual>
</VisualBrush>
                        </DiffuseMaterial.Brush>
                    </DiffuseMaterial>
                </GeometryModel3D.Material>
            </GeometryModel3D>
        </ModelVisual3D.Content>
    </ModelVisual3D>
```

```xml
                        <!-- Light sources. -->
                        <ModelVisual3D>
                            <ModelVisual3D.Content>
                                <Model3DGroup>
                                    <AmbientLight Color="#404040" />
                                    <DirectionalLight Color="#C0C0C0"
                                                    Direction="2 -3 -1" />
                                </Model3DGroup>
                            </ModelVisual3D.Content>
                        </ModelVisual3D>

                        <!-- Camera. -->
                        <Viewport3D.Camera>
                            <PerspectiveCamera Position="0 0.25 4"
                                            LookDirection="0 0 -4"
                                            UpDirection="0 1 0"
                                            FieldOfView="20" />
                        </Viewport3D.Camera>
                    </Viewport3D>
                </Border>

                <ControlTemplate.Triggers>

                    <!-- Animation to close the switch. -->
                    <EventTrigger RoutedEvent="CheckBox.Checked">
                        <BeginStoryboard>
                            <Storyboard TargetName="rotate"
                                    TargetProperty="Angle">
                                <DoubleAnimation To="90" />
                            </Storyboard>
                        </BeginStoryboard>
                    </EventTrigger>

                    <!-- Animation to open the switch. -->
                    <EventTrigger RoutedEvent="CheckBox.Unchecked">
                        <BeginStoryboard>
                            <Storyboard TargetName="rotate"
                                    TargetProperty="Angle">
                                <DoubleAnimation To="-90" />
                            </Storyboard>
                        </BeginStoryboard>
                    </EventTrigger>
                </ControlTemplate.Triggers>
            </ControlTemplate>
        </Page.Resources>

        <!-- Display two sample CheckBox controls using the template. -->
        <StackPanel Orientation="Horizontal">
            <CheckBox Template="{StaticResource templateKnifeSwitchCheckBox}"
                    Foreground="White"
                    Margin="24"
                    HorizontalAlignment="Center"
                    VerticalAlignment="Center">
                Lights
            </CheckBox>
```

```
      <CheckBox Template="{StaticResource templateKnifeSwitchCheckBox}"
                Foreground="White"
                Margin="24"
                HorizontalAlignment="Center"
                VerticalAlignment="Center">
          Camera
      </CheckBox>
    </StackPanel>
  </Page>
```

Notice that the *ControlTemplate* itself has a Resources section that contains much of the markup dedicated to defining all the parts of the switch. Like some other programs you've already seen, it builds everything from a unit cube that is scaled to various sizes, so I've abridged the file here. The Resources section defines two models named "base" and "switcher." Following the Resources section, the markup defines the appearance of the control itself. Very often a control template begins with a *Border* element. In this template, a *Viewport3D* is a child of that *Border*. Much of the markup in the *ControlTemplate* resembles markup you'd write normally for creating graphical figures. One big difference is the presence of *TemplateBinding* extensions that reference properties of the *CheckBox* control. For a control like *CheckBox* that derives from *ContentControl*, often the *ControlTemplate* definition includes a *ContentPresenter* element that displays the *Content* property of the control. I've based a *VisualBrush* on that *ContentPresenter* so that the content is displayed in the center of the switch's base.

A Triggers section usually concludes the *ControlTemplate*. Here is where changes in control properties can trigger changes in the appearance of the control, including animations. I have ignored the customary triggers for showing text in gray when the control is disabled and outlining the content when the control has input focus. Instead, I've defined two animations that flip the switch whenever it's clicked.

In an article for the January 2007 issue of *MSDN Magazine* I presented a template for the *Slider* control that used 3D graphics to create a control resembling a potentiometer that might be found on a mixing board in a sound studio. (The original article is online at *http://msdn.microsoft.com/msdnmag/issues/07/01/Foundations*.) I was never completely happy with that template because it had two big problems: It could only be used for vertical sliders and the range was fixed to a *Minimum* value of −25 and *Maximum* value of 25. I cleverly used the *Value* property of the *Slider* to set the *Angle* property of an *AxisAngleRotation3D*, but in doing so I didn't leave the application programmer much leeway in using the control.

Generally, controls that can be displayed in either a horizontal or vertical orientation use two different templates for these orientations, and that's the approach I decided to use for the enhanced version of my 3D slider. If you're writing the templates only for your own use, you can select which template to use in the Triggers section of a *Style* definition. However, if you're creating a custom control for others to use, it really should have a null *Style* property and shouldn't require a specific *Style* to use the control. In other words, code within the control should select the template to use based on the *Orientation* property.

It also became obvious to me that I'd need to write some code anyway for handling the range problem. A custom slider control really should *not* require the range to be fixed between −25 and 25. I decided to derive a new class from *Slider* named *Slider3D* and add a get-only *Angle* property that the template could use directly. Here's the code part of the *Slider3D* class.

```
Slider3D.cs
//------------------------------------------
// Slider3D.cs (c) 2007 by Charles Petzold
//------------------------------------------
using System;
using System.Windows;
using System.Windows.Controls;

namespace Petzold.Slider3D
{
    public partial class Slider3D : Slider
    {
        // Constructor.
        public Slider3D()
        {
            InitializeComponent();

            // Default Orientation is Horizontal, so load that template.
            Template =
                (ControlTemplate)FindResource("templateHorizontalSlider3D");
        }

        // Get-only Angle property and dependency property.
        static readonly DependencyPropertyKey AngleKey =
            DependencyProperty.RegisterReadOnly("Angle",
                typeof(double),
                typeof(Slider3D),
                new PropertyMetadata(-25.0));

        public static readonly DependencyProperty AngleProperty =
            AngleKey.DependencyProperty;

        public double Angle
        {
            protected set { SetValue(AngleKey, value); }
            get { return (double)GetValue(AngleProperty); }
        }

        // Static constructor.
        static Slider3D()
        {
            OrientationProperty.OverrideMetadata(typeof(Slider3D),
                new FrameworkPropertyMetadata(PropertyChanged));

            ValueProperty.OverrideMetadata(typeof(Slider3D),
                new FrameworkPropertyMetadata(PropertyChanged));
```

```
        MinimumProperty.OverrideMetadata(typeof(Slider3D),
            new FrameworkPropertyMetadata(PropertyChanged));

        MaximumProperty.OverrideMetadata(typeof(Slider3D),
            new FrameworkPropertyMetadata(PropertyChanged));

        IsDirectionReversedProperty.OverrideMetadata(typeof(Slider3D),
            new FrameworkPropertyMetadata(PropertyChanged));
    }


    // PropertyChanged event handlers.
    static void PropertyChanged(DependencyObject obj,
                            DependencyPropertyChangedEventArgs args)
    {
        (obj as Slider3D).PropertyChanged(args);
    }

    void PropertyChanged(DependencyPropertyChangedEventArgs args)
    {
        if (args.Property == OrientationProperty)
        {
            Template = (ControlTemplate)FindResource(
                Orientation == Orientation.Horizontal ?
                    "templateHorizontalSlider3D" :
                    "templateVerticalSlider3D");
        }
        else
        {
            Angle = (IsDirectionReversed ? -1 : 1) *
                    (50 * (Value - Minimum) / (Maximum - Minimum) - 25);
        }
    }
}
}
}
```

The class defines one new property named *Angle* backed by a dependency property. But this *Angle* property is dependent on five other properties of the *Slider* class, as the code at the very end of the listing makes clear. The static constructor calls the *OverrideMetadata* method for each of these five *Slider* properties to set a new *PropertyChanged* handler that's called whenever the properties change. Despite the name of the *OverrideMetadata* method, this new *PropertyChanged* handler is called *in addition to* any handlers for these properties defined in the *RangeBase* or *Slider* class.

The code part of the *Slider3D* class assumes the existence of two templates stored as resources with the text keys of "templateHorizontalSlider3D" and "templateVerticalSlider3D." The XAML part of *Slider3D* consists solely of a Resources section that references two XAML files with a root element of type *ResourceDictionary*. These are the files that contain the actual templates.

Slider3D.xaml

```
<!-- =============================================
        Slider3D.xaml (c) 2007 by Charles Petzold
     ============================================= -->
<Slider xmlns="http://schemas.microsoft.com/winfx/2006/xaml/presentation"
        xmlns:x="http://schemas.microsoft.com/winfx/2006/xaml"
        x:Class="Petzold.Slider3D.Slider3D">
    <Slider.Resources>
        <ResourceDictionary>
            <ResourceDictionary.MergedDictionaries>
                <ResourceDictionary Source="HorizontalSlider3DTemplate.xaml" />
                <ResourceDictionary Source="VerticalSlider3DTemplate.xaml" />
            </ResourceDictionary.MergedDictionaries>
        </ResourceDictionary>
    </Slider.Resources>
</Slider>
```

I toyed around with sharing some resources between the two sliders, but in the end I decided to make each template entirely independent of the other. Here's the template for the slider in its vertical orientation.

VerticalSlider3DTemplate.xaml

```
<!-- =========================================================
        VerticalSlider3DTemplate.xaml (c) 2007 by Charles Petzold
     ========================================================= -->
<ResourceDictionary
        xmlns="http://schemas.microsoft.com/winfx/2006/xaml/presentation"
        xmlns:x="http://schemas.microsoft.com/winfx/2006/xaml"
        xmlns:src="clr-namespace:Petzold.Slider3D">
    <ControlTemplate x:Key="templateVerticalSlider3D"
                     TargetType="src:Slider3D">

        <!-- Border properties are probably unused. -->
        <Border BorderBrush="{TemplateBinding BorderBrush}"
                BorderThickness="{TemplateBinding BorderThickness}"
                Background="{TemplateBinding Background}">

            <!-- Grid layout accommodates two TickBars and Track. -->
            <Grid>
                <Grid.ColumnDefinitions>
                    <ColumnDefinition Width="Auto" />
                    <ColumnDefinition Width="50" />
                    <ColumnDefinition Width="Auto" />
                </Grid.ColumnDefinitions>

                <!-- TickBars are collapsed (invisible) by default. -->
                <TickBar Grid.Column="0" Name="LeftTick"
                         Width="10" Placement="Left" Visibility="Collapsed"
                         Fill="{TemplateBinding Foreground}" />
```

```xml
                            <TickBar Grid.Column="2" Name="RightTick"
                                    Width="10" Placement="Right" Visibility="Collapsed"
                                    Fill="{TemplateBinding Foreground}" />

                        <!-- The groove image is provided by this Border. -->
                        <Border Grid.Column="1"
                                Margin="21 22 21 22" CornerRadius="2 2 2 2"
                                BorderBrush="Black" BorderThickness="1"
                                Background="LightGray" />

                        <!-- That same Grid cell is occupied by the Track. -->
                        <Track Grid.Column="1" Name="PART_Track">
                            <Track.DecreaseRepeatButton>

                                <!-- The two RepeatButtons are transparent. -->
                                <RepeatButton Command="Slider.DecreaseLarge"
                                            IsTabStop="False" Focusable="False">
                                    <RepeatButton.Template>
                                        <ControlTemplate>
                                            <Border Background="Transparent" />
                                        </ControlTemplate>
                                    </RepeatButton.Template>
                                </RepeatButton>
                            </Track.DecreaseRepeatButton>

                            <Track.IncreaseRepeatButton>
                                <RepeatButton Command="Slider.IncreaseLarge"
                                            IsTabStop="False" Focusable="False">
                                    <RepeatButton.Template>
                                        <ControlTemplate>
                                            <Border Background="Transparent" />
                                        </ControlTemplate>
                                    </RepeatButton.Template>
                                </RepeatButton>
                            </Track.IncreaseRepeatButton>

                            <!-- The Thumb is basically a Visual3D element. -->
                            <Track.Thumb>
                                <Thumb Height="50">
                                    <Thumb.Template>
                                        <ControlTemplate>
                                            <Border Background="Transparent">
                                                <Viewport3D>

<!-- Shift the rest of this left to avoid excessive indents. -->
<ModelVisual3D>
    <ModelVisual3D.Content>
        <GeometryModel3D>
            <GeometryModel3D.Geometry>
```

```
                              <!-- Slider lever: rectangular pyramidal frustum. -->
                              <MeshGeometry3D
                                  Positions="-1  0.25 4, -1 -0.25 4, -2  1 0, -2 -1 0,
                                             -1 -0.25 4,  1 -0.25 4, -2 -1 0,  2 -1 0,
                                              1 -0.25 4,  1  0.25 4,  2 -1 0,  2  1 0,
                                              1  0.25 4, -1  0.25 4,  2  1 0, -2  1 0,
                                             -1  0.25 4,  1  0.25 4, -1 -0.25 4, 1 -0.25 4"

                                  TriangleIndices=" 0  2  1,  1  2  3,
                                                    4  6  5,  5  6  7,
                                                    8 10  9,  9 10 11,
                                                   12 14 13, 13 14 15,
                                                   16 18 17, 17 18 19" />
                          </GeometryModel3D.Geometry>

                          <GeometryModel3D.Material>
                              <DiffuseMaterial Brush="LightGray" />
                          </GeometryModel3D.Material>
                      </GeometryModel3D>
                  </ModelVisual3D.Content>
          </ModelVisual3D>

          <!-- Light sources. -->
          <ModelVisual3D>
              <ModelVisual3D.Content>
                  <Model3DGroup>
                      <AmbientLight Color="#808080" />
                      <DirectionalLight Color="#808080" Direction="2 -3 -1" />
                  </Model3DGroup>
              </ModelVisual3D.Content>
          </ModelVisual3D>

          <!-- Set up the camera looking head on down the Z axis. -->
          <Viewport3D.Camera>
              <PerspectiveCamera Position="0 0 18" LookDirection="0 0 -1"
                                 UpDirection="0 1 0" FieldOfView="15">
                  <PerspectiveCamera.Transform>
                      <RotateTransform3D>
                          <RotateTransform3D.Rotation>

                              <!-- Bind rotation angle to Angle property. -->
                              <AxisAngleRotation3D Axis="1 0 0"
                                  Angle="{Binding RelativeSource={RelativeSource
                                          AncestorType={x:Type src:Slider3D}},
                                          Path=Angle}" />
                          </RotateTransform3D.Rotation>
                      </RotateTransform3D>
                  </PerspectiveCamera.Transform>
              </PerspectiveCamera>
          </Viewport3D.Camera>
```

```
                                        <!-- Back to normal indenting. -->
                                    </Viewport3D>
                                </Border>
                            </ControlTemplate>
                        </Thumb.Template>
                    </Thumb>
                </Track.Thumb>
            </Track>
        </Grid>
    </Border>

    <!-- Define triggers to make the TickBars visible. -->
    <ControlTemplate.Triggers>
        <Trigger Property="Slider.TickPlacement" Value="TopLeft">
            <Setter TargetName="LeftTick" Property="Visibility"
                                          Value="Visible" />
        </Trigger>
        <Trigger Property="Slider.TickPlacement" Value="BottomRight">
            <Setter TargetName="RightTick" Property="Visibility"
                                           Value="Visible" />
        </Trigger>
        <Trigger Property="Slider.TickPlacement" Value="Both">
            <Setter TargetName="LeftTick" Property="Visibility"
                                          Value="Visible" />
            <Setter TargetName="RightTick" Property="Visibility"
                                           Value="Visible" />
        </Trigger>
    </ControlTemplate.Triggers>
</ControlTemplate>
</ResourceDictionary>
```

Notice that this template references other WPF elements. The *TickBar* element is responsible for displaying the optional tick marks on each side of the slider, and the *Track* element extends the length of the slider and incorporates two *RepeatButton* controls. This *Track* element must be given a name of "PART_Track" because that's how the code implemented in the *Slider* control accesses that element. The two *RepeatButton* controls must be associated with commands defined by the *Slider* code named *DecreaseLarge* and *IncreaseLarge*.

The 3D graphics come into play in the definition of the slider *Thumb* control. The *Slider* code expects the template to include a control of type *Thumb*, but because *Thumb* is a control, it has a default appearance defined by its own *Template* property of type *ControlTemplate*. The template for the *Slider* replaces this *Thumb* template with markup based around a *Viewport3D*.

The template for the horizontal slider (which I won't show here) is very similar in structure. The two templates and the *Slider3D* files are part of a project named Slider3DDemo, which also includes this small XAML file to demonstrate a pair of horizontal sliders with their values displayed in *TextBlock* elements.

Slider3DDemo.xaml

```xml
<!-- ==============================================
        Slider3DDemo.xaml (c) 2007 by Charles Petzold
        ============================================== -->
<Page xmlns="http://schemas.microsoft.com/winfx/2006/xaml/presentation"
      xmlns:x="http://schemas.microsoft.com/winfx/2006/xaml"
      xmlns:src="clr-namespace:Petzold.Slider3D"
      WindowTitle="Slider3D Demo"
      Title="Slider3D Demo">
    <StackPanel Orientation="Vertical">
        <!-- Create a Slider3D control. -->
        <src:Slider3D x:Name="slider1"
                    Orientation="Horizontal" Margin="12"
                    Minimum="-100" Maximum="100"
                    LargeChange="10" SmallChange="1" />

        <!-- Display Slider3D value in a TextBlock -->
        <TextBlock Text="{Binding ElementName=slider1, Path=Value}"
                    HorizontalAlignment="Center" />

        <!-- Create another Slider3D with tick marks. -->
        <src:Slider3D x:Name="slider2"
                    Orientation="Horizontal" Margin="12"
                    Minimum="0" Maximum="2.5"
                    LargeChange="0.1" SmallChange="0.01"
                    TickPlacement="Both" TickFrequency="0.1"
                    IsDirectionReversed="true" />

        <!-- Display Slider3d value in a TextBlock. -->
        <TextBlock Text="{Binding ElementName=slider2, Path=Value}"
                    HorizontalAlignment="Center" />
    </StackPanel>
</Page>
```

An application definition file completes the project.

Slider3DDemoApp.xaml

```xml
<!-- ==============================================
        Slider3DDemoApp.xaml (c) 2007 by Charles Petzold
        ============================================== -->
<Application xmlns="http://schemas.microsoft.com/winfx/2006/xaml/presentation"
          StartupUri="Slider3DDemo.xaml" />
```

And here's a pair of *Slider3D* controls with the thumbs seen in perspective.

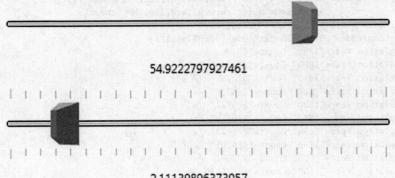

54.9222797927461

2.11139896373057

3D Visualization of Data

As we accumulate more and more data in our computers, we need better ways to visually represent that data. Animation and 3D graphics can help. Animation can be automatically initiated, triggered with a button, or controlled wholly by the user through a scrollbar or slider.

As a simple example, suppose you want to represent the population of the individual states of the United States, but you want to include census data dating from the very first census in 1790 up to the most recent census in 2000. One possible approach is to use little bars to show the population for each state on a map of the United States, and then let the user set the year using a scrollbar. In this way, it's easy to visualize the change in population both geographically and temporally.

I began this project by cobbling together some data from disparate sources, including Wikipedia, the United States Census Bureau, and the Geospatial & Statistical Data Center at the University of Virginia Library (*http://fisher.lib.virginia.edu*). Because I wanted bar graphs on a map of the United States, I also obtained the longitude and latitude of all the state capitals. The program that accessed all the individual data and assembled them into one file wasn't pretty, but all the data came together in a single XML file generated by the *Serialize* method of the *XmlSerializer* class. Following is an excerpt of this data file.

StatePopulationData.xml

```xml
<StatePopulationData xmlns:xsi="http://www.w3.org/2001/XMLSchema-instance"
                     xmlns:xsd="http://www.w3.org/2001/XMLSchema">
  <State Name="Alabama" Capital="Montgomery"
         Longitude="86.36667" Latitude="32.3833351">
    <Population Year="1790" Count="0" />
    <Population Year="1800" Count="0" />
    <Population Year="1810" Count="0" />
    <Population Year="1820" Count="144317" />
    <Population Year="1830" Count="309527" />
    <Population Year="1840" Count="590756" />
    <Population Year="1850" Count="771623" />
    <Population Year="1860" Count="964201" />
    <Population Year="1870" Count="996992" />
    <Population Year="1880" Count="1262505" />
    <Population Year="1890" Count="1513017" />
    <Population Year="1900" Count="1828697" />
    <Population Year="1910" Count="2138093" />
    <Population Year="1920" Count="2348174" />
    <Population Year="1930" Count="2646248" />
    <Population Year="1940" Count="2832961" />
    <Population Year="1950" Count="3061743" />
    <Population Year="1960" Count="3266740" />
    <Population Year="1970" Count="3444000" />
    <Population Year="1980" Count="3891000" />
    <Population Year="1990" Count="4041000" />
    <Population Year="2000" Count="4447100" />
  </State>
  <State Name="Alaska" Capital="Juneau"
         Longitude="134.583328" Latitude="58.3666649">
```

• • •

For each of the states, population values prior to the state joining the nation are zero, so the populations don't reflect people living in these areas while they were territories.

For ease in serialization and deserialization, the elements of this XML file are based on C# classes not shown here because they're simple and don't really do anything. A *StatePopulationData* class represents the root element of the file. It's basically a collection of objects of type *State*, which is a collection of objects of type *Population*. These classes simply define the structure of the XML data. I used them first in the ugly program that accessed the raw data and serialized them into the StatePopulationData.xml file. These classes also play a role when accessing the file and deserializing it from XML back into objects.

The project is named StatePopulationAnimator, and it requires the Petzold.Media3D library. A XAML file defines the basic layout of the program's page.

StatePopulationAnimator.xaml

```xml
<!-- =========================================================
         StatePopulationAnimator.xaml (c) 2007 by Charles Petzold
     ========================================================= -->
<Page xmlns="http://schemas.microsoft.com/winfx/2006/xaml/presentation"
      xmlns:x="http://schemas.microsoft.com/winfx/2006/xaml"
      xmlns:cp="http://schemas.charlespetzold.com/2007/xaml"
      x:Class="Petzold.StatePopulationAnimator.StatePopulationAnimator"
      WindowTitle="State Population Animator"
      Title="State Population Animator"
      Background="Transparent">
    <DockPanel>
        <!-- ScrollBar for rotating camera. -->
        <ScrollBar Name="scroll" DockPanel.Dock="Right"
                   Minimum="-180" Maximum="180"
                   SmallChange="10" LargeChange="10" />
        <Grid>
            <Grid.RowDefinitions>
                <RowDefinition Height="*" />
                <RowDefinition Height="Auto" />
                <RowDefinition Height="Auto" />
            </Grid.RowDefinitions>

            <Grid.ColumnDefinitions>
                <ColumnDefinition Width="*" />
                <ColumnDefinition Width="Auto" />
            </Grid.ColumnDefinitions>

            <!-- Viewport3D shows map and graph. -->
            <Viewport3D Name="viewport3d"
                        Grid.Row="0" Grid.Column="0" Grid.ColumnSpan="2"
                        ClipToBounds="False">

                <cp:Billboard UpperLeft="-1 0 -1" UpperRight="1 0 -1"
                              LowerLeft="-1 0  0" LowerRight="1 0  0">
                    <cp:Billboard.Material>
                        <DiffuseMaterial>
                            <DiffuseMaterial.Brush>
                                <!-- Image courtesy of NASA/JPL-Caltech
                                     (http://maps.jpl.nasa.gov). -->
                                <ImageBrush Viewbox="0 0 0.5 0.5"
                                            ImageSource="ear0xuu2.jpg" />
                            </DiffuseMaterial.Brush>
                        </DiffuseMaterial>
                    </cp:Billboard.Material>
                </cp:Billboard>

                <!-- Light source. -->
                <ModelVisual3D>
                    <ModelVisual3D.Content>
                        <AmbientLight Color="White" />
                    </ModelVisual3D.Content>
                </ModelVisual3D>
```

```
                    <!-- Camera with rotation transform. -->
                    <Viewport3D.Camera>
                        <OrthographicCamera Position="0 3.5 2"
                                            LookDirection="0 -2.5 -2"
                                            UpDirection="0 1 0"
                                            Width="2.5">
                            <OrthographicCamera.Transform>
                                <RotateTransform3D
                                        CenterX="0" CenterY="0" CenterZ="-0.5" >
                                    <RotateTransform3D.Rotation>
                                        <AxisAngleRotation3D Axis="0 1 0"
                                            Angle="{Binding ElementName=scroll,
                                                             Path=Value}" />
                                    </RotateTransform3D.Rotation>
                                </RotateTransform3D>
                            </OrthographicCamera.Transform>
                        </OrthographicCamera>
                    </Viewport3D.Camera>
                </Viewport3D>

                <!-- Canvas displays state names. -->
                <Canvas Grid.Row="0" Grid.Column="0" Grid.ColumnSpan="2">
                    <TextBlock Name="txtblkTip" TextAlignment="Center" Padding="2"
                            Background="{DynamicResource
                                {x:Static SystemColors.InfoBrushKey}}"
                            Foreground="{DynamicResource
                                {x:Static SystemColors.InfoTextBrushKey}}" />
                </Canvas>

                <!-- Other elements and controls go down at bottom. -->
                <TextBlock Name="txtblkYear"
                            Grid.Row="1" Grid.Column="0" Grid.ColumnSpan="2"
                            Text="1790"
                            HorizontalAlignment="Center"
                            FontSize="36" Margin="12" />

                <Slider Name="sliderYear"
                            Grid.Row="2" Grid.Column="0"
                            Minimum="1790" Maximum="2000"
                            Margin="12"
                            ValueChanged="YearSliderOnValueChanged" />

                <CheckBox Name="chkboxNormalize"
                            Grid.Row="2" Grid.Column="1"
                            Content="Show Proportion of Total"
                            Margin="12"
                            Checked="NormalizeCheckBoxOnChecked"
                            Unchecked="NormalizeCheckBoxOnChecked" />
            </Grid>
        </DockPanel>
</Page>
```

The *Billboard* class from the Petzold.Media3D library provides a simple rectangular surface. On this surface appears a bitmap named ear0xuu2.jpg. This is a map of the earth that I downloaded from the Web site of the Jet Propulsion Laboratory at *http://maps.jpl.nasa.gov*. Notice that the *VisualBrush* indicates that only the upper-left quarter of the map is used, which includes longitudes from the International Date Line to Greenwich, England, and latitudes from the equator to the North Pole. This area is a little larger than what I required, but it simplified the calculations.

Also notice that I'm using an *OrthographicCamera*. When graphing data, it's very easy to introduce inadvertent visual distortions. Entire books have been written on this subject. (See the works of Edward Tufte.) You don't want a perspective effect adding to your problems!

The XAML file gives names to many of its elements. Within the XAML file, the *ScrollBar* at the right edge of the page is linked to the camera transform so that you can view the map from different directions. However, the *Slider* and *CheckBox* at the bottom of the page are handled entirely in code, which is the following file.

```
StatePopulationAnimator.cs
//-----------------------------------------------------------
// StatePopulationAnimator.cs (c) 2007 by Charles Petzold
//-----------------------------------------------------------
using System;
using System.IO;
using System.Windows;
using System.Windows.Controls;
using System.Windows.Controls.Primitives;
using System.Windows.Input;
using System.Windows.Media;
using System.Windows.Media.Media3D;
using System.Windows.Resources;
using System.Xml.Serialization;
using Petzold.Media3D;

namespace Petzold.StatePopulationAnimator
{
    public partial class StatePopulationAnimator: Page
    {
        StatePopulationData data;
        Cylinder[] cyls;

        // Constructor.
        public StatePopulationAnimator()
        {
            // Get XML data.
            Uri uri = new Uri("pack://application:,,/StatePopulationData.xml");
            StreamResourceInfo info = Application.GetResourceStream(uri);
            XmlSerializer xml = new XmlSerializer(typeof(StatePopulationData));
            data = xml.Deserialize(info.Stream) as StatePopulationData;
            info.Stream.Close();
```

```
            // Initialization will cause slider event.
            InitializeComponent();
        }

        // Event handler for slider.
        void YearSliderOnValueChanged(object sender,
                            RoutedPropertyChangedEventArgs<double> args)
        {
            int year = (int)Math.Round(args.NewValue);
            txtblkYear.Text = year.ToString();
            bool willNormalize = false;

            if (chkboxNormalize != null)
                willNormalize = (bool)chkboxNormalize.IsChecked;

            Recalc(year, willNormalize);
        }

        // Event handler for CheckBox.
        void NormalizeCheckBoxOnChecked(object sender, RoutedEventArgs args)
        {
            Recalc((int)Math.Round(sliderYear.Value),
                            (bool)chkboxNormalize.IsChecked);
        }

        // Calculates heights of cylinders.
        void Recalc(int year, bool willNormalize)
        {
            // Create cylinders for first time.
            if (cyls == null)
            {
                cyls = new Cylinder[50];

                for (int i = 0; i < data.States.Count; i++)
                {
                    State state = data.States[i];
                    cyls[i] = new Cylinder();
                    cyls[i].Material = new DiffuseMaterial(Brushes.Pink);

                    double x = 1 - state.Longitude / 90;
                    double z = -state.Latitude / 90;

                    cyls[i].Radius1 = cyls[i].Radius2 = 0.005;
                    cyls[i].Point1 = new Point3D(x, 0, z);
                    cyls[i].Point2 = new Point3D(x, 0, z);

                    viewport3d.Children.Add(cyls[i]);
                }
            }

            int popTotal = 0;
```

```
            // Find total population for normalization.
            if (willNormalize)
            {
                for (int i = 0; i < data.States.Count; i++)
                    popTotal += InterpolatePopulation(i, year);
            }

            // Redo cylinder Point2 values with data.
            for (int i = 0; i < data.States.Count; i++)
            {
                int pop = InterpolatePopulation(i, year);
                double y;

                if (willNormalize)
                {
                    y = 10.0 * pop / popTotal;
                    cyls[i].Name = String.Format("{0}\n{1:P0}",
                                            data.States[i].Name,
                                            (double)pop / popTotal);
                }
                else
                {
                    y = pop / 10000000.0;
                    cyls[i].Name = String.Format("{0}\n{1:N0}",
                                            data.States[i].Name, pop);
                }

                Point3D point = cyls[i].Point2;
                point.Y = y;
                cyls[i].Point2 = point;
            }
        }

        // Returns interpolated population for iState (0 to 49)
        //   and year (1790 through 2000).
        int InterpolatePopulation(int iState, int year)
        {
            State state = data.States[iState];
            int i1 = (year - 1790) / 10;
            int i2 = (year - 1781) / 10;
            double weight = (year % 10) / 10.0;
            double pop = (1 - weight) * state.Populations[i1].Count +
                            weight * state.Populations[i2].Count;
            return (int)pop;
        }

        // Monitor MouseMove messages to display fake tool tips.
        protected override void OnPreviewMouseMove(MouseEventArgs args)
        {
            txtblkTip.Visibility = Visibility.Hidden;
            Point ptMouse = args.GetPosition(viewport3d);
            HitTestResult result =
                        VisualTreeHelper.HitTest(viewport3d, ptMouse);
```

```
        if (result is RayMeshGeometry3DHitTestResult)
        {
            RayMeshGeometry3DHitTestResult result3d =
                result as RayMeshGeometry3DHitTestResult;

            if (result3d.VisualHit is Cylinder)
            {
                Canvas.SetLeft(txtblkTip, ptMouse.X + 12);
                Canvas.SetTop(txtblkTip, ptMouse.Y + 12);
                txtblkTip.Text = (result3d.VisualHit as Cylinder).Name;
                txtblkTip.Visibility = Visibility.Visible;
            }
        }
    }
  }
}
```

The constructor loads the data from the XML file. Any change to the *Slider* or *CheckBox* control causes a call to the *Recalc* method. The first time *Recalc* is called, it takes the opportunity to create 50 *Cylinder* objects from the Petzold.Media3D library. The height of these cylinders indicates the population of each state, which requires an interpolation to be performed. Dividing the population by 10,000,000 to convert to 3D coordinates seemed to give about the right results. When the user checks the *CheckBox*, the program displays the proportion of total population in each state. The total height of all the cylinders remains constant so that you can see the geographic change in population distribution over the course of time.

I had originally used *ToolTip* controls to display the state names and population, but when preparing the program to be a XAML Browser Application, I discovered that *ToolTip* controls were not allowed. Instead I mimicked them using a *TextBlock* that is positioned on a *Canvas* panel that overlays the *Viewport3D* in the same grid cells.

The project is completed with an application definition file.

StatePopulationAnimatorApp.xaml
```
<!-- ============================================================
        StatePopulationAnimatorApp.xaml (c) 2007 by Charles Petzold
     ============================================================ -->
<Application xmlns="http://schemas.microsoft.com/winfx/2006/xaml/presentation"
             StartupUri="StatePopulationAnimator.xaml" />
```

Here's a little image of the program with the *ScrollBar* set to give a little offset to the common view.

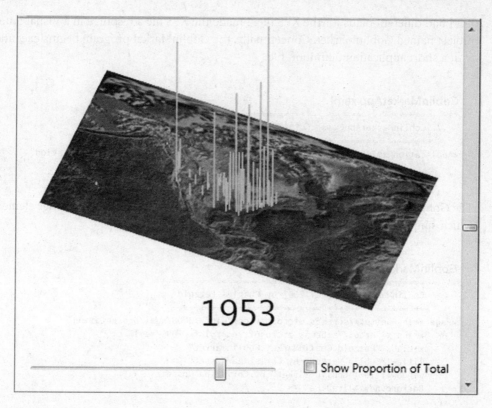

The *ScrollBar* lets you essentially swing around the country if a particular view obscures what you want to see. It's not too difficult to imagine more interactive graphs that let you explore the data in more creative ways.

Mimicking Real World Objects

In one of the first public presentations of a WPF application, the British Library digitized several of their treasures to offer them in a XAML Browser Application called "Turning the Pages" (*http://www.bl.uk/onlinegallery/ttp/ttpbooks.html*). It's quite enjoyable, and the 3D effect adds greatly to the experience.

I decided to try to imitate this program, not with a digitization of a physical book, but with a Word 2007 document file of Christina Rossetti's poem "Goblin Market," written in 1859 and published in 1862. Within my WPF program I wanted easy access to this document with a minimum of extra work, so I saved the document in the new XPS (XML Paper Specification) format that was developed in conjunction with WPF. The document has a total of 34 pages, including a cover page and a blank page following the cover page. XPS documents are stored in ZIP files that contain all the components of the documents, which is mostly text (in XAML files) and any bitmap images that might be involved. If you launch the XPS file from Windows Explorer, you can read it in a *DocumentViewer* object within Internet Explorer.

But I had different plans for the XPS file. I made the XPS file a resource in a Visual Studio project named GoblinMarket. Conceptually, the GoblinMarket program begins execution with a short application definition file:

GoblinMarketApp.xaml
```
<!-- =================================================
       GoblinMarketApp.xaml (c) 2007 by Charles Petzold
     ================================================= -->
<Application xmlns="http://schemas.microsoft.com/winfx/2006/xaml/presentation"
             StartupUri="GoblinMarket.xaml" />
```

The GoblinMarket.xaml file is quite short. It contains a brief definition of a *Page* element, which simply defines a class name and specifies titles.

GoblinMarket.xaml
```
<!-- =================================================
       GoblinMarket.xaml (c) 2007 by Charles Petzold
     ================================================= -->
<Page xmlns="http://schemas.microsoft.com/winfx/2006/xaml/presentation"
      xmlns:x="http://schemas.microsoft.com/winfx/2006/xaml"
      x:Class="Petzold.GoblinMarket.GoblinMarket"
      Title='"Goblin Market" by Christina Rossetti'
      WindowTitle='"Goblin Market" by Christina Rossetti'
      Background="AliceBlue" />
```

The rest of the *GoblinMarket* class that derives from *Page* actually does some real work. The constructor is responsible for accessing the XPS file that's compiled with the rest of the program as a resource. This process begins with the normal *Application.GetResourceStream* call to get a memory stream object to the resource, but then a *Package* object needs to be created with that memory stream. At that point, the constructor accesses the *XpsDocument* object within the package and gets a *DocumentPaginator* object. This *DocumentPaginator* has a *GetPage* method to obtain a *DocumentPage* object for each page. The *DocumentPage* class defines a *Visual* property that obtains a *Visual* object for the page. That's very fortunate because we know exactly how to cover 3D figures with brushes made from *Visual* objects.

GoblinMarket.cs
```
//-------------------------------------------
// GoblinMarket.cs (c) 2007 by Charles Petzold
//-------------------------------------------
using System;
using System.IO;
using System.IO.Packaging;
using System.Windows;
using System.Windows.Controls;
using System.Windows.Documents;
using System.Windows.Media;
```

```
using System.Windows.Resources;
using System.Windows.Xps.Packaging;
using Petzold.BookViewer3D;

namespace Petzold.GoblinMarket
{
    public partial class GoblinMarket : Page
    {
        public GoblinMarket()
        {
            // Access the document stored as an application resource.
            StreamResourceInfo info = Application.GetResourceStream(
                    new Uri("pack://application:,,/GoblinMarket.xps"));

            // Open a package from the resources stream.
            Package pack = Package.Open(info.Stream, FileMode.Open,
                                                    FileAccess.Read);

            // Add a URI to the package store.
            string strUri = "memorystream://GoblinMarket.xps";
            Uri uriPackage = new Uri(strUri);
            PackageStore.AddPackage(uriPackage, pack);

            // Get the XPS file.
            XpsDocument xps = new XpsDocument(pack, CompressionOption.Normal,
                                            strUri);

            // Get a paginator for the fixed documents in the XPS file.
            FixedDocumentSequence seq = xps.GetFixedDocumentSequence();
            DocumentPaginator paginator = seq.DocumentPaginator;

            // Plan is to get a Visual for each page in the document.
            Visual[] visuals = new Visual[paginator.PageCount];

            for (int i = 0; i < paginator.PageCount; i++)
                visuals[i] = paginator.GetPage(i).Visual;

            // Close the file.
            xps.Close();

            // Create BookViewport to display book.
            BookViewport viewer = new BookViewport(visuals);
            Content = viewer;
        }
    }
}
```

Even as I was first writing this code to obtain an array of *Visual* objects corresponding to all the pages in the document, I was perfectly aware that this strategy might not be suitable for larger documents. For longer books with many more pages, a program might want to obtain each *Visual* object only when it's actually required for display. But that's an enhancement for another day.

The constructor of this class concludes by creating an object of type *BookViewport*—the following class that derives from *Viewport3D*—passing to it the array of *Visual* objects corresponding to the pages of the book.

The *BookViewport* class consists of both a XAML file and a C# file. The XAML file simply defines light sources and a camera.

```
BookViewport.xaml
<!-- =============================================
       BookViewport.xaml (c) 2007 by Charles Petzold
     ============================================= -->
<Viewport3D xmlns="http://schemas.microsoft.com/winfx/2006/xaml/presentation"
            xmlns:x="http://schemas.microsoft.com/winfx/2006/xaml"
            x:Class="Petzold.BookViewer3D.BookViewport">
    <ModelVisual3D>
        <ModelVisual3D.Content>
            <Model3DGroup>
                <AmbientLight Color="#404040" />
                <DirectionalLight Color="#C0C0C0" Direction="1 -1 -4" />
            </Model3DGroup>
        </ModelVisual3D.Content>
    </ModelVisual3D>

    <Viewport3D.Camera>
        <PerspectiveCamera Position="0 -6 24"
                           LookDirection="0 6 -24"
                           UpDirection="0 1 0"
                           FieldOfView="45"
                           FarPlaneDistance="30" />
    </Viewport3D.Camera>
</Viewport3D>
```

As you'll soon see, the book will be positioned so that the "spine" is parallel to the Y axis with the origin in the center. The back of the book sits on the XY plane with the pages spread out along the negative and positive X axes, and facing toward the positive Z axis. Because I made the page of the book 8.5 by 11 units in size (just because it helped me think about coordinates less abstractly), the camera is considerably farther away from the origin than it has been in previous programs in this book. It is also a little below the XZ plane so that it looks up at the book, much like the view of a book laid open on a desk. The light is somewhat offset from direct illumination so that each page will be slightly off-white.

The remainder of the *BookViewport* class is in the following C# file. The sole constructor has an argument that's an array of *Visual* objects, and it begins by creating one *Billboard* object for each leaf. One leaf is required for every two pages in the book. When creating each leaf, the constructor uses the array of *Visual* objects to create a series of *VisualBrush* objects, one for the front (the *Material* property) and one for the back (the *BackMaterial* property) of each leaf. When I first wrote this code, the recto pages (those on the right side) looked fine but the verso pages (on the left) displayed mirror images of the text! A little transform applied to the brush solved that problem.

Again, let me remind you that for a longer book, it might be better to delay the process of creating the *VisualBrush* objects and applying them until it's time to view a particular page. It might also be advantageous to convert these *Visual* objects into bitmaps using *RenderTarget-Bitmap*.

The constructor positions the leaves as if they were standing straight up from the spine—that is, parallel to the YZ plane. The leaves of the book cannot be positioned right against each other because they might start blending into each other. The *leafGap* constant indicates the spacing of the leaves; for a longer book it might be worthwhile to experiment with this value. I use this constant to apply a *TranslateTransform3D* to each *Billboard* object to position the leaves in increments of *leafGap* units along the negative and positive X axes.

BookViewport.cs

```
//--------------------------------------------
// BookViewport.cs (c) 2007 by Charles Petzold
//--------------------------------------------
using System;
using System.Collections.Generic;
using System.Windows;
using System.Windows.Controls;
using System.Windows.Input;
using System.Windows.Media;
using System.Windows.Media.Animation;
using System.Windows.Media.Media3D;
using Petzold.Media3D;

namespace Petzold.BookViewer3D
{
    public partial class BookViewport : Viewport3D
    {
        // Distance between leaves.
        const double leafGap = 0.05;

        // Duration of animation.
        static readonly Duration durAnimation =
                        new Duration(TimeSpan.FromSeconds(3));

        // Other variables needed during mouse clicks.
        int leafCount = 0;
        int leafView = 0;
        List<Billboard> lstBillboards = new List<Billboard>();
        Random rand = new Random();

        // Precreated DoubleAnimation objects.
        DoubleAnimation animaAngle = new DoubleAnimation(0, durAnimation);
        DoubleAnimation animaRadius = new DoubleAnimation(0, durAnimation);
```

```
            // Only constructor.
            public BookViewport(Visual[] visuals)
            {
                InitializeComponent();

                // Get the number of leaves.
                leafCount = (visuals.Length + 1) / 2;

                for (int i = 0; i < leafCount; i++)
                {
                    // Create Billboard object for each leaf.
                    Billboard board = new Billboard();
                    board.Slices = 48;
                    board.Stacks = 24;
                    board.UpperLeft = new Point3D(0, 5.5, 0);
                    board.UpperRight = new Point3D(0, 5.5, 8.5);
                    board.LowerLeft = new Point3D(0, -5.5, 0);
                    board.LowerRight = new Point3D(0, -5.5, 8.5);

                    // Set the top brush to a recto.
                    VisualBrush visbrush = new VisualBrush(visuals[2 * i]);
                    RenderOptions.SetCachingHint(visbrush, CachingHint.Cache);
                    board.Material = new DiffuseMaterial(visbrush);

                    // Set the back brush to a verso.
                    visbrush = new VisualBrush(visuals[2 * i + 1]);
                    visbrush.Transform = new ScaleTransform(-1, 1, 0.5, 0);
                    RenderOptions.SetCachingHint(visbrush, CachingHint.Cache);
                    board.BackMaterial = new DiffuseMaterial(visbrush);

                    // Calculate the offset from the center for the leaf.
                    double spineOffset = leafGap * (i - leafCount / 2);
                    board.Transform = new TranslateTransform3D(spineOffset, 0, 0);

                    // Create a PageTurner object for each leaf.
                    PageTurner pgturn = new PageTurner();
                    pgturn.Angle = 90;
                    pgturn.Radius = (leafCount - i) * leafGap;
                    board.AlgorithmicTransforms.Add(pgturn);

                    // Add the board to the Viewport3D and also a collection.
                    Children.Add(board);
                    lstBillboards.Add(board);
                }
            }
```

```
        // Animate leaf when user clicks a page.
        protected override void OnMouseLeftButtonDown(MouseButtonEventArgs args)
        {
            Point pt = args.GetPosition(this);
            HitTestResult result = VisualTreeHelper.HitTest(this, pt);

            if (result is RayMeshGeometry3DHitTestResult)
            {
                RayMeshGeometry3DHitTestResult result3d =
                            result as RayMeshGeometry3DHitTestResult;

                if (result3d.VisualHit is Billboard)
                {
                    // Get the clicked billboard and prepare for animations.
                    Billboard board = result3d.VisualHit as Billboard;
                    int indexBillboard = lstBillboards.IndexOf(board);
                    Billboard boardAnimate = null;

                    // Clicked a recto: forward page turn (right to left).
                    if (indexBillboard >= leafView)
                    {
                        boardAnimate = lstBillboards[leafView];
                        animaAngle.To = -90;
                        animaRadius.To = (leafView + 1) * leafGap;
                        leafView++;
                    }
                    // Clicked a verso: back page turn (left to right).
                    else
                    {
                        boardAnimate = lstBillboards[leafView - 1];
                        animaAngle.To = 90;
                        animaRadius.To = (leafCount - leafView + 1) * leafGap;
                        leafView--;
                    }
                    // Start the animations.
                    PageTurner turn =
                            boardAnimate.AlgorithmicTransforms[0] as PageTurner;

                    turn.Random1 = rand.NextDouble() - 0.5;
                    turn.Random2 = rand.NextDouble() - 0.5;
                    turn.BeginAnimation(PageTurner.AngleProperty, animaAngle);
                    turn.BeginAnimation(PageTurner.RadiusProperty, animaRadius);
                }
            }
        }
    }
}
```

Now for the hard part: Toward the end of the constructor you'll notice that the class creates a *PageTurner* object for each *Billboard*, and adds that object to the *AlgorithmicTransforms* collection of the *Billboard*. A little explanation is required: In the Petzold.Media3D library, the *Billboard* class derives from the *ModelVisualBase* class, which supports a feature that I call "algorithmic transforms." These are transforms that can't be done with the normal matrix transform objects, and so must be implemented in code. *ModelVisualBase* defines a property named *AlgorithmicTransforms* that is a collection of objects of type *AlgorithmicTransform*. The abstract *AlgorithmicTransform* class itself is tiny:

```
namespace Petzold.Media3D
{
    public abstract class AlgorithmicTransform : Animatable
    {
        public abstract void Transform(Point3DCollection points);
    }
}
```

To write your own algorithmic transform, you need to derive from the *AlgorithmicTransform* class and implement the *Transform* method. Whenever this method is called, it must perform an in-place transform of the points in the collection. Because *AlgorithmicTransform* derives from *Animatable*, and hence also *Freezable*, any non-abstract derivative must also override the *CreateInstanceCore* method.

Your *AlgorithmicTransform* derivative will probably define some of its own properties. It should define these properties as dependency properties so that they can be animated. But your class doesn't need to worry about notifications: The *AlgorithmicTransforms* property that *ModelVisualBase* defines is backed by a dependency property and implemented with a *FreezableCollection* containing all the algorithmic transforms defined for an object. *ModelVisualBase* is notified whenever a dependency property in one of the classes in this *FreezableCollection* changes. The class then regenerates its *MeshGeometry3D* object by consecutively calling all the *Transform* methods in all the objects in the *AlgorithmicTransforms* collection. These transforms affect the *Positions* and *Normals* collections of the *MeshGeometry3D* so that they conceptually occur before any regular transforms that might be defined for the *GeometryModel3D* or the *ModelVisual3D*.

The *PageTurner* class derives from *AlgorithmicTransform* and is essential for the realistic look of this 3D book. Basically, *PageTurner* curls the edge of the *Billboard* object at the spine so that the page can turn from right to left and back again. This curling effect is controlled by an animation applied to two properties of the *PageTurner* object.

I toyed around with making the *PageTurner* class implement a generalized "curling" transform, but the application-specific code was hard enough, and that's why it's not part of the Petzold.Media3D library. Recall that each *Billboard* object is positioned parallel to the YZ plane with one edge on the XY plane and extending in the direction of the positive Z axis. The *PageTurner* class defines an *Angle* property that swivels the bulk of that *Billboard* object by *Angle* degrees. When *Angle* is 90 degrees, the page sits on the right side of the book, and when *Angle* is −90 degrees, the page sits on the left side of the book. The program turns the pages by animating between these two angles.

However, this is not simply a rotation transform, because the edge of the *Billboard* at the spine must remain fixed, which means that a portion of the *Billboard* at the spine must curl. The degree of this curling is governed by a property named *Radius*. When all the pages are stacked up at the right side of the book at the beginning, the bottommost page has a small *Radius* value and the topmost page has a large *Radius* value. These *Radius* values are in increments of *leafGap* units, just like the spacing of the pages along the spine.

To turn a page from one side of the book to another, the program animates the *Angle* property of the *PageTurner* object. The *Angle* goes from 90 degrees to −90 degrees to turn the page from right to left, and oppositely to go back. However, the program must also animate the *Radius* value, decreasing it if the page is moving to a side of the book with fewer leaves, or increasing it if the page is moving to a side with more leaves. The *OnMouseLeftButtonDown* override in *BookViewport* class makes this determination, and concludes by initiating animations on both the *Angle* and *Radius* properties.

Here's the *PageTurner* class that handles the actual curling transform.

```
PageTurner.cs
//-------------------------------------------
// PageTurner.cs (c) 2007 by Charles Petzold
//-------------------------------------------
using System;
using System.Windows;
using System.Windows.Media.Media3D;
using Petzold.Media3D;

namespace Petzold.BookViewer3D
{
    public class PageTurner : AlgorithmicTransform
    {
        // Radius dependency property and property.
        public static readonly DependencyProperty RadiusProperty =
            DependencyProperty.Register("Radius",
                typeof(double),
                typeof(PageTurner),
                new PropertyMetadata(0.0));

        public double Radius
        {
            set { SetValue(RadiusProperty, value); }
            get { return (double)GetValue(RadiusProperty); }
        }

        // Angle dependency property and property.
        public static readonly DependencyProperty AngleProperty =
            DependencyProperty.Register("Angle",
                typeof(double),
                typeof(PageTurner),
                new PropertyMetadata(0.0));
```

```
public double Angle
{
    set { SetValue(AngleProperty, value); }
    get { return (double)GetValue(AngleProperty); }
}


// Random dependency properties and properties.
public static readonly DependencyProperty Random1Property =
    DependencyProperty.Register("Random1",
        typeof(double),
        typeof(PageTurner),
        new PropertyMetadata(0.0), ValidateRandom);

public double Random1
{
    set { SetValue(Random1Property, value); }
    get { return (double)GetValue(Random1Property); }
}


public static readonly DependencyProperty Random2Property =
    DependencyProperty.Register("Random2",
        typeof(double),
        typeof(PageTurner),
        new PropertyMetadata(0.0), ValidateRandom);

public double Random2
{
    set { SetValue(Random2Property, value); }
    get { return (double)GetValue(Random2Property); }
}


static bool ValidateRandom(object obj)
{
    double doub = (double)obj;
    return doub <= 1 && doub >= -1;
}


// Transform property required for AlgorithmicTransform.
public override void Transform(Point3DCollection points)
{
    if (Angle == 0)
        return;

    double factor = Radius * 90 / Angle;
    double cutoff = Math.PI * Radius / 2;
    double x = 0, y = 0, z = 0;
    double a = (Random1 + Random2) / 5.5 / 5.5;
    double b = (Random1 - Random2) / 5.5;

    for (int i = 0; i < points.Count; i++)
    {
        y = points[i].Y;
        double random = a * y * y + b * y;
```

```
                    // This is the part of the page that curves.
                    if (points[i].Z < cutoff)
                    {
                        double radians = points[i].Z / factor;
                        x = factor * (1 - Math.Cos(radians));
                        z = factor * Math.Sin(radians);
                    }
                    // This is the part of the page that stays straight.
                    else
                    {
                        double radians = Math.PI * Angle / 180;
                        x = factor * (1 - Math.Cos(radians)) +
                                    (points[i].Z - cutoff) * Math.Sin(radians);
                        z = factor * Math.Sin(radians) +
                                    (points[i].Z - cutoff) * Math.Cos(radians);

                        x += random * points[i].Z * (90 - Math.Abs(Angle)) / 1000;
                    }
                    // Set the recalculated point.
                    points[i] = new Point3D(x, y, z);
                }
            }


        // CreateInstanceCore required when deriving from Freezable.
        protected override Freezable CreateInstanceCore()
        {
            return new PageTurner();
        }
    }
}
```

After everything seemed to be working well, I added *Random1* and *Random2* properties to *PageTurner* so that the pages turn with a little random variation. A program using this class just sets these properties once for each page turn. The random effect is greatest when the page is in the middle of a turn (that is, when *Angle* equals zero degrees) and at the part of the page farthest from the spine.

And here it is, unfortunately so reduced in size that you probably can't read it.

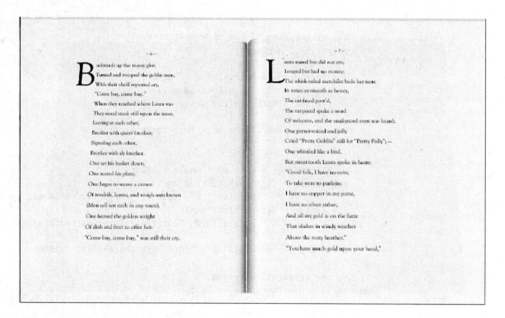

Interactive Mouse Tracking

I first used the *VisualTreeHelper.HitTest* method in the TableForFour program in Chapter 3, "Axis/Angle Rotation." The StatePopulationAnimator.cs and BookViewport.cs files demonstrate a simpler version of that method that doesn't require a callback function. You can use this simpler variation when you only need the topmost *ModelVisual3D* under a particular point.

Although the hit-testing facility in WPF 3D certainly provides you with a convenient way to determine the *ModelVisual3D* under the mouse pointer, it is not a general-purpose coordinate conversion. For example, if the user clicks an area of the *Viewport3D* where no *ModelVisual3D* resides, you can't determine what three-dimensional point corresponds to that click, and it's not just one point: An infinite number of 3D points correspond to every 2D point. Nor does WPF 3D provide you with the easier transform in the other direction: from the 3D space of the *Viewport3D* to the 2D space of the screen.

The *ViewportInfo* class in the Petzold.Media3D library can help fill the gaps here, and the purpose of the MouseTracking project is to show you how to use this class. The MouseTracking program begins with an application definition file.

```
MouseTrackingApp.xaml
<!-- =================================================
     MouseTrackingApp.xaml (c) 2007 by Charles Petzold
     ================================================= -->
<Application xmlns="http://schemas.microsoft.com/winfx/2006/xaml/presentation"
             StartupUri="MouseTracking.xaml" />
```

The XAML part of the *MouseTracking* class displays the standard 3D coordinate axes and three cubes colored red, green, and blue.

MouseTracking.xaml

```xml
<!-- =============================================
        MouseTracking.xaml (c) 2007 by Charles Petzold
        ============================================= -->
<Page xmlns="http://schemas.microsoft.com/winfx/2006/xaml/presentation"
      xmlns:x="http://schemas.microsoft.com/winfx/2006/xaml"
      xmlns:cp="http://schemas.charlespetzold.com/2007/xaml"
      x:Class="Petzold.MouseTracking.MouseTracking"
      WindowTitle="Mouse Tracking"
      Title="Mouse Tracking"
      Focusable="True">
    <Page.Resources>
        <cp:BoxMesh x:Key="cube" />
    </Page.Resources>

    <DockPanel>
        <!-- Scrollbars for rotating camera. -->
        <ScrollBar Name="vscroll" DockPanel.Dock="Right"
                   Orientation="Vertical" Minimum="-180" Maximum="180" />
        <ScrollBar Name="hscroll" DockPanel.Dock="Bottom"
                   Orientation="Horizontal" Minimum="-180" Maximum="180" />

        <Viewport3D Name="viewport">
            <cp:Axes />

            <!-- Red cube. -->
            <ModelVisual3D>
                <ModelVisual3D.Content>
                    <GeometryModel3D
                            Geometry="{Binding Source={StaticResource cube},
                                               Path=Geometry}">
                        <GeometryModel3D.Material>
                            <DiffuseMaterial Brush="Red" />
                        </GeometryModel3D.Material>
                    </GeometryModel3D>
                </ModelVisual3D.Content>

                <ModelVisual3D.Transform>
                    <TranslateTransform3D OffsetX="-2" />
                </ModelVisual3D.Transform>
            </ModelVisual3D>

            <!-- Green cube. -->
            <ModelVisual3D>
                <ModelVisual3D.Content>
                    <GeometryModel3D
                            Geometry="{Binding Source={StaticResource cube},
                                               Path=Geometry}">
                        <GeometryModel3D.Material>
                            <DiffuseMaterial Brush="Green" />
                        </GeometryModel3D.Material>
                    </GeometryModel3D>
                </ModelVisual3D.Content>
```

```xml
            <ModelVisual3D.Transform>
                <TranslateTransform3D OffsetX="0" />
            </ModelVisual3D.Transform>
        </ModelVisual3D>

        <!-- Blue cube. -->
        <ModelVisual3D>
            <ModelVisual3D.Content>
                <GeometryModel3D
                        Geometry="{Binding Source={StaticResource cube},
                                           Path=Geometry}">
                    <GeometryModel3D.Material>
                        <DiffuseMaterial Brush="Blue" />
                    </GeometryModel3D.Material>
                </GeometryModel3D>
            </ModelVisual3D.Content>

            <ModelVisual3D.Transform>
                <TranslateTransform3D OffsetX="2" />
            </ModelVisual3D.Transform>
        </ModelVisual3D>

        <!-- Light sources. -->
        <ModelVisual3D>
            <ModelVisual3D.Content>
                <Model3DGroup>
                    <AmbientLight Color="#808080" />
                    <DirectionalLight Color="#808080" Direction="2 -3 -1" />
                </Model3DGroup>
            </ModelVisual3D.Content>
        </ModelVisual3D>

        <!-- Camera with transforms. -->
        <Viewport3D.Camera>
            <PerspectiveCamera Position="0 0 10" UpDirection="0 1 0"
                            LookDirection="0 0 -1" FieldOfView="45">
                <PerspectiveCamera.Transform>
                    <Transform3DGroup>
                        <RotateTransform3D>
                            <RotateTransform3D.Rotation>
                                <AxisAngleRotation3D Axis="1 0 0"
                                    Angle="{Binding ElementName=vscroll,
                                                    Path=Value}" />
                            </RotateTransform3D.Rotation>
                        </RotateTransform3D>

                        <RotateTransform3D>
                            <RotateTransform3D.Rotation>
                                <AxisAngleRotation3D Axis="0 1 0"
                                    Angle="{Binding ElementName=hscroll,
                                                    Path=Value}" />
                            </RotateTransform3D.Rotation>
                        </RotateTransform3D>
                    </Transform3DGroup>
```

```
                </PerspectiveCamera.Transform>
            </PerspectiveCamera>
        </Viewport3D.Camera>
    </Viewport3D>
  </DockPanel>
</Page>
```

The C# part of this program lets you grab a cube with the mouse and move it in 3D space. I certainly won't claim that this is the most spectacular application of 3D interactivity, but it's something that's not possible without supplementary code. Notice that each cube has a *TranslateTransform3D* element attached to it: The program moves the cube by modifying the properties of this transform.

One challenge in a program like this is defining the exact relationship between what the user does with the mouse and what happens in three-dimensional space. Sometimes the exact problem isn't obvious until it comes time to code the routines, and then you're stuck with a variable (often named *x*, *y*, or *z*) that you don't know how to set.

For this little exercise, I took a very simple approach: I decided that horizontal and vertical movements of the mouse would translate into movements of the cube parallel to the XY plane. I also decided to let the user move the cube parallel to the Z axis by turning the mouse wheel (with the left mouse button simultaneously depressed). You can use the scrollbars to alter your view of 3D space but the mouse still works the same way, and the result can seem somewhat peculiar.

Much of the mouse-tracking logic implemented in the C# code is similar to standard two-dimensional mouse tracking. Mouse tracking is initiated when the mouse button is pressed. At that time, the program accumulates information to store in fields and calls *CaptureMouse*. Thereafter, all mouse input comes to the page. The program releases the mouse capture when the user releases the mouse button. However, a program can also lose mouse capture in other ways, such as when a system modal dialog box is displayed on the screen. It's also polite to implement the Escape key to abort the mouse tracking and return everything to the way it was before. That's why the class overrides *OnPreviewTextInput* and *OnLostMouseCapture*.

MouseTracking.cs

```
//--------------------------------------------
// MouseTracking.cs (c) 2007 by Charles Petzold
//--------------------------------------------
using System;
using System.Windows;
using System.Windows.Input;
using System.Windows.Media;
using System.Windows.Media.Media3D;
using Petzold.Media3D;
```

```
namespace Petzold.MouseTracking
{
    public partial class MouseTracking
    {
        bool isTracking;
        Point3D pointOriginal;
        TranslateTransform3D transOriginal;
        TranslateTransform3D transTracking;

        public MouseTracking()
        {
            InitializeComponent();
        }

        // Left mouse button click initiates tracking operation.
        protected override void OnMouseLeftButtonDown(MouseButtonEventArgs args)
        {
            base.OnMouseLeftButtonDown(args);

            Point ptMouse = args.GetPosition(viewport);
            HitTestResult result = VisualTreeHelper.HitTest(viewport, ptMouse);

            // We're only interested in 3D hits.
            RayMeshGeometry3DHitTestResult result3d =
                            result as RayMeshGeometry3DHitTestResult;
            if (result3d == null)
                return;

            // We're only interested in ModelVisual3D hits.
            ModelVisual3D vis3d = result3d.VisualHit as ModelVisual3D;
            if (vis3d == null)
                return;

            // We're only interested in visuals with translate transforms.
            transTracking = vis3d.Transform as TranslateTransform3D;
            if (transTracking == null)
                return;

            LineRange range;
            ViewportInfo.Point2DtoPoint3D(viewport, ptMouse, out range);
            pointOriginal = range.PointFromZ(transTracking.OffsetZ);
            transOriginal = transTracking.Clone();
            isTracking = true;
            CaptureMouse();
            Focus();

            args.Handled = true;
        }
```

```
            // Mouse moves occur in the Z=0 plane.
            protected override void OnMouseMove(MouseEventArgs args)
            {
                base.OnMouseMove(args);

                if (!isTracking)
                    return;

                // Get the mouse position and adjust the translate transform.
                Point ptMouse = args.GetPosition(viewport);
                LineRange range;
                ViewportInfo.Point2DtoPoint3D(viewport, ptMouse, out range);
                Point3D pointNew = range.PointFromZ(transTracking.OffsetZ);
                AdjustTranslateTransform(pointNew);
            }

            // Mouse wheel moves forward and backward along Z axis.
            protected override void OnMouseWheel(MouseWheelEventArgs args)
            {
                base.OnMouseWheel(args);

                if (!isTracking)
                    return;

                // Get the mouse position and adjust the translate transform.
                Point ptMouse = args.GetPosition(viewport);
                LineRange range;
                ViewportInfo.Point2DtoPoint3D(viewport, ptMouse, out range);
                Point3D pointNew = range.PointFromZ(transTracking.OffsetZ);
                pointNew.Z += args.Delta / 1200.0;
                AdjustTranslateTransform(pointNew);
            }

            // Called from OnMouseMove and OnMouseWheel.
            void AdjustTranslateTransform(Point3D pointNew)
            {
                Vector3D vectMouse = pointNew - pointOriginal;
                transTracking.OffsetX = transOriginal.OffsetX + vectMouse.X;
                transTracking.OffsetY = transOriginal.OffsetY + vectMouse.Y;
                transTracking.OffsetZ = transOriginal.OffsetZ + vectMouse.Z;
            }

            // End the tracking normally.
            protected override void OnMouseLeftButtonUp(MouseButtonEventArgs args)
            {
                base.OnMouseLeftButtonUp(args);

                isTracking = false;
                ReleaseMouseCapture();
            }
```

```
      // Abort the tracking operation.
      protected override void OnPreviewTextInput(TextCompositionEventArgs args)
      {
          base.OnPreviewTextInput(args);

          if (!isTracking)
              return;

          // End mouse tracking with press of Escape key.
          if (args.Text.IndexOf('\x1B') != -1)
              ReleaseMouseCapture();
      }

      // Clean up for aborted tracking operation.
      protected override void OnLostMouseCapture(MouseEventArgs args)
      {
          base.OnLostMouseCapture(args);

          // If tracking has been aborted, return to original values.
          if (isTracking)
          {
              transTracking.OffsetX = transOriginal.OffsetX;
              transTracking.OffsetY = transOriginal.OffsetY;
              transTracking.OffsetZ = transOriginal.OffsetZ;
              isTracking = false;
          }
      }
    }
  }
}
```

This program makes use of the *ViewportInfo* class included in the Petzold.Media3D library. This class takes account of the camera transforms and the aspect ratio of the *Viewport3D* to allow conversions between 2D and 3D coordinates. As I discussed in Chapter 7, "Matrix Transforms," WPF 3D uses the transforms associated with the camera to translate points in 3D space to normalized two-dimensional coordinates that are then mapped to the screen. It should be possible to convert from 2D coordinates back to 3D coordinates using the inverse of these transforms, and that's one feature that *ViewportInfo* provides. However, this mapping is not free from ambiguity, and *ViewportInfo* must take the *NearPlaneDistance* and *FarPlaneDistance* settings into account when deriving a three-dimensional point that corresponds to the mouse position. Even then, it's not guaranteed to work: In general, the camera transforms map a three-dimensional point to a four-dimensional point, which is then mapped back to three-dimensional space by dividing all coordinates by the *W* value of the *Point4D* structure. To go back the other way, you really need to begin with a *Point4D* object, but the information to reconstitute that object has been lost. Fortunately, the problem doesn't show up except with non-standard projection transforms.

Even so, the static *ViewportInfo.Point2DToPoint3D* method in the Petzold.Media3D library doesn't return a 3D point: It returns a *LineRange* object that consists of two 3D points, one corresponding to *NearPlaneDistance* and the other corresponding to *FarPlaneDistance*. The *LineRange* structure, which is also in the Petzold.Media3D library, includes methods to help you resolve that line to a point. The *OnMouseLeftButtonDown* method in the *MouseTracking* class uses the *PointFromZ* method to translate the *LineRange* object to a *Point3D* where the Z coordinate is set from the *OffsetZ* property of the *TranslateTransform3D* object associated with the clicked cube.

When the user then moves the mouse with the button pressed, another call to *Viewport-Info.Point2DToPoint3D* obtains the new 3D coordinate corresponding to the mouse position, and uses that to set the properties of the *TranslateTransform3D*, hence moving the cube in 3D space.

Printing in 3D

Printing the contents of a *Viewport3D* is almost ridiculously easy. In the Windows Presentation Foundation, printing is based on objects of type *Visual*. *Visual* is the base class to *UIElement*, which is the base class to *FrameworkElement*, which is the base class to *Viewport3D*, so a *Viewport3D* certainly qualifies. If all you want to do is print a single *Viewport3D* object on a printer page, the job is as easy as creating an object of type *PrintDialog* and calling the *PrintVisual* method. Printing multiple pages is a bit tougher; see Chapter 17 of my book *Applications = Code + Markup* for details.

What you'll find, however, is that you're really printing the contents of the *Viewport3D* object, and that can actually be a problem. Let's look at an example.

I'm going to be discussing inches and device-independent units here, and some confusion can arise. In the WPF, an inch is always equivalent to 96 device-independent units. However, an inch on the screen is not something you can measure with a ruler. Windows assumes a certain resolution of the video displays in dots per inch. Very often Windows assumes that the video display has 96 pixels to the inch, which means that WPF device-independent units are the same as pixels. However, you can use the Display Properties dialog box under Windows XP or the DPI Scaling dialog box, which you can invoke from the left column of the Personalization panel under Windows Vista to change that assumed resolution. If you set it to 120 DPI, for example, Windows assumes that 120 pixels on the screen are equivalent to one metrical inch, and each WPF device-independent unit is equivalent to 1.25 pixels.

The following XAML file displays a unit cube, but it's not a standalone XAML file because the root element is *Window*, the *x:Class* attribute appears in that element, and an event handler is defined for a Print menu item.

PrintViewport3D.xaml

```xml
<!-- ==================================================
        PrintViewport3D.xaml (c) 2007 by Charles Petzold
     ================================================== -->
<Window xmlns="http://schemas.microsoft.com/winfx/2006/xaml/presentation"
        xmlns:x="http://schemas.microsoft.com/winfx/2006/xaml"
        x:Class="Petzold.PrintViewport3D.PrintViewport3D"
        Title="Print Viewport3D">
    <DockPanel>
        <Menu DockPanel.Dock="Top">
            <MenuItem Header="_Print!" Click="PrintOnClick" />
        </Menu>

        <Viewport3D Name="viewport3d">
            <ModelVisual3D>
                <ModelVisual3D.Content>
                    <Model3DGroup>
                        <GeometryModel3D>
                            <GeometryModel3D.Geometry>
                                <MeshGeometry3D
                                    Positions="-0.5  0.5  0.5,  0.5  0.5  0.5,
                                               -0.5 -0.5  0.5,  0.5 -0.5  0.5,
                                                0.5  0.5 -0.5, -0.5  0.5 -0.5,
                                                0.5 -0.5 -0.5, -0.5 -0.5 -0.5,
                                               -0.5  0.5 -0.5, -0.5  0.5  0.5,
                                               -0.5 -0.5 -0.5, -0.5 -0.5  0.5,
                                                0.5  0.5  0.5,  0.5  0.5 -0.5,
                                                0.5 -0.5  0.5,  0.5 -0.5 -0.5,
                                               -0.5  0.5 -0.5,  0.5  0.5 -0.5,
                                               -0.5  0.5  0.5,  0.5  0.5  0.5,
                                                0.5 -0.5 -0.5, -0.5 -0.5 -0.5,
                                                0.5 -0.5  0.5, -0.5 -0.5  0.5"

                                    TriangleIndices=" 0  2  1,  1  2  3,
                                                      4  6  5,  5  6  7,
                                                      8 10  9,  9 10 11,
                                                     12 14 13, 13 14 15,
                                                     16 18 17, 17 18 19,
                                                     20 22 21, 21 22 23" />
                            </GeometryModel3D.Geometry>

                            <GeometryModel3D.Material>
                                <DiffuseMaterial Brush="Cyan" />
                            </GeometryModel3D.Material>
                        </GeometryModel3D>

                        <AmbientLight Color="Gray" />
                        <DirectionalLight Color="Gray" Direction="2, -3 -1" />
                    </Model3DGroup>
                </ModelVisual3D.Content>
            </ModelVisual3D>
```

```
                <Viewport3D.Camera>
                    <PerspectiveCamera Position="-1 1 3"
                                       LookDirection="1 -1 -3"
                                       UpDirection="0 1 0"
                                       FieldOfView="45" />
                </Viewport3D.Camera>
            </Viewport3D>
        </DockPanel>
    </Window>
```

The *PrintOnClick* event handler is implemented in the C# part of the class. The following file completes the PrintViewport3D project.

PrintViewport3D.cs

```
//------------------------------------------------
// PrintViewport3D.cs (c) 2007 by Charles Petzold
//------------------------------------------------
using System;
using System.Windows;
using System.Windows.Controls;
using System.Windows.Media;

namespace Petzold.PrintViewport3D
{
    public partial class PrintViewport3D
    {
        [STAThread]
        public static void Main()
        {
            Application app = new Application();
            app.Run(new PrintViewport3D());
        }

        // Constructor.
        public PrintViewport3D()
        {
            InitializeComponent();
        }

        // Event handler for Print command.
        void PrintOnClick(object sender, RoutedEventArgs args)
        {
            PrintDialog dlg = new PrintDialog();

            if (dlg.ShowDialog().GetValueOrDefault())
            {
                dlg.PrintVisual(viewport3d, "PrintViewport3D: 3D Cube");
            }
        }
    }
}
```

The event handler for the Print menu item creates an object of type *PrintDialog* and calls *Show-Dialog* to display the dialog box and allow the user to make changes to the default settings. If the user clicks the OK button, the program then calls *PrintDialog* with the *Viewport3D* object created from the XAML file. If you want to print without displaying the dialog box—perhaps from a console program—you don't need to call *ShowDialog*. You can just call *PrintVisual* from the *PrintDialog* object and the visual will go to the default printer. If you comment out the *ShowDialog* call, for example, the program prints when you click the Print menu item. Your program itself can also change the destination printer and characteristics of that printer by accessing properties of the *PrintDialog* object.

Now for the problems I promised you: Because you're printing the same *Viewport3D* displayed within the program's window, it looks almost exactly the same as the version you see on the screen. What you see is what you get, but not necessarily what you want.

If the program's window is much wider than 8.5 inches (the customary width of a printer page in the United States), the cube will be large and it's likely that part of the cube will be truncated in the printed version. If you make the window very narrow to display a tiny cube, that's the size of the cube you'll see on the printer page. If that narrow window is very tall and the cube is several inches from the top of the window, that's what you'll see on the printer page. If the window is not tall enough to fit the entire height of the cube, that's what you'll see on the printer page.

In fact, if your actual display resolution (the number of pixels you count per inch when you hold a ruler up to the screen) matches the display resolution that Windows assumes, you can hold the printer page up to the window client area with the upper-left corners aligned and marvel at how close they are.

You can make the display of the cube more suitable for a printer page by setting the *Viewport3D* to be the same size as the page:

```
<Viewport3D Name="viewport3d" Width="8.5in" Height="11in"
                              HorizontalAlignment="Left"
                              VerticalAlignment="Top">
```

Now the cube doesn't change size as you resize the window, but you still need to get the whole cube in the window for the whole cube to print.

Yes, you can print a *Viewport3D* but it's not the best way to go. You gain much more control over the size and rendering of the 3D figures on the printer page by switching to the *Viewport3DVisual* for printing purposes.

Viewport3DVisual supports the same *Children* and *Camera* properties as *Viewport3D*, but it's one of only three classes that derive *directly* from *Visual*, and the class supports several other properties that let you control how it's printed. Internally, *Viewport3D* makes use of a *Viewport3DVisual*.

You can build a *Viewport3DVisual* entirely in code, of course, but you can also define a *Viewport3DVisual* in a XAML file much like you would define a *Viewport3D*. The difference is how you view it: *Viewport3D* derives from *FrameworkElement*, so you can make the *Viewport3D* a child of a *Window* or *Page* or *Panel* as you've seen. But a *Viewport3DVisual* derives from *Visual*, and the most convenient way to view a *Visual* is by setting it to the *Visual* property of a *VisualBrush*.

The following XAML file is part of a project named PrintViewport3DVisual. Much of the client area of the window consists of a *Border* element that has its *Background* property set to a *VisualBrush* based on a *Viewport3DVisual*. I've reduced the indentation of the *Viewport3DVisual* element so that the lines won't run off the end of the pages of this book, but notice that it's virtually identical to a *Viewport3D* element.

PrintViewport3DVisual.xaml

```
<!-- ======================================================
        PrintViewport3DVisual.xaml (c) 2007 by Charles Petzold
     ====================================================== -->
<Window xmlns="http://schemas.microsoft.com/winfx/2006/xaml/presentation"
        xmlns:x="http://schemas.microsoft.com/winfx/2006/xaml"
        x:Class="Petzold.PrintViewport3DVisual.PrintViewport3DVisual"
        Title="Print Viewport3DVisual">
    <DockPanel>
        <Menu DockPanel.Dock="Top">
            <MenuItem Header="_Print!" Click="PrintOnClick" />
        </Menu>

        <Border>
            <Border.Background>
                <VisualBrush Stretch="None">
                    <VisualBrush.Visual>

<Viewport3DVisual x:Name="visual3d" Viewport="0 0 384 384">
    <ModelVisual3D>
        <ModelVisual3D.Content>
            <Model3DGroup>
                <GeometryModel3D>
                    <GeometryModel3D.Geometry>
                        <MeshGeometry3D
                            Positions="-0.5  0.5  0.5,   0.5  0.5  0.5,
                                       -0.5 -0.5  0.5,   0.5 -0.5  0.5,
                                        0.5  0.5 -0.5,  -0.5  0.5 -0.5,
                                        0.5 -0.5 -0.5,  -0.5 -0.5 -0.5,
                                       -0.5  0.5 -0.5,  -0.5  0.5  0.5,
                                       -0.5 -0.5 -0.5,  -0.5 -0.5  0.5,
                                        0.5  0.5  0.5,   0.5  0.5 -0.5,
                                        0.5 -0.5  0.5,   0.5 -0.5 -0.5,
                                       -0.5  0.5 -0.5,   0.5  0.5 -0.5,
                                       -0.5  0.5  0.5,   0.5  0.5  0.5,
                                        0.5 -0.5 -0.5,  -0.5 -0.5 -0.5,
                                        0.5 -0.5  0.5,   0.5 -0.5  0.5"
```

```
                                        TriangleIndices=" 0  2  1,  1  2  3,
                                                          4  6  5,  5  6  7,
                                                          8 10  9,  9 10 11,
                                                         12 14 13, 13 14 15,
                                                         16 18 17, 17 18 19,
                                                         20 22 21, 21 22 23" />
                    </GeometryModel3D.Geometry>

                    <GeometryModel3D.Material>
                        <DiffuseMaterial Brush="Cyan" />
                    </GeometryModel3D.Material>
                </GeometryModel3D>

                <AmbientLight Color="Gray" />
                <DirectionalLight Color="Gray" Direction="2, -3 -1" />
            </Model3DGroup>
        </ModelVisual3D.Content>
    </ModelVisual3D>

    <Viewport3DVisual.Camera>
        <PerspectiveCamera Position="-1 1 3"
                           LookDirection="1 -1 -3"
                           UpDirection="0 1 0"
                           FieldOfView="45" />
    </Viewport3DVisual.Camera>
</Viewport3DVisual>

                </VisualBrush.Visual>
            </VisualBrush>
        </Border.Background>
    </Border>
  </DockPanel>
</Window>
```

Take note of the setting of the *Viewport* property in the *Viewport3DVisual* tag:

```
<Viewport3DVisual x:Name="visual3d" Viewport="0 0 384 384">
```

The *Viewport* property is a *Rect* structure, and the four numbers correspond to the *X* and *Y* properties of the structure (indicating the coordinate of the upper-left corner) and the *Width* and *Height* properties.

The *Width* and *Height* numbers I've used are equivalent to 4 inches in device-independent units. This means that the image rendered by this *Viewport3DVisual* is equivalent to what you'd see with a *Viewport3D* displayed in a window client area that is 384 device-independent units wide and high. I've set the *Stretch* property of the *VisualBrush* to *None* so that this image is displayed in actual size rather than being stretched to the size of the brush.

The project is completed with this C# file.

PrintViewport3DVisual.cs

```
//-------------------------------------------------------
// PrintViewport3DVisual.cs (c) 2007 by Charles Petzold
//-------------------------------------------------------
using System;
using System.Windows;
using System.Windows.Controls;
using System.Windows.Media;

namespace Petzold.PrintViewport3DVisual
{
    public partial class PrintViewport3DVisual
    {
        [STAThread]
        public static void Main()
        {
            Application app = new Application();
            app.Run(new PrintViewport3DVisual());
        }

        // Constructor.
        public PrintViewport3DVisual()
        {
            InitializeComponent();
        }

        // Event handler for Print command.
        void PrintOnClick(object sender, RoutedEventArgs args)
        {
            PrintDialog dlg = new PrintDialog();

            if (dlg.ShowDialog().GetValueOrDefault())
            {
                dlg.PrintVisual(visual3d, "PrintViewport3DVisual: 3D Cube");
            }
        }
    }
}
```

The logic is basically the same as in the previous project, but this time the *PrintVisual* call gets a *Viewport3DVisual* object rather than a *Viewport3D* object.

When you print from this program, the resultant cube will be approximately 2 inches wide and 2 inches high on the printer page, and located about an inch from the left and top edges of the paper. Why is that?

If you look at the window of the previous program (PrintViewport3D), you'll see that the width of the cube occupies approximately the center 50 percent of the entire width of the window client area. If you make the client area approximately square, you'll find that the height of the cube similarly occupies about 50 percent of the height of the window. For example, if the window client area is made 4 inches square, the cube is about 2 inches wide and 2 inches high, with a space of about 1 inch on all four sides.

In the new program (PrintViewport3DVisual), the *Viewport3DVisual* object is given a *Viewport* property 4 inches square, so the cube will be about 2 inches wide and 2 inches high with a 1-inch space on all four sides. That's what you're seeing in the upper-left corner of the printer page.

You can set the *Viewport Width* and *Height* to 6 inches, for example:

```
<Viewport3DVisual x:Name="visual3d" Viewport="0 0 576 576">
```

Now the cube is about 3 inches wide and 3 inches high, and about 1.5 inches from the edge of the page. You can also set the *X* and *Y* properties of the *Viewport* rectangle to positive or negative values:

```
<Viewport3DVisual x:Name="visual3d" Viewport="-96 96 576 576">
```

Now when you print the cube, it is still about 3 inches in size but it's an inch closer to the left edge of the page and an inch lower on the page. Notice that these changes to these *X* and *Y* properties of *Viewport* don't affect the cube displayed on the brush in the program's window. The brush ignores everything in the *Viewport3DVisual* that's transparent.

You can set the *Viewport* property of the *Viewport3DVisual* object in code right before calling *PrintVisual*. For example, try this:

```
visual3d.Viewport = new Rect(0, 0, dlg.PrintableAreaWidth,
                                   dlg.PrintableAreaHeight);
```

These two properties of the *PrintDialog* class don't exactly have proper names. In reality the properties report the total size of the page in device-independent units. For 8.5-by-11-inch paper, the numbers are 816 and 1056. You can try the program with this code in both portrait and landscape mode and you'll discover in both cases that the width of the cube now occupies about the center 50 percent of the paper width, although what constitutes the width depends on the printing mode.

When you look at the PrintViewport3D window, it's easy to see that the cube and camera are defined so that the width of the cube occupies about the middle half of the *Viewport3D*, and we also get that sense when we use the size of the printer page to set the *Viewport* in the PrintViewport3DVisual program. But that's something we're *seeing*. Is it possible to obtain the relationship of the dimensions of the cube relative to the dimensions of the viewport programmatically?

Yes. The *Viewport3DVisual* class defines a get-only *DescendantBounds* property specifically for this purpose. This is another property of type *Rect*, and it provides the total rectangular bounds of all the *ModelVisual3D* objects in the *Viewport3DVisual* relative to the dimensions of the *Viewport* property.

In this particular example, if you set the *Viewport* property to the rectangle (0, 0, 100, 100), for example, *DescendantBounds* is approximately (28, 29, 49, 50), which agrees with our observation that the cube occupies about the center 50 percent of the viewport.

What this means is that you can obtain sufficient information in your program to size and position 3D figures on the printer page intelligently.

For example, suppose you want to print the cube so that it is 2 inches wide, positioned on the printer page 3 inches from the top, and horizontally centered. Here's some code that does what you want:

```
// Normalize viewport.
visual3d.Viewport = new Rect(0, 0, 1, 1);
Rect rectBounds = visual3d.DescendantBounds;
// Want cube to be 2 inches (192 units) wide.
double scale = 192 / rectBounds.Width;
// Want cube centered horizontally.
double x = (dlg.PrintableAreaWidth - 192) / 2 - scale * rectBounds.X;
// Want cube 3 inches (288 units) from top.
double y = 288 - scale * rectBounds.Y;
// Set the new Viewport.
visual3d.Viewport = new Rect(x, y, scale, scale);
```

You can insert this code right before the *PrintVisual* call and try it.

Anaglyphs

The graphics in this book achieve a three-dimensional look from perspective effects and hidden-surface removal. A wholly different approach to three-dimensional graphics takes account of stereoscopic vision. In real life we see depth because our two eyes receive two slightly different views.

One of the common ways of displaying stereoscopic scenes is the *anaglyph*, which is a composite image that consists of a left-eye view and a right-eye view. Quite commonly, the left-eye view is tinted red, and the right-eye view is tinted cyan. Put on a pair of 3D glasses with a red filter over the left eye and a cyan filter over the right, and the picture seems to have depth.

The project that concludes this book attempts to create a red/cyan anaglyph on the screen that you can view with 3D glasses.

Because the red tinting and the cyan tinting correspond to the views from our two eyes, this anaglyph will require two cameras slightly offset from each other. The need for two cameras implies two *Viewport3D* objects, one overlaid on top of the other. The overlaying itself is fairly easy: Just put both of the *Viewport3D* objects in the same cell of a *Grid* panel.

One of these *Viewport3D* objects should display red figures and the other should display cyan figures. The areas where the red figures and cyan figures overlap should be gray. This implies that something needs to be transparent, but it's not immediately obvious how transparency will become part of this program.

To avoid a lot of repetitive markup, you probably want to define as much of the scene as you possibly can as shared resources, and then reference these resources from the two *Viewport3D* objects. But is this even possible? These resources will probably include *GeometryModel3D* objects, which means they have *Material* properties assigned, and that seems to conflict with the need to have separate colors in the two *Viewport3D* objects. After giving this matter much thought, I decided that the *Material* properties of all the *GeometryModel3D* objects should be assigned *White* brushes. It is then possible to handle the red and cyan tinting with the light sources.

The following XAML file begins by building a space station entirely from unit cubes. Notice that the background of the *Page* is set to black—just like real space. I've abridged the file here because the Resources section does nothing but tediously construct a space station of type *Model3DGroup* with a resource key of "station."

```
SpaceStation.xaml
<!-- ================================================
        SpaceStation.xaml (c) 2007 by Charles Petzold
     ================================================ -->
<Page xmlns="http://schemas.microsoft.com/winfx/2006/xaml/presentation"
      xmlns:x="http://schemas.microsoft.com/winfx/2006/xaml"
      Title="Space Station"
      WindowTitle="Space Station"
      Background="Black">
    <Page.Resources>

        • • •

    </Page.Resources>

    <Grid>
        <!-- Cyan light Viewport3D. -->
        <Viewport3D Name="cyan" Opacity="0.62">
            <ModelVisual3D x:Name="modvis">
                <ModelVisual3D.Content>
                    <Model3DGroup>
                        <StaticResource ResourceKey="station" />
                        <Model3DGroup.Transform>
                            <RotateTransform3D>
                                <RotateTransform3D.Rotation>
                                    <AxisAngleRotation3D x:Name="rotate" />
                                </RotateTransform3D.Rotation>
                            </RotateTransform3D>
                        </Model3DGroup.Transform>
                    </Model3DGroup>
                </ModelVisual3D.Content>
            </ModelVisual3D>
```

```xml
                <ModelVisual3D>
                    <ModelVisual3D.Content>
                        <Model3DGroup>
                            <AmbientLight Color="#008080" />
                            <DirectionalLight Color="#008080" Direction="2 -3 -1" />
                        </Model3DGroup>
                    </ModelVisual3D.Content>
                </ModelVisual3D>

                <Viewport3D.Camera>
                    <PerspectiveCamera Position="0 3 6"
                                       LookDirection="0 -4 -6"
                                       UpDirection="0 1 0"
                                       FieldOfView="75" />
                </Viewport3D.Camera>
            </Viewport3D>

            <!-- Red light viewport3D. -->
            <Viewport3D Opacity="0.38">
                <ModelVisual3D Content="{Binding ElementName=modvis,
                                         Path=Content}" />
                <ModelVisual3D>
                    <ModelVisual3D.Content>
                        <Model3DGroup>
                            <AmbientLight Color="#800000" />
                            <DirectionalLight Color="#800000" Direction="2 -3 -1" />
                        </Model3DGroup>
                    </ModelVisual3D.Content>
                </ModelVisual3D>

                <Viewport3D.Camera>
                    <PerspectiveCamera Position="-0.2 3 6"
                                       LookDirection="0.2 -4 -6"
                                       UpDirection="0 1 0"
                                       FieldOfView="75" />
                </Viewport3D.Camera>
            </Viewport3D>
        </Grid>

    <!-- Animation. -->
    <Page.Triggers>
        <EventTrigger RoutedEvent="Page.Loaded">
            <BeginStoryboard>
                <Storyboard TargetName="rotate" TargetProperty="Angle">
                    <DoubleAnimation From="0" To="360" Duration="0:0:10"
                                     RepeatBehavior="Forever" />
                </Storyboard>
            </BeginStoryboard>
        </EventTrigger>
    </Page.Triggers>
</Page>
```

After the Resources section come two *Viewport3D* objects. The first *Viewport3D* references the total space station stored as a *Model3DGroup* resource and applies an animated *Rotate-Transform3D* to that model to rotate it in space. Remember that visuals cannot be shared. The second *Viewport3D* has a separate *ModelVisual3D* with a binding to that animated model.

Both *Viewport3D* objects get similar light, except that one is cyan and the other is red. I originally believed I could make the figures semi-transparent with a semi-transparent brush in the *DiffuseMaterial* object. But this didn't work well at all: For example, if multiple cyan objects overlaid one another, they would be different shades of cyan depending on how many layers were involved. I decided that the *DiffuseMaterial* had to be based on an opaque white. I handled the transparency by setting the *Opacity* properties of the two *Viewport3D* objects, empirically choosing values that seemed to result in a gray composite.

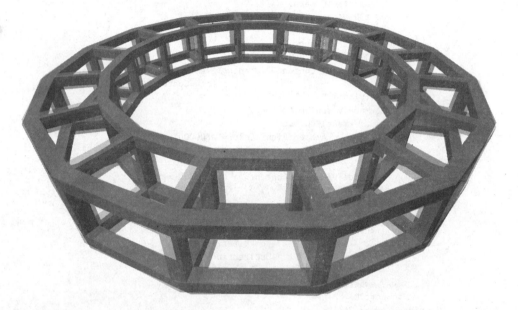

You can't get a good sense of the stereo effect from this black-and-white page, but you can probably imagine it.

Imagination is always the first step in graphics programming, so let your imagination run wild and strive to make your programming nimble enough to fulfill your vision.

Index

Symbols and Numbers

Charles Petzold

Charles Petzold has been writing about personal computer programming for two decades. His classic book *Programming Windows*, now in its fifth edition, has influenced a generation of programmers and is one of the best-selling programming books of all time. He is also the author of *Code: The Hidden Language of Computer Hardware and Software*, the critically acclaimed narrative on the inner life of smart machines. Charles is also a Microsoft MVP for Client Application Development. His Web site is *www.charlespetzold.com*.